JUDGES AND GENERALS IN THE MAKING OF MODERN EGYPT

Why do authoritarian regimes survive? How do dictators fail? What role do political institutions play in these two processes? Many of the answers to these questions can be traced to the same source: the interaction between institutions and preferences. Using Egypt as a case study, Professor Mahmoud Hamad describes how the synergy between judges and generals created the environment for the present government and a delicate balance for its survival. The history of modern Egypt is one of the struggle between authoritarian governments, and forces that advocate for more democratic rights. While the military has provided dictatorial leaders, the judiciary provides judges who have the power to either support or stymie authoritarian power. *Judges and Generals in the Making of Modern Egypt* provides a historically grounded explanation for the rise and demise of authoritarianism, and it is one of the first studies of Egypt's judicial institutions within a single analytical framework.

Mahmoud Hamad is an assistant professor of political science at Cairo University and the founding secretary general of the Arab Association of Constitutional Law (2016–2018). He previously taught at the University of Utah, Drake, and Brigham Young University. During his graduate studies, he won two Fulbright awards at the University of Washington and the University of Utah.

Judges and Generals in the Making of Modern Egypt

HOW INSTITUTIONS SUSTAIN AND UNDERMINE AUTHORITARIAN REGIMES

MAHMOUD HAMAD

Cairo University

CAMBRIDGE
UNIVERSITY PRESS

CAMBRIDGE
UNIVERSITY PRESS

University Printing House, Cambridge CB2 8BS, United Kingdom

One Liberty Plaza, 20th Floor, New York, NY 10006, USA

477 Williamstown Road, Port Melbourne, VIC 3207, Australia

314-321, 3rd Floor, Plot 3, Splendor Forum, Jasola District Centre, New Delhi - 110025, India

103 Penang Road, #05-06/07, Visioncrest Commercial, Singapore 238467

Cambridge University Press is part of the University of Cambridge.

It furthers the University's mission by disseminating knowledge in the pursuit of education, learning and research at the highest international levels of excellence.

www.cambridge.org
Information on this title: www.cambridge.org/9781108442442
DOI: 10.1017/9781108559393

First published 2019
First paperback edition 2022

A catalogue record for this publication is available from the British Library

ISBN 978-1-108-42552-0 Hardback
ISBN 978-1-108-44244-2 Paperback

Contents

Figures

Tables

Acknowledgments

This book is based on extensive field and archival research conducted between 2004 and 2018. While the shortcomings in this work are mine and mine alone, the virtues are widely shared. I am indebted to numerous individuals who helped me through the life and academic journey. I am enormously grateful for many of my family, friends, and colleagues who encouraged me to commence the work, preserve with it, and finally publish it. The list is long, and I surely forget many. For those who are not individually mentioned, I am exceedingly appreciative.

My late father planted in me thrust for political knowledge that I carried until the present day. My mother has been the central figure in my life since my father's early departure. She provided guidance, support, dedication, and boundless love for which I am forever grateful. My wife and my children had to endure the long hours, exhaustion, and attention deficit that such massive work entails.

My professors at Cairo University provided a world-class education. To name just a few: Ali Eddin Hilal, Kamal El-Menoufi, Mostafa Kamel El-Sayed, Mohamed Safi Eddin Kharboush, Hala El-Said, Galal Mouawad, Ahmed Yousef, Nevine Mossaad, Nazli Moawad, Ibrahim Darwish, Laila El-Khawaga, Gaber Awad, Hamed Quisay, Wadoda Badran, Nasr Arif, Heba Rauf, Mohamed Kamal, Ola Abouzeid, Saif Eldin Abdelfatah, Hamdy Abdelrahman, and Heba Rauf.

The Fulbright program fellowships were instrumental in allowing me to study at the University of Washington and the University of Utah. My fellowship at the University of Washington was a window into American graduate education. During my time in Seattle, I was fortunate to meet Tamir Moustafa for whom I am grateful for asking me to read his dissertation proposal which ignited my interest in studying the political role of the courts. My host family during my time in Seattle provided a second home. Thank you, Emily M. Wilson and Mike Rich.

At the University of Utah, Susan Olson has been the perfect adviser, mentor, and friend. I was fortunate to have her advice and support over the past 15 years. I was privileged also to have outstanding mentors: Matthew Burbank, Claudio Holzner, M. Hakan Yavuz, Ibrahim Karawan, Jim Gosling, and Mushira Eid. My colleague and friend Melissa Goldsmith provided insightful comments on drafts of the work for which I am thankful.

I also wish to thank several colleagues for reading and commenting on this work at different stages of the project, including Tom Ginsburg, Nathan Brown, Bruce Rutherford, Mary Volcansek, Zaid El-Ali, Kate Malleson, and Michael Tolley.

A particular word of gratitude is due to the scores of Egyptian judges, prosecutors, scholars, policymakers, and activists, who opened their minds and their hearts to give me the opportunity to understand the inner workings of the Egyptian courts, its complicated relationship with the executive, and the deep imprint courts have had on the politics and society.

Finally, I would like to thank my editor at Cambridge University Press, John Berger, and his entire team, for their excellent guidance through the book publishing process.

This book is dedicated to my mother, wife, and sons: Omar and Ali.

Abbreviations and Acronyms

ACA   Administrative Control Authority
APA   Administrative Prosecution Authority
CA   Constituent Assembly
ESSC   Emergency State Security Courts
FJP   Freedom and Justice Party
GID   General Intelligence Directorate
GCA   Government Cases Authority
HAC   High Administrative Court
HJC   High Judicial Council
HSSC   High State Security Court
JID   Judicial Inspection Department
JPC   Judicial Personal Circuit
MIRA   Military Intelligence and Reconnaissance Administration
NAM   Non-Aligned Movement
NDP   National Democratic Party
NEA   National Elections Authority
OSSA   Office of State Security Affairs
PP   Public Prosecutor
PPC   Political Parties Committee
PPD   Public Prosecution Department
PSSC   Permanent State Security Courts
RCC   Revolutionary Command Council
RSF   Regime Survival Functions
SCA   State Cases Authority
SCAA   Special Council for Administrative Affairs
SCAF   Supreme Council of the Armed Forces
SCC   Supreme Constitutional Court

SCJB   Supreme Council of Judicial Bodies
SPEC   Supreme Presidential Election Commission
SPP   Socialist Public Prosecutor
SSIS   State Security Investigations Service
SSPD   State Security Prosecution Department
UMC   Urgent Matters Circuit

Introduction

July 3, 2013, was a typical warm summer day in Cairo (temperature was 95°
Fahrenheit – 35° Celsius), but it was an even more blistering politically. That
afternoon, army chief General Abdel Fattah Al-Sisi deposed Mohamed Mursi,
Egypt's first democratically elected president. In making this momentous
proclamation the general was naturally flanked by the top brass of the army,
navy, and air force. But the carefully choreographed picture put front and
center Egypt's most senior judge (the president of the Supreme Judicial
Council and the Court of Cassation). Sisi also announced the appointment
of the chief justice of the Supreme Constitutional Court (SCC) as interim
president of the republic. The junta, it appears, was eager to demonstrate that
the guardians of the rule of law supported these actions, which had no
constitutional or legal basis.[1]

Chief Justice (President) Adly Mansour promoted Sisi to the rank of field
marshal, oversaw the writing of an army-backed constitution, and guaranteed
the election of the field marshal to the presidency. This heavy judicial
involvement in politics was, nevertheless, the tip of the iceberg of an extended
and protracted judicialization of pure politics since and even before the
removal of Mubarak.[2]

The post-Mubarak era was the most judicialized in recent memory if not
the most court-centered transition ever. The judiciary molded every aspect of
the transition(s) from devaluation of the old order to building (and dismantling) political institutions and writing of new constitution(s). Administrative

---

[1] An added benefit from the generals' perspective was to tie the fate of senior judges and hence
their respective institutions to the lot of the army takeover itself, "We must, indeed, all hang
together, or most assuredly we shall all hang separately" as Benjamin Franklin memorably stated.
[2] About the definition of "pure politics," see Ran Hirschl, "The New Constitutionalism and
the Judicialization of Pure Politics Worldwide, " *Fordham Law Review* 75, no. 2 (2006):
721–754.

courts disbanded Egypt's ruling and de facto single party for more than thirty years, dissolved all of Egypt's municipal councils, and suspended the Constituent Assembly (CA). The criminal courts were visited by the who's who of the old regime, including Mubarak, his two sons, the speakers of the two houses of parliament, two prime ministers, many cabinet members, chieftains of the interior ministry, and scores of leading business tycoons. The SCC did not let other courts surpass it. They dissolved the parliament less than six months after it was elected, annulled a law preventing Mubarak's lieutenants from contesting elections, and almost handed over the presidency to Mubarak's last prime minister.

Off-the-bench judicial acts were not less impressive. The judiciary managed the first free and fair parliamentary and presidential elections. A senior judge became the first-ever civilian vice-president, and another senior judge headed the nation's CA that drafted the 2012 Constitution. Furthermore, judicial rulings and actions were instrumental in undermining the Mursi regime and laying the groundwork for army takeover. After July 3rd, it was Mursi's turn to appear before the courts, accompanied by the main pillars of his regime and thousands of his supporters.

The amplified role of Egyptian courts came as a surprise to many. In reality, the judiciary played a crucial political role in Egyptian politics during the First Republic (1954–2011). The Egyptian experience of the existence of active judiciary within a fundamentally illiberal authoritarian environment is a truly unique phenomenon. Why would an authoritarian regime allow an independent center of power to exist outside its control?

This book engages with some of the most enduring issues of politics and political science. Why do authoritarian regimes survive? How do dictators fail? What role do political institutions play in these two processes? As I will explain, many of the answers to these questions can be traced to the same source: the interaction between institutions and preferences. These answers in turn present another indulgence: to build bridges between the recent scholarly work on institutionalism, regime transition, and judicialization, which appear to be isolated and detached islands.

This work asserts that much of Egypt's modern political history could be understood through studying the relation between the bench and the army command, the gavel and the tank. Generals, who ruled Egypt since the military takeover of July 1952, needed the collaboration of judges to supplement might with right, power with legitimacy, and dominance with respect.

In this chapter, I first start by presenting the commonly accepted explanation of judicial independence in Egypt and show why this explanation is lacking. I then introduce an account of judicial independence under Sadat and Mubarak. My analysis highlights the role of long-term regime survival strategies in the decision to grant courts a high degree of institutional independence. This work, therefore, focuses on the rich, dynamic, and politically relevant interaction between the regime and the courts. Judicialization of politics in Egypt went through waves of expansion and contraction but remains vital to the political future of Egypt in the twenty-first century.

JUDICIAL INDEPENDENCE UNDER AUTHORITARIANISM

The main explanation of the independence of the Egyptian judiciary under the authoritarianism of the First Republic is "credible commitment."[3] According to Moustafa, government officials in Egypt noted the connection between the existence of an independent judiciary capable of upholding property rights, enforcing business contracts, and attracting investment to achieve economic development.[4] The creation of an independent judicial body, the SCC, was intended to provide assurance to the badly needed domestic and international investment.

I see many major problems at the outset with this thesis. First, the 1971 Constitution, issued by Sadat, emphasized the socialist nature of the state and did not provide any genuine guarantees of private ownership. If judicial review means ensuring the conformity of legislation to the supreme law of the land, no court should reject nationalism or any other form of public control over private capital. For instance, the very first article asserted the socialist nature of the state, "The Arab Republic of Egypt is a democratic, *socialist state based on the alliance of the working forces of the people* " while article 4 clearly stated the socialist nature of the Egyptian economy: "The economic foundation of the Arab Republic of Egypt is a *socialist* democratic system based on sufficiency and justice in a manner preventing exploitation, conducive to liquidation of income differences, protecting legitimate earnings, and guaranteeing

---

[3] Tamir Moustafa, *The Struggle for Constitutional Power* (Cambridge: Cambridge University Press, 2007).

[4] The credible commitment thesis was built on the work of North and North and Weingast on the importance of institutions in minimizing transaction costs and advancing economic development Douglass C. North, *Structure and Change in Economic History* (New York: W. W. Norton, 1981), Douglas North and Barry Weingast, "Constitution and Commitment: The Evolution of Institutions Governing Public Choice in Seventeenth-Century England," *The Journal of Economic History* 49, (1989): 97–109.

the equity of the distribution of public duties and responsibilities." Other articles leave no doubt of this constitutional commitment.[5]

If Sadat did want to provide credible commitment, as argued by Moustafa, it would have been much easier to change the constitution than to empower the SCC. Notwithstanding, Sadat amended the constitution in 1981, two years after the establishment of the SCC, without touching these socialist provisions; which did not change until 2007. Under the 1971 Constitution it was perfectly legal for the rubber-stamp parliament to change the maximum land ownership and confiscate private properties. It was also lawful for the legislature to draft a law to nationalize, sequestrate, or expropriate private properties. As Magaloni notes, in his analysis of the Mexican Supreme Court, "when the existing constitutional framework is not liberal, judicial review does not provide stronger limits on government predation."[6]

Second, for the SCC to provide these commitments credibly, the constitution must be self-enforcing through a degree of a balance of power in the polity. North and Weingast, in their study of the constitutional development in the United Kingdom argued, "The constitution must be self-enforcing in the sense that the major parties to the bargain must have an incentive to abide by the bargain after it is made."[7] This is hardly the case in Egypt. The

---

[5] Article 24 was another classic provision emphasizing the socialist notion of control of means of production: "The people shall control all the means of production and direct their surplus in accordance with the development plan laid down by the State." Article 30 highlights public ownership as the norm and the leading role the public sector plays in national development: "Public ownership is the ownership of the people and it is confirmed by the continuous consolidation of the public sector. The public sector shall be the vanguard of progress in all spheres and shall assume the main responsibility in the development plan." Article 37 mandates sitting maximum limit of land ownership, hardly a guarantee of private ownership: "The law shall fix the maximum limit of land ownership with a view to protecting the farmer and the agricultural laborer from exploitation and asserting the authority of the alliance of the people's work forces at the level of the village." Article 32 put severe restrictions on private ownership: "Private ownership shall be represented by the non-exploitative capital. The law organizes the performance of its social function in the service of national economy within the framework of the development plan so that it may not be in conflict, in the ways of its use, with the general welfare of the people." Article 34 provided some guarantees for private ownership but permitted the legislature to curb it: "Private ownership shall be safeguarded and may not be put under sequestration except in the cases specified in the law and with a judicial decision. It may not be expropriated except for the general good and against a fair compensation in accordance with the law." Article 35 again gave the parliament the authority to nationalize private properties: "Nationalization shall not be allowed except for considerations of public interest, in accordance with a law and subject to compensation."

[6] Beatriz Magaloni, "Enforcing the Autocratic Political Order and the Role of the Courts," in Tamir Moustafa and Tom Ginsburg (eds.), *Rule by Law: The Politics of Courts in Authoritarian Regimes*, (Cambridge: Cambridge University Press, 2008), 204.

[7] North and Weingast, "Constitution and Commitment," 623.

emergence of the SCC, and for that matter the courts and the Council of State, is by no stretch of the imagination a product of a bargain between semiequal political powers. This has grave consequences for Moustafa's views because in the absence of a viable balance of power, at any given moment, the authoritarian ruler could alter the institutional structure – as well as its diverse functions. The Amendment of Article 88 of the constitution, which removed the full judicial oversight of the elections, is a case in point.[8]

Third, unlike the US Supreme Court and other high courts in the West, the Egyptian SCC does not control its docket. No party in a legal dispute can directly bring a case before the SCC. A foreign investor, negatively affected by governmental action, must file a case before the courts or the Council of State, and the merit court has the sole jurisdiction to certify the case to the SCC.[9] Hence, the institutional independence of the SCC is of little value, if any, where petitioners could not request the SCC to adjudicate their complaints.[10]

Fourth, Moustafa provided a partial explanation for the creation of independent courts in Egypt. Moustafa limited his analysis to the SCC. The conformity in regime behavior toward the different branches of the judiciary suggests that the regime's strategy toward the courts had a unified logic. It was not a mere historical coincidence that all of Egypt's judicial institutions lost a great deal of independence and powers under Nasser and regained these institutional guarantees and prerogatives under Sadat and Mubarak. If the same regime treated different courts similarly, why should we assign independent causes for its behavior toward each judicial institution?

Fifth, the examples of authoritarian regimes that were able to attract massive sums of foreign direct investment such as China and Singapore are illustrative of the fact that judicial independence is not a prerequisite for foreign

---

[8] North and Weingast accentuated this aspect, asserting the crucial importance of multiple veto points to ensure the continuity of the political equilibrium that provides for the credible commitment. North and Weingast, "Constitution and Commitment," 623–625. During the reigns of Sadat and Mubarak no such veto points existed. The regimes of Sadat and Mubarak had the political power to alter institutional arrangements whenever they so choose.

[9] For instance, when minister of trade and industry, *Rashid Mohamed Rashid*, issued an administrative decree to stop exporting Clinker and Portland cement to meet the growing local demand, the cement companies publicly threatened to file a lawsuit before the Council of State, not the SCC. *Al-Masry Al-Youm*, March 28, 2008.

[10] Furthermore, because of the chronic delay in the adjudication of cases by the exceptionally busy lower courts, the value of constitutional adjudication seems of little value in economic and financial matters where timing is the essence of success. The Egyptian government in 2007 became aware of such a problem and proposed legislation to establish special economic circuits within every appeals court to be exclusively responsible for the speedy settlement of economic legal disputes.

investment. Egypt itself saw an increase in foreign investment after the 2005 crack on the judiciary. The same happened in Singapore. After the government emasculated the independence of the courts, some experts expected a negative effect on the economy. "Not at all. No corporations fled the country. Singapore's competitiveness ranking held strong and capital continued to flow in. Singapore therefore presents countries like China with the possibility of an alternative model: while economic reform and prosperity demand the rule of law, the rule of law does not necessarily mean that judiclization – and the expansion of individual rights – necessarily will follow. It is possible to de-link economic and political/social reform (Silvertein 2003)."[11]

Therefore, this work does not find the credible commitment thesis satisfactory. This theory fails to grasp the complicated and dynamic web of relationships within authoritarian regimes and between those regimes and their regional and international partners. In the following section, I present an alternative explanation that takes all of these shortcomings into account.

REGIME SURVIVAL AND JUDICIAL INDEPENDENCE

Political survival is the fundamental objective that all leaders embrace. To stay in power, democratic leaders win elections (after all, the cardinal difference between democracy and authoritarianism is the existence of competitive, free, and fair elections). Authoritarian leaders do not have to worry about such trivial matters. Electoral contestations either do not exist altogether or are generally perceived as sham exercises of political theater with little meaning or value.[12] Autocrats, nevertheless, face two types of domestic threats: those that emerge from within the ruling elite (horizontal threat) and those that come from outsiders within society (vertical threat).[13] While these two threats appear as distinct, in fact they are not mutually exclusive. Horizontal threats could have the potential of enticing popular uprising, and vertical threats could lead to defection from within the regime.

---

[11]   Gordon Silverstein, "Singapore: The Exception That Proves Rules Matter," in Tom Ginsburg and Tamir Moustafa (eds.), *Rule by Law*, 83.

[12]   The 2018 presidential elections in both Russia and Egypt are excellent examples in this regard.

[13]   In addition to "domestic" threats, de Mesquita and Smith add foreign threat. "Threats to political survival can arise from three distinct sources: rivals within the current political order; domestic mass movements that seek to revolutionize the extant political system by replacing it with new institutions of governance; and foreign enemies who seek to take control of national resources or policies." Bruce Bueno de Mesquita and Alastair Smith, "Political Survival and Endogenous Institutional Change," *Comparative Political Studies* 42, no. 2 (2009): 171. In the Egyptian context, regime change through foreign intervention lost value since British forces departed from Egypt in the mid 1950s.

Hence, a critical task for any dictator is to manage potential threats with the aim of forestalling popular revolutions and/or elite defections. In *The Economic Origins of Dictatorship and Democracy*, Acemoglu and Robinson write, "the major constraint that faces those controlling political power in non-democracy is a danger that those excluded from political power might attempt to gain political power or to overthrow those who are in control."[14] To avoid this, authoritarian rulers use a mixture of punishments and rewards. In fact, authoritarian rule could be understood as a balancing act involving

> The supply of carrots and sticks. Carrots are measures intended to buy loyalty or acquiescence, while sticks are repressive measures that raise the costs of collective action against the ruler. It has become common in the growing literature on authoritarian politics to describe rulers' policy choices using some formulation of this dichotomy.[15]

Tales of repression are well documented in Egypt and many authoritarian regimes, but tyrannical governments survive in the long run because they do more than (just) repression. They ought to provide or promise to provide some benefits for the society. The problem, however, is the fact that "the promises of an autocrat are never completely credible."[16] To mitigate this "creditability deficit" authoritarian leaders build institutions that have the potential of making their promises more credible and hence help sustain their power.[17]

Researchers came to conclude that authoritarian institutions are much more than "window dressing." After all, "why would some autocrats care to dress their windows?"[18] These political structures are the result of elite strategic choices and have a real impact on the survival of autocrats. The literature on authoritarian institutions generally examined one of two questions: (1) why authoritarian regimes have political institutions similar to those in

---

[14] Daron Acemoglu and James A. Robinson, *Economic Origins of Dictatorship and Democracy* (New York: Cambridge University Press, 2010), 120.

[15] Mary Gallagher and Jonathan K. Hanson, "Coalitions, Carrots and Sticks: Economic Inequality and Authoritarian States," *PS: Political Science & Politics* 42, no. 4 (2009): 667–672.

[16] Mancur Olson, "Dictatorship, Democracy, and Development," *American Political Science Review* 87, no. 3 (September 1993): 571.

[17] Political scientists did not always pay due attention to political institutions. Gandhi and Przeworski summed this nicely: "Blinded by ideological antagonisms of the Cold War, we paid little attention to the institutional structure of authoritarian regimes. Announcing their plan for a seminal analysis of "totalitarianism," Friedrich and Brzezinski (1961, p. 18) refused to bother with institutions: "The reader may wonder why we do not discuss the 'structure of government,' or perhaps 'the constitution,' of these totalitarian systems. The reason is that these structures are of very little importance." Jennifer Gandhi and Adam Przeworski, "Authoritarian Institutions and the Survival of Autocrats," *Comparative Political Studies* 40, no. 11 (November 2007): 1292.

[18] Olson, "Dictatorship, Democracy, and Development," 571.

democracies and (2) how these institutions influence political and economic outcomes such as economic development and regime endurance.[19]

Over the past two decades, a growing body of scholarship has begun to systematically examine authoritarian political institutions such as parties, legislatures, and elections.[20] The majority opinion among scholars (if we use courtroom terminology) holds that institutions are important for the survival of durable authoritarianism. Large-N statistical analysis and detailed case studies of one or a few cases agree that institutions are critical to the survival of authoritarian leaders. This body of research argues that "repression only goes so far in perpetuating autocratic rule and that elections, political parties, legislatures and courts are tools used by autocratic regimes to co-opt regime opponents and make concessions to regime insiders."[21]

Political institutions perform two critical functions: division and co-optation or, in the language of O'Donnell, "encapsulate" potential opposition.[22] Authoritarian institutions are consequential because elites can use them to cement or protect their hold on power. Authoritarian leaders devise a complex set of institutions to control the polity and society and increase chances of political survival. Ezrow and Frantz put it elegantly, "At the most fundamental level, they [political institutions] are tools for the regime's survival."[23] Political

---

[19] Joseph Wright, "Do Authoritarian Institutions Constrain? How Legislatures Affect Economic Growth and Investment," *American Journal of Political Science* 52, no. 2 (2008): 322.

[20] For an extensive discussion of how parties, elections, and legislatures function under dictatorships, see Jennifer Gandhi, *Political Institutions under Dictatorship* (Cambridge, UK: Cambridge University Press, 2008); Beatriz Magaloni, *Voting for Autocracy: Hegemonic Party Survival and Its Demise in Mexico* (Cambridge, UK: Cambridge University Press, 2006); Jennifer Gandhi and Adam Przeworski, "Cooperation, Cooptation and Rebellion under Dictatorships," *Economics and Politics* 18, no. 1 (March 2006): 1; Erica Frantz and Natasha Ezrow, *The Politics of Dictatorships: Institutions and Outcomes in Authoritarian Regimes,* (Boulder: Lynne Rienner, 2011); Jason Brownlee, Authoritarianism in an Age of Democratization (Cambridge, UK: Cambridge University Press, 2007); Jennifer Gandhi and Adam Przeworski, "Authoritarian Institutions and the Survival of Autocrats," *Comparative Political Studies* 40, no. 11 (November 2007): 1279–1301, Carles Boix, *Democracy and Redistribution* (Cambridge: Cambridge University Press, 2003); Benjamin Smith. "Life of the Party: The Origins of Regime Breakdown and Persistence under Single-Party Rule," *World Politics* 57 (2005), 421–451; Beatriz Magaloni, "Credible Power-Sharing and the Longevity of Authoritarian Rule," *Comparative Political Studies* 41 (2008), 715–741. Valerie Bunce, *Subversive Institutions: The Design and the Destruction of Socialism and the State* (New York: Cambridge University Press, 1999).

[21] Michael Albertus and Victor Menaldo. "Dictators as Founding Fathers? The Role of Constitutions under Autocracy," *Economics & Politics* 24, no. 3 (2012): 281.

[22] Guillermo O'Donnell, *Modernization and Bureaucratic-Authoritarianism: Studies in South American Politics* (Berkeley, CA: Institute of International Studies, 1973).

[23] Natasha M. Ezrow and Erica Frantz, "State Institutions and the Survival of Dictatorships," *Journal of International Affairs* 65, no. 1 (Winter 2011): 10.

liberalization in the form of the introduction of multiparty system, "competitive" elections, and more active legislatures once perceived as steps in the long road to democracy are now considered tools of autocratic regime entrenchment. As Volpi and Cavatorta recognized, "authoritarian incumbents utilize the procedures and the discourse of democracy to strengthen the iron arbitrary rule."[24]

Autocratic rulers survive when they meet threats with "an adequate degree of institutionalization."[25] Scholars disagree, however, about what "adequate degree of institutionalization" entails. They also disagree about how institutions facilitate regime survival. For instance, Boix and Svolik argue, "institutions contribute to authoritarian stability by reducing informational asymmetries among the governing elite."[26] They went further to add,

> Formal political institutions have the potential to facilitate power-sharing and thus enhance the survival of authoritarian regimes: once such institutions are in place, the dictator and his allies can maintain a more stable ruling coalition under less favorable circumstances than would be possible without those institutions.[27]

Geddes concluded that party-based regimes survive longer than other non-party authoritarian regime, regardless of whether they hold elections.[28] Brownlee found no relationship between holding limited elections and authoritarian regime survival.[29] Magaloni demonstrated that hegemonic party survival and demise is explained by four central independent variables: elite unity, mass electoral support, manipulation of electoral institutions, and coordination dilemmas among oppositional parties.[30]

---

[24] Frédéric Volpi and Francesco Cavatorta, "Introduction: Forgetting Democratization? Recasting Power and Authority in a Plural Muslim World," in Frédéric Volpi and Francesco Cavatorta (eds.), *Democratization in the Muslim World: Changing Patterns of Authority and Power* (New York: Routledge, 2007), 3.

[25] Jennifer Gandhi and Adam Przeworski, "Authoritarian Institutions and the Survival of Autocrats," *Comparative Political Studies* 40, no. 11 (November 2007): 1284.

[26] Carles Boix and Milan W. Svolik. "The Foundations of Limited Authoritarian Government: Institutions, Commitment, and Power-Sharing in Dictatorships," *Journal of Politics* 75, no. 2 (2013): 313.

[27] Ibid., 301.

[28] Barbra Geddes, "What Do We Know about Democratization after Twenty Years?" *Annual Review of Political Science* 2 (1999): 115–144.

[29] Thomas Pepinsky, "The Institutional Turn in Comparative Authoritarianism," *British Journal of Political Science* 44, no. 3 (July 2014): 641.

[30] Beatriz Magaloni, *Voting for Autocracy: Hegemonic Party Survival and Its Demise in Mexico* (Cambridge, UK: Cambridge University Press, 2006).

Institutions are critical to streamline authoritarian succession. Ezrow and Frantz encapsulated the significance of institutions for authoritarian survival stating,

> Dictatorships rely on parties and legislatures because they help to prolong their survival. Indeed, regimes that use these institutions are longer lasting than those that do not. On average, dictatorships with neither a party nor a legislature rule for three and a half years, dictatorships with at least one-party rule for eight and a half years and dictatorships with at least one party and a legislature rule for eighteen years.[31]

Another important contribution of this line of scholarship is investigating the conditions under which institutions succeed in performing their regime survival functions (RSFs). "It may be that the real difference between successful autocracies (resilient autocracies) and breakdown is the relative strength and health of institutions that facilitate the efficient allocation of punishments and rewards."[32] For Brownlee, institutions enhance regime durability when they remain strong and independent; "ruling parties create durable authoritarian rule 'unless institutions weaken and elites destroy them, which happens because 'elites behave opportunistically in response to the political context that surrounds them'."[33] Another group of scholars maintained, "Recent work clearly demonstrates that, depending on their origins and external factors, institutions such as elections, parliaments, parties and courts may stabilize but also destabilize autocratic regimes."[34]

Several scholars utilized this institutional approach to examine the durability of authoritarianism in Egypt.[35] Maye Kassem's *In the Guise of Democracy: Governance in Contemporary Egypt* and William Zartman's

[31] Natasha M. Ezrow and Erica Frantz, "State Institutions and the Survival of Dictatorships," 1.
[32] Mary Gallagher and Jonathan K. Hanson, "Authoritarian Survival, Resilience, and the Selectorate Theory," in Martin K. Dimitrov (ed.), *Why Communism Did Not Collapse: Understanding Authoritarian Regime Resilience in Asia and Europe* (New York: Cambridge University Press, 2013), 186.
[33] Brownlee, *Authoritarianism in an Age of Democratization*, 37 & 40.
[34] Dag Tanneberg, Christoph Stefes, and Wolfgang Merkel, "Hard Times and Regime Failure: Autocratic Responses to Economic Downturns," *Contemporary Politics* 19, no. 1 (2013): 125.
[35] This book subscribes to the view that Egypt has been an authoritarian state under Nasser, Sadat, and Mubarak. While the regime since the 1970s could fall under what Brumberg may term "liberalizing autocracy," in reality this was nothing other than a newer, sleeker form of authoritarianism. Daniel Brumberg, "The Trap of Liberalized Autocracy," *Journal of Democracy* 13, no. 4 (2002): 56–68.

Beyond Coercion: The Durability of the Arab State have shown how, paradoxically, party polarization can reinforce authoritarian rulers.[36] Ellen Lust-Okar, using Egypt and Morocco as her case studies, argued that formal political institutions are the means whereby rulers can shape the actions of actual and potential opposition groups, can co-opt or exclude them, and can manage contest so as best to preserve their own monopoly on power.[37] Blaydes argued that highly contested elections act as "a decentralized distribution mechanism that aids authoritarian survival by regulating intra-elite competition, while at the same time outsourcing the cost of political mobilization and redistribution."[38] Clientelism, she added, during electoral campaigns strengthened the regime by shifting costs normally borne by the state to candidates. Absent these elections, "the regime would not be so durable."[39]

Although this body of work has made important contributions to the study of dictatorships, it remains incomplete. Judicial institutions are generally absent from this debate. The literature, in general or those studies that focused on Egypt, largely neglected the analysis of courts as institutions that sustain autocratic rule. Little attention is paid to the genesis and development of institutions such as the judiciary that could bolster autocratic regimes. Pereira recognized this stating, "Most studies of authoritarianism assume that regimes that come to power by force cannot rely on law to maintain control of society or to legitimize themselves; their unconstitutional origins are seen as making such an effort contradictory and impossible."[40] In addition to parties, legislatures, and constitutions, "judicial institutions merit systematic examination as well."[41] Courts, provided they enjoy a socially accepted degree of institutional independence, could be at least as significant as legislatures, multi-parties, and elections in sustaining autocracy.

---

[36] Maye Kassem, *In the Guise of Democracy: Governance in Contemporary Egypt* (Ithaca Press, 1999), William Zartman, "Opposition as Support of the State," in Adeed Dawisha and I. William Zartman (eds.), *Beyond Coercion: The Durability of the Arab State* (London: Croom Helm, 1988), 61–87.

[37] Ellen Lust-Okar, *Structuring Conflict in the Arab World: Incumbents, Opponents, and Institutions* (Cambridge: Cambridge University Press, 2005).

[38] Lisa Blaydes, *Elections and Distributive Politics in Mubarak's Egypt* (New York: Cambridge University Press, 2010), 8–9.

[39] Ibid., 237.

[40] Anthony W. Pereira, *Political (In)Justice: Authoritarianism and the Rule of Law in Brazil, Chile, and Argentina* (Pittsburgh, PA: University of Pittsburgh Press, 2005), 5.

[41] Joseph Wright and Abel Escribà-Folch, "Authoritarian Institutions and Regime Survival: Transitions to Democracy and Subsequent Autocracy," *British Journal of Political Science* 42, no. 2 (April 2012): 308.

The Model

While all regimes establish some type of courts, few authoritarian regimes make their courts sufficiently institutionally independent. Socially acceptable institutional independence is a prerequisite for the courts to be recognized by the populace as political structures of the state not mere extensions of the regime repressive apparatus. "In certain regimes, a range of 'pathologies' of authoritarian rule prompted authoritarian regimes to rediscover the utility of courts, thereby generating a seeming paradox of relatively strong and independent judiciaries coexisting with unbridled personalized and discretionary rule."[42] Existing research does not adequately explain the emergence and viability of independent courts in Egypt.

Both Sadat and Mubarak expected to stay in power for an extended period of time. This longtime horizon enticed the two leaders to build an institutional base of their authoritarian rule. As Olson once correctly noted, when discussing the significance of legislatures, "a dictator should only invest in a binding legislature if he expects to remain in power for a long time."[43] The regimes of Sadat and Mubarak enhanced the institutional independence of the judiciary in order to allow the courts to command the social acceptance needed to perform crucial RSFs. The judiciary played a direct and indirect role in providing the institutional foundations for durable authoritarianism.

Political liberalization, including the rule of law and judicial independence, was a consequence of the failure of Sadat and Mubarak to sustain the extensive welfare state installed by Nasser. Populist-authoritarian regimes can survive by supplying an extensive social remuneration. When the state must reduce social welfare because of financial constraints, it substitutes political rights in order to maintain public support. When the regimes of Sadat and Mubarak failed to maintain the Nasserite's commitment to providing full employment, free affordable healthcare, and food subsidy for the masses political liberalization was introduced, including expanding judicial independence.

Sadat and Mubarak sought to use the courts as survival tools. However, in order for the courts to fulfill their RSFs, the two authoritarian leaders had to grant judges a degree of institutional independence. The presence of popular support and faith in the judiciary is a prerequisite for such a strategy. In order for courts to

---

[42] Reinoud Leenders, "Prosecuting Political Dissent: Courts and the Resilience of Authoritarianism in Syria," in Steven Heydemann and Reinoud Leenders (eds.), *Middle East Authoritarianisms: Governance, Contestation, and Regime Resilience in Syria and Iran* (Stanford, CA: Stanford University Press, 2013), 170.

[43] Wright, "Do Authoritarian Institutions Constrain?" 327.

be able to supply the critically needed RSFs for the regime, judges need to be regarded as professional, independent, and concerned political actors.

The model presented here is based on the following ten assertions:

1. (Authoritarian) Leaders want to stay in power.
2. Lacking massive financial resources to pay off the society, authoritarian leaders with longtime horizon build (or reconfigure) institutions.
3. The specific institutional mix is regime-specific.
4. These institutions serve critical RSFs.
5. Autonomy and influence are vital prerequisites for institutions to perform these RSFs.
6. Institutional autonomy and influence would create tension within the regime.
7. The regime seeks to maintain control over political institutions without undermining the image of institutional autonomy and influence.
8. During critical junctures, the regime could decide to overtly exert control by scraping or minimizing institutional autonomy and influence.
9. Absence of autonomy and influence undermines the capacity of institutions to perform the RSFs.
10. Deprived of these RSFs, the regime becomes exposed to horizontal threats and prone to demise.

Nasser built a full-fledged "populist authoritarian" regime. He used charisma, nationalism, and populist economic policies to attract support from critical segments of the society, namely laborers, farmers, and university graduates. The regime was reasonably successful in the 1950s and the first half of the 1960s. High GDP growth, agrarian reform, massive industrialization, free university education, guaranteed employment for university graduates, and subsidized food, housing, and clothing helped to keep the population content. However, the regime was immensely weakened after the crushing defeat of the Six-Day War. The 1968 massive demonstrations, was the first anti-regime mass actions since 1954.

In retrospect, it is clear that the stability of Nasser's regime in its essence was "performance-based." So long as the leader could fulfill the social contract, the regime remained resilient. When dearth of resources made the provision of social spending unsustainable, the regime faced serious problems. Tanneberg, Stefes, and Merkel put it nicely:

> Autocrats lack the safety valve of democratic elections and they do not have much else but economic output to show for their denial of basic rights and

TABLE 1.1 *Historical map of the important dates in the development of the Egyptian judiciary*

Event		Regime
	1805	*Muhammad 'Ali*
Establishment of Mixed Courts	1876	*Ismail, khedive*
	1882	*British Occupation*
Establishment of National Courts	1883	
	1922	*Fuad I, King*
The Constitution	1923	
Establishment of Court of Cassation	1931	
	1936	*Faruq, King*
Judicial Independence Act	1943	
Establishment of Council of State	1946	
Dissolution of Mixed Courts	1949	
	1952	*Army Takeover*
Attack on the Council of State	1954	*Nasser, President*
Massacre of the Judiciary	1969	
	1970	*Sadat, President*
The Permanent Constitution	1971	
Judicial Authority Law	1972	
Establishment of the SCC	1979	
	1981	*Mubarak, President*
Restoration of the HJC	1984	
SCC's Historic Ruling on Elections	2000	
Constitutional Amendment, Art 76	2005	
Amendment of Judicial Authority Law	2006	
Constitutional Amendment, Art 88	2007	
Amendment of SCC Law	2011	*SCAF Assumes Power*
Constitution	2012	*Mursi, President*
	2013	*Army Takeover*
Constitution	2014	*Sisi, President*
Amendment of Judicial Laws	2017	

liberties if the source of ideological support has dried out or has been absent from the very beginning. In fact, the trade-off between political rights and material well-being is often at the heart of non-ideological autocratic, developmental states. If this trade-off turns into a false promise that leaves citizens with nothing but a repressive *and* ineffective leadership.[44]

Nasser, however, did not survive long enough to see anti-regime antagonism crystalize. Following in Nasser's footsteps, Sadat (and Mubarak) managed the ruling elite through monopoly over force, distributing spoils (symbolic and materialistic), and "coup-proofing."[45] Cultivating support within the society was a different story. The economic crises became so severe that it threatened to undermine the regime itself. The 1967 war exacerbated the worsening economic conditions. "Economic growth, which had averaged 6 percent per year from 1960 to 1965, slowed to one percent in 1966–1967. The decline was even steeper after the war."[46] Egypt lost critical sources of income: foreign revenues from Suez Canal and oil deposits in Sinai. The war-streaking economy was further undermined by the growing spending on the military during the War of Attrition against Israel and the forced resettlement of nearly one million inhabitants of the Suez Canal region to Cairo and the Delta. This was a serious challenge to a performance-based authoritarian regime without a source of ideological support. The newly minted leader did not have the resources to continue the "populist authoritarian" tradition of Nasser. Sadat, however, was not willing to relinquish ultimate power.

The solution was to move in the direction of "bureaucratic authoritarianism," with emphasis on institutions.[47] These institutions performed critical RSFs needed for regime survival in the long term. The judiciary, for several reasons, became the cornerstone of this "regime change."[48] First, the courts

---

[44] Tanneberg, Stefes, and Merkel, "Hard Times and Regime Failure: Autocratic Responses to Economic Downturns," 124.

[45] Coup-proofing refers to the institutional and personal arrangements to prevent an individual or a group from within the armed forces or the security apparatus from challenging the ruler. See, for example, James T. Quinlivan, "Coup-proofing: Its Practice and Consequences in the Middle East," *International Security* 24, no. 2 (Fall 1999): 131–165.

[46] Lust-Okar, *Structuring Conflict in the Arab World*, 9.

[47] The Arab Socialist Union, the Soviet-style single party could not "penetrate" society and incorporate constituencies and was controlled by Sadat's enemies.

[48] The regime linked judicial independence and the rule of law to its legitimation strategy. "Hence, unless we are convinced that legitimacy does not matter at all for the survival of autocratic regimes (Przeworski 1992, p. 107), more research into the 'legitimacy foundations' of autocratic regimes is necessary." I am sympathetic toward the ideas and theories presented by Weber (1956 [1921]), Arendt (1951), Friedrich and Brzezinsky (1956), Easton (1979 [1965]), or Linz (1975), which assert that ideological or normative support matters for the stability of an

were the most credible state institutions. A stock of trust and confidence has accumulated during the 1923–1952 era, which facilitated the role the courts were expected to perform to aid the regime's goals. Second, the weakness of the judiciary was appealing to Sadat. After all, Sadat wanted to institutionalize the regime without relinquishing power. The judiciary lacked a material power base (unlike the army, the security establishment, or the Arab Socialist Union). It seems that the relative weakness of the judiciary among other institutions that endured it to Sadat. Third, a decade of tension between lawyers/judges and Nasser meant that, "Legal professionals were largely uninvolved in the political maneuvering that surrounded Nasser's succession and the institution of the judiciary was on bad terms with Nasser's regime. When Sadat needed a new base of support, the legal profession was ready and waiting."[49] Judges, who suffered under Nasser, were willing partners.

It is important to note early on that I am not claiming here that Sadat or Mubarak were inherently ideologically different from Nasser. Both came from the ranks of the armed forces, where the emphasis has always been on discipline and deference rather than the free exchange of ideas. What I am arguing instead is that both Sadat and Mubarak found it politically expedient to emphasize democracy, the rule of law, and judicial independence in order to achieve a degree of political acceptance at home and abroad. The two autocrats used these values instrumentally to boost their regime's survival while striving to maintain their unquestionable authority. Rational calculations rather than ideological commitments are credited with the change in the regimes' discourse and policies after Nasser's departure.

In the post-Nasser era, Sadat and Mubarak only wanted to depict an image of the rule of law rather than a genuine, powerful judicial role. The regime had to negotiate its way between two competing objectives: the quest to enhance its authority in the long term and the desire to maintain firm control over all state institutions and preventing the emergence of independent centers of power. Judges, however, sought to expand their domain of influence, and this created tension with the regime.[50]

autocratic – political systems. Tanneberg, Stefes, and Merkel, "Hard Times and Regime Failure: Autocratic Responses to Economic Downturns," 124.

[49] Bruce K. Rutherford, "The Struggle for Constitutionalism in Egypt" Ph. D. diss., Yale University, 1999, 286–287.

[50] The move by Sadat and Mubarak to invigorate a limited type of rule of law or Rechtsstaatand as well as to introduce a limited degree of political liberalization went hand in hand with the great transformation in Egypt's international alliance. Sadat, as well as Mubarak, replaced Egypt's political alliance with the Soviet Union with a strategic relationship with the West, particularly the United States. The two leaders wanted to portray an image of liberalism and democracy to appeal to their new international partners.

The courts became a cornerstone of the rules and procedures made by the regime to manage "government-opposition interactions."[51] The judiciary was the most important institution in the regime survival strategy. Courts provided numerous critical RSFs. Courts "legalized" political conflicts that could turn into violence if they were not channeled in nonviolent routes. Courts served as avenues where demands were revealed without appearing as acts of resistance and where accommodations were reached in a legalistic form and publicized as such. Participation in the litigation process absorbed opposition activities into the institutional framework of the regime, according to the rules established by the ruler. Legalized opposition becomes domesticated opposition. Here, the courts performed functions similar to the legislature and parties, "by creating parties and a legislature, a dictator draws his potential opposition out of the general public and into state institutions."[52]

Hence, the judiciary functioned to create a divided structure of contestation, which created divided loyalties. Moderates became increasingly less willing to mobilize against the government. Lust-Okar argued that Mubarak's ability to use the rules and procedures of a divided structure of contestation aimed at preserving the status quo, confronting radical oppositions, and unifying the regime.[53] In addition, judicialized repression is much preferred to naked force "because they [political trials] demobilize popular oppositional movements; garner legitimacy for the regime by convincing key audiences that it 'plays fair' in dealing with opponents; create positive political images for the regime and negative ones for the opposition."[54]

The courts were part and parcel of the dictators' strategy to split potential political opponents. By offering a "legalistic" route to "contest" policies of the regime and secure some of the opposition demands, at least part of the opposition did "fill to the legal trap" and refrained from challenging the regime by more violent means. The rest of the opposition that refused to play the judicious game were isolated, portrayed as extremist, and dealt with the harsh repression tools of the regime. Those who refused to play the regime legal game were doomed: enemies of the state.

---

[51] This is different from the simplistic view of the "domesticated" judiciary as a purely coercive tool. "Syria's judiciary should be regarded as part and parcel of the regime's repressive apparatus and as such has played an important role in the resilience of authoritarian rule." Leenders, "Prosecuting Political Dissent: Courts and the Resilience of Authoritarianism in Syria," 169.

[52] Erica Frantz and Andrea Kendall-Taylor, "A Dictator's Toolkit: Understanding How Co-optation Affects Repression in Autocracies," *Journal of Peace Research* (2014): 51, 332.

[53] Lust-Okar, *Structuring Conflict in the Arab World*, 66.

[54] Pereira, *Political (In)Justice*, 33

For the opposition, in turn, participation in the litigation processes provided an opportunity to pursue interests with limited political cost. The mere existence of "independent" courts implied that there were some internal rules that regulate the prerogatives of power. The courts' legalistic and judicious decision-making method appeared to be much fairer if compared with the arbitrary modus of the ruler or the majoritarian approach of the legislature. Prereira recognized that independent judicial institutions in authoritarian regimes could help sustain the dictator in power by making the dispute-solving mechanisms more credible. "Where repression is judicialized, regime opponents are likely to have a few more rights and a little more space in which to contest regime prerogatives."[55]

The courts also can vouch for the regime. It was a common practice under Mubarak, and currently under El-Sisi, that whenever complaints emerge about the inhumane conditions in Egypt's detention centers, the Public Prosecutor (PP) would dispatch prosecutors to examine the centers. In all cases, the reports attested to the reasonable conditions and recommended minor changes. The reports revealed nothing damaging or troubling to the regime.[56]

The courts also handled sensitive issues that the regime feared would shoulder huge costs if dealt with directly. The SCC, for example, was tasked with undermining the legal foundations of the socialist state inherited from Nasser.[57] After the removal of Mubarak, the SCAF utilized the same court to get rid of the first parliament elected after the January uprising. Landry argued, "Authoritarian regimes rely on courts because formal legal institutions are expected to bring legitimacy to decisions that may not be fair or equitable."[58] The same could be said about the sentences of political dissidents. Courts provide a patina of legality that surely appears much better than extrajudicial killings or disappearing of regime opponents.

The courts performed the added benefit of monitoring subordinates. While authoritarian leaders have great latitude to intervene and impose their will, independent of the courts if they choose to, those leaders might utilize the hierarchical nature of the court structure to impose discipline upon various

---

[55] Ibid., 198.

[56] *Youm7*, June 26, 2014.

[57] The socialist nature of the 1971 Constitution forced the SCC to utilize a great deal of judicial creativity to uphold the scorers of free-market legislation enacted in the 1990s. Chief Justice Al-Morr introduced the principle of a "living constitution" borrowed from the US Supreme Court's liberal jurisprudence to accomplish this goal. Personal interview with a deputy chief justice of the SCC, March 13, 2018.

[58] Pierre Landry, "The Institutional Diffusions of Courts in China: Evidence from Survey Data," in Ginsburg and Moustafa (eds.), *Rule by Law*, 207.

agents of the states. Additionally, courts might act as watchdogs to prevent the emergence of power centers outside the regime's control.[59]

Furthermore, judicial independence and active courts helped the regime develop a rule-of-law image. "Building the rule of law is part of the political process in which the state acquires its legitimacy as upholder of the law, and in which the organs of state power are viewed as existing to enforce the law."[60] In his study of Latin American courts, Domingo argued, "Judicialization of politics reflects the degree to which regime legitimacy is increasingly constructed upon the public perception of the state's capacity and credibility in terms of delivering on rule of law, and rights protection."[61] Domingo advanced the argument further:

> The judicialization of politics may also be discursively linked to regime legitimization around the rule of law and rights-based democracy. In appearing to bow before the court rulings, power-holder can stake a more credible claim to be observing the principles of rule of law and limited government. In times of regime or political crisis this may emerge as a useful strategy in terms of bolstering legitimacy. Where other branches of power are perceived as deficient or lacking in credibility, facilitating the judicialization of politics can give credence to a public discourse of attachment to rule of law, acceptance of limited government, and commitment to strengthening rights protection mechanisms.[62]

In addition to all these functions that independent courts can perform in any political context, the judiciary in the Egyptian case played an indirect role as well. In fact, Egypt depicts a case where the judiciary was at least as important if not more important than the other survival institutions of parties, elections, and the legislature. After all, judicial independence preceded the establishment of the multi-party system and "competitive" elections. Moreover, judicial

---

[59] Rosberg highlighted the failure of centralized monitoring machineries as the reason for the emergence of an independent judiciary in Egypt. He argued that Sadat granted more independence to the judiciary in order to effectively monitor powerful state institutions (e.g., the central bureaucracy, local governments, labor unions, the intelligence apparatus, the police, and the army) that increasingly challenged the government's central control. He did so when it became apparent that the centralized monitoring strategies (through intelligence service, police, and the single political party) had failed to produce reliable information on the activities of these state institutions. James Rosberg, "Roads to the Rule of Law: The Emergence of an Independent Judiciary in Contemporary Egypt" (PhD diss. MIT, 1995).

[60] Hilton L. Root and Karen May, "Judicial Systems and Economic Development," in Ginsburg and Moustafa (eds.), *Rule by Law*, 321.

[61] Pilar Domingo, "Judicialization of Politics or Politicization of the Judiciary? Recent Trends in Latin America," *Democratization* 11, no. 1 (February 2004): 110.

[62] Ibid., 22.

rulings were responsible for the establishment of many significant political parties. The regime, in its effort to manage political liberalization, created the Political Parties Committee (PPC), which routinely rejected applications to form new parties. The only remedy was to appeal to the Council of State. Many political parties were granted the legal license to operate through judicial rulings. Secondly, the 1971 Constitution mandated judicial oversight of all electoral contestations. Judges stepped off their bench to be the umpires of elections, a responsibility that the regime managed to keep rather symbolic for thirty years. Lastly, and as consequences of their influence over parties and elections, courts had a large say on parliament composition.

Because the courts performed critical RSFs, they were granted more latitude than typical authoritarian institutions. This is not unique to Egypt. In Brazil and Argentina, "Judges are allowed to express their criticism publically, from the bench [and] their views are accorded serious consideration because their participation is regarded as indispensable to the regime's effective operation and to its continued acceptance among an influential sector of the public."[63]

From the regime perspective, judicial independence was a low-risk game. The regime believed that most of the cases appearing on the judicial docket had limited political significance. Adverse judicial rulings would not undermine the pillars of authoritarian rule. The regime would also seek to maintain influence over critical legal matters (judicial review, prosecution, etc.). Therefore, the regime devised a set of strategies to exercise control over judges without publically appearing to infringe on judicial independence.

After all, the regimes of Sadat, Mubarak, and Sisi wanted a "sham constitution" with high de jure rights protection and law de facto enforcement of these rights. Judges, either for ideological commitment to the rule of law or out of professional interest in furthering their bureaucratic authority, sought to move into a status of "strong constitutions." Under "strong constitutions," constitutional rhetoric enjoys applicability on the ground (high de facto rights protection).[64] Martin Shapiro argued that it is imperative to distinguish two norms when speaking of the rule of law:

> The first is that the powers that be shall rule by, and themselves obey, enacted, general rules, and that they shall change their policies by changing

[63] Mark J. Osiel, "Dialogue with Dictators: Judicial Resistance in Argentina and Brazil," *Law and Social Inquiry* 20, no. 2 (Spring 1995): 486.

[64] This typology of constitutions was developed by David S. Law and Mila Versteeg, "Constitutional Variations among Strains of Authoritarianism," in Ginsburg and Simpser (eds.), *Constitutions in Authoritarian Regimes*, 166–167.

those rules rather than by arbitrary deviations for or against particular persons. The second is that there is a core of individual human rights inherent in law itself, so that the rule of law must include the protections of rights ... authoritarian regimes with no real allegiance to rights may, nevertheless, wish to pledge themselves, or at least their subordinate agents, to the rule of law in the first sense and to institutionalize courts as guarantors of that pledge. They may wish to do so because, quite apart from rights, they see some advantage to themselves in doing so.[65]

Even with evidence of expanding judicialization beyond what the regime initially envisioned, Sadat and Mubarak concluded that the benefits dwarfed the costs. This *modus vivendi* lasted for three decades. By the third millennia, however, courts started to throw curve balls at the regime. The SCC ruling mandating full judicial oversight of the elections was a turning point. It represented from the regime perspective a "clear and present danger." Not only could the ruling transform the balance of power in the legislature (and hence the presidency, which at this point was selected by the People's Assembly), but also the ruling threatened the essence of authoritarianism in Egypt. El-Ghobashi, an expert in Egypt's constitutional politics, accurately summarized the significance of the historic ruling:

> Authoritarian regimes work by combining uncertain procedures with near-certain political results. However, some of these regimes develop elaborate judicial systems and legal procedures that may end up unwittingly providing opportunities for varieties of societal petitioning. By insisting on the legal armature of limited elections, Egyptian judges, opposition candidates and domestic monitors have worked to undermine the authoritarian equation, establishing certain procedures in order to maximize the uncertainty of results. In so doing, they have demonstrated that in the details of authoritarian laws and statutes lurks the devil of anti-authoritarian mobilization.[66]

In stepping out of the prearranged field of influence, Egyptian courts were not an anomaly. As Gandhi and Przeworski correctly noticed, "Institutions that facilitate policy concessions run the risk of generating outcomes that run counter to the ruler's policy preferences."[67] For courts to perform its function as a constraint, leaders must fear that the overt manipulation of institutional rules would be self-defeating, and therefore not manipulate them. Rosberg

---

[65] Martin Shapiro, "Courts in Authoritarian Regimes," in Ginsburg and Moustafa (eds.), *Rule by Law*, 329.

[66] Mona El-Ghobashy, "Egypt's Paradoxical Elections," *Middle East Report Online* 238, (Spring 2006). Available from: www.merip.org/mer/mer238/elghobashy.html.

[67] Gandhi and Przeworski, "Authoritarian Institutions and the Survival of Autocrats," 1283.

contends, "If law is meant to legitimate domination, we should also expect legal outcomes that defy the interest of elites. Law can only be a source of legitimacy if it plausibly applies logical criteria with reference to standards of universality and equity."[68]

Mubarak seemed to take this lesson to heart for two decades. The regime refrained from overtly challenging judicial rulings or undercutting judicial role. However, the shortsighted calculations behind the grooming of prince-regent Gamal Mubarak drove the young lieutenants astray. Short-term goals undermined the regime survival strategy. To make sure that the SCC would not trouble the regime with more adverse rulings, the regime successfully implemented a "court-packing plan," which ended the court's active era and undermined its independence. Furthermore, to prevent the emergence of a viable opposition candidate that could command the required parliamentary votes to validate his nomination, the regime thought to tightly control the 2010 parliament. To accomplish this goal, the regime enacted constitutional amendments that effectively removed judicial oversight of the elections. This ruined the ability of the judiciary to act as a safety valve for the regime.

These measures undermined the value of courts as constraints on the regime. The young Mubarak's eminent assumption of power undermined the hope of policy change after Mubarak's natural departure. Furthermore, the tight control of the elections negated any hope of peaceful, albeit gradual, regime change in the foreseeable future. The declining share of the ruling party in parliament in the 2000 and 2005 legislative elections gave hope that Egypt's future would be not unlike Mexico, where the PRI's hegemonic party autocracy of seventy-one years eventually ended. Elections create hope for future spoils. The completely rigged 2010 elections ended any shred of hope.

When the regime sealed off the legislature and ventured to limit the public space, the courts became the only nonviolent avenue to challenge regime actions. Adjudication related to "pure-politics" increased in number and significance. Adverse rulings condemned critical regime policies. The courts issued a whole array of rulings against the regime's foreign, economic, and social policies. The regime started to openly defy rulings for the first time since 1970. This further undermined the value of the judiciary as a survival tool. The regime had forgotten that a prerequisite for courts to perform their RSFs is for rulings to be respected and enforced, even if these rulings run counter to regime wishes.

---

[68]   Rosberg, "Roads to the Rule of Law," 59.

It has only been since the third millennia that the regime dismantled its own equilibrium that more social forces started to advocate for the regime downfall. Popular protests have increased in intensity and frequency since 2001.[69] The regime seems to have forgotten that institutions over time become "sticky," not in the sense that thereby constraining political actors even when their interests change, but in the sense that they alter the costs and benefits of actors' actions. Nasser could undermine judicial power with minimal political costs. Sadat, on the other hand, would have paid a higher price, and Mubarak the ultimate one. A leader (such as Nasser) that clearly stated his rejection of the principle of judicial independence was not expected to suffer deeply when he undermined this institutional independence. On the other hand, a regime that preached judicialization and judicial independence for several decades was expected to pay a hefty political price for snubbing its own rhetoric.[70]

The inability of the judiciary to regulate social, economic, and political conflicts heightened the allure of working from the outside. The regime became susceptible to previously "encapsulated" opponents. Faced with no institutional remedy for their problems, millions of Egyptians flocked to the streets overpowering the regime's oppressive arm and forcing the removal of Mubarak.

The post-Mubarak era was a different story. The courts benefited from the open space created after the January 25th uprising to expand its domain of influence and play a critical role in the transition processes (2011–2014). Sisi's first term was very much similar to the first few years under Nasser. Early on, the regime highlighted the role of the courts and did not impede its independence. Afterwards, the story was completely different. A military dictatorship that consolidated its grip on the society and the polity would most surely try to subjugate all institutions of the state, including the courts.

In a nutshell, Egypt's politics in the last five decades could be understood as a collision between the need for survival and the desire for political supremacy. Judicial independence and judicialization were at the center of this struggle. When the regime's survival calculations outweighed the longing for

---

[69] Rabab El-Mahdi, "Egypt: A Decade of Rupture," in Lina Khatib and Ellen Lust (eds.), *Taking to the Streets: The Transformation of Arab Activism* (Baltimore: Johns Hopkins University Press, 2014), 52–75.

[70] I am not urging here that courts constrain ruling elites' choices by binding them to their prior actions and rhetoric, but that courts' rulings and judicial actions put a political cost on regime choices, and in certain occasions, the cost might be very high indeed. Mubarak's advisors probably knew they would have to shoulder the costs of undermining the standing of the same institution that facilitated regime survival since Sadat but mistakenly assumed that they could create a new equilibrium after the succession processes concluded.

control, judicial independence expanded. This usually happened early on during the reigns of the authoritarian leaders, when rulers focus on laying down the political foundations of the regime. However, over time the regime grew confident of its hegemony over the society, and the yearning for total control prevailed. This explains the cycle of expansion and retraction of rights and liberties under Sadat and Mubarak. When Mubarak broke the balance to ensure ultimate political control and facilitate hereditary succession, the regime undermined its own survival strategy. This crucial miscalculation set the background conditions for the popular uprising that ended the First Republic.

The model presented here is not a mere formality, I subsequently derived from it three principal hypotheses that, based on the data, appear well founded. The first hypothesis is that judicial institutional independence (and judicialization) would take place in a regime that lacks other survival resources. The second is the regime would expand and deepen institutionalization during periods of regime vulnerability and could detract when the leader felt confident of his grab on the society and the polity. Hence, the judicial role would receive a boast early in the life of the dictator and would suffer later.[71] This explains the cycle of expansion and contraction of judicialization and liberalization in Egypt's First Republic. The final hypothesis derived from the model is that weakening the judiciary would undermine the ability of the courts to foster the survival of the regime. Without a judicial cover, the regime would be weakened and prone to collapse. This is applicable not only to Mubarak but also to Sisi. These three hypotheses, which we will discuss in the subsequent chapters, were derived from the development of the model.

Significance of Work

This book is guided by two cardinal concerns. The first is to explain the political development of Egypt – by engaging in serious and deep excavation of the institutional foundations of the authoritarian state with special focus on the courts. The other is to use this analysis to say something of broader relevance about institutionalism, judicialization, and regime change. My effort relies on a large data collection and a deep understanding of the inner workings of Egypt's institutions.

This work offers a singular analytical framework that explains both the durability and collapse of authoritarian rule. This is a powerful heuristic of explaining regime survival and demise. I argue for examining Egypt's past, present, and

---

[71] This is similar to the view that holds that "autocratic rulers adopt constitutions in the nascent stages of an autocratic coalition taking power, when uncertainty about leader intentions is high." Albertus and Menaldo, "Dictators as Founding Fathers?" 279.

future through a judicial lens to analyze the political dynamisms on the banks of the Nile. This book differs from most existing research in the explicit focus on the courts as survival mechanisms for authoritarian leaders. Thus, I believe my contribution is to offer a more general account than that suggested by others and to do so within a unified theoretical approach, an approach that also provides explanations of how authoritarian governments survive through institutionalization and how political institutions influence regime change. In previous studies, institutions are either understood as to undermine authoritarian regimes or to sustain autocratic rule. The case of Egypt is noteworthy because the institution that helped maintain the regimes of both Sadat and Mubarak was the one that facilitated the demise of the latter (and Mursi as well).

The second main goal of this study is to underscore some principle theoretical issues related to the role of political institutions, authoritarian politics, and success and failure of democratization. This book seeks to advance the integration of the judiciary into the literature on authoritarian durability. The careful examination of Egypt makes a convincing argument that scholars need an account for both the processes through which courts form and change, on the one hand, and the consequences of those processes for the outcomes that judicial institutions are thought to explain. The central message for future research is that the effects of courts as authoritarian institutions cannot be studied separately from the concrete calculations of political survival that motivate regime behavior and judicial attitudes that shape judicial rulings and actions. Institutions are not empty vessels without interests and culture. This could open a new avenue of research not previously driven.

Sophisticated studies of politics within authoritarian institutions (like the Egyptian courts) are still rare; this work seeks to provide one detailed example of how a very careful study of one country's authoritarian political system can illustrate some of the foundations of broader theoretical claims. While this work focuses on a single case study, its theoretical implications are much wider. At this stage in our knowledge of courts as authoritarian institutions, a study that shows rigorously that a judiciary affects political outcomes in one country is preferable to a study that can elicit a conditional correlation between institutions and some outcome across all dictatorships. "It is, of course, difficult to generalize any conclusions beyond this single case, but internal validity should be privileged over external validity when it is difficult to defend the assumptions about measurement validity and data generating processes that are necessary for making externally valid inferences."[72]

---

[72] Pepinsky, "The Institutional Turn in Comparative Authoritarianism," 649.

RESEARCH APPROACH AND METHODS

This research offers a longitudinal analysis of the state-court relationship in Egypt. With the purpose of situating the judiciary within the broader process of political contestation, this study embraces the historical-institutional model.[73] This approach is best suited to explain the puzzle of independent, politically relevant, and liberal courts within authoritarian settings, as well as state-court interactions thereafter. As Pierson and Skocpol argued, "the problems that interest historical institutionalisms often come from identifying heretofore unexplained real-world variations – or from realizing that empirical patterns run counter to received academic and popular wisdom," such as the existence of independent liberal judiciary outside the realm of democratic politics.[74]

This approach examines the connections, disjunctions, and interactions between the law, the courts, and other political and social institutions. Gillman and Clayton outlined the premises of this approach, stating historical

---

[73] In the study of American courts, three main approaches are particularly prominent: the attitudinal model, the strategic model, and the historical-institutional model. The attitudinal model posits that judicial attitudes are measured "objectively" and quantified. According to proponents of this model, attitudes convincingly explain the behavior of Supreme Court justices, without the need to refer to any "external" factors, such as the constitution, the statutes, the behavior of Congress, or the values of the society. This model presented a straightforward claim that, in the end, the impact of nonattitudinal factors on judicial decisions appears to be minimal. "Simply put, Rehnquist votes the way he does because he is extremely conservative; Marshall voted the way he did because he is extremely liberal." Jeffrey Segal and Harold J. Spaeth, *The Supreme Court and the Attitudinal Model* (New York: Cambridge University Press, 1993), 65. On the other hand, the strategic model involves the application of a positive theory of institutions (PTI) that challenges the legal and attitudinal approaches to the study of the Supreme Court. Those who adhere to this model argued that the law, as it is generated by the Supreme Court, is the long-term product of short-term strategic decision-making. Epstein and Knight sum it up nicely: "Justices are strategic actors who realize that their ability to achieve their goals depends on a consideration of preferences of others, and of the institutional context in which they act." Lee Epstein and Jack Knight, *The Choices Justices Make* (Washington DC: CQ Press, 1998), 10. The historical-institutional model is a reaction to the stylized, ahistorical formalism of much of the scholarship that relies on the assumptions of the strategic model coming from economic theory. This model depicts judicial decision-making as a process in which judicial values and attitudes are shaped by judges' distinct professional roles, their sense of obligation, and salient institutional perspectives. "Central to this approach then is the use of interpretive methodologies to describe the historic evolution of these institutionalized perspectives or patterns of meaningful action." Cornell W. Clayton and Howard Gillman, eds., *Supreme Court Decision-Making: New Institutionalist Approaches* (Chicago: University of Chicago Press, 1999), 32.

[74] Paul Pierson and Theda Skocpol, "Historical Institutionalism in Contemporary Political Science" in Ira Katznelson and Helen V. Milner (eds.) *Political Science: The State of the Discipline* (New York, NY: Norton, 2002), 697.

institutionalism seeks to emphasize the connections "that attach courts and judges in general to culture and society."[75] Historical institutionalists tend to be concerned with placing the judiciary and the law within a larger social and intellectual context that both shapes the course of law and helps define legal meaning.

New historical institutionalists propose a macro-level analysis of the court's decision-making within the political system that incorporates a concern for history, institutional development and interaction, context, and the relationship between ideas and institutions. This feature of historical institutionalism is particularly important to the study of Egyptian courts for many reasons: first, the courts in Egypt issue a single opinion and no dissent is published. Moreover, rulings do not disclose how judges cast their votes. Indeed, the law classifies such information, and judges or court officials who reveal this information are subject to discipline.[76]

In addition, Egypt embraced the model of bureaucratic judiciary of continental Europe. In this type of judicial institutions, a distinct institutional culture dominates judicial decision-making.[77] Therefore, the judicial institutional arrangements in Egypt do not fit the microanalysis of both attitudinal and rational choice approaches. The bulk of the contemporary judicial behavior research focuses on the micro-analytical level of examining the voting behavior of individual justices.[78] The role historical legacies have played in shaping Egypt's judicial institutions make historical institutionalism a perfect fit for understanding the dynamism of judicial politics. Without grounding courts and judges in their history, it is exceptionally difficult to understand the judicial activism on the bench.

Historical institutionalism, nonetheless, accepts that judges, and for that matter all political actors, are sophisticated, rational actors who seek to maximize their interests within a certain environment. Scholars, therefore, consider the role of strategic interaction between the judiciary as an institution and other branches of government in the judicial decision-making process.[79]

---

[75] Howard Gillman and Cornell Clayton, eds., *The Supreme Court in American Politics: New Institutionalist Interpretations* (Lawrence: University Press of Kansas, 1999), 3–4.

[76] Kevin Boyle and Adel Omar Sherif, eds., *Human Rights and Democracy* (London: Kluwer Law International, 1996) 42–43.

[77] Carlo Guarnieri and Patrizia Pederzoli, *The Power of Judges: A Comparative Study of Courts and Democracy* (Oxford: Oxford University Press, 2002).

[78] For example, Lawrence Baum, *The Puzzle of Judicial Behavior* (Ann Arbor: University of Michigan Press, 1997).

[79] See, for example, Susan Burgess, "Beyond Instrumental Politics: The New Institutionalism, Legal Rhetoric, and Judicial Supremacy," *Polity* 25 (1993): 445–459; John Gates, "Theory, Methods, and the New Institutionalism in Judicial Research." in John Gates and Charles

This is particularly relevant for judicial institutions operating within a context of uncertainty created by authoritarian political arrangements, as Egyptian courts have been since the end of the liberal era in 1952.

To understand the dynamic of the state-court relationship in Egypt, I used a variety of research methods. These included textual analysis of legal documents related to the judiciary, judicial rulings, presidential speeches, and newspapers. I conducted numerous interviews with judges, public officials, oppositional parties and groups, and civil society leaders. I used participant observation of many judicial professional and social gatherings.

TEXTUAL ANALYSIS

This analysis of texts included the following: legal documents (constitutional and statutory); presidential discourse of Nasser, Sadat, Mubarak, Mursi, Mansour, and Sisi; judicial rulings germane to basic regime interests or citizens' and groups' civil and political rights; and other relevant public records.[80]

Legal Documents

The first type of texts analyzed was constitutional and statutory provisions regarding the judiciary during the period of study. I examined primary sources (official documents) published in the *Official Gazette* and supplemented the analysis with secondary reviews and assessment. The main goal of this legal analysis was to pinpoint the changes in institutional independence (e.g., judicial selection, promotion, security of tenure) since 1952.

Presidential Speeches

The second type of text analyzed was regime leaders' discourse. The primary focus was major public presidential addresses. This was an obvious choice because of the central role the chief executive played in the Egyptian political landscape, a position so crucial that one seasoned observer describes it as "a

---

A. Johnson (eds.), *The American Courts: A Critical Assessment* (Washington DC: CQ Press, 1991); and Paul W. Khan, "Independence and Responsibility in Judicial Rule," in Irwin Stotzky (ed.), *The Role of the Judiciary in the Transition to Democracy in Latin America* (Boulder: Westview, 1993).

[80] Unless otherwise noted, translation is conducted by the author. This includes presidential speeches, courts' rulings, legal documents, newspapers, interviews' transcripts, etc.

one man show."[81] I selected one speech per year for each of the three presidents, with attention to the representativeness and comparability of the three presidential discourse samples.

After consultation with a number of Egyptian specialists, I decided to focus on Nasser's annual revolutionary day speeches.[82] This choice proved compelling for a number of reasons. First, Nasser, since 1954, kept the habit of delivering a speech in every year of his reign. Second, these annual speeches were highly regarded, extremely popular, and extensive. Third, the set date of the speeches, generally between July 22 and 26 minimized the significance of temporal events and focused the speeches more on politics and policies, rather than commentary on current events.

For Sadat, I analyzed the president's annual speeches and messages in commemoration of the May 15 Revolution (sometimes called the Corrective Movement or the Rectification Revolution). With Sadat, the 1952 Revolution receded into the shadows. This May Revolution was "Sadat's counterpart to the 1952 Revolution. Having put his own stamp on the regime, Sadat produced his own parallels for the dates and emblems, which Nasser had declared symbolic of the Revolution. Thus, May 15 supplanted July 23."[83] The May Revolution speeches, hence, represent Sadat's chosen emphases about his rule, his perceptions of the polity and society, his appraisal of the past, and his vision for the future.

Mubarak had no revolution to his credit. His presidential addresses in the opening sessions of the parliament are the most significant speeches of the year and the ones that receive unparalleled attention from the state-controlled press and media. Hence, this equivalent to the state of the union address was the obvious choice when analyzing Mubarak's discourse.

Mursi had neither a revolution nor a parliament. I examined his inauguration speech and the last address before his removal from office. To

---

[81] Personal interview with former minister of youth and National Democratic Party's General Secretariat Member, November 5, 2005.

[82] Initially, I began by analyzing Nasser's speeches in the opening of the parliament (the equivalent to State of the Union Address in the US context). However, this initial choice proved lacking for a plethora of reasons: for one thing, in some years, he would deliver two opening addresses per year and nothing at all in others. Another more qualitative problem was that Nasser's speeches to the parliament were not particularly important politically because the parliament was a rather insignificant institution for much of Nasser's reign. During the 1952–1970 period, the parliament was absent altogether for nine full years. See: Azzah Wahbī, *al-Sulṭah al-tashrīʿīyah fī al-niẓām al-siyāsī al-Miṣrī baʿda Yūliyū 1952* (al-Qahirah: Markaz al-Dirāsāt al-Siyāsīyah wa-al-Istirātījīyah, 1993).

[83] Raphael Israeli, *"I, Egypt": Aspects of President Anwar al-Sadat's Political Thought*, Jerusalem Papers on Peace Problems (Jerusalem: Magnes Press, 1981), 20.

compensate for the lack of speeches, I investigated the discourse of his top lieutenants in the Muslim Brotherhood, the Shura Council, and the Freedom and Justice Party.

Interim President Adly Mansour delivered very few addresses. Sisi as well did not give many formal speeches, but he spoke about many different issues during many occasions, such as visits to military posts, factories, and government institutions.

Judicial Rulings

The third type of text analyzed is selected major judicial rulings regarding the basic regime interests (e.g., control of the Parliament, opposition political parties, civil society, and freedom of speech). I examined rulings delivered by the SCC, the Council of State, and the courts. To identify major rulings, I followed a similar strategy to the one employed by Mayhew.[84] Any ruling featured in one of the major newspapers, *Al-Masry Al-Youm, Al-Ahram, Al-Akhbar, Al-Gomhouria, Al-Wafad, Al-Ahaly, Al-Araby, Al-Fager, Al-Osoboa, El-Waten, Al-Mesryoon* and *shorouk*, was included in the analysis. Additionally, I included any ruling mentioned during my interviews as well as those rulings documented in scholarly works. In most cases, secondary sources were sufficient to understand the direction of ruling (for or against regime interest), as well as its significance in the Egyptian political context.[85]

Publications

The fourth type of text analyzed was publications: newspaper, statements, and judicial periodicals. The objective was to understand the regimes' behavior toward the courts. This included, among other things, appointment of judges to non-judicial positions, changing justices' compensation, or purging judges from their judicial posts. I also examined selective writings by judges. This included articles published in *Majallat Majlis al-Dawlah*, the State Council's annual periodical (1950–present), the Judges Club periodical *Al-Qada*, as well as writings in newspapers, academic periodicals, conference presentations, and books. Judges' writings can tell us a great deal about how they approach

[84] David R. Mayhew, *Divided We Govern: Party Control, Lawmaking, and Investigations, 1946–1990* (New Haven: Yale University Press, 1991).

[85] If the directions of the rulings or their substances were unclear in the secondary sources, I consulted the official rulings issued by the court and published either by the court itself or in other secondary sources.

their vocation and perceive their role.[86] However, they need to be interpreted with care as judges usually speak and write with the audience in mind.[87]

INTERVIEWS

The second research method was semistructured interviews with senior and rank and file judges, prominent leaders in civil society, and oppositional parties and groups, as well as government officials, especially in the Ministry of Justice, and leaders of the National Democratic Party (NDP). These interviews were critical to better understand two interrelated issues: the political role of the judiciary as perceived by judges, politicians, activists, and government officials in addition to the relation between the state and courts, the balance between state interests and citizens' rights. These interviews facilitated the understanding of different attitudes and political leanings within the judiciary. Furthermore, interviews shed light on regime leaders' perceptions of major judicial rulings and their positions on judges' demands.

It goes without saying that the feasibility of this project depended on my access to interview subjects in the legal and political institutions. I was fortunate through professional and personal ties to secure access to judges, public prosecutors, and lawyers in different levels of the Egyptian judicial structure as well as influential regime officials, oppositional parties' and groups' high-ranking members, and civil society leaders.

Because conducting field research on politically sensitive matters within an authoritarian context can create risks for interview subjects, I provided individuals with anonymity for all comments or selected comments that they identified when they volunteered opinions that they had not previously stated in public and were concerned about encountering social or political harm from the government or others disagreeing with those opinions. Hence, in most cases, I refer to the position of the person interviewed rather than stating his/her name. In other occasions, the name and position of the individual interviewed is mentioned. A few officials were interviewed on background basis only with the understanding their names and positions were not to be revealed.

---

[86] C. K. Rowland and Robert A. Carp, *Politics and Judgment in Federal District Courts* (Lawrence: University Press of Kansas, 1996), 146–147.

[87] Thomas B Marvell, *Appellate Courts and Lawyers: Information Gathering in the Adversary System* (Westport: Greenwood Press, 1978), 9–13.

PARTICIPANT OBSERVATION

The third research method in this study is participant observation of a variety of formal and non-formal judicial behavior between 2005 and 2017. "Participant observation refers to a research approach in which the major activity is characterized by a prolonged period of contact with subjects in the place in which they normally spend their time. During the encounters, data, in the form of field notes, are unobtrusively and systematically collected."[88] This approach emphasizes participation as an opportunity for in-depth systematic study of a particular group.

This approach aims to gain a close and intimate familiarity with Egypt's judicial community. Between 2005 and 2017, I attended and participated in rallies to support the call for judicial independence, court proceedings of the Council of State's administrative court, three general assemblies of the Judges Club, confidential meetings of the Alexandria Judges Club, and countless social gatherings of judges at different levels of the Egyptian judiciary. This intensive involvement with judges in their natural environment provided a clearer understanding of the judicial mind.

The variety of methods used made possible the examination of the complex behavior of the regime, the court, and other relevant actors. For example, analyzing legislation, presidential speeches, regime actions, and interviews with leading executive personnel was sufficient to understand regime behavior toward the judiciary. On the other hand, judicial rulings, judges' speeches and writings, and interviews with judges and justices, as well as participation in many judicial gatherings were adequate for analyzing the courts jurisprudence. The behavior of the judicial support structure was examined through interviews, statements by political parties and civil society personnel, and coverage by independent newspapers.

ORGANIZATION OF THE BOOK

In addition to this introductory chapter, this book includes eight other chapters. Chapter 2, *The Historical Legacies and the Institutional Culture of the Egyptian Judiciary*, explores the main attributes of the institutional culture of the modern Egyptian judiciary. Egypt's judicial culture brings together features of the religious Islamic heritage with modern liberal political ideals. The culture and structure of the modern Egyptian judicial system is an

---

[88] Robert Bogdan, "Participant Observation," *Peabody Journal of Education* 50, no. 4. (July 1973): 303.

amalgamation of two different institutional experiences: the Islamic courts and the Mixed Courts. These two historical legacies left enduring marks on the structure and culture of the modern Egyptian judiciary.

The practices, norms, and rulings of the Islamic Courts (800–1950s), Mixed Courts (1876–1949), the National Courts (1883–present), and the Council of State (1946–present) embedded the activist role of Egyptian judges and cultivated the popular respect for the judiciary. These two features – the self-proclaimed activism and the widespread public support for the judicial institutions, especially in comparison to the executive and the legislative branches – became defining attributes of the modern judicial politics of Egypt.

Chapter 3, *Nasser's Egypt: Charisma, Populism, and the Attacks on Judicial Independence,* investigates the state-court interaction during the reign of Nasser (1952–1970). Nasser based his regime survival on direct personal appeal and was not particularly concerned with emphasizing the rule of law or judicial independence. The regime was able to attract mass support through socialist economic programs and the populist policies. In addition, revolutionary leaders generally demonstrate a lack of interest in legalists' concern for protecting the status quo or incrementally changing it.

Populist revolutionary leaders seek to mold both the society and the polity according to their revolutionary perceptions and norms. Legal institutions, including the courts, were regarded as a reservoir of reactionary ideas and an obstacle for change rather than a vehicle for reform. No wonder that the relation between the regime and the courts was strained. This chapter is divided into two sections. The first outlines the emergence and significance of Nasser's revolutionary charismatic leadership. The second examines the Nasserite regime's policy toward courts and judges, especially in matters related to judicial independence. This section analyzes the change in judicial behavior from an independent, active, and liberal role to a much more timid, limited, and conservative role.

Chapter 4, *The Years of Sadat: Crisis, Regime Survival, and the Awakening of Judicial Activism (1970–1981),* introduces the linkage of the regime's bid for political survival to the restoration of judicial institutional independence. Furthermore, it studies the slow emergence of liberal judicial activism and investigates its effect on the Egyptian polity. It also underscores the regime's effort to control the judicial institutions without damaging the liberal image it sought to portray to serve its domestic and international agenda.

The sudden death of Nasser in September 1970 dealt a massive blow to the charisma-reliant populist political regime. Sadat had to establish his own survival strategy that distinguished his regime from that of his predecessor.

This was no easy task as Sadat lacked Nasser's charisma and revolutionary credentials. The struggling war economy denied any hopes of legitimacy based on entitlement or social programs for the lower classes. Sadat decided to embrace institutionalism to shore up his regime. The regime became dependent on the courts' RSFs. The regime's rule of law orientations had a positive effect on judicial independence directly and indirectly. Directly, the regime strengthened the rule of law institutions, particularly the judiciary. The courts' institutional independence grew under Sadat. Indirectly, courts benefited from the atmosphere of political openness, the multi-party system, and a freer press. This context enabled the reconstitution of the judicial support structure, i.e., the bar, civil society organizations, professional syndicates, and later oppositional parties that became instrumental in defending judicial independence.

Chapter 5, *Judicial Politics under Mubarak: Judges and the Fall of the Pharaoh (1981–2011)*, further advances the argument linking regime survival to judicial independence. It examines the profound political role courts and judges played from under Mubarak. Mubarak relied on courts' RSFs as a principal foundation of his political system. This had positive implications on the judiciary. The regime's tolerance toward the expansion of judges' role in the political process came to a holt in the early years of the new millennia. The regime attacks on judicial activism and its feverish efforts to reassert control wrecked its survival strategy. The regime first undermined the institutional independence of the SCC. It then moved to domesticate the Judges Club. Lastly, it ended judicial oversight of the elections that the regime itself previously endorsed. The regime started to defy rulings openly for the first time since the death of Sadat. This prevented the courts from delivering the needed RSFs and opened the floodgates of popular protests that ended Mubarak's oppressive rule.

Mubarak's bid for political survival and the impact on the political role of the judiciary is the subject of this chapter, which is divided into four main sections. The first section outlines Mubarak's embrace of institutionalism, focusing on the president's rhetoric and legislative changes related to the courts. The second section investigates the expansion of the liberal-activist judicial role. The third section examines the regime's policies to influence and control courts and judges. The fourth focuses on the state-courts' interaction in the third millennia up until Mubarak's abdication.

Chapter 6, *The SCAF, the Courts, and Islamists: Judges and Political Transition (2011–2012)*, sheds light on judicial activism in post-Mubarak Egypt. Mubarak's departure marked the beginning of the era of the Supreme Council of the Armed Forces (SCAF). The SCAF sought to limit the revolutionary change to a minimum and keep the main pillars of the first republic that dominated Egypt's politics since 1952.

This chapter investigates the oversized role the courts played in the transition process. It analyzes the legal changes related to the institutional independence and the political role of the courts, particularly the SCC. Understanding the active role courts played in 2011–2012 as well as judges' intense interactions with generals and Islamists is the locus of this chapter, which is divided into three sections. The first examines how did the courts destroy the pillars of the old regime. The second accentuates how judges help build and dismantle the political institutions of the new political order. The third section investigates the courts' actions that influenced the constitutional-drafting process under the SCAF leadership.

Chapter 7, *Mursi and the Judiciary: The Self-Fulfilling Prophecy* (2012–2013), underscores the role courts and judges played in undermining the regime of Mohamed Mursi, Egypt's first democratically elected civilian president. This chapter contends that a reservoir of mistrust between the courts and Mursi coupled with the regime's inability to devise a suitable policy to manage its relationship with the judiciary had devastating consequences.

The executive–judicial confrontations under Mursi are the nucleus of this chapter, which is divided into two sections. In section one, I analyze the regime's discourse and policies toward the courts, with a focus on two case studies: the conflict over the PP and the constitutional-drafting process. I conclude with an analysis of the changes related to the judiciary in the 2012 Constitution. In section two, I move to study judicial counteroffensives on the regime. Judicial rulings and actions were instrumental in the coordinated strategy to delegitimize the presidency. Furthermore, judicial rulings were the *raison d'etre* for postponing legislative elections. Judicial actions on and off the bench dealt a massive blow to the regime's public standing and facilitated conditions that enabled the army takeover on July 3rd, 2013.

Chapter 8, *Patricians and Plebeians: The Chief Justice Paves the Road to the General* (2013–2014), explores how judicial behavior shaped the second transition period and facilitated the ascendance of Gen. Sisi to power. The removal of Mursi marked the beginning of a new era in Egypt's history. An age when the counterrevolutionary forces were able to scale back the revolutionary wave of 2011–2013. The 2013–2014 period presents striking similarities to the post-1952 period. Both eras witnessed an intense program to consolidate powers at the hands of the military leadership. Judges collaborated with both army takeovers and helped shore up the two military regimes.

The deep, profound, and widespread role the courts played in the restoration of the old order is the center of this chapter, which is divided into three sections. The first covers the role of the Interim President Adly Mansour in restoring the old order through the enactment of a series of laws and executive orders. The second investigates the judicial policies and explains the marked transformation of judicialization from challenging the regimes of Mubarak and Mursi to supporting the heavy hand after July 3, 2013. The third section highlights the changes pertaining to the judiciary in the 2014 Constitution.

Chapter 9, *Old Wine in a New Bottle: Sisi, Judges, and the Restoration of the Ancien Régime (2014–2018)* underscores the generals and judges' interaction during Sisi's first term in office. This chapter highlights the general's strategy to achieve complete political consolidation over all aspects of the political, social, and economic life. It details how courts facilitated many of the regime's heavy-handed policies. It also highlights the pockets of judicial resistance and how Sisi sought to assert control over all judicial institutions. It concludes by offering a window on the judicial-military relationship in the future. If the model presented in this work holds, the synergy between judges and generals will not last. Confrontation is likely to come, and it is not going to be pleasant. Sisi's actions to fully subordinate the justice system to presidential dictates and regime interests would likely undermine the residual faith in the courts and would negate any hope of democratization, rule of law, or checks and balances.

Egypt under Sisi and judicial politics during general's first term in office is the subject of this chapter, which is divided into two sections. The first investigates Sisi's program to establish full presidential hegemony over the state and society. This section details the regime policies to consolidate power in the security and civilian sectors of government. It then moves to underscores the strategies to restore the state's control over the polity and the society. Section two analyzes the state-courts' interaction. This section details the RSFs provided by the judiciary in service of the regime, investigates judicial rulings and actions that defied the regime's policies, and concludes by examining Sisi's legal changes to the laws governing judicial institutions to increase executive control over the courts.

2

The Historical Legacies and the Institutional Culture of the Egyptian Judiciary

I love this country, and you and I cannot live elsewhere ... However, without laws and courts in this country, it will be impossible for me to continue residing here. I am suffering and injustice makes me miserable. We ought to establish courts to safeguard us from the Europeans. *We ought to establish courts to safeguard us from the ruler. We need courts in order to live in security and dignity.*[1]
Nubar's letter to his wife dated February 25, 1867.[2]

Judicial autonomy is crucial to allow judges the necessary freedom to play a significant political role if they so wish. That being said, after securing their institutional independence, judges can behave in many different ways. Courts are not empty vessels made in the image and to serve the purpose of the regime. Institutions are more than an equilibrium that is dictated by the preferences and actions of outside actors. Institutions are living, breathing creatures that have its institutional cultures and goals. If comprehending the regime's incentives provides us with a clear understanding of the policies toward the polity and courts, it is imperative to shed some light on judicial culture. These cultural attributes influence the adjudication process and other forms of judicial behavior. Without studying the collective identity of Egyptian judges, it is unfeasible to understand the role that courts and judges played (and will continue to play) in Egyptian politics. We need to open the black box that is the Egyptian judiciary.

In a civil law bureaucratic judiciary, looking back at the critical junctures in the creation and sustaining of the institutions is of paramount importance. The institutional culture of the modern Egyptian judiciary brings together

---

[1] Nubar Pasha, *Nubar fī Misr*, 'arḍ wa-taqdīm Nabīl Zakī (al-Qahirah: Mu'assasat Akhbār al-Yawm, 1991), 173–174, emphasis added.

[2] Boghos Nubar Pasha (1825–1899), an Egyptian statesman of Armenian descent, was Egypt's first prime minister, a position he held on three different occasions. He also served as minister of foreign affairs under Isma'il Pasha (1863–1897).

features of the Islamic religious heritage with modern liberal political ideals. The culture and structure of the modern Egyptian judicial system is an amalgamation of two different institutional experiences: the Islamic courts and the Mixed Courts. These two historical legacies left enduring marks on the structure and culture of Egypt's courts.

In this chapter, I scrutinize how these two foundational institutions influenced the development of the modern courts in Egypt. I devote increasing attention and space as the institutional experience comes nearer to the present day. Then I move to underscore the experiences of the National Courts (courts of general jurisdiction) and the Council of State (administrative tribunals). These two institutions represent the backbone of the Egyptian judiciary today.

THE ISLAMIC COURTS AND THE CENTRALITY OF JUDGESHIP

During the reign of the second caliph Umar ibn Al-Khattāb (c. 634–644), Egypt became part of the Islamic empire. Nevertheless, Christianity remained the dominant religion for a few centuries. Islam became the religion of choice for the majority of Egyptians early in the second millennium and has remained the religion of the majority of Egyptians ever since. The role of judges in Islam and Islamic history has influenced the judicial practices of Egypt in the past and present.

In Islam, judgeship emerged as a position of high stature. After all, the prophet Muhammad was the first judge in Islam. He ruled in disputes amongst Muslims and between Muslims and non-Muslims. In early Islam, the Judge, *qadi*, was the second most important position after the caliph in the capital or the governor in the provinces. In the initial periods of Islamic history, the caliph himself directly appointed all judges. Later, a two-tier system emerged by which the caliph was to appoint the chief justice, which in turn had the power to dispatch judges to the different prefectures of the empire.

Judges were appointed from amongst the ranks of renowned religious scholars, who were known for their integrity, impartiality, and good moral character. Islam emphasized judges' personal independence from social and political pressures. Islam mandated judges' financial independence by assigning them salaries from the public treasury. At that time in human history, it was customary for judges to collect fees from the parties appearing before them, a practice that the Islamic practices forbade. Early Muslims recognized how receiving compensation from the parties appearing before a judge can damage his independence and credibility.

Islam also fostered judicial creativity. Many instances of judicial creativity are evident in Quran. The judges-made law became a staple of judges who were also *fuqaha* – persons trained in *fiqh* (singular *faqih*). Beyond the provisions of Quran and Sunnah (the body of Islamic custom and practice based on Muhammad's words and deeds) and the principal directions of *fiqh* (Islamic jurisprudence), Judges had the latitude in using their ingenuity to solve legal problems. If the judge could not find legal guidance in those three sources, he had the freedom to make his ruling. *Qadis* were not bound by previous judgments, and no rule of binding precedent emerged in Islamic law.

Islam also instituted the right to appeal rulings to a higher authority, the prophet during his life, and the caliph or the ruler in later times. *Fiqh* established two conditions for overturning a ruling: procedural and substantive. The ruling is procedurally invalid if the person who issued it lacked the qualifications of the judge. On the other hand, the ruling was deemed void if it contradicted the principles of Islamic jurisprudence. This is very similar to the modern appeal practices in Egypt.

The *qadi* was obliged to follow certain basic procedures. Chief amongst them was to consider all people equally and to act impartially. The *qadi* was supposed to listen carefully to the evidence given by the witnesses, to encourage compromise between parties given that the agreement did not violate principles of Islam or was otherwise illegal, and to give judgment.

Some distinguished judges in Islam became part of the popular culture that judges and non-judges embrace and seek to imitate. One prominent figure that was repeatedly mentioned in my interviews with judges is Al-Ezz Ibn Abd-Elsalam. Ibn Abd-Elsalam (1182–1262) was an Islamic scholar and a judge who repeatedly challenged unjust rulers. He was imprisoned and had to emigrate from Syria to Egypt, but in the end, the ruler submitted to his authority and justice prevailed over the objection of the ruling elite. Many conversations with judges reveal a sense of judgeship as seeking justice, not merely applying procedures. Another story that was also repeatedly mentioned is related to the fourth Caliph Ali. This is how one judge put it:

> Ali lost his shield and saw a Jewish man selling it in the market. Ali claimed the shield, but the man insisted of his ownership and asked to see the judge. The judge, Umar, asked Ali if he has witnesses to collaborate his story. Ali said his two sons (prophet Muhammad's grandsons) know what happened and they can testify. Umar refused to allow the testimony of the two sons on behalf of their father. His ruling was that Ali could not verify his claim and that the man can keep the shield.[3]

---

[3]   Personal Interview with Hussam Al-Ghariani, vice-president of the Court of Cassation, June 26, 2016. Judge Al-Ghariani assumed the presidency of the Court of Cassation and the High

The main lesson, I was told, is that a judge should not consider the social status of the persons in the dispute and should only serve justice. Islamic folk culture is also full of stories of noted scholars who refused to assume judgeship because of the severity of the position.

The Islamic religious courts dominated Egypt's adjudication for more than a millennium. These courts served the populous reasonably well until the great decline in the Middle Ages. Ottoman judicial practices were not particularly hospitable to Egyptians. The administrative deterioration of the Ottoman Empire left its mark on Egypt. The judicial administration of Egypt in the seventeenth and eighteenth centuries mostly resembled other Ottoman provinces. The justice system was corrupt, outdated, and dominated by officials who were neither versed in law nor Arabic.[4] Egypt's modern judicial history finds its earlier ancestors in the administrative innovations of Muhammad 'Ali. In addition to the religious courts (courts of general jurisdiction), "Of particular significance for the future were councils (*majalis*, sing. *majlis*) with judicial powers that were established throughout Egypt in the 1840s, and the *Majlis al-Ahkam*, a kind of supreme court."[5] Moreover, there were special councils for trade disputes called merchants' councils. Those new judicial bodies slashed parts of the jurisdiction of the long-standing Shari'a or Islamic religious courts.[6] During this era, "the most characteristic and remarkable feature of the Egyptian legal system consists in the multiplicity of jurisdictions which divide among them the litigious business of the country."[7]

Under British occupation, the imperial power sought to bring the Shari'a Courts under their authority. Nevertheless, a reorganization proposal was defeated after fierce opposition from the religious judges and *Al-Azhar*. Shari'a Courts continued to function in legal disputes related to personal matters until the 1950s when these courts were absorbed in the secular judiciary. Shari'a, however, is still applied in personal disputes until the present day.

Judicial Council (HJC) (2011–2012). He then chaired the Constituent Assembly that drafted the 2012 Constitution.

[4] Galal H. El-Nahal, *The Judicial Administration of Ottoman Egypt in the Seventeenth Century* (Minneapolis, MN: Bibliotheca Islamica, 1979).

[5] Enid Hill, "Courts and the Administration of Justice in the Modern Era," in *The State and Its Servants: Administration in Egypt from Ottoman Times to the Present*, ed., Nelly Hanna (Cairo: The American University in Cairo Press, 1995), 98.

[6] Hāmid Muhammad Abū Tālib, *Nizām al-qadā' al-Misrī fī mīzān al-sharī'ah* (al-Qahirah: Dār al-Fikr al-'Arabī, 1993), 52–53.

[7] Maurice S. Amos, Legal Administration in Egypt, *Journal of Comparative Legislation and International Law* 12, no. 4, (1930): 168–169.

The Islamic influence over modern judicial attitudes is powerful and viable. For instance, Badawi Hamouda, the first chief justice of the Supreme Court, argued that it was Mohamed Abdou, Egypt's most distinguished Islamic scholar of the modern age, who first championed the principle of judicial immunity in the nineteenth century.[8] The emphasis on religion as a way to empower judicial activism and guide judicial actions was exceptionally evident in many judges' speeches and interviews. The references to the experience of many past Muslim judges who defied the executive and enforced the rule of law was also evident.

Judge Mahmoud Mekki's writings and public statements emphasize the role of Islam in the struggle for political freedom. He repeatedly spoke of early Muslim judges as role models.[9] Ahmed Mekki, the first vice-president of the Court of Cassation 2009–2011, and minister of justice under Mursi highlighted how Islam offers solutions to the problem of despotism, a solution that structures the rapport between judges and the political authority. He maintained that Islam, in principle, is no different from the liberal European aspirations for a free system of government:

> 1) Islam believes in the rule of law principle ... 2) Islam has known the separation of powers principle ... 3) Furthermore, the sovereignty of the people or that of the nation as the source of powers was mentioned in the Quran and Sunnah [the Prophet's heritage and commandments] in requiring Shura [consultation] and acceptance and prohibiting coercion.[10]

Besides, judges, particularly within the Council of State, buttress their opposition to allowing females to sit on the bench by frequently pointing out the Islamic prohibition on women assuming the position of a judge. Those judges often cite religious opinions attributed to Prophet Muhammad and other notable scholars against such an appointment. They also point to the lack of female judgeship in the lengthy Islamic history.

---

[8] Meeting No. 12, Al-legna al-tahdeereyya li wada'a mashrua'a al-dustur, 23. Judicial immunity in Egypt has an expanded meaning. In addition to the legal immunity, which protects judges from lawsuits brought against them for official conduct in office, Egyptian judges enjoy personal immunity in the form of protection for them and their homes from search, arrest, or other form of legal action. That was particularly important in a country where the security forces had expanded authority to detain without a court order.

[9] Personal interviews with Mahmoud Mekki, vice-president of the Court of Cassation, multiple interviews in 2006. Mekki served as vice-president of the Republic under President Mursi until the office was abolished in the 2012 Constitution.

[10] Ahmed Mekki, "al-ṣidām bin al-niẓām al-Nāṣiri wa al-quḍāt," in Nabīl ʿAbd al-Fattāḥ (ed.), *al-Quḍāh wa-al-iṣlāḥ al-siyāsī*, 83.

THE MIXED COURTS AND THE LIBERAL INFLUENCE

The Mixed Courts' experience has not been particularly popular among Egyptian scholars. Until recently, most Egyptian jurists and judges tended either to ignore the Mixed Courts' experience altogether or evaluate its impact on the national judiciary unenthusiastically.[11] Nonetheless, the Mixed Courts put their enduring mark on the structure of the Egyptian judiciary and, more importantly, on judicial practices, attitudes, and behavior.

In the nineteenth century, Egypt suffered from the principle of *extraterritoriality*. This meant that European laws, not Egyptian, applied to Europeans residing in Egypt. Extraterritoriality was an upshot of the *Capitulations System*. Under this system, foreigners and others who enjoyed expatriate status were immune from prosecution in Egyptian courts. All litigation between foreigners and Egyptians had to be brought before one or more of the Consular Courts of the seventeen capitulatory states, recognized by the Ottoman Sultan. Egyptians and their government were in an extremely vulnerable or helpless position for two reasons. First, the Consular Courts tended to favor their compatriots. Second, all appeals had to be heard before appellate courts on the Consular Courts' own soil. No wonder that the Consular Courts were notorious in their judgments against Egyptians as well as the Egyptian government.[12]

While Muhammad 'Ali's (1805–1849) heavy hand kept the Consular Courts at bay, after his death, the Capitulations System expanded enormously. A French Investigatory Committee of 1876 argued, "The Capitulations has been replaced by unrestrained customary situations molded according to the European representatives' views."[13] It would not be a surprise that many Egyptian officials explored legal alternatives to either eliminate or minimize the impact of the Consular Courts. This led, in the end, to the establishment of the Mixed Courts.[14]

---

[11] It's rather interesting that the evaluation of the Mixed Courts experience is more positive today among Egyptian judges than any point in history. In my interviews, notable reformist judges praised the independence of the courts and its practices.

[12] Azīz Khānkī, *al-Mahākim al-mukhtalitah wa-al-mahākim al-ahlīyah: mādīhā, hādirhā, mustaqbalahā* (al-Qahirah: al-Matba'ah al-'Asrīyah, 1939), 24–27.

[13] Abd al-Hamid Badowi pasha, "athr al-amtizat fi al-qudaa wa al-tashrea' fi misr", in *al-Kitāb al-dhahabī lil-mahākim al-ahlīyah*, Mahkamt al-Naqd, al-juz' 1 (al-Qahirah: al-Matba'ah al-Ami'ri'yah, 1937), 1–61.

[14] The Mixed Courts were initially called "the 'Courts of the Reform' and were composed of 'mixed magistrates: that is, judges from some fourteen capitulatory powers, as well as Egyptian judges, hence the name by which they came to be known." Enid Hill, "The Golden

Nubar Pasha, the founder of the Mixed Courts, sought to mitigate the Capitulations' problems by establishing a modern judicial system. This was not an easy task; neither European countries nor the Khedive (the title of Egypt's ruler) could be expected to welcome any institution, legal or otherwise, that might constrain their authority. Nubar had first to persuade the Khedive. He drew on Ismail's fury toward the immense power of the European consulates, stressing how these consulars exerted their authority over all Egyptians, governed and governors alike. Nubar argued, "If you want to be really independent, you have to be your own master. Your government now is composed of 17 different consulars. There are 17 consulates, each of which has as much moral clout and practical power as you and occasionally hinder your authority."[15]

Nubar not only wanted to get rid of the Capitulations but also sought to liberalize the political structure in Egypt. Cannon stated, "There may also have been more direct political implications. According to Nubar's memoirs, his original plan sought to eliminate the causes, not merely mitigate the symptoms of insecurity among local subjects and foreign residents in Egypt."[16] Brown agreed and suggested that Nubar sought "to restrict the power of the khedive."[17] Therefore, "the operation of the system [he envisaged] was safe from – and even circumscribed – the power of the Khedive."[18]

Nubar wanted to check the unrestricted power of the Khedive by establishing an independent judiciary. He sought to limit the ruler's absolute power by expanding the scope and jurisdiction of the proposed Mixed Courts. Nubar suggested that the new courts have jurisdiction over all individuals in Egypt: citizens, residents, and foreigners. Furthermore, he suggested that these courts have jurisdiction over all matters, civil and criminal. It was clear that "Nubar's *ideal would have been to establish legal limits on the arbitrary use of executive powers in Egypt* ... This was his assumption that the most effective check on abusive personal power rested in the administrative apparatus of the courts themselves, not in some form of representative body."[19] Nubar designed the system to achieve these objectives. This decision would have enduring

---

Anniversary of Egypt's National Courts," in Jill Edwards (ed.), *Historians in Cairo: Essays in Honor of George Scanlon* (Cairo: American University in Cairo Press, 2002), 204.

[15] Pasha, *Nūbār fī Misr*, 175.

[16] Byron Cannon, *Politics of Law and the Courts in Nineteenth-Century Egypt* (Salt Lake City: University of Utah Press, 1988), 46–47.

[17] Nathan J. Brown, "The Precarious Life and Slow Death of the Mixed Courts of Egypt," *International Journal of Middle East Studies* 25, no. 1. (February 1993): 35.

[18] Ibid., 35.

[19] Cannon. *Politics of Law and the Courts in Nineteenth-Century Egypt*, 46–47.

implications. This historical mission could still be sensed today among many
Egyptian judges.[20]

After Nubar Pasha convinced the Khedive, he had to obtain the approval of
the capitulatory powers.[21] It took long and arduous negotiations between
Egypt and the capitulatory powers, but on June 28, 1875, an agreement was
signed establishing the Mixed Courts.[22] The Mixed Courts began to operate in
1876. The courts' structure and jurisdiction were a radical reform of Egypt's
chaotic nineteenth-century legal system, where Consular Courts competed
with government tribunals and religious courts for jurisdiction over and
enforcement of a multitude of claims.[23]

The 1875 Charter of the Mixed Courts established their locations and
jurisdiction. There was one Court of Appeal in Alexandria and three courts
of the first instance: Alexandria, Cairo, and Mansura. According to Article 9 of
its Charter, "These courts had exclusive jurisdiction in all litigation involving
civil and commercial matters arising between natives and foreigners and
between foreigners of different nationalities, with the exception of personal
status matters. They shall also have exclusive jurisdiction in all suits concerning real estate between natives and foreigners and between foreigners of the
same nationality or different nationalities."[24] The Mixed Courts radically
changed the Egyptian judicial process. For the first time in Egypt's long

---

[20] Even judges who were well-known advocates of judicial restraint could not ignore this
institutional mission. Mohamed *Fathi Najib*, a well-known regime loyalist, former president of
the Court of Cassation and the SCC argued that the Egyptian judiciary "has grown out of only
performing its justice function to emerge as a balancing power that manages to control the
rhythm of the other two authorities within the requirements and principles of democracy."
Muḥammad Fatḥi Najib, *al-Tanẓim al-qadai al-Misri* (al-Qahirah: Dar al-Ṭiba'ah al-Ḥadithah,
1998), 9.

[21] It seems that Khedive Ismail did not forgive Nubar Pasha for his efforts to establish the Mixed
Courts and consequently limited his power. The British and French consulars narrated that
Ismail clearly indicated that he did not trust Nubar and "firmly believe that he has worked to
undermine and limit his authority." Ilyas Ayyubī, *Ta'rikh Misr fī 'ahd al-Khidiw Isma'il Pasha:
min sanat 1863 ila 1879* (al-Qahirah: Matba'at Dar al-Kutub al-Misrīyah, 1923), al-juz' 2, 470.

[22] B. A. Roberson, "The Emergance of the Modern Judiciary in the Middle East: Negotiating the
Mixed Courts of Egypt," in Chibli Mallat (ed.), *Islam and Public Law* (London: Graham &
Trotman, 1993), 107–139.

[23] According to Goldberg, "These courts saw themselves as the protectors not only of natural
individuals but also of foreign companies (imbued with legal personality after all) even if only
partly owned by foreigners." Ellis Goldberg, *Tinker, Tailor, Textile Worker* (Berkeley: University
of California Press, 1986), 62.

[24] Herbert J. Liebesny, *The Law of the Near & Middle East: Readings, Cases, & Materials*
(Albany: State University of New York Press, 1975), 72. It is important to note that the
establishment of the Mixed Courts did not abolish the Consular Courts altogether. The former
continued to adjudicate criminal cases as well as civil and commercial matters (excluding
real estate disputes) if all parties in the dispute were from one nationality. See Latifah

history, the government and the Crown could be sued in the courts. Article 10 of the Charter stated, "The Egyptian Government, the administrative offices, and the estates of the Khedive and of members of his family shall be subject to the jurisdiction of these courts."[25]

The Mixed Courts had some specific provisions that enabled them to fulfill their legal and political mission. One article added to the mixed codes (and borrowed neither from *Code Napoléon* nor from English law) required the government to enforce judgments against itself. That is, if a foreigner sued the government and won, the government was obligated to carry out the ruling. When the courts issued a ruling against the Khedive and the government refused to enforce it, judges declared their intention to leave Egypt. Some judges abstained from issuing rulings. These actions generated mounting pressure on the government. In the end, the Khedive caved and gave assurance that all rulings would be enforced in the future.[26]

In addition, Egypt agreed to adopt the French *parquet* or *ministère public* system. This system designated officers of the court to investigate and prosecute crimes, advise the court on legal matters, and represent the general interest of the state.[27] The construction of the *parquet* and its removal from the Egyptian government's control limited the degree to which Egypt's rulers could influence the courts.[28] This is the primary foundation of the work of the Public Prosecution Department (PPD).

The Mixed Courts' adjudication provided compelling examples of judicial activism. The courts' powers even extended to the legislative domain. Taking advantage of the absence of a functional legislative council in Egypt since the beginning of British occupation, the Mixed Courts in 1911 obtained legislative powers in matters related to the codes it applied. Law 7/1911 granted "a legislative assembly, consisting of all appeals-court judges and lower-court judges from those capitulatory powers not represented on the appeals court, was granted the authority to approve legislation and also to propose legislation to the government relating to foreigners."[29] This expanded political role is

---

Muhammad Salim, *Tarikh al-qadai al-Misri al-hadith, (al-juz' 1), 1875–1914* (al-Qahirah: al-Hayah al-Misriyah al-'Ammah lil-Kitab, 2000), 187.

[25] Liebesny, *The Law of the Near & Middle East*, 72–73.

[26] Salim, *Tarikh al-qadai al-Misri al-hadith, al-juz' 1, 1875–1914*, 136.

[27] In Egypt, this office, in either the Mixed or the National Court was called *al-Niabba* named hereafter, public prosecution. It is "a government bureau for the investigation and prosecution of crimes and other activities in the public interest; the officials are in hierarchy parallel to the hierarchy of the judges." Enid Hill, *Mahkama!: Studies in the Egyptian Legal System: Courts & Crimes, Law & Society* (London: Ithaca Press, 1979), 171–172.

[28] Brown, *The Precarious Life and Slow Death of the Mixed Courts of Egypt*, 35.

[29] Ibid., 40.

unmatched in other judicial experiences. Only the Egyptian Council of State has secured similar powers under the 2014 Constitution. Article 174 states that the State Council "reviews and drafts bills and resolutions of legislative character referred to it."

Sixty years after the establishment of the Mixed Courts, the Egyptian jurist Ramzi Saif argued for the first time, citizens and residents of Egypt experienced the practice of truly modern courts, where independent and qualified judges issued rulings out of conviction.[30] In retrospect, the Mixed Courts had lasting imprints on the Egyptian judicial structure, practices, and personnel.

First, the courts were remarkably independent institutionally and financially. Article 5 of the Mixed Courts Charter instituted a multilateral appointment process. It stated, "The choice and appointment of the judges shall be made by the Egyptian Government; but in order to be assured of the qualification possessed by the persons whom it may select, it shall address itself unofficially to the ministers of justice abroad and shall only engage persons who have received the approval and authorization of their government." Once appointed, those judges cannot be removed. Article 19 of the Charter states, "The judges who compose the Court of Appeal and the District Courts shall not be removable."[31] This institutional independence withstood the Egyptian Government and the British authorities' attempts to control or influence its functions. Brinton, an American judge who sat on the courts, wrote that the Mixed Courts' existence was "altogether independent of the existing political regime."[32] In addition to the institutional independence, the Mixed Courts enjoyed splendid financial autonomy. Judicial fees were a primary source of income. The Mixed Courts controlled their finances, removed the government hand from interference, and benefited from the continuous appreciation of their resources. Nonetheless, the Mixed Courts requested and usually secured increases in their government allotted budgets.[33]

Hoyle, in his comprehensive assessment of the Mixed Courts' legacy, maintained, "The judiciary could not be pressured or induced into a particular decision, whether directly or indirectly. Judges were honest, and there was equality before the law."[34] This would become an inspiring model for Egyptian judges in the years to come. Therefore, the Egyptian judicial

---

[30] Faruq Abd Al-Barr, *Dawr majlis al-Dawlah al-Misri fi himayat al-huquq wa-al-hurriyat al-`ammah* al-juz' 1, (al-Qahirah: n.p., 1988), 36.

[31] Liebesny, *The Law of the Near & Middle East: Readings, Cases, & Materials*, 72–73.

[32] Jasper Yeates Brinton, *The Mixed Courts of Egypt* (New Haven: Yale University Press, 1968), ix–x.

[33] Salim, *Tarikh al-qadai al-Misri al-hadith, al-juz'* 1, 1875–1914, 79.

[34] Mark Hoyle, *Mixed Courts of Egypt* (London: Graham & Trotman, 1991), 185–186.

community's struggle for judicial independence was due, at least partly, to the unprecedented degree of freedom that the Mixed Courts enjoyed.[35] This is practically true because a number of Egyptians serving on the mixed bench increased as time elapsed. Many distinguished Egyptian judges started their judicial career in the Mixed Courts and moved later to the National Courts or the Council of State. These judges brought with them an appreciation for the importance of strict judicial independence. When the Mixed Courts came to an end in 1949, most Egyptian judges that did not retire joined the ranks of the National Courts.[36]

Second, the Mixed Courts created, for the first time in the Egyptian judicial history, an institution with corporate interests that used its collective action resources to achieve institutional goals. Judges' lobbying compelled the government to enforce their rulings against the Khedive and sway legislation related to their jurisdiction. This corporate nature became one of the defining characteristics of the modern Egyptian judiciary. Modern Egyptian courts have used collective actions to achieve institutional goals. It is noticeable that the contemporary judges' array of collective action techniques to exert pressure on the political establishment is derivative of the strategies used by the Mixed Courts. Recent examples of collective judicial actions include the struggle between the Judges Club and the Mubarak's regime during the 2005–2006 judicial revolt and when different courts suspended their work to protest President Mursi's Constitutional Declaration that infringed on judicial independence in 2012.

Third, the Mixed Courts brought a sense of professionalism to the legal community. Supporters of the courts had no difficulty explaining the courts' resilience and longevity. The system, as Brinton observed in 1949, "had brought order out of chaos and, by endowing the country with a judicial system second to none on the continent of Europe."[37] This professionalism extended beyond judges themselves to lawyers and other administrative staff of the courts. This professionalism and professional pride could easily be traced

---

[35] The Mixed Courts' Code of 1875 granted their general assemblies the authority to elect the courts' presidents. This provided an important guarantee of institutional independence. This practice is still active in the institutional memory of the Egyptian courts. In 2002, then deputy-president of the Judges Club *Nagy Derbalah* wrote an article in the Judges Club periodical to argue for the restoration of the elected members in the HJC; surprisingly the first justification he provided was the Mixed Courts' experience. See Nagy Derbalah, *Al-Quda*, al-Sanah 19 (September 2002): 56–58.

[36] Latifah Muhammad Salim, *Tarikh al-qadai al-Misri al-hadith, al-juz' 2, 1914–1952* (al-Qahirah: al-Hayah al-Misriyah al-ʿAmmah lil-Kitab, 2000), 207.

[37] Brinton, *The Mixed Courts of Egypt*, 210.

through the sense of commitment to their profession that Egyptian judges express today.[38]

Fourth, the Mixed Courts had an enduring influence on the judicial decision-making processes. While Egyptian law and courts were modeled after the Napoleonic Code and the French judiciary, the increasing number of British and American judges serving in the courts, especially after the British Occupation in 1882, introduced elements of the common-law system. This development was critical for enhancing judicial decision-making discretion. The Egyptian judiciary developed beyond the strict application of the law that usually characterizes the civil law and bureaucratic judiciaries to include the latitude in the decision-making process, which common-law judges usually enjoy. This is a salient feature of Egypt's until the present day.

Fifth, the Mixed Courts helped spread public awareness of and augmented trust in the litigation process. Because the courts were independent, they were able to stand up to the government and issue rulings that ran counter to the government's interests. This added to the courts' legitimacy and contributed to the positive attitudes toward the judicial system. This would be vital to Sadat and Mubarak's regimes strategy of using the courts to perform Regime Survival Functions. Hoyle encapsulated this eloquently:

> All in all, a feeling of confidence in, and the fairness of, the Mixed Courts existed. Parties felt that disputes could and should be left to settlement by the courts, even if they did not know the specific legal term of what was claimed. They became conscious, nevertheless, of having certain loosely defined rights.[39]

Last but not least, the Mixed Courts preached a sense of liberalism among the Egyptian judicial community. The Mixed Courts "instructed Egyptians in the constitutional foundations of Western law... and civil liberties which become the basis of nationalist movement."[40] This manifested itself in the courts' apparent willingness to rule against the Egyptian Government or even against the Crown. This liberalism has been integrated into the professional socialization of judges and is still considered a salient attribute of the judicial political culture in Egypt. The example set by the Mixed Courts is still alive and well in the minds of many Egyptian judges.

---

[38] It was notable through all the interviews I conducted with different junior and senior judges, that only one junior judge (*n* of 50) thought he might want to change his professional career and work in the private sector.

[39] Hoyle, *Mixed Courts of Egypt*, 187–188.

[40] Nadav Safran, *Egypt in Search of Political Community* (Cambridge: Harvard University Press, 1961), 36.

Yahia Al-Rifai, arguably the godfather of the modern judicial independence movement, is a prominent example of the influence of European liberal intellectuals. Al-Rifai, while preaching judicial independence, quotes Montesquieu in his emphasis on the separation of power, "each branch of government could limit the power of the other two branches. Therefore, no branch of the government could threaten the freedom of the people."[41] The logical conclusion is that the judiciary ought to be independent and far from the undue influence or pressure from the holders of the "sword" or keepers of the "purse."

In making a case for democracy as a prerequisite for full judicial independence, Ahmed Mekki heavily leaned on liberal ideals:

> The European political thought, especially in England and France, engineered the democratic liberal political system that prevails today in the nations of the free world ... and that is the system that most people of the world aspire to imitate ... From the writings of Rousseau, Locke, Hobbes, and Montesquieu, the European and Western civilization devised a liberal democratic system that has three principles: first, the sovereignty of the people ... second, the principle of rule of law. ... third, the separation of power ... because the absolute power is absolute corruption as shown in Baron Acton's famous statement.[42]

Although the Mixed Courts were a modern and efficient judicial system, their jurisdiction was limited. Egyptian nationals were not subject to the Mixed Courts and continued to suffer from the most primordial courts and unqualified judges. Many Egyptian jurists aspired to benefit from the experience of the Mixed Courts in establishing the national courts. Another group of intellectuals was disgruntled with the Mixed Courts, arguing that the Mixed Courts were foreign courts that undermined Egyptian sovereignty.[43] Frequently, "the Mixed Courts were attacked as a colonial vestige detracting from the nation's sovereignty and independence."[44] Therefore, many nationalist leaders sought to establish modern national courts in order to abolish the Mixed Courts altogether or at least limit their jurisdiction.[45]

---

[41] Yahia Al-Rifai's introduction to Hamadah Husni, *'Abd al-Naṣir wa-al-qaḍaā*, 5.

[42] Mekki, "al-ṣidām bin al-niẓām al-Nāṣiri wa al-quḍāt," 81.

[43] See, for example, Abd al-Rahmān al-Rāfiʿī, *'Asr Ismāʿīl*, 270 and beyond.

[44] Amr Shalakany, "'I Heard It All Before': Egyptian Tales of Law and Development," *Third World Quarterly* 27, no. 5 (July 2006): 845.

[45] Curiously, this issue became one of the few areas where the views of Egyptian nationalists and the occupation authorities converged. Both wanted to abolish the Mixed Courts. Egyptians desired this because the Mixed Courts embodied the foreign encroachment on their rights, the British because of the obstacle the capitulations system continued to present in their attempt to

THE NATIONAL COURTS AND THE STRUCTURAL
FOUNDATIONS OF THE JUDICIARY

The establishment of a national judiciary modeled after the Mixed Courts but independent from them became an objective embraced by many Egyptians for a variety of different reasons. Enhancing state's national autonomy became a judicial aim in itself. Many judges configured their roles as guardians of the Egyptian state vis-à-vis foreign domination and domestic threats. This "state-center" tradition has stood shoulder to shoulder to "right-center" tradition within Egypt's judicial corps.

The establishment of the National Courts (*al-mahakim al-ahliya*), in 1883, was a fundamental addition to the Egyptian judicial system.[46] The structure of Egyptian judiciary today generally resembles that of the National Courts.[47] The National Courts were the first truly modern Egyptian judicial institution. Brown argued, "The decision to establish the National Courts in 1883 represented a shift in several ways: it established a separate, professional judiciary; it involved borrowing large parts of the French legal code; and it established a hierarchy of courts that has been greatly supplemented but not to this day replaced."[48] The Egyptian elite exploited the dominance of the civil law legal tradition and the commanding presence of Mixed Courts to create a civil law judicial system that would minimize British influence. Brown maintained:

> In Egypt, legal reform was largely the fruit of efforts undertaken by centralizing elite that sought to circumscribe foreign influence even when it collaborated with it. The national elite used law to preempt imperial penetration and strengthen the administrative capacity of the Egyptian state.[49]

secure complete control over Egyptian affairs. See Jasper Y. Brinton, "The Closing of the Mixed Courts of Egypt," *The American Journal of International Law* 44, no. 2 (April 1950): 303–312.

[46] The term National Courts will be used interchangeably with the courts of general jurisdiction to refer to the plethora of civil and criminal courts in Egypt.

[47] Referred to at their founding and at the time of their fiftieth anniversary as *al-mahakim al-ahliya*, these courts are now known as *al-mahakim al-wataniya*. "Whereas the initial designation could be translated National Courts, the English referred to them as 'native courts' and the French as 'tribunaux indignés' – admittedly unfaltering, indeed patronizing expressions in the charged nationalistic atmosphere of Egypt." Hill, "The Golden Anniversary of Egypt's National Courts," 220.

[48] Nathan J Brown, "Law and Imperialism: Egypt in Comparative Perspective Retrospective," *Law & Society Review* 29, no. 1 (1995): 109.

[49] Ibid., 109–110.

The story of the National Courts started in 1882 when the minister of justice commissioned a committee to recommend measures for judicial reform. The committee proposed an institution drawn from the Mixed Codes but adjusted to the local circumstances. It recommended that judges should be qualified and independent-minded, as well as empowered with guarantees of judicial independence. The committee advocated the appointment of some Mixed Courts' Egyptian and European judges as well as other European jurists acquainted with the Egyptian society in order to cultivate social trust for the new courts.[50] The National Courts with jurisdiction over civil and criminal cases were first implemented in the Delta in 1883, and when they proved successful, they were introduced to Upper Egypt in 1889.[51] Following in the Mixed Courts' footsteps, the National Courts were established with two levels: courts of first instance, and a court of appeals in Cairo. The second court of appeals in *Assuit* (Upper Egypt) was established in 1925.[52] From the outset, the salience and significance of judicial independence were evident. The memorandum argued that judges should be knowledgeable and independent. The minister stated:

Whereas administrative officers can be guided in their decisions by their superiors, judges cannot receive any sort of orders. Therefore, judges have to be more educated and endowed than senior government officials. Hence, they have to be chosen by a select committee and confirmed by the cabinet itself. In regard to independence ... judges' salaries must be sufficient and any judge should feel safe about his life, income, and position.[53]

In the period between their establishment and the 1952 Revolution, the National Courts passed through three different phases.[54] The first was the

---

[50] A Transcript of the Deliberations of the Council of Ministers on 2 November 1882 in Mahkamt al-Naqd, *al-Kitāb al-dhahabī lil-mahākim al-ahlīyah*, al-juz' 1 (al-Qahirah: al-Matba'ah al-Ami'ri'yah, 1937), 102–106.

[51] While the National Courts curtailed the jurisdiction of the religious *"Shari'a"* courts, they did not eradicate it altogether. These courts continued to have jurisdiction over personal matters for the Egyptian citizens. Those courts had jurisdiction over all citizens, Muslims and non-Muslims. However, if all parties in the dispute agreed, they could choose one of the three officially recognized religious or *Meli* councils: Coptic Orthodox, Anglican Protestant, and Armenian Catholic. For more details see Ahmed Safout Bek, "al-mahakim al-ahliya wa quda' al-majlis al-meli fi al-ahoual al-shakhsia legher al-muslimen," in Mahkamt al-Naqd, *al-Kitāb al-dhahabī lil-mahākim al-ahlīyah*, al-juz' 1, 257–278.

[52] Hill, *Mahkama!*, 50.

[53] Memorandum by Minister of Justice Husayn Fakhri pasha to the Council of Ministers, in Mahkamt al-Naqd, *al-Kitāb al-dhahabī lil-mahākim al-ahlīyah*, al-juz' 1, 111–115.

[54] This historical assessment mirrors the one advocated by Al-Sanhuri, Nadiyah and Tawfiq al-Shawi, eds., 'Abd al-Razzāq Ahmad Sanhuri, *Majallat Majlis al-Dawlah*, 2, (January 1951): viii–xii.

establishment phase when the courts were in their infancy. Judicial knowledge, language, and adjudication were underdeveloped and many of the judges lacked sufficient legal training. However, the courts were reinforced by the infusion of new personnel from *Al-Azhar* and the new school of *Dar El-Ulum*.[55] Those judges albeit not properly trained according to Western standards, were nonetheless men of high stature and had a profound knowledge of Islam and society.

The second phase, which followed the 1919 Revolution, came about when this old generation was approaching retirement. The new judges were young professionals who received advanced judicial training in France or in Egypt by European professors. This generation strived to develop the National Courts' jurisprudence to match that of the Mixed Courts. They struggled to create an independent legal tradition and national jurisprudence. Judge Al-Bishri pointed rightly to the socioeconomic background of this generation, arguing that judges came, for the first time, from outside the Turkish ruling elite that dominated the judiciary in the pre-1919 era. He also demonstrated, using rates of conviction in political cases, that this new generation's jurisprudence was far more liberal and nationalistic in comparison to the founding fathers.[56]

The third phase was marked by the inauguration of the Court of Cassation in 1931. In this "renaissance" period, the National Courts established their unique judicial jurisprudence and legal language. By their golden anniversary, the National Courts developed a distinct judicial culture.[57] The National Courts enormously helped the modernization of the legal profession as a whole. The Egyptian Bar Association was founded in 1912. For the first time in Egypt's legal history, lawyers became well-respected professionals requiring an advanced legal education. The association became a vocal center for nationalistic and liberal ideals; a tradition that the bar would strive to keep after 1952.[58] Furthermore, the Egyptian School of Law (*Madrasat al-Huquq*) was established in 1886 and educated the first generation of Egyptian lawyers and judges. In 1925 it became part of the Egyptian University (later Cairo

---

[55] Established 988 A.D., Al-Azhar University is the oldest Islamic university in the world. For over one thousand years, Al-Azhar was the acclaimed cultural and educational center for all Muslims.

[56] Tariq Al-Bishri, *Dirasat fi al-dimuqratiyah al-Misriyah* (al-Qahirah: Dar al-Shuruq, 1987), 159–160.

[57] Hill, *"The Golden Anniversary of Egypt's National Courts,"* 204.

[58] Ahmad Abd Al-Hafiz, *Niqabat al-Muhamin: surat Misr fi al-qarn al-`ishrin* (al-Qahirah: Markaz al-Dirasat al-Siyasiyah wa-al-Istiratijiyah, 2003), 16–21 and Donald M. Reid, *Lawyers and Politics in the Arab World, 1880–1960* (Minneapolis, MN: Bibliotheca Islamica, 1981), 56–62.

University). Following the French tradition, the Arabic name still today *Qualiti al-Huquq* (literally School of Rights) is illustrative of the self-proclaimed function of the school as an educational institute that produces defenders of citizens, society, and state's rights.

The Mixed Courts had a significant imprint on the National Courts. The Courts' structure and codes were modeled after the Mixed Courts. The 1883 Codes were based on the 1875 Codes of the Mixed Courts. Judges, mostly Egyptians, "tended to follow the Mixed Courts' interpretation of the law."[59] European influence manifested itself in the National Courts. For example, the country's highest court, Cairo Appeals Court, had four European judges on its bench and all other courts of the first instance had at least one foreign judge.[60]

In some cases, the National Courts followed in the footsteps of the Mixed Courts. With the establishment of the Court of Cassation, the National Courts resisted the expanded jurisdiction of the Mixed Courts vigorously. Cairo's First Instance Court ruled on May 24, 1933, "The jurisdiction of the National Courts is the standard in the judicial system, only what is excluded from its jurisdiction can come under the jurisdiction of other judicial institutions like the Mixed and Religious courts."[61] Additionally, many Egyptian judges, whether they had served on the mixed bench or not, had a sort of professional jealousy of the remarkable degree of institutional independence that the Mixed Courts enjoyed. The institutional independence of the Mixed Courts became the benchmark by which judicial independence was measured. Therefore, many National Courts' judges in the 1920s and 1930s struggled to expand judicial independence. They argued that the courts' general assemblies, rather than the executive branch, should control the appointment of presidents and deputy-presidents of primary courts. Additionally, all judges should be immune from dismissal and arbitrary changes in the retirement age. They forcibly argued, "Those demands were granted to the Mixed Courts, and there should not be two judicial systems in a single country, one enjoys privileges and the second is deprived of them."[62]

In the 1923 Constitution, the judiciary received substantial attention. Chapter Four, with eight relatively long articles, is devoted entirely to the judicial

---

[59] Mark S. W. Hoyle, "The Mixed Courts of Egypt: An Anniversary Assessment," *Arab Law Quarterly* 1, no. 1 (November 1985): 60.

[60] Azīz Khānkī, *al-Mahākim al-mukhtalitah wa-al-mahākim al-ahlīyah: mādīhā, hādirhā, mustaqbalahā* (al-Qahirah: al-Matba'ah al-'Asrīyah, 1939), 5–6.

[61] Latifah Muhammad Salim, *Tarikh al-qadai al-Misri al-hadith*, al-juz' 2 (al-Qahirah: al-Hayah al-Misriyah al-'Ammah lil-Kitab: 2000), 379.

[62] Ibid., 307.

authority. Article 124 is particularly significant; it stated, "Judges shall be independent, only the law, and no other authority, shall influence their judgments, and no branch of government has any right to intervene in the litigation." However, the subsequent articles were not as assertive. Articles 125, 126, 127, and 128 authorized statutory determination of 1) judicial structure and jurisdiction, 2) appointment of judges, 3) the application of judicial immunity and reassignment, and 4) appointment and dismissal of the public prosecutors (*Niabba*).[63]

Reviewing the transcripts of the 1923 Constituent Assembly shows that most members supported judicial independence in principle but were not satisfied with the current personnel on the bench. This explains the rationale behind stating the policy and delegating its application to subsequent legislation. The idea was to allow unqualified judges to retire and to provide further guarantees for future judicial appointments.[64] The awareness of the significance of judicial independence manifested itself early on in the House of Representatives' deliberations over the government budget in 1926. One leading MP of the *Al-Wafd* Party criticized the government for raising the salaries of three selected senior judges (*mustasharin*, sing. *mustashar*: senior judge in high courts). Sa'd Zaghlul, the leader of the nationalist movement and a former judge himself, led the charge, stating,

> The judiciary cannot be independent except if the executive branch refrains from interference ... In this incident executive infringement is illegal and a bribe to judges. You, as representatives of the nation, have to strike hard any hand that infringes on judicial independence. It is not appropriate at all that the President of the Appeal Court receives a special pay increase. This does not square with the dignity of judges, and it might adversely affect the President's reputation himself.[65]

Zaghlul went further to add:

If the Ministry of Justice has no shame; what would deter it from promising the President a special pay-increase if he followed the Ministry's line? It cannot be that a judge has an advantage over another who sits beside him, except because of age or seniority. However, if a minister can grant a judge an extraordinary salary increases, this would be a bribe in its clearest form. You,

[63] Majlis al-shuyukh. *al-Dastur: wa-al-qawanin al-muttasilah bih* (al-Qahirah: al-Matba'ah al-Amiriyah, 1938), 22.

[64] Muhammad Al-Sharif, '*Alā hamish al-dustur* (al-Qahirah: n.p., 1938), 520–533.

[65] Majlis al-Nuwab, *Majmu'at madabit*, Session 3, al-juz' 1, (al-Qahirah: al-Matba'ah al-Amiriyah, 1926), 433–434.

members, if you decided to terminate this pay increase … would be eliminating an offense against judicial independence.[66]

Consequently, the House of Representatives voted to remove this particular
pay increases from the budget, and the three judges were to receive the same
salary as their counterparts.[67] While the discussion mentioned above might
appear to be distant history, it is, nevertheless, still very relevant in Egyptian
judicial discourse today.[68] In one other incident, the government provided
official cars to the presidents of the three criminal circuits at the Cairo Court
of Appeal. This came after the assignation of a senior judge. The three judges,
however, refused to use these cars because other judges on the court did not
receive the same privilege.[69]

Law-decree 68/1931, which established the Court of Cassation (*Mahkamat
al-Naqd*), further enhanced the institutional independence of the judicial
branch.[70] This legislation provided substantial guarantees for legal autonomy.
Article 51 states, "The General Assembly of the Court of Cassation is responsible for disciplining judges as well as judges of the appeals courts and Court
of Cassation."

Furthermore, Law-decree 31/1936 established the first High Judicial Council (HJC), with powers over all judicial affairs. The minister of justice chaired
the HJC, and it included eight other members. Four of those were members
by the virtue of their positions: The president of the Court of Cassation, the
president of Cairo's Court of Appeal, the Permanent Undersecretary of the
Ministry of Justice, and the Public Prosecutor (PP). Another four members
were elected by the general assemblies of the Court of Cassation and Cairo's
Court of Appeal.[71] However, this law decree was not properly authorized by
the Parliament according to the 1923 Constitution and therefore was nullified.
The government introduced a new draft to the Parliament in 1938, and when
the preliminary deliberations elongated, the Ministry of Justice issued an
executive order to establish a provisional committee to provide input on

---

[66] Ibid., 434.

[67] Granting financial benefits, in one form or another, will become an extremely politically
sensitive issue in the judicial politics that will appear in the following chapters.

[68] In 2006 this parliamentary debate was quoted in length in a number of books, publications,
and pamphlets published by pro-judicial independence institutions, including the Judges
Club. Please refer to the discussion in the final chapter of this work.

[69] Tariq Al-Bishri, *al-Qada al-Misri bayna al-istiqlal wa-al-ihtiwa*, 30.

[70] Amin Anis Pasha, "mahkamt al-naqd wa al-abram fi misr," in Mahkamt al-Naqd, *al-Kitāb al-
dhahabī lil-mahākim al-ahlīyah*, al-juz' 1, 185–195.

[71] Muḥammad Kāmil 'Ubayd, *Istiqlāl al-qaḍā': dirāsah muqāranah* (al-Qahirah: Nādī al-Quḍāh,
1991), 270.

matters such as appointment, promotion, transfer, and retirement of judges. The president of the Court of Cassation chaired this committee, which included the Permanent Undersecretary of the Ministry of Justice, the president of Cairo's Court of Appeal, the president of Assuit's Court of Appeal, the PP; and three members of the Court of Cassation elected by its General Assembly.[72] This provisional committee continued to perform its duties until 1943.[73]

In 1943, the al-Wafd government issued The Judicial Independence Act. The legislation aimed at strengthening the prime minister's political standing. It came amidst a major internal crisis within the ruling party that undermined the trust in the party's leadership. These events provide an early indication of the linkage between promoting judicial independence and regime survival. The Judicial Independence Act substantially enhanced judicial independence. Before that law, judicial independence depended on the customs, public opinion, and balance of power in the political system. This legislation codified customary practices and enshrined new guarantees.

Article 10 of the Judicial Independence Act maintained that judges of the Court of Cassation and the Courts of Appeal and the presidents and vice presidents of the first-instance courts, as well as first-instance courts' judges who served for at least three years, could not be removed. Article 11 added that those first-instance courts' judges, who did not serve the three minimum years, could not be dismissed without the consent of the HJC.[74] The establishment, composition, and powers of the HJC have been integral parts of the judicial independence discourse. Subsequent governments attempted to maintain their control over the HJC's composition and to keep its powers ceremonial. On the other hand, the judges advocated a Council that, at least partially, was elected by judges, and with an expanded authority over all matters related to courts and magistrates.

These guarantees coupled with the fractured nature of the political system helped to ensure judicial independence. In addition, the institutional weakness

---

[72] Ibid., 270.

[73] This led to the establishment of the Judges Club in 1939. The Judges Club, since its establishment, became an extremely active organization in defending judicial independence and political democracy.

[74] However, this legislation and the subsequent laws did not provide many guarantees for members of the Public Prosecution Office (Niabba). The executive authority could transfer or dismiss any prosecutor. The executive branch has controlled the appointment of the Public Prosecutor (PP) and, until 1984, his tenure in office. The appointment of the PP and his assistants is still a contentious issue in the Egyptian judicial discourse. The 2006 Law gave more powers to the HJC regarding the appointment of assistants to the PP but kept the appointment of the PP himself exclusively in the hands of the president of the Republic.

of the Ministry of Justice denied the executive branch the opportunity to exercise its heavy hand. Between 1923 and 1952, the intense social and political struggle for national independence, democracy, and social justice led to extreme government instability.[75] This situation resulted in frequent reshuffles of cabinet personnel. The Ministry of Justice had, in a seventy-five-year span (1878–1953), a record number of sixty ministers. Under the 1923 Constitution and until the establishment of the Republic in 1953, it had thirty-eight ministers. This constant reshuffling undermined the power of the Ministry of Justice over the courts. The judiciary functioned as an independent organization with minimal interference from the executive branch.[76]

The existence of the Mixed Courts helped to buttress the National Courts' quest for judicial independence. The National Courts benefited from the Mixed Courts' experience, especially using collective action to exert pressure on the regime. For example, in 1921, following in the Mixed Courts' footsteps the entire judicial corps protested to the King the infringements on rights and liberties and demanded its restoration.[77] Many National Courts' judges were fierce defenders of judicial institutional independence.[78] On many occasions, senior judges had vigorously protested remarks that might infringe upon their independence. Abd Al-Aziz Fahmi, the first president of the Court of Cassation, threatened to resign after the Cairo's chief of police, in a memorandum to his officers, stated that they could use whatever measures to stifle demonstrations, "with an absolute guarantee of support from the courts." The chief had to publicly assert that he was far from even thinking about any infringement on judicial independence.[79] Fahmi was duly praised for his stand and for the tradition of independence he established. He was later called Egypt's greatest judge and until the present day, the largest hall in the Court of Cassation carries his name.[80]

Another similar incident happened shortly after the proclamation of the Judicial Independence Act. After the minister of justice visited *Assuit* Court of

---

[75] During the era, three main political forces competed for power; the King and a number of minority political parties, national movements led by *Al-Wafd*, and the British authorities. This led to extreme government instability. Tariq Al-Bishri, *al-Qada al-Misri bayna al-istiqlal wa-al-ihtiwa* (al-Qahirah: Maktabat al-Shuruq al-Dawliyah, 2006), 10–11.

[76] Ibid., 10–11.

[77] Salim, *Tarikh al-qadai al-Misri al-hadith*, al-juz' 2, 320–321.

[78] Saad Zaghlul, the leader of Egypt's 1919 Revolution, worked as a prosecutor and a judge.

[79] Sabri Abu Al-Majd, *Sanawat ma qabla al-thawrah: Yanayir 1930–23 Yuliyu 1952*, al-juz' 1 (al-Qahirah: al-Hayah al-Misriyah al-`Ammah lil-Kitab: 1987), 674–677.

[80] It was not surprising, therefore, that the Judges Club had issued in 2003 and 2004, during its intense struggle with the executive branch, commemorative editions of its periodical to celebrate the memory of Fahmi and Al-Sanhuri as exemplars of judicial independence.

Appeals, he sent a thank-you note to the president of the court to express the Ministry's gratitude for him and the justices. The president of the court resolutely returned the letter to the minister stating, "Kindly accept my regrets for not being able to receive your message. As the person who can show gratitude, can also reprimand, and the Minister of Justice can do neither to judges." This incident was recalled more than half a century later amidst the struggle between Mubarak and the judiciary.[81]

The National Courts, especially the Court of Cassation, became the guardians of civil and political rights. For example, these courts granted Egyptians the right to form political parties. In a landmark decision in 1925, Cairo Court of First Instance ruled that the establishment of political parties was an integral component of the right to form a political association guaranteed under the 1923 Constitution. The court stated that in the absence of a specific legislation, this right was unrestricted, provided that the objectives of the proposed party were within the limits of the law. This unlimited political freedom guarded by the courts permitted the establishment of many political parties and the development of a vibrant party-system.[82]

The National Courts were genuinely supportive of the freedom of the press. In 1922, the courts acquitted a journalist and his editor-in-chief of an accusation of defaming the Crown.[83] In 1935, another court acquitted the owner and editor-in-chief of the opposition publication *Al-siyassa* accused of libeling the government. The court's verdict came despite the government and the British authorities public appeal for their conviction.

In addition, the courts demonstrated their nationalistic aspirations and independence from the occupying British authorities. In many cases, the National Courts acquitted Egyptians accused of attacking British officials and soldiers. In a famous case, a court found many Al-Wafd leaders not guilty in the assassination of the highest British general in the Egyptian army. The British authorities publicly criticized this verdict, but the court was unwavering in its position.[84]

Unsurprisingly, public opinion became increasingly aware of the courts' activities. The public concluded that empowering the judiciary was the best guarantee for the protection of rights and liberties. Popular support and respect for judges enabled them to exert pressure on the government to

[81] Yaḥyá Jamal, Asharq Al-Awsat, May 12, 2006.
[82] Faruq Abd Al-Barr, *Dawr majlis al-Dawlah al-Misri fi himayat al-huquq wa-al-hurriyat al-'ammah*, al-juz' 1 (al-Qahirah: Matabi' Sijill al-'Arab, 1988), 417–418.
[83] Salim, *Tarikh al-qadai al-Misri al-hadith*, al-juz' 2, 239.
[84] Ibid., 243–244.

expand the scope of judicial independence.[85] For instance, in 1951, the public opinion compelled the government to issue the Code of Penal Procedure (*Code de procédure pénale*), which removed the authority to investigate cases from the executive-dominated PPD to an investigating judge (*juge d'instruction*), who enjoyed guarantees of judicial independence. This penal code mandated that an independent and impartial magistrate would investigate criminal cases. This system was revoked after the 1952 Revolution. Demands from judges, lawyers, and human rights activists to restore it are still echoed in the contemporary legal and political discourse of twenty-first-century Egypt.[86]

Evidently, many of the customary judicial practices that are considered the backbone of the Egyptian judicial independence today were established during this era. Notable among them is the privilege of the Court of Cassation's general assembly to select its members. In 1951, the minister of justice violated this norm and appointed two judges that were not nominated by the court. This resulted in a storm of criticism from the court's justices. For the first time in Egyptian judicial history, the two judges that were not selected filed a lawsuit against the minister of justice before the Court of Cassation, requesting it to revoke the minister's decree. The intense debate forced the minister of justice to resign. Thus, an assemblage of judges emerged and was able to challenge and overcome the executive intrusion.[87] This collective judicial action and the appeal to the Court of Cassation to overturn executive orders in relation to judges became distinctive features of the modern Egyptian judiciary.

In addition, the Judges Club's political role started to mature by the 1940s. Before this period, the board of the Judges Club was largely composed of senior judges, who were keen to keep good ties with the administration, especially the minister of justice. In the 1948 election, a number of junior public prosecutors and judges ran and won seats on the board. That was a blunt challenge to the minister of justice Mursi Badr Pasha who had a troubling relationship with the judicial corp.[88] The new board confronted the regime on a number of occasions. In 1951, the Judges Club clashed with the Al-Wafd government over decreasing the judges' benefits. The Judges

---

[85] Al-Bishri, *Dirasat fi al-dimuqratiyah al-Misriyah*, 161.

[86] While, theoretically, both bodies belong to the same judicial organization, the difference between the courts and the public prosecution office is as wide today as it was in the prerevolutionary era. The executive branch was able to increase its influence over the latter but not the former. Ibid., 160–161.

[87] Salim, *Tarikh al-qadai al-Misri al-hadith*, al-juz' 2, 316–317.

[88] Isam Hassūnah, *23 Yūliyū– wa-'Abd al-Nasir: shahādatī* (al-Qahirah: Markaz al-Ahram lil-Tarjamah wa-al-Nashr, 1990), 28–31.

Club convened its general assembly and threatened a general strike. This threat was efficient and credible enough that the government backed down and reinstated the judges' specialized payroll scheme.[89] This collective action, which probably was influenced by the experience and practices of the Mixed Courts, has become an important method to achieve judges' institutional demands.

Another case, a few months before the 1952 Revolution, highlighted the emerging role of the Judges Club in defense of judicial independence. The government prosecuted the leader of the Socialist Party on charges of inciting violence that led to the massive "Cairo Fire" of January 1952, when downtown Cairo was torched. The composition of the circuit, and especially its president, meant that the defendant could be easily convicted. The proceedings started in mid-May, and it was common knowledge that the circuit's president would retire on June 7, 1952. The presiding judge tried to speed the trial and deliver a verdict before that day. However, defense lawyers used all legal maneuvers to delay the proceedings. The government floated the idea to pass a law to increase the retirement age from sixty to sixty-five years and, hence, keep the circuit composition intact. In order to induce judges to support the proposed legislation, the government promised a substantial increase in judicial salaries. The Judges Club publicly denounced the bill and ensured its demise.[90] In the end, another circuit continued the trial, and the leader of the Socialist Party was acquitted. Both these matters – judicial salaries and retirement age – are still hotly contested political issues in the twenty-first century. A similar confrontation between the government and Judges Club over the same problems took place more than fifty years later in 2005–2006.

The National Courts, especially since the establishment of the Court of Cassation in 1931, became well known for their liberal inclination and their support of civil and political rights. The courts' hands, however, were somewhat tied. Judges were not permitted to repeal administrative decrees. Thus, the need emerged for administrative courts empowered to strike down unlawful administrative decisions. This need was the driving force behind the creation of Egypt's second judicial institution, the Council of State.

THE COUNCIL OF STATE

The Council of State (*Conseil d'État* or *Majlis al-Daula*), hereafter simply the Council, was first proposed during Ismail's reign as a completion of the Mixed

---

[89] Ibid., 32–35.
[90] Al-Bishri, *Dirasat fi al-dimuqratiyah al-Misriyah*, 162.

Court reform. The government was to consult the proposed Council on all "projects of law" submitted to the House of Representatives. The Council would "judge the acts of public functionaries and sit as an administrative tribunal."[91] This body was called *Majlis Shura al-Hukuma* (government consultative council) and, following its French counterpart, was to be part of the executive branch.[92] The prime minister was to be the presiding officer, with two foreign vice presidents and eight other members, half of them Egyptians and half of them foreigners. The Council's functions included participating in drafting legislation, offering legal advice on matters concerning public property, and adjudicating cases of administrative conflicts.

Although presented as a continuation of the 1876 judicial reform, it might be argued that Ismail was trying to circumvent the European-imposed institutions that crippled his authority.[93] However, the Khedive maneuvers did not bear fruit. Ismail was deposed in June 1876, and the first project for an Egyptian *Conseil d'État* vanished with him. In the same year, the government created *Hayat Qadaya al-Hukumah*, or the Government Lawsuits Authority (GLA), to act as the government attorney.[94] However, this institution lacked any adjudication power. The British authorities, after their occupation of Egypt in 1882, rebuffed any ideas of establishing an administrative judiciary, national or mixed, that might act as a check on their powers.[95]

Until the establishment of the Council, the government, and its institutions were subjects of the ordinary courts. In order to shield government actions from judicial intervention, courts were denied the right to invalidate or suspend administrative orders. Individuals could only sue for damages incurred because of government decrees and actions. Early on, several National Courts ruled they did not have the jurisdiction to review administrative decisions. This tendency changed gradually and many courts, using French administrative judicial practices, started to challenge administrative decrees and award compensation to remedy government's actions.[96]

In 1936, during the legislative activities that accompanied the end of capitulations, the government put together the first draft of legislation for

---

[91] Cannon, *Politics of Law and the Courts in Nineteenth-Century Egypt*, 82.

[92] Hill, *"Courts and the Administration of Justice in the Modern Era,"* 102.

[93] Ibid., 81.

[94] Within the Ministry of Justice, the primary function of the GLA, later named *Hayat Qadaya al-Dawlah* or State Lawsuits Authority, is to supervise and conduct government litigation in the courts. Its duties are very similar to those of the Solicitor-General Office in common-law legal systems like the United States and the United Kingdom.

[95] Al-Bishri, *Dirasat fi al-dimuqratiyah al-Misriyah*, 178–179.

[96] Salim, *Tarikh al-qadai al-Misri al-hadith*, al-juz' 2, 283–286.

the Council, but the bill languished in the House of Representatives. Abd Al-Hamid Badawi, a jurist and a minister at that time, argued a storm of criticism met his proposal to establish the Council. It was claimed that the Council would be superior to state institutions, subdue the executive branch, eliminate the cabinet power of legislative interpretation, be a power above all powers, and transcend the jurisdiction of the courts. Badawi, however, maintained that the real underlying rationale was the fear that the government that would oversee the establishment of the Council would pack it with its supporters and therefore would restrain future cabinets.[97] In the context of extreme government instability that existed before 1952, it was natural to fear that the party in power during the foundation of the Council would appoint its supporters as a form of insurance policy. This is an early indication of the political elite's apprehension of the substantial role the courts could play in the political process.

The legislative efforts continued in the 1930s and 1940s. In 1945, a bill was introduced to establish an administrative court. Law 112/1946 instituted the Council as an independent judicial body within the Ministry of Justice. The Council was to be composed of a president, a vice-president, and judges appointed by a decree after the approval of the Council's General Assembly.[98] The legislation that created the Council placed limitations on the administrative courts' jurisdiction and narrowly defined who had standing to bring a case. Nonetheless, the act "established a general assembly [composed of all judges of the Council] for the new judicial body that gave the administrative judiciary a corporate voice. Later, the Council's General Assembly lobbied to expand the parties who could bring cases and to expand the jurisdiction of the Majlis al-Dawla."[99] The jurisdiction of the administrative courts covered the following legal matters:

1. Provincial and municipal elections.
2. Administrative decisions pertaining to civil servants' appointment, promotion, discipline and financial compensation.
3. Annulment of final administrative decisions.[100]

---

[97] Abd Al-Hamid Badawi, *Majallat Majlis al-Dawla*, al-Sanah 1, (Yanayir 1950).
[98] Salim, *Tarikh al-qadai al-Misri al-hadith*, al-juz' 2, 287.
[99] Brown, "*Arab Administrative Courts and Judicial Control of the Bureaucracy*," 4.
[100] In order to expand its jurisdiction, the Administrative Court ruled that the refusal or the failure of an administrative agency to make a decision that it is required to make by virtue of existing laws or orders is considered equivalent to a decision, and therefore within the jurisdiction of the court. See Jasper Yeates Brinton, *The Council of State in Egypt* (Cairo: American Embassy, 1951), 15–16.

The new Council was divided into three sections: (1) The General Assembly of the Council of State (the highest authority within the Council), (2) The Judicial Section or the Court of Administrative Justice (has a separate general assembly), and (3) The Advisory and Legislative Section (has a separate general assembly as well). The Council was fortunate with its personnel, especially its first two presidents: Dr. Mursi and Dr. Al-Sanhuri. Both were among Egypt's highly respected jurists.[101] Their stature, commitment, and vast legal knowledge augmented the Council and shaped its institutional culture and jurisprudence.[102] In his memoir, Al-Sanhuri was open about his preference for judicial activism.[103] Echoes of this judicial supremacy mindset could well be heard among administrative judges in this day and age. During the writing of the 2013 and 2014 Constitutions, the administrative courts asserted their authority to examine the composition and procedures of the constitutional drafting committees. In this, the Council was following in Al-Sanhuri's footsteps. Al-Sanhuri attempted to formulate a theory of the boundaries of legislative authority in his seminal study entitled, "Unconstitutional Legislation and the Abuse of Legislative Authority."[104]

The new body did not only lobby to extend its legal jurisdiction, but it also pursued its mandate with vigor. In 1948, the Administrative Court decided in favor of the principle of judicial review of the constitutionality of legislation.[105] This decision resolved a long-standing debate among Egyptian courts that

---

[101] *Mohamed Kamel Mursi Pasha* was the first president of the Council of State, a leading jurist, and a prominent professor and dean of the Faculty of Law.

[102] Al-Bishri, *Dirasat fi al-dimuqratiyah al-Misriyah*, 182–194.

[103] Nadiyah Al-Sanhuri and Tawfiq Al-Shawi, eds., *'Abd al-Razzāq al-Sanhuri min khilāl awrāqihi al-shakhiīyah* (al-Qahirah: al-Zahrā' lil-I'lām al-'Arabī, 1988), 82–83.

[104] *'Abd al-Razzāq Al-Sanhuri* "Unconstitutional Legislation and the Abuse of Legislative Authority," Majallat Majlis al-Dawlah, 1952. Mohamed Nour Farahat, "The Rule of Law: Can the Constitution be Unconstitutional?" *Al-Ahram Weekly*, 2–8 February 2006.

[105] Legal thinking in Egypt has been strongly influenced by French traditions, which, by a strict interpretation of the principle of separation of powers, would deny courts the right to examine the constitutionality of legislation. However, an opposing view emerged in Egyptian legal circles in the 1940s. This view was influenced by new streams of legal thought from the United States and changes in French legal thought, led by the esteemed Professor Duguit, of the University of Bordeaux, perhaps the leading European authority of his day in the field of constitutional law, and whose lectures at the Egyptian University in 1926 were remarkable cultural events. Professor Duguit strongly defended the doctrine of judicial review and urged its acceptance in Egypt. See Brinton, *The Council of State in Egypt*, 24–25. Duguit aptly noted, "As I grow older and delve deeper into the study of law, the more convinced I become that law is not a creation of the state, but rather something outside the state; and that the idea of the law is totally independent from the idea of the state; and that legal principle is equally binding on the state as well as the individual." Duguit concluded from this that the state is subject to a higher legal principle from which it cannot escape.

started when a lower court asserted the principle in 1941, only to have this reasoning rejected by an appeals court.[106] The Council wasted no time in expanding its jurisdiction and asserting its liberal jurisprudence.[107] This was most remarkable, perhaps, when dealing with sensitive security measures. As consecutive Egyptian governments turned to extraordinary measures invoking the martial law against their domestic opponents (the Muslim Brotherhood, radical nationalists, and leftist groups), the Administrative Court increasingly stood in their way.

The Council incorporated government powers under martial law in its jurisdiction. The Council ruled that while the declaration of martial law itself is a sovereign decision and hence not subject to administrative courts' scrutiny, all measures taken during martial law were subject to judicial review.[108] The Council ruled that, even under martial law, the government could not issue law-decrees to expand its emergency powers. The administrative courts exercised their jurisdiction in this regard on the occasion of the Cairo Fire in 1952. The courts repealed many executive decisions of house arrest, administrative detention, and domestic deportation as unlawful. The courts ruled that the government could be held responsible for its decisions under martial law and individuals or institutions affected by an unjust decision could seek remedy in the form of compensation in courts.[109]

A 1951 verdict questioned the legal status of the government's dissolution of the Muslim Brotherhood. A year later, in the wake of the January riots in Cairo, the Administrative Court revoked arrest warrants for two radical critics of the regime, Fathi Radwan and Yusuf Hilmi. When the government issued a new arrest order, hoping to meet the court's objections, the court again overturned it.

---

[106] Before this landmark ruling, judicial review (in its abstention form) was a highly contested legal matter. Different courts, including the Court of Cassation, issued conflicting opinions. See Kulliyat al-Huquq, *al-Mutamar al-`Ilmi al-Awwal li-Kulliyat al-Huquq: dawr al-Mahkamah al-Dusturiyah al-`Ulya fi al-nizam al-qanuni al-Misri* (al-Qahirah: Jami`at Hulwan, 1998), 287.

[107] Al-Sanhuri's daughter Nadiyah Al-Sanhuri and his student Tawfiq Al-Shawi argued that the idea of judicial supremacy over both the legislative and executive branches was, in the 1920s, not present in the French judiciary or jurisprudence and it has no place in the Anglo-Saxon law. They argued that Al-Sanhuri derived this idea from the Islamic principles, which make Sharia supreme over legislation and hence empower the judiciary to ensure that all legislation adhere to Sharia principles. Nadiyah Al-Sanhuri and Ibid., 265.

[108] Abd Al-Barr, *Dawr majlis al-Dawlah al-Misri fi himayat al-huquq wa-al-hurriyat al-`ammah*, al-juz' 1, 479–482.

[109] Ibid., 484–522.

While it accepted the French legal theory of sovereign acts, the Council endeavored to limit its applications.[110] The Council narrowly defined "matters of sovereignty" to include only measures enacted by the government as the supreme authority charged with protecting national sovereignty and statehood in Egypt and abroad.[111] Furthermore, Egyptian courts have developed a doctrine by which the courts themselves decide which legislative act falls under as "sovereign" and which does not. The administrative courts, therefore, were able to scrap many executive orders that infringed upon citizens' rights and liberties as well as the freedom of the press. In many occasions, the courts ordered a reversal of (or compensation for) government decisions to close down newspapers.

The Council repeatedly affirmed its commitment to the freedom of expression. In 1950, it quashed the dismissal of an employee and awarded damages, where removal from office had no basis other than a frank expression of personal opinion before the employee's supervisor. The courts held that as a matter of general interest, each citizen could express his or her opinion freely.[112] In addition, the Council adopted an active role in issues related to the separation of powers.[113] Throughout the Al-Sanhuri presidency, the Council stood firm against government agencies that refused to enforce its judgments. The Council deemed this class of action a felony. Furthermore, any cabinet member that authorized such an action would be held *personally* responsible for the damages and have to pay compensation from *his own funds* rather than the state treasury.[114]

Predictably, the al-Wafd government was not particularly impressed with Al-Sanhuri's judicial activism. Especially since prior to presiding over the Council, Al-Sanhuri was a leading member and minister of a number of anti-Wafd governments. In 1950, the government asked Al-Sanhuri to step down, on the pretext that formerly partisan ministers should not occupy judicial posts.[115] Al-Sanhuri immediately convened the Council's General

---

[110] This theory developed by the French *Conseil d'État* is comparable to the principle of sovereign immunity in common-law countries. Generally, it is the doctrine that the sovereign or government cannot commit a legal wrong and is immune from civil suit or criminal prosecution. The sovereign acts theory had been applied in Egypt before the establishment of the Council of State.

[111] Al-Bishri, *Dirasat fi al-dimuqratiyah al-Misriyah*, 190–191.

[112] Brinton, *The Council of State in Egypt*, 42.

[113] Ibid., 33–34.

[114] Muhammad `Imarah, *al-Duktur `Abd al-Razzaq Al-Sanhuri: Islamiyah al-dawlah, wa-al-madaniyah, wa-al-qanun* (al-Qahirah: Dar al-Rashad, 1999), 72.

[115] `Abd al-Halim Jindi, *Nujum al-muhamah fi Misr wa-Urubba: al-Halbawi, Al-Sanhuri, Mustafá Mar`i, Marshal Hawl, Hanri Rawbayr* (al-Qahirah: Dar al-Ma`arif, 1991), 211–213.

Assembly. The General Assembly, under the leadership of the deputy-president, defended both the president and the principle of judicial independence arguing,

> Article 50 of the Council of State Law postulates that the Council's presidents, deputy-presidents, and judges cannot be removed. This provision is a strong guarantee of the Councils' independence. Particularly taking into account that the Council adjudicates cases in which the government is one of the parties involved. Furthermore, as the government did not inform the Council of charges that hinder the credibility and trust required for the President's post, according to Section 2 of the previously mentioned Article 50; therefore, demanding the retirement of the President of Council of State in such a manner is a gross violation of the law and an infringement on the Council's independence that is not approved by the Assembly. The General Assembly authorizes the Council's President to undertake the measures he deems necessary to protect the Council's independence and asks him to inform the Minister of Justice of such a decision.[116]

Al-Sanhuri and other members knew that this was a test of the Council's resolve, and the Council proved its ability to guard institutional independence. After failing to depose Al-Sanhuri, the government tried to limit his discretionary power. The government succeeded in revoking the president's prerogative to suspend administrative decree adjudicated before the court if he deemed that the consequences of execution might be irreparable. The al-Wafd government issued legislation that transferred this right to the Administrative Court. In addition, the government also continued to pressure the Council and its members. The government refused to confer promotions of Council members. The cabinet declined to appoint more members and to grant Council members the same pay scale as their counterparts in the National Courts.[117] However, the Council and its president were steadfast and did not restrain their judicial activism. The public and particularly politically active institutions such as the bar became fierce defenders of the Council.

In 1951, the King pressured the government to draft legislation to abolish the Council and merge its members and functions with the Court of Cassation. However, many members of the cabinet threatened to resign in protest and

---

[116] The president of the Council of State Annual Report (4th year), in *Majallat Majlis al-Dawlah*, al-Sanah 2, (Yanayir 1951): 500.

[117] Ibid., 504–508.

argued that public opinion was unwavering in its support to the Council and its members.[118] The prime minister had to yield.[119] Al-Sanhuri wrote in his memoir praising the public opinion, "In Egypt there is a public opinion that is feared by all authorities: feared by the government, the Parliament, and all superior authorities [properly he meant the Crown]." By 1952, the Council's slogan as "the fort of rights and liberties" became a *lingua franca* in the popular political discourse. The founding fathers of the Council endowed subsequent generations with a wealth of liberal precedents and legal reasoning that were overwhelmingly protective of citizens' rights and liberties. As one contemporaneous senior Council justice puts it, "Al-Sanhuri and his generation set the tone for the future jurisprudence of the Council. Therefore, any judge or group of judges that deviate from this heritage under regime's pressure would generally be the exception, not the norm."[120]

The eminent journalist Ahmed Bahaa Eddin encapsulated the central position the Council commanded in the political process and the legitimacy it cultivated, stating,

> When the Council of State was established, and Al-Sanhuri became its president, he became a hero to all segments of the Egyptian people. Before the Revolution, the political struggle was at its climax and most political conflicts would end at the Council of State, Al-Sanhuri issued courageous and impartial verdicts that followed not only the letter of the law but also, and more importantly, its spirit. Al-Sanhuri's presidency of the Council of State was one of the substantial transformations in Egypt's life before the Revolution.[121]

THE INFLUENCE OF THESE INSTITUTIONAL EXPERIENCES ON THE INSTITUTIONAL CULTURE OF THE MODERN EGYPTIAN JUDICIARY

Prior to 1952, Egypt had vibrant parliamentary politics, with active political parties, the well-developed labor movement, energetic professional societies,

---

[118] Al-Sanhuri and Shawi, *'Abd al-Razzāq al-Sanhuri min khilāl awrāqihi al-shakhiīyah*, 266. The revolutionary government in 1954, after suppressing public opinion and abolishing the parliament, political parties and other civil society organizations will secure the passage of such legislation.

[119] Tariq al-Bishri, *al-harakah al-siyāsīyah fī Misr, 1945–1952* (al-Qahirah: al-Hay'ah al-Misrīyah al-'Ammah lil-Kitāb, 1972), 346–348.

[120] Faruq 'Abd al-Barr, *Mawqif 'Abd al-Razzaq Al-Sanhuri min qadaya al-hurriyah wa-al-dimuqratiyah* (al-Qāhirah: n.p., 2005), 68–69.

[121] Ahmad Baha Al-Din, *Shar'iyat al-sultah fi al-'alam al-'Arabi* (al-Qahirah: Dar al-Shuruq, 1984), 24.

and mostly free press. Political participation, while narrow, was higher than most Third World countries. During this period, the judiciary enjoyed substantial independence and played an increasingly important political role. Judges solidified a reputation for independence and impartiality and attracted increasing support and respect among the masses.

During this liberal era (1923–1952), the Egyptian judiciary, including the National Courts and the Council, was at the heart of the political process. The courts developed liberal jurisprudence and judicial independence traditions. The courts, especially the Court of Cassation and the Administrative Court, established a large volume of liberal legal precedents and deeply instituted liberal tradition within Egypt's judicial and legal culture.

The courts made the most out of the political and cultural conditions of this era to expand judicial independence and judicialization. Abraham identified five preconditions for independent judicial behaviour: "(1) regime stability, (2) a competitive political party system, (3) significant horizontal power distribution, (4) a strong tradition of judicial independence, and (5) a high degree of political freedom."[122] During this era, the judiciary benefited from a level of political liberalism and parliamentary democracy that existed in Egypt under the 1923 Constitution.[123] In this period, no single authority had ultimate control over the state, its apparatus, or the political process in general. This period was marked by acute competition between the British as the occupying power, the Crown armed with both its constitutional prerogatives and its subservient minority parties, and the Al-Wafd that enjoyed unwavering public support.[124]

Judicial independence, liberal judicialization, and political legitimacy became increasingly intertwined and entangled. Al-Bishri persuasively summarized this relationship: "Legitimacy was to take a stand against the Crown and the British occupation's infringement on recognized rights. The judiciary was a forum for defending the national movement and democracy, and judicial independence was a proper guarantee of those rights."[125]

These foundational institutions and their legacies and practices left enduring marks on the structure and institutional culture of the Egyptian judiciary.

---

[122] Henry J. Abraham, *The Judicial Process* (New York: Oxford University Press, 1998), 300.

[123] The 1923 Constitution included an expanded Bill of Rights. Chapter II included twenty-one articles that granted Egyptians a whole array of social, economic and political rights and liberties. See Ahmad Faris Abd Al-Mun`im, *al-Dawr al-siyasi li-Niqabat al-Muhamin*, (1912–1981) (Cairo: n.p., 1984), 118–126, and Majlis al-Shuyukh, *al-Dastur: wa-al-qawanin al-muttasilah bih*, 7–70.

[124] See Al-Bishri, *al-harakah al-siyāsīyah fī Misr*, 1945–1952; Usamah Ahmad al-'Adili, *al-Nizam al-siyāsī al-Misrī wa-al-tajribah al-lībirālīyah* (al-Jīzah: Maktabat Nahdat al-Sharq, 1996).

[125] Al-Bishri, *Dirasat fi al-dimuqratiyah al-Misriyah*, 159–160.

Personal interviews with scores of junior and senior judges at the civil and criminal courts, the Council and the Administrative Prosecution Authority (APA), the examination of rulings and writings by current and former judges, the analysis of statements and actions by judges, judicial councils, and judicial associations reveal the significant traits of Egyptian judicial culture.

While this work does not marginalize the differences among judges, it argues that the majority of judges embrace a core set of values. The book studies judges as a collective entity for two main reasons: sociological and methodological. First, as a civil law judiciary, all of Egypt's judges undergo the same professional socialization at an early age.[126] It is within the judiciary that judges develop their career outlook. Egyptian law schools, since the 1960s, admit students with below average high school grades. The quality of legal education has deteriorated with the surge in the number of admitted students. Hence, most of what judges learn takes place after joining the judiciary either through on-the-job training or the specific professional courses through the National Center for Judicial Studies.[127] Furthermore, judges typically enter the different judicial institutions in their early twenties (legal education in Egypt is an undergraduate degree) and usually stay until they reach the mandatory age of retirement (now seventy years). They all go through the same cycle of training and advancement. All these factors mold judges in a very similar image and increase the similarities amongst the judicial corps.

Secondly, all courts' rulings in Egypt are issued as an opinion of the tribunal, and no dissent is published. The rulings do not reveal the individual vote of each judge. In fact, disclosing such information is unlawful. Other than personal off-the-record conversations, we cannot tell how each judge voted. Hence, we cannot, with any degree of certainty, analyze individual judicial attitudes or behavior.[128] In fact, on some occasions, a judge might be asked to write a ruling that he did not support.[129]

---

[126] The bureaucratic and professional nature of the Egyptian judiciary aided the socialization process from senior to junior judges. This is one of the main characteristics of bureaucratic judiciaries. For more about this issue, please see Carlo Guarnieri and Patrizia Pederzoli, *The Power of Judges: A Comparative Study of Courts and Democracy*, 18–77.

[127] The National Center for Judicial Studies (NCJS) was established in 1981. The NCJS under the auspices of the minister of justice and its managed senior judge selects. The Center was tasked with "Preparation and training of all members of the judicial institutions as well as educating them scientifically and practically to practice of judicial work." (Article 2 of Presidential Decree No 347 of 1981).

[128] That being said, the careful examination of rulings, writings, and personal interviews conducted reveal some attitudinal difference between ordinary and administrative judges. The latter are more assertive, inclined to limit governmental actions.

[129] Personal interview with a Deputy Chief Justice of the Supreme Constitutional Court (SCC), March 13, 2018.

It seems correct to argue that judges during their professional socialization develop a set of goals. The relative ranking of each of these goals changes from one judge to another, from one judicial institution to another and from one era to another. Nevertheless, all judges agree about the significance of these goals. The first goal is personal welfare. Like other members of bureaucratic institutions, Egyptian judges want to protect and expand their corporate rights and privileges: materialistic and symbolic. Judges aspire for greater salaries, faster promotions, better medical insurance, and higher pensions. They also seek to increase the social standing of the profession in comparison to other state employees. Judges pursue nicer courthouses and better judicial infrastructure. The higher the stature the judiciary command, the better social standing judges enjoy.

The second related collective objective is institutional independence. Judges seek to preserve and expand the guarantees of institutional and financial autonomy from other institutions of the state. All judges interviewed, regardless of seniority or age, expressed their interest in achieving judicial self-governance, rendering the courts free from influence by or control from other branches of government or political parties and social groups. Judges jealously guard their autonomy even against "infringements" by other judicial institutions. In many occasions, the Council refused to revoke administrative judges' legal immunity to allow the PPD to question them.[130] The same "protective" attitude was also evident in the SCC.[131] All judicial associations refused to get audited by the executive branch. The SCC and the Court of Cassation and High Administrative Court all issued rulings exempting their professional organizations from government oversight.

Judges also care about guarding their tariff against infringements by other authorities of the state: executive and legislative. Different judicial institutions fight over jurisdiction and powers. On many occasions, the administrative courts fought with the courts of general jurisdiction. During the drafting process of the 2014 Constitution, the Council was locked in a bitter struggle with the APA and State Cases Authority, and none of the three institutions pulled no punches.

---

[130] The PP sent an official memo to the Council's requesting lifting judicial immunity of four members who publically quarreled with a Court of Cassation vice-president over the Council's powers under the 2014 Constitution. The Council refused the request arguing instead that the members were defending the Council rights and authority. The Council vice-president Ahmed El-Fekki stated in a newspaper interview, "Only the Special Council has the exclusive power over Council members." Shrouk, November 13, 2014.

[131] In a recent case, the SCC refused to revoke the immunity of Hatem Bagato who served as minister of legislative affairs under Mursi. *Al-Wafd*, August 9, 2014.

The third goal that Egyptian judges embrace is to ensure respect for the rule of law. As judges are the guardians of the legal system, this would mean respect for the state institutions and the public for their authority. Judges could and do disagree about a whole range of issues, but all agree that their rulings should be respected and enforced. Judges, at least for purely selfish reasons want to expand their influence over the society and the polity. Because the rule of law ties well to liberal political ideology, judges during the First Republic were the most liberal among state institutions. Rutherford acknowledged this:

> The only consistent advocate of LC [liberal constitutionalism] throughout modern Egyptian history is the judiciary. It developed a commitment to LC in the late 19th century, when judicial reforms led to the training of Egyptian lawyers and judges in accordance with French standards. This commitment to LC was sustained throughout the repression of the Nasser era.[132]

This is akin to Charles Epp's notion of "rights-enhancing judicialization," whereby courts create or expand individual rights and liberties through their evolving jurisprudence.[133] In the case of authoritarian regimes, that would entail challenging the executive branch and providing a legal shield for opposition parties and groups vis-à-vis the state.[134] Many judges used their legal power to expand the courts' jurisdiction and broaden the protection of civil and political rights beyond the extent initially authorized by the regime. A Deputy Chief Justice of the Supreme Constitutional Court (SCC) has stated that the main objective of any judge is to protect citizens' rights and liberties, and that this goal surpasses any other objective.[135]

The fourth objective is to protect the state. As civil servants, judges value the judiciary as a state institution and understand that both a failed state or a weak government will harm the judicial system. The analysis of judicial behavior reveals a sense of elitism in comparison to other segments of the society,

---

[132] Bruce K. Rutherford, *Egypt after Mubarak: Liberalism, Islam, and Democracy in the Arab World* (Princeton: Princeton University Press, 2008), 458–459.

[133] Charles R. Epp, *The Rights Revolution: Lawyers, Activists, and Supreme Courts in Comparative Perspective* (Chicago: University of Chicago Press, 1998).

[134] Even in their liberal or even activist role, Egyptian judges have always maintained that they have been serving the law and upholding the constitution. Shapiro and Stone Sweet rightly highlighted this, claiming "In democratic states most government officials achieve legitimacy by acknowledging their political role and claiming subordination to the people through elections or responsibility to those elected. Judges, however, claim legitimacy by asserting that they are non-political, independent, neutral servants of 'the law'." Martin Shapiro and Alec Stone Sweet, *On Law, Politics, and Judicialization* (New York: Oxford University Press, 2002), 3.

[135] Personal interview with a Deputy Chief Justice of the SCC, March 13, 2018.

a sense of pride in the role within the state. This created a practical affinity with other "guardian elites" such as the military. The relationship between generals and judges is akin to the relations among *patricians* in ancient Rome. Patricians used to compete amongst themselves for control of Rome's premier offices and over the direction of state policies. However, patricians normally collaborated to prevent the advancement of *plebs* into what they perceived as their domain of influence. Many judges believe long-term interests are best served by remaining within "statist coalition." This is not particularly unique to Egypt. Studies of other bureaucratic judiciaries such as Brazil, Chile, and Turkey revealed similar types of relations.[136] Pereira straightforwardly states, "The degree of military and judicial consensus, integration, and cooperation is a key neglected variable in unlocking the puzzle of variation in authoritarian legality."[137]

The significance of any of these objectives would depend on the socio-political situation. The ranking depends on the political context and the positions of the other principal actors in the political process. Judges who act as reformers in a stagnant political environment can be a conservative force in a rapidly changing revolutionary sitting. Egyptian courts picked up the mantle of reform within the stagnate-conservative regime of Mubarak and Sadat but expressed a strong commitment to limited change within the revolutionary environment since the end of the First Republic. This is not a schizophrenic institutional behavior. Judges are reformers, not revolutionaries. They will always prefer the status quo if they believe that the state, which they serve and receive their institutional rule from, is threatened.

Nevertheless, the role of agency in shaping judicial behavior deserves recognition. Influential leaders have been able to frame the debate in a way that advanced one institutional goal over the others. The imprint that Al-Sanhuri left on the ideological foundations of the Council could be easily sensed until the present day.[138] Besides, presidents of the Judges Club as representatives of the collective interests had vast impact on judicial behavior. Mumtaz Nasar, Yahia Al-Refai, and Zakria Abd Al-Aziz framed their main task

---

[136] Lisa Hilbink, *Judges beyond Politics in Democracy and Dictatorship: Lessons from Chile* (Cambridge: Cambridge University Press, 2007). Hootan Shambayati, "A Tale of Two Mayors: Courts Politics in Iran and Turkey," *International Journal. Middle East Studies* 36, no. 2 (2004): 253–275.

[137] Pereira, *Political (In)justice*, 191.

[138] Even judges who belong to the more conservative and regime-friendly camp within the judiciary, such as Jamal Dahroug, stated that they joined the Council because of the Al-Sanhuri experience: "I was influenced by Dr. Sanhuri and I wanted to serve like him in the Council." Personal interview with Jamal Dahroug, December 17, 2005.

as defending the "honor of the bench," meaning the institutional independence and social standing of judges and hence could justify anti-regime actions as preferential to judicial interests. Other presidents such as Moqbel Shaker or Ahmed El-Zend publically advocated closer ties with the executive to further the materialistic privileges of judges.

Judges, however, use claims to legal formalism or judicial activism on and off-the-bench, to serve their personal and institutional goals. Some judges did advocate judicial restraint under Mubarak and then defended judicial activism after his departure or vice versa. As Shetreet put it, "Although the two approaches are distinct in theory, in practice it is not always possible to make clear-cut, precise distinctions between 'conservative' (restrained) and 'liberal' (activist) judges, or between 'formalist' and 'nonformalist' judges. Indeed, on occasion, a single judge might select one of the two approaches according to the particular circumstances of a case."[139]

To conclude, the institutional culture of the modern Egyptian judiciary brings together features of the Islamic religious heritage with modern liberal, political ideals and civil-law bureaucratic judiciary. The Islamic tradition puts a premium on judges' independence, impartiality, aspirations for justice, and a broad social and political mandate. The Mixed Courts (liberal) influence accentuates courts' institutional and financial independence, the corporate nature and collective action, professionalism and citizens' rights and freedoms. The National Court and the Council of State established the structural foundations of the modern court system, engraved many of the practices, and crystallized a unique institutional cultural.

---

[139] Shimon Shetreet, "Creating a Culture of Judicial Independence: The Practical Challenge and the Conceptual and Constitutional Infrastructure," in Shimon Shetreet and Christopher Forsyth (eds.), *The Culture of Judicial Independence: Conceptual Foundations and Practical Challenges* (Boston: Martinus Nijhoff Publishers, 2012), 60.

3

Nasser's Egypt

Charisma, Populism, and the Attacks on Judicial Independence

The Master retired,	السيدُ نام
How could I believe, the Fourth Pyramid perished?	وكيف أصدق الهرم الرابع ماتْ؟
The Leader has never left,	القائد لم يذهب أبداً
He just entered the room to rest,	بل دخل الغرفة كى يرتاخ
And, He will rise with the Sun.	وسيصحو حين تطل الشمسُ

– Nizār Qabbānī *"The Fourth Pyramid"* speaking of Nasser

The dawn of July 23, 1952, marked the beginning of a new phase in Egypt's modern history. A handful of officers known as the Free Officers carried out a bloodless coup d'état, deposed King Farouk, and ended a century-and-a-half of Muhammad Ali's dynasty. The political inclinations of the clandestine Free Officers and their Revolutionary Command Council (RCC) were not entirely clear. Old regime politicians did not take them seriously, believing that the officers would return to their barracks quickly. Nasser and his cohorts proved those veteran politicians thoroughly wrong. The army was to dominate Egypt's political life until the present day.

In the first few weeks after the coup, Nasser and the RCC's aspirations seemed to be non-militaristic. They struggled to seek closer ties with the old regime's parties, especially the majority party, Al-Wafd. However, Nasser and other Free Officers soon relinquished any hopes of reforming the old political system and its veteran leaders. It became apparent that all party leaders including Al-Wafd "planned to climb aboard the army train for a return to power without giving the least assurance that their political policies would change."[1] Moreover, power with its symbolic and material rewards became increasingly appealing to the young officers and their supporters as time elapsed.

---

[1] Jean Lacouture, *The Demigods: Charismatic Leadership in the Third World* (New York: Knopf, 1970), 93.

Early on, the Free Officers presented a well-known and respected senior officer, Gen. Mohamed Naguib, as the leader of their movement. This choice proved vital for the largely unknown young officers. The Free Officers succeeded, aided by the general's humility and stature, to assert control over the army swiftly and to gain increasing support among the masses.[2] However, Naguib, who commanded at one time the-all-important positions of president, prime minister, commander-in-chief, and head of the RCC, strived to be more than a symbolic figurehead of the new regime. Naturally Nasser, who was "the brains of the movement," became increasingly irritated with the power and popularity that the General enjoyed. Nasser and the other young officers thought Naguib was harvesting the fruits of their labor and seizing their preeminence. Nasser, in early 1954, crudely tried to depose him. Faced with massive popular opposition coupled with unrest within the officer corps, Nasser and the RCC tactically recoiled.

To cleanse the house, the *junta* had a three-point plan. First, bowing to pressure, they conceded and reinstated the old general as president, however, without much real power. Next, Nasser consolidated his power base within the army and stirred up the officer corps against Naguib and his allies of "corrupt civilians." Lastly, the RCC's members used their control over the bureaucracy to recruit supporters within the labor unions. By the end of March 1954, the balance of power tipped in favor of the RCC. Seizing the opportunity of a failed assassination attempt against Nasser, the RCC accused the Muslim Brotherhood, Naguib's largest sympathetic group, of carrying out the plot. The RCC spread allegations about Naguib's involvement in the conspiracy. Nasser removed Naguib from all his official posts and placed the General under house arrest.[3] This was the real beginning of Nasser's era in Egypt's history.

THE NASSERITE ERA

By the end of 1954, Nasser became the indisputable leader of the new regime. It has become clear that he was no longer the *primus inter pares*, but rather, the center of gravity in the political system. Nasser's authority was based largely on his control of the military, security apparatus, and civilian

---

[2] Ulwī Ḥāfiz, *al-Fasād* (al-Jīzah: al-Sharikah al-'Arabīyah al-Duwalīyah lil-Nashr wa-al-I'lām, 1991), 22 and Fathi Radwan, *72 shahran ma'a 'Abd al-Nasir* (al-Qāhirah: Dar al-Hurriyah, 1986), 12–15.

[3] Rif'at Sayyid Aḥmad, *Thawrat al-Jinarāl: qiṣṣat Jamāl 'Abd al-Nāṣir kāmilah, min al-milād ilá al-mawt, 1918–1970: mawsū'ah fikrīyah wa-siyāsīyah* (al-Qāhirah: Dār al-Hudá, 1993), 190–215.

bureaucracy. He knew that his regime required a new source of popular acceptance in order to survive.

The careful construction of the popular image of the "young colonel" as Egypt's new savior coincided with the overthrow of Naguib. Two events were crucial in establishing Nasser's public persona: his role in the creation of the Non-Aligned Movement (NAM) and the defeat of the Tripartite Aggression. Nasser's leading role in creating the NAM was critical to his primacy. Nasser's stood toe-to-toe with Third World icons: Nehru, Tito, Sukarno, and Nkrumah. Lacouture highlighted Nasser's participation in the Bandung Conference of 1955 in Indonesia, which established the NAM, stating,

> Colonel Nasser's courtship of the Egyptian people may be said to date from his return from Indonesia: the marriage took place in 1956. Before 1955 his relation to the people was totally different from what it was the day he entered Cairo, April 22, 1955, his portrait flanked by the mob to indicate the significance of the event: identification had taken place. Nasser was no longer the product of some Western intrigue; he spoke as an Egyptian nationalist about an Egyptian revolution that purported to be something more than a successful coup d'état. *He spoke in the name of Egypt.*[4]

The nationalization of the Suez Canal and the defeat of the Tripartite Aggression in 1956 were indispensable events in building Nasser's public image. The Suez Crisis was a "great leap forward" for Nasser's leadership. The nationalization of the Suez Canal Company was widely perceived as an act of vengeance. For Egyptians, Arabs, and citizens of colonized nations, the Evil West that occupied, humiliated, and exploited Egypt has been insulted, embarrassed, and defeated by Nasser (*our* leader). Nasser became the spokesperson for the masses, not only in Egypt but also all over the Third World. The late Nobel laureate Naguib Mahfouz illustrated this, maintaining, "I have long felt that Nasser was one of the greatest political leaders in modern history. I only began to fully appreciate him after he nationalized the Suez Canal."[5]

Therefore, by the mid-1950s Nasser became the dominant figure in Egypt and the Arab world. In January 1956, he legalized his grip on power by drafting a constitution with an all-powerful executive, with himself as its chief. Nonetheless, it was Nasser's popular appeal more than his official positions that furnished a new basis for his authority. Egyptians attached themselves to Nasser as their charismatic leader. Nasser became recognized as more than a mere ruler. Egyptians, who had traditionally deified their leaders, now

---

[4] Lacouture, *The Demigods*, 108.
[5] *Al-Ahram Weekly* online, September 24–30, 1998.

looked upon Nasser as both a pharaoh with divine powers and a messiah with a noble cause.[6]

An amalgamation of personal, domestic, regional, and international factors enabled Nasser to develop his charismatic credentials. For one thing, Egypt's conditions were fertile soil for Nasserism. The country suffered from extreme underdevelopment, severe social and economic injustices, and widespread corruption.[7] Hence, any reform, however minor, would be an improvement on the despondent status quo. In addition, Egypt had suffered from seventy years of national humiliation under the heavy hand of the British occupation. Putting an end to British imperialism and foreign domination became the chief objective of several generations of Egyptian nationalists. Most Egyptians in 1952 believed that profound socioeconomic development was impossible until the imperialist yoke was lifted. For some, this also meant stripping power from the aristocratic class. British withdrawal, agrarian reform, nationalization of foreign properties, and dismantling of aristocratic privileges all were extremely popular demands.[8]

At a personal level, Nasser was all that King Farouk was not. While the King was a descendant of an Albanian family, "Nasser's family roots, on the other hand, have hugged the soil of deep Upper Egypt for centuries."[9] In fact, Nasser was the first truly Egyptian ruler of Egypt for more than two millennia. Since the Persian conquest had destroyed the twenty-sixth pharaonic dynasty in 525 BC, Egypt was under the authority of the Greeks, Romans, Byzantines, Arabs, Kurdish, Turkish, French, or British at one point or another.[10] In his appearance, speech, and lifestyle, Nasser was also noticeably different from his predecessor. While King Farouk's lavish life and his appreciation for beauty,

---

[6] Anthony Nutting, *Nasser* (New York: E. P. Dutton, 1972), 194.

[7] Bill and Leiden summarized the country's miserable conditions: "Egypt is one of the poorest and most densely populated societies in the world. Just before the 1952 military coup, a Rockefeller Foundation team reported that the situation of the peasants in Egypt was worse than that of the peasants in any other country in which they had carried out investigations – and this included China and India. According to their report, on a scale of 106.5 for perfect health, India reached 54 and Egypt 15. In one of the villages surveyed north of Cairo, nearly 100 percent of the population had bilharzia, a debilitating parasitical disease that attacks the kidneys and liver; 89 percent had trachoma; over 20 percent were typhoid or paratyphoid carriers." James A. Bill and Carl Leiden, *Politics in the Middle East* (Boston, MA: Little, Brown, 1979), 225.

[8] Kirk J. Beattie, *Egypt during the Nasser Years: Ideology, Politics, and Civil Society* (Boulder, CO: Westview Press, 1994), 18–19.

[9] Wilton Wynn, *Nasser of Egypt: The Search for Dignity* (Cambridge: Arlington Books, 1959), 18–19.

[10] Nutting, *Nasser*, 1.

money, and gambling were common knowledge, Nasser was a simple man who dressed, lived, and died like a middle-class Egyptian.[11] Nasser was corruption-free whereas King Farouk was allegedly implicated in a number of corruption scandals.[12]

Nasser was fortunate with the expansion of radio and print media as well as the introduction of television. The mass media facilitated the establishment and development of Nasser's charisma; "Songs were composed to give praise to the new deity and throughout the land of the pharaohs Nasser's subjects gave thanks to divine providence for having sent him to deliver them from the hands of their enemies."[13] The public became charmed with Nasser's character, which the media glorified despite the later national and military defeats. Dekmejian rightly articulated this, stating, "The high degree of residual legitimacy that *Nasir* [Nasser] possessed by virtue of his leadership during the fifties – a legitimacy too great to be erased overnight by a defeat."[14] As the highly respected author Tawfiq Al-Hakim, who was critical of Nasser, wrote,

> [Nasser] had inundated us with magic and dreams in such a way that we did not know how he inundated us. Perhaps as they said it was his personal magic when he spoke to the masses, or perhaps it was the dream in which we had begun to live because of those hopes and promises. Whatever the fact, those glowing images of the accomplishments of the revolution made out of us instruments of the broad propaganda apparatus with its drums, its horns, its odes, its songs, and its films.[15]

Furthermore, whereas King Farouk was not known for his public-speaking skills, Nasser was the great orator of his time. At the peak of his popularity, he could captivate his audiences, inside and outside Egypt. Not surprisingly, Nasser delivered a record number of 1,359 public speeches in his eighteen

[11] Even a highly unsympathetic writer such as Ivor Powell could not ignore these facts. See Ivor Powell, *Disillusion by the Nile: What Nasser Has Done to Egypt* (London: Solstice Production, 1967), 38.

[12] Salah Nasr, one of the Free Officers, later the Director of National Intelligence and a close confidant of Field Marshall Amer, who was imprisoned after the 1967 defeat, stated, "I have known Nasser till 26/8/1967, we bitterly disagreed and he imprisoned me. In spite of the fierce dispute between us, I cannot believe that Nasser could be a crook or a thief. It has been always my conviction that Nasser is the greatest Egyptian." 'Abd Allāh Imām, *Salāh Nasr yatadhakkar: al-mukhābarāt wa-al-thawrah* (al-Qahirah: Mu'assasat Rūz al-Yūsuf, 1984), 96.

[13] Nutting, *Nasser*, 194.

[14] R. Hrair Dekmejian, *Egypt under Nasir; a Study in Political Dynamics* (Albany: State University of New York Press, 1971), 245.

[15] Tawfiq Al-Hakim, *The Return of Consciousness* (New York: New York University Press, 1985), 28.

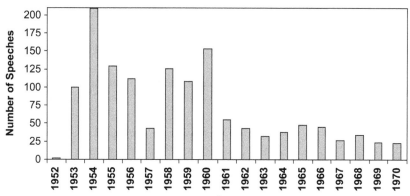

FIGURE 3.1 Nasser speeches per year (1952–1970).[16]

years in power – an average of seventy-five speeches per year. Nasser was especially busy during the buildup of his charismatic leadership 1953–1956.

Ironically, Nasser's enemies unintentionally helped the augmentation of his charisma. The fierce attack and the personal insults inflicted on him in the Western and Israeli press – the historical enemies in the mind of many Arabs – managed only to affirm Nasser's image as the leader long waited for. To many Egyptians, Nasser was the beloved son who endowed them with a sense of dignity and national pride after more than two thousand years of national humiliation.[17] Many Egyptians believed that Nasser possessed extraordinary qualities, and he applied those qualities for their benefit and well-being of the people.[18] The depth of their devotion and attachment to him was evident in the mass grief after his death.

NASSER'S POPULIST-CHARISMATIC REGIME

Early on, the revolutionary government demonstrated that it had little interest in legal documents, with their "obstructionist" nature. When advisors complained that provisions in the 1923 Constitution obstructed the purge of old regime enthusiasts from the administrative apparatus, the RCC abrogated the constitution on December 10, 1952. A month later, in January 1953, the RCC

---

[16] Unless noted otherwise, all speeches are from Nasser webpage maintained by Gamal Abdel Nasser Foundation, available from: http://nasser.bibalex.org/

[17] Nutting, *Nasser*, 477.

[18] Kamal El-Menoufi, "The Orientations of Egyptian Peasants towards Political Authority between Continuity and Change," *Middle Eastern Studies* 18, no. 1 (January 1980): 82–93.

banned all political parties and confiscated all their properties. On February 10, 1953, a Constitutional Declaration was issued. Article 8 of this declaration granted the RCC the power to take any necessary measures to protect the revolution and achieve the revolutionary objectives.

The new regime was not particularly interested in constitutional salience. In eighteen years (1952–1970), Egypt had six different constitutions and constitutional proclamations: 1953, 1956, 1958, 1962, 1964, and 1969. It was noticeable that all of Nasser's constitutions were provisional. This signaled the apparent insignificance of the constitutional foundations of the state and the ability of the regime to change them at any time to accommodate the whims of the leader.

Nasser became synonymous with the political authority, the regime, and the state itself. While the personification, centralization of power, and pyramid-shaped political entity are as ancient as Egypt itself; Nasser brought it to new levels. Nasser's regime illustrated two fundamental principles: concentration of power and lack of checks and balances. The consecutive constitutions entrusted the president of the Republic with vast powers, unmatched by any other institution. All constitutions subscribed to a presidential system of government. The president assumed executive power, including appointing the prime minister, his deputies, and all ministers; relieving them of their duties; appointing civil and military officials; and devising social, economic, and foreign policies of the state. In addition, he had the power to dissolve the parliament and could veto legislation and issue decrees that had the force of law. The president could put questions to a national referendum, proclaim a state of emergency, and declare war. He was also the head of the Supreme Councils of the Armed Forces, the police, and the judiciary. "The Egyptian Constitution gave the president of the Republic a curious mixture of powers. He practically had powers equivalent to those of the prime minister in the British system and to those of the president of the French Fifth Republic."[19]

In addition to controlling the executive branch, the president was the chief executive and head of the single party – the Liberation Movement (1953), the National Union (1956), and lastly the Arab Socialist Union (1962) – which had the power to select members of the legislature. A constitutional provision mandated that all MPs must be members of the regime-controlled single party. Losing the single party's membership meant surrendering the parliamentary seat. Membership in the legislature was controlled from above.

---

[19] Noha El-Mikawy, *The Building of Consensus in Egypt's Transition Process* (Cairo: American University in Cairo: 1999), 101.

Even after the end of the transient period (the period between the annulment of the 1923 Constitution and the proclamation of the 1956 Constitution), the executive continued to dominate the legislature. In fact, the legislature did not play any significant role in the political process during the Nasser's entire tenure in office.

This concentration of power had a damaging effect on judicial independence. Al-Bishri pointed out, rightly, that judicial independence springs from "the symmetry between the executive and the legislative. If the legislative authority lost its autonomy ... the judiciary will be circumscribed."[20] He maintained, "Naturally, administrative or political scrutiny of government activities diminished. The fusion of legislative authority in the executive branch obliterated the judiciary's capacity to perform independently."[21]

In addition to tightly controlling all institutions of the state and the political system, the regime marginalized all civil society organizations. By the early 1960s, the government control over the economy coupled with restrictive legislations systematically drained resources that enabled the vibrant civic space that Egypt enjoyed prior to 1952. This guaranteed the absence of any collective action against the regime's policies at least until the Six-Day War. This was bad news for judges who lost any support from the judicial support structures. An indication of the tightened regime control of the civil society was the bar association's discourse and actions under Nasser. Traditionally a fierce defender of judicial independence in the pre-1952 era, the bar did not utter a word against the "Massacre of the Judiciary" in 1969.[22]

Consequently, a single leader, who assumed unequivocal political and moral authority, personified the state, which in turn controlled all aspects of the social and political life of its citizens. In this political environment, the ideas and ideals of the leader commanded center stage in the political process. Early on, it became clear that Nasser and most of the RCC emphasized social problems rather than political ones. As early as 1953, Nasser publicly stated, "Our most vicious enemies are three: social injustice, political dictatorship, and the British occupation." He repeated this phrase, leaving no doubt that social injustice came at the pinnacle of this ranking of Egypt's problem.[23] The socialist orientation was evident in Nasser's bible *The Philosophy of the Revolution*.[24]

---

[20] Tariq Al-Bishri, *al-Dimuqratiyah wa-nizam 23 Yuliyu 1952–1970* (al-Qahirah: Dar al-Hilal, 1991), 207.

[21] Tariq Al-Bishri, *al-Dimuqratiyah wa-al-Nasiriyah* (al-Qahirah: Dar al-Thaqafah al-Jadidah, 1975), 22.

[22] Ahmad Faris Abd Al-Munim, *al-Dawr al-siyasi li-Niqabat al-Muhamin (1912–1981)*, 204.

[23] Nasser speech in Mansoura on 4 April 1953.

[24] Gamal Abdel Nasser, *Egypt's Liberation: The Philosophy of the Revolution* (Washington, DC: Public Affairs Press, 1955), 39–40.

Nasser had a profound conviction that social and economic equality was a prerequisite for democracy and political participation. In this, he was no different from other Third World revolutionaries in the 1950s and 1960s: "Socialism, not democracy, was the call of revolutionary movements of the time."[25] Nasser's confidant Heikal argued that under Nasser priority was given to social democracy. There was a conviction that political democracy is derivative of social democracy.[26] In addition, Nasser apparently believed that discipline and hierarchy of the army are the only remedies for Egypt's massive problems. Nasser believed that "only the army can meet and solve the praetorian conditions of Egypt and that the army played the role of the 'vanguard' in the Egyptian revolution."[27] The motto of the Liberation Union "Unity, Discipline, Work" captured Nasser's preference for stability. The militaristic nature of the regime manifested itself in the pivotal positions that army officers occupied in the executive, the legislative, and the foreign service of the Nasserite regime.[28]

In fairness, Nasser's regime was no different from the authoritarian-populist regimes that came to dominate Middle Eastern politics in the postcolonial era. This model, originally introduced to the region by Ataturk, was also popular in Africa and Latin America. Hinnebusch put this eloquently stating, "It appears to be a function of a specific stage of state formation and social modernization."[29]

From Nasser's perspective, the regime had a social contract with people. This arrangement highlighted the significance of social justice and down-played the participatory and democratic principles. The government was entrusted to provide economic and social welfare in exchange for popular support of the regime's domestic and international policies.[30] The careful analysis of Nasser's political discourse is particularly revealing of his political ideology. Nasser's use of the five concepts, democracy, freedom, justice, the

---

[25] Lust-Okar, *Structuring Conflict in the Arab World: Incumbents, Opponents, and Institutions*, 61.

[26] Muhammad Hasanayn Heikal, *Ahādīth fī al-'āsifah* (al-Qahirah: Dar al-Shurūq, 1987), 59.

[27] Amos Perlmutter, *Egypt, the Praetorian State* (New Brunswick: Transaction Books, 1974), 19.

[28] Alī Al-Dīn Hilāl, *Taṭawwur al-niẓām al-siyāsī fī Miṣr, 1803–1997* (al-Qahirah: Markaz al-Buḥūth wa-al-Dirāsāt al-Siyāsīya, 1997), 185.

[29] Raymond A. Hinnebusch, Jr, *Egyptian Politics under Sadat: the Post-populist Development of an Authoritarian-Modernizing State* (Cambridge: Cambridge University Press, 1985), 2.

[30] The analysis of political leaders' discourse as an indication of their political ideology and political values is a widely accepted practice. A number of Egyptian and foreign scholars have already analyzed Nasser's discourse, but not in relation to judicial independence and the rule of law. See, for example, Muḥammad Al-Sayyid Salīm, *al-Taḥlīl al-siyāsī al-Nāṣirī: dirāsah fī al-'aqā'id wa-al-siyāsah al-khārijīyah* (Bayrūt: Markaz Dirāsāt al-Waḥdah al-'Arabīyah, 1983) and Rif'at Sayyid Aḥmad, *Thawrat al-Jinarāl*.

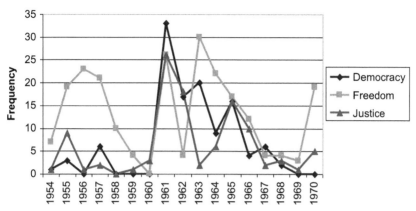

FIGURE 3.2 The frequency of democracy, freedom, and justice in Nasser's Revolution Day speeches (1954–1970)

rule of law, and judicial independence, varied significantly. It is particularly noticeable that in more than two hundred pages of transcribed speeches (or about 150,000 words), Nasser did not mention even once the concept of judicial independence. The "rule of law" fared just a little bit better, with two mentions in a single year (1968).[31] Nasser also rarely referred to the constitution, the parliament, or the judiciary in his speeches.

Freedom was the central value in Nasser's Revolution Day speeches. It had the highest salience in Nasser's discourse, followed by democracy and justice. Freedom was mentioned 224 times (just a little bit above thirteen mentions a year). Democracy came a distant second with 117 citations (or about seven citations per year). Lastly, was justice with 106 references (an average of slightly more than six references every year). A more careful yearly analysis reveals that democracy was not mentioned even once in six of the seventeen speeches – or one-third of the time, while freedom and justice were absent only once (1960 and 1958 respectively). Excluding the high anomalies (democracy mentioned thirty-three times in 1961, freedom mentioned thirty times

---

[31] After the 1967 defeat, the regime's widespread support weakened. Many claimed that the absence of the rule of law, democracy, and freedom as well as the massive power of the security establishment was to blame for the defeat. Pressure for democracy from intellectuals, journalists, and university professors and students intensified. Nasser started to bow to the pressure and acknowledged the need for some sort of representation and legality. However, this was short lived. After cementing his popularity, the regime did not change its practices. Rather, in the following months, Nasser opted to root out all opposition within the judiciary. This led to what has been known as "the Massacre of the Judiciary."

in 1963, and justice mentioned twenty-six times in 1961),[32] the average per-year mention was twelve references for freedom and five references for democracy and justice.

It is important, nonetheless, to analyze how Nasser used the three concepts. For Nasser, parliamentary democracy, legal and political liberalism did not solve Egypt's problems. Nasser determined that liberal democracy within a semi-feudal and highly non-egalitarian society was counterproductive. Social justice, a classless society, and a socialist economy were necessary conditions for a "true democracy." The prerevolution procedural democracy was a sham. "Dictatorship of feudalism and capital ... used the name of democracy to preserve the control of the owning class" (1962 speech). "Democracy is actually the embellishment of social justice," Nasser maintained in his 1962 speech. The president, also, stated in his 1967 Revolution Day address that political democracy is built on the foundation of social and economic democracy.

Freedom to Nasser was generally confined to the macro or national level and did not accentuate individual liberties. In most of his references to the concept, Nasser referred to freedom from foreign influence. Freedom was intimately associated with national independence: "We long for freedom and independence" (1958). At the societal level, freedom was the lack of economic need; "the first goal of agrarian reform is to free farmers from the domination of massive landholders, which denied them [farmers] freedom and development," Nasser stated in his 1954 speech.

In the same vein, Nasser's discourse revealed that justice was not understood as procedural or legal as in the liberal tradition. Justice denoted social equality among citizens and classes, or at the international level among equal, sovereign, and independent nations. Most often, Nasser would couple the term justice with the modifier social. In fact, the two terms coincided in 80 of the 106 mentions of justice. In another nine references, it can be inferred that Nasser referred to social justice. Therefore, in the 106 mentions of justice, he meant social justice 89 times or about 84 percent.

The lack of emphasis on liberal democracy, the rule of law, and judicial independence, as well as the far-reaching emphasis on social justice, independence, and national freedom can be attributed to the influence of Nasser's environment on his political ideology. Nasser was a pure product of his socioeconomic upbringing; the miserable political, economic, and social

---

[32] This was the year of the breakup of the United Arab Republic. Many blamed Syria's separation on the lack of freedom and democracy under Nasser.

conditions; as well as Egypt's national humiliation as a British colony since 1882. Most Egyptians in this era bonded all these problems together.

Besides, Nasser was also deeply affected by socialism. In the 1950s and 1960s, the economic development model of the communist regimes in the Soviet Union and Eastern Europe was particularly influential among the revolutionary-populist leaders of the newly independent Third World states. These socialist governments highlighted social justice as the principle political value and downplayed the significance of liberal democracy. The emphasis on social justice as a prerequisite for political democracy in Nasser's discourse clearly reflected the influence of Marxism on his political ideology.

It was no surprise, therefore, that political and legal liberalism disappeared altogether from Nasser's discourse. The low salience of liberal democracy, the rule of law, and judicial independence, on the one hand, and the extensive focus on socioeconomic justice and national independence confirms the proposition of this research linking revolutionary-charismatic appeal to the decline of rational-legal sources of legitimacy. For most of his rule, Nasser did not feel the need to base his public appeal on rational-legal grounds. Comfortable in his role as a populist-charismatic leader, Nasser stressed the significance of social justice and national independence over all other values.

In addition to the limited political value of judicial independence for a revolutionary-charismatic leader, Nasser did not personally believe in separation of powers or check and balances. He was blunt in his rejection of judicial independence:

> I believe that separation of power is a significant fraud ... In fact, there is no such thing as the separation of powers, because the party that has a majority in parliament controls the executive branch and of course, the legislature ... Therefore, the political leadership that has the majority controls two branches, the executive branch, and the legislative branch. And because it controls the legislative branch, it controls the judicial branch as well, just because the judiciary is controlled by the legislative branch, regardless of what has been said about its independence.[33]

In fact, Nasser was not shy to publicly state:

> We did not interfere in the judiciary since 1952 ... however if there is a political case, we create a political court; in which, we ourselves were the judges, hence, we kept the judges away from politics and kept us away from the judiciary. This starts with the People's Court, where members of the Revolutionary Command Council were the judges. This arrangement

---

[33] Hamadah Husni, *'Abd al-Nāṣir wa-al-qaḍā': dirāsah wathā'iqīyah* (al-Qahirah, n.p., 2005), 29.

denoted to the public the political nature of the case, about which we have an opinion. Therefore, we keep it away from the judiciary, and we personally take responsibility for it.[34]

To Nasser, judges were no different from other civil servants. He was in favor of including judges in the single party in order to tie them to the revolutionary objectives. "In my opinion, judges should join in the national work . . . In fact, the Socialist Union is a coalition of all the different forces of the people and so they [the judges] must join it," the president maintained. The Socialist Union Law of 1962 included judges in its membership.[35] In Nasser's mind, the judiciary was not inherently different from other state institutions. When the minister of justice Isam Hassūnah complained to the president about the Socialist Union's effort to infiltrate the judiciary and institute a clandestine organization from within to direct and supervise judges, Nasser responded saying, "If *Shaarawy Gomaa* [minister of interior] has established, within the police, a secret organization composed of police officers that believe in the Revolution, and so did *Shams Badran* [minister of war] in the armed forces; why do not you do the same within the judiciary?"[36]

The miniature value for and appreciation of judicial independence and the rule of law had a destructive effect on the judiciary, especially the courts' role in defense of rights, liberties, the rule of law, and democracy. True to form, the revolution had an uneasy relationship with legal professionals. In this, it is not different from most major leftist revolutions in modern history.[37] We rarely found a revolutionary regime that managed to attain power and kept, at the same time, healthy relationships with jurists: judges, lawyers, or law professors. Most historians of major revolutions in the last two centuries cannot but accept the unavoidable conflict between revolutionaries and legal professionals as a rule in political life.[38]

THE REGIME AND THE JUDICIARY

Nasser's political philosophy and discourse had an adverse effect on the rule of law in general and the judicial institutions in particular. This section

---

[34] Quoted in: Abd Allah Imam, *Inqilab al-Sadat: ahdath Mayu 1971* (al-Qahirah: Dar al-Khayyal, 2000), 366–367.

[35] Abd Al-Fattah Murad, *al-Mukhalafat al-tadibiyah lil-qudah wa-ada' al-niyabah: dirasah tahliliyah wa-ta'siliyah muqaranah* (al-Iskandariyah: A. al-F. Murad, 1993), 1424.

[36] Hassūnah, *23 Yūliyū– wa-'Abd al-Nasir: shahādatī*, 192–194.

[37] The regimes of Allende in Chile and Chavez in Venezuela are but a couple of modern examples of this diffuclut relationship.

[38] Ḥusni, *'Abd al-Naṣir wa-al-qaḍā'*, 7.

investigates the policies of the revolutionary-charismatic regime toward courts and judges, as well as judicial behavior in response to these policies. Analytically, we could distinguish between three different phases in regime-court interaction.

The Regime and the Courts: The Early Years

The revolutionary regime, in its first two years in power, sought to use judicial independence and the rule of law to enhance the regime's public support. The 1952 Revolution did not launch a full-scale attack against judicial independence in its early days. In fact, with the exception of a limited purge of some well-known aristocratic or corrupt judges, which a Court of Cassation's review committee deemed unfit for judicial posts, the regime did not impede the courts.

Remarkably, some legislation enhanced judicial independence. Noticeable among the first pieces of legislation under the new regime was the amendment of the Council of State law to provide for additional guarantees of judicial independence. These safeguards included placing the Council under the auspices of the Council of Ministers, rather than the Ministry of Justice; granting the Council full responsibility for the appointment, promotion, and discipline of its members; equalizing position and pay between the administrative judges and their counterparts in the courts. All these significant amendments were issued, published, and enacted merely four days after the birth of the July 1952 regime.[39] The Council's annual report confirmed this regime objective. Al-Sanhuri stated, "The Revolution has venerated the Council for its courageous stands in the darkest and most undemocratic ages. Therefore, the Revolution swiftly amended the Council's legislation to remove the vicious oversight and interference [of the Ministry of Justice]."[40] Senior Council members including Al-Sanhuri provided valuable legal advice to the RCC in the early days after the coup.

As for the courts, the regime issued Law-decree 188/1952 – generally known as the Second Judicial Independence Law. This law reorganized the High Judicial Council (HJC), removing from its membership the president of Cairo's First Instance Court, a change that the majority of judges championed. The new composition of the HJC enhanced judicial independence by drawing the absolute majority of the Council (five out of seven) from the ranks of the most senior judges. The executive branch entirely controlled the

---

[39] Law 115/1952, issued July 27, 1952.
[40] Quoted in: *Majallat Majlis al-Dawlah*, al-Sanah 20–25, (1971): 14.

selection of only two members: the Public Prosecutor (PP) and the Under-Secretary of the Ministry of Justice.[41]

Nevertheless, the desire to achieve control over the legal process manifested itself in the regime's move to amend the Code of Penal Procedure in December 1952. Five months after the success of the revolution, the RCC issued Law 353/1952. This legislation and subsequently Law 121/1956 removed the powers of the investigating judges and transferred this jurisdiction to the executive-dominated Public Prosecution Department (PPD).[42] Until the present day, the use of the PPD to target political opposition members has been a frequent complaint from civil society activists, lawyers, and legal scholars.

The collaboration between generals and judges was evident in the early days after the coup. Al-Sanhuri and other fellow judges who came to resent the corruption, anarchy, and instability of the Farouk's regime provided a way out of many legal dilemmas in the early days of the coup. The 1923 Constitution mandated the recall of the dissolved parliament if the seat of the monarchy became vacant. The Wafd-dominated House of Representatives could have posed quite the problem for the Free Officers. Al-Sanhuri and the Council of State issued a legal opinion allowing the transfer of power to the Council of Minister and negating the need to convene the House. This consolidated the authority in the hands of the revolutionary officers, a decision that many judges shortly came to regret.

The first major revolutionary assault on the judiciary occurred during the March Democracy Crisis of 1954. At the height of the struggle between the then President Mohamed Naguib, on the one side, and the RCC led by Nasser, on the other – the RCC mobilized its supporters and staged a demonstration outside the headquarters of the Council of State. The RCC was fearful that the Council, which was holding a meeting presided over by Al-Sanhuri, would lend its moral and legal weight behind Naguib at this critical moment. Demonstrators attacked the Council's building, physically beating Al-Sanhuri, who had publicly adopted a pro-democracy position.[43]

---

[41] Yaḥya Rifai, *Tashri'at al-sulṭah al-qada 'iyah mu'allaqan 'alá nuṣusihā* (al-Qahirah, Nadi al-Quda, 1991), 490–500.

[42] The Public Prosecution is an integral component of the Egyptian judiciary. Every judge must serve as a prosecutor in the early stages of his career (roughly ten years). Senior positions, including the Public Prosecutor (PP), assistant public prosecutor, first public attorneys and public attorneys are filled with mid-career or senior judges. This last group traditionally selected by the Ministry of Justice. Prosecutors enjoy more power, benefits, and relatively higher salaries than their counterparts who sit on the bench.

[43] Beattie, *Egypt during the Nasser Years*, 96–97.

The protesters outside shouted, "down with democracy, down with ignorant judges!"[44] Historians are divided about the real mastermind behind this vicious attack. Some accept Nasser and other RCC members' claim that they had no relation to or prior knowledge of this episode. However, most experts argued otherwise. Abd Al-Latif Al-Baghdadi, a member of the RCC, later admitted, "Al-Sanhuri infuriated the RCC members when he suggested that the RCC should be abolished. This suggestion made the Free Officers believe that Al-Sanhuri backed Naguib."[45]

Therefore, fearing that Al-Sanhuri might persuade the Council to issue a public statement supporting Naguib's camp, some RCC members authorized the use of force to silence the Council. Naguib acknowledged this in his memoir, stating that the RCC orchestrated this attack to force the Council to side with the junta and abandon the demands for the return of civilian rule and democratic institutions.[46]

This incident revealed that the *junta* was loyal to its radical and militaristic nature. All "enemies of the Revolution" regardless of their rank, position, or stature were to be sidelined. Al-Sanhuri, who had initially supported the July regime and had helped draft the abdication proclamation of King Farouk in 1952, was now an enemy of the officers.[47] This attack, the first of its kind in Egyptian judicial history, had an enormous impact. The revolution and the RCC indicated it could use its heavy hand in a way unmatched by any government under the monarchy. Al-Sanhuri never returned to the Council. Two weeks later, on April 15, the RCC issued a decree, which stripped all individuals that held ministerial posts between 1943 and July 1952 of their political rights and, consequently, the competency to serve the state in any capacity. Al-Sanhuri was the prime target of this decree, particularly when he refused to receive Nasser after the assault, publically accusing him of the responsibility for this attack.[48] By removing Al-Sanhuri, the revolution was able to achieve what the King and the al-Wafd governments failed to accomplish years before.

---

[44] Al-Sanhuri and al-Shawi,'*Abd al-Razzāq Al-Sanhuri min khilāl awrāqihi al-shakhiīyah*, 283–284.

[45] Abd Al-Latif Al-Baghdadi, *Mudhakkirāt 'Abd al-Latif al-Baghdadi* (al-Qahirah: al-Maktab al-Misrī al-Hadīth, 1977), 127.

[46] Mohammed Naguib, *Kalimati lil-ta'rikh* (Al-Qahirah: Dār al-Kitāb al-Namūzaji, 1975), 224.

[47] Robert St. John, *The Boss: The Story of Gamal Abdel Nasser* (New York: McGraw-Hill, 1960), 174.

[48] Al-Sanhuri and al-Shawi, eds., *'Abd al-Razzāq Al-Sanhuri min khilāl awrāqihi al-shakhiīyah*, 284.

Less than a year later, the regime aspired to "clean the house" – getting rid of all administrative judges known for their liberal stands as well as Al-Sanhuri supporters.[49] In March 1955, the RCC issued Law 165/1955 on the reorganization of the Council of State. Article 77 granted the Council of Ministers the power to dismiss and reappoint all Council of State's members. The Council of Ministers issued a decree dismissing eighteen judges – including the Council's deputy-president. This purge had direct and indirect consequences. At one end, the regime removed the most liberal members of the Council, who might be expected to scrutinize and reverse regime policies. At a broader level, all judges became aware of the cost of opposing the regime. Security of tenure, a pivotal pillar of judicial independence, lost any real meaning or value. It became apparent that the regime had the power and the audacity to circumvent any legal guarantees at any point in time.[50] Nasser forced judges to self-censorship if they wished to keep their titles and stature.

REGIME POLICIES TOWARD THE COURTS (1955–1967)

By 1955, Nasser became the unequivocal leader of a stable and popular government, and there were no more overt assaults on judicial independence. The regime, however, developed a whole array of strategies to dominate judicial affairs. First, the executive repeatedly sidestepped the judiciary by establishing a full range of exceptional tribunals to adjudicate politically sensitive cases. Second, the legislature narrowed the scope of judicial scrutiny through legislations that denied courts the power to decide various actions and policies of the regime. Third, the president appointed highly trusted judges to critical positions in the court system. These select senior judges ensured judicial conformity with the regime's interests. Thus, the government

---

[49] *El-Akhbar*, August 31, 1975.

[50] This intimidation strategy forced most judges to focus on their welfare (keeping their job and derivative symbolic and materialist benefits). Shetreet explained a similar outcome in Russia. "After the collapse of the Soviet Union, the constitutional court was led by Chief Justice Valery Zorkin in several cases involving the transition of rule from the Soviet to the post-Soviet era. These cases were controversial and included both an invalidation of one of President Yeltsin's decrees and a finding that Yeltsin's actions were unconstitutional. In response to these and other decisions, Yeltsin shut down the constitutional court for several years. Valery Zorkin remained with the court. However, the court's perspective was notably different after its reopening: it began to regularly agree with government actions." Shimon Shetreet, "Creating a Culture of Judicial Independence: The Practical Challenge and the Conceptual and Constitutional Infrastructure," In C. F., Forsyth, and Shimon Shetreet, eds., *The Culture of Judicial Independence: Conceptual Foundations and Practical Challenges* (Boston: Martinus Nijhoff Publishers, 2012) 24.

dominated the courts, as it did with all other state institutions such as Al-Azhar, the universities, the army, the police, and the civil bureaucracy. Because the regime did not need the Regime Survival Functions (RSFs) that the courts can provide, Nasser could quickly weaken the judicial system and circumnavigate the courts altogether without the fear of shouldering severe political costs. Socioeconomic achievements at home and political victories abroad provided a reliable social base until the 1967 Six-Day War.

Exceptional Courts

The revolutionary regime established ad hoc tribunals, whose composition, mandate, and procedures the government controlled. Through these "courts" the regime was able to secure its preferred verdicts without radically changing judicial structure or personnel. This was the preferred government strategy to ensure desirable decisions in sensitive cases. While the use of exceptional courts started in the first months after the revolution, the regime used it systematically and with high frequency since 1954.

The first such exceptional tribunal was established less than a month after the revolution when trouble erupted in a textile factory in the rural town of Kafr Al-Dawar, north of Cairo. This plant had a labor union that the management claimed was Communist; creating accusations in Cairo that "enemies of the Revolution" inspired the strike.[51] Early on, Nasser was adamant to present his movement as anti-Communist. This was critical to garner support from the United States and avoid a military intervention by the large British forces stationed less than a hundred miles from Cairo. The RCC acted swiftly. It appointed one of their members to preside over a court martial in Alexandria; "You must make an example out of those responsible," Nasser instructed the chief judge.[52] The trial was held on the factory grounds, and it took the court less than a single week to decide that two of the workers were guilty and to order their execution.

The Court of Treason was to hear cases of corruption and abuse of power under the *ancien régime*. It was presided over by a Court of Cassation's justice and three judges of Cairo's Court of Appeal, all chosen by the minister of justice and four high army officers selected by the commander-in-chief of the armed forces. This tribunal had jurisdiction over all prime ministers, ministers, members of parliament, and other high-ranking officials accused of offenses, detailed in the law, committed since September 1, 1939. The court's

---

[51] Abd Al-Latif Al-Baghdadi, *Mudhakkirāt 'Abd al-Latif al-Baghdadi*, 68–69.
[52] St. John, *The Boss*, 147

prosecution of several of the old regime's prominent politicians was intended to intimidate and silence civilian partisans. This combined with a purge of individuals with "suspicious conduct" from the bureaucracy, cleared the way for RCC control of the government.[53] Nonetheless, because of its hybrid composition that privileged professional judges, the RCC did not welcome some of this court's rulings. The composition and type of verdicts might explain the short life of the Court of Treason, which lasted only for a few years, in comparison to other exceptional courts that lasted much longer.[54]

Another high profile exceptional tribunal was the "Revolution Court." The court was composed of three members from the RCC, with the following justification:

> This Court is going to pass judgments on any individual accused of acting against the interest of the state and the Revolution; it will pass its judgment in the name of the RCC. Therefore, despite our high regard to our judicial institutions ... These crimes cannot be assigned to the ordinary judiciary and the regular courts. No single revolution in the history of any revolutions has adjudicated its affairs according to the ordinary judiciary. Conventional legislation has its limitations and boundaries and judges cannot transcend those limits and boundaries, as they were legislated for normal circumstances.

This statement and many others demonstrated the limited role the regime ascribed to the courts. The Revolution Court initially targeted Al-Wafd and leaders of other political parties. All leading Wafd leaders less than sixty-five years old were brought to trial before the Revolution Court. These trials aimed at destroying the party's credibility, influence, and any aspiration for playing a political role in the future.[55] Later, the Revolution Court ruled on the highly publicized case involving the Muslim Brotherhood's alleged attempt to assassinate Nasser. The Revolution Court delivered unusually harsh judgments by sentencing many senior Muslim Brotherhood leaders to death.

Another exceptional tribunal was the "People's Court." Established by an RCC decree in November 1954 and composed entirely of military officers, this court had jurisdiction over all crimes, including those crimes committed before its establishment, against the state, the revolution, the regime, or any

---

[53] In addition, the rapid proliferation of officers turned representatives of the revolution throughout the civilian bureaucracy served to consolidate RCC control. Beattie, *Egypt during the Nasser Years*, 79.

[54] Wahid Ra'fat, *Fusul min Thawrat 23 Yulyu* (al-Qahirah: Dar al-Shuruq, 1978), 32.

[55] Tal'at Al-Ghiryānī, *Fu'ād Sirāj al-Dīn: ustūrah. . .ākhir bāshawāt Misr* (al-Qahirah: Dar Sfinks, 1995), 24–25.

cases transferred to the court by the RCC; even if these cases were under review by the regular courts.[56]

However, the most important exceptional court, because it lasted for the entire duration of the First Republic, is the Emergency State Security Courts (ESSC).[57] Established by Articles 7, 8, and 9 of Law 162/1958 (in regard to the state of emergency and government powers under its application), the ESSC became a long-term Achilles' heel in the Egyptian judicial system.[58] Consecutive constitutions granted the president of the Republic the authority to declare, unilaterally, a state of emergency. Nasser, Sadat, and Mubarak all used this power to rule the country under emergency law for prolonged periods. The state of emergency became the norm, rather than the exception, until 2012.

The aforementioned law granted the ESSC jurisdiction in all matters related to the defiance of orders by the president or any person that he designates. Article 9 of the Law bestowed on the president or any presidential designee the authority to transfer to the ESSC any public law offenses. Nasser used this power to transfer cases to the ESSC after declaring a state of emergency on June 5, 1967.

If the broad jurisdiction of these exceptional tribunals is disconcerting, its composition is even more alarming. The legislation permitted the president to control the courts' composition. At the lower level, the ESSC may be composed of a judge and two armed forces officers. The high ESSC might be staffed with three judges and two senior officers. In all cases, judges (civilian and military) are appointed by a presidential decree after conferring with the minister of justice and the minister of defense respectively. Moreover, according to Article 12 of the abovementioned law, state security courts' verdicts were not subject to appeal and became final only after the president approves the judgment. The president had the authority to pardon, commute the sentence, or order a new trial before another circuit.

The military courts have been another example of extraordinary courts. Law 25/1966 instituted the courts and defined their composition, competence, and jurisdiction.[59] According to this law, the military courts have exclusive jurisdiction over all legal offenses by officers, soldiers, and civilians within the

---

[56] Ibid., 32.

[57] Instead of using martial law, the regime uses the "state of emergency." Nonetheless, both are very similar in nature. Law 533/1954 (the first legislation about the state of emergency under the Revolution) is an identical copy of Law 15/1923 (about the martial law under the monarchy). Law 162/1958 replaced Law 533/1954 and gave the executive the same sweeping rights.

[58] *Al-Jarida al-Rasmiyya*, Issue 29, September 28, 1958.

[59] *Al-Jarida al-Rasmiyya*, Issue 23, June 1, 1966.

Ministry of Defense (at this time was called the minister of war). Most concerning, however, is the provision of the law that granted the president the authority to transfer legal offenses by civilians to military courts, a prerogative that Nasser and his successors repeatedly used to ensure their preferred legal outcomes in politically or security-sensitive cases.[60]

The first article of this law left no doubt about the military courts' lack of independence. It clearly stated that the military judiciary is an integral part of the general hierarchy of the armed forces. In addition, the minister of defense appointed all judges in these courts. According to Article 55 of the law, judges in the military courts are selected from among the officer corps and are subject to the code of military service. Verdicts issued by the military courts are not subject to any judicial appeal. The verdicts, however, are subject to ratification of a designated officer. This officer, usually the president of the Republic, has the right to rescind the rulings altogether, shorten the sentence, or order another trial.

In addition to creating exceptional courts to handle sensitive matters, the regime issued restrictive legislation. These laws stripped the courts, especially the Council of State, of much of its jurisdiction over many matters.

Prohibitive Legislation

The revolutionary regime exempted its actions and policies from any independent legal scrutiny. Appealing to the courts to challenge abusive government decisions was commonplace in the pre-1952 era. Nasser's regime used its exclusive control over the legislative machinery to issue prohibitive legislation. These acts ensured the regime's control over the society by reducing access to courts. Among the first legislation that denied the courts any power over fundamental regime interests was "the Court of Treason Law," Law-decree 344/1952. This law-decree sheltered verdicts issued by the Court of Treason from all sorts of review or appeal.

This prohibitive legislation became commonplace practice. As one senior adminstartive court judge noted, "It seems that the regime became captivated by such medicine, as a cure for its problems."[61] Furthermore, the regime's

---

[60] In 2007, President Mubarak ordered military tribunals for a number of Muslim Brotherhood leaders. After Mubarak, generals would insist on keeping civilians under the mercy of military tribunals in the 2012 and 2014 Constitutions.

[61] Abd Al-Barr, *Dawr majlis al-Dawlah al-Misri fi himayat al-huquq wa-al-hurriyat al-`ammah*, al-juz' 2, 97.

prohibitive legislation extended well beyond the security realms. There were many examples of these prohibitive laws.

- Law 178/1952 concerning agriculture reform, which denied all courts the power to adjudicate petitions to rescind or suspend seizure decrees and all legal disputes related to the ownership of requisitioned properties.
- Law 181/1952 ruled out judicial review of orders dismissing civil servants without disciplinary procedures.
- Law 270/1956 banned all courts from reviewing all orders by the military governor.
- Law 345/1956 and Law 184/1958 denied administrative tribunals the authority to adjudicate university administrations' decisions related to students.
- Law 106/1957 considered all decisions by the minister of interior related to dismissing mayors and deputy-mayors as final and outside judicial scrutiny.
- Law 31/1963 regarded all presidential decrees to dismiss or involuntarily retire civil servants as "matters of sovereignty" hence excluded from judicial review.
- Law 119/1964 exempted all presidential decrees related to state security from all types of review by any institution, judicial or otherwise.

The regime used this prohibitive legislation to aid its quest to tighten its control over the most active sectors of the society – students, workers, civil servants, and local-council officials. The regime strived to control those important sectors of the society entirely. These groups were placed under the regime's mercy without any legal remedy. According to a survey conducted by the Ministry of Justice in the early 1990s, eighty different major prohibitive laws passed between 1948 and 1968.[62] Al-Bishri rightly pointed out that,

> In the 1950s and 1960s, there were hundreds of laws that proscribed adjudication and removed a significant portion of administrative acts away from judicial scrutiny. Prohibition on adjudication became almost a norm. It was included in all administration proposals for every administrative activity.[63]

In addition to the countless laws that prohibited seeking judicial remedies from executive decisions, restrictions on judicial review were enshrined in the

---

[62] Ali El-Sadek, "Istqlal al-sultah al-qudae 'an al-sultah al-tashreaa,' *al-Majallah al-Jinā'īyah al-qawmīyah* 38, Issues: 1, 2, and 3, (March, July, and November 1995), 65–66.

[63] Al-Bishri, *al-Dimuqratiyah wa-al-Nasiriyah*, 23.

revolutionary constitutions. Article 191 of the 1956 Constitution stipulated that "All decisions, actions, and orders enacted by the Revolutionary Command Council and all institutions created to protect the Revolution are not subject to any review by any institution: judicial or otherwise."

The regime went as far as utilizing its legislative supremacy to reverse individual cases adjudicated before the courts. On one occasion, a former judge won a case against a presidential decree that mandated his dismissal from the bench.[64] In order to stall the enforcement of the verdict, the government attorneys petitioned the High Administrative Court (HAC) to reverse the lower court's verdict. During the deliberations of the case, the president issued Law-decree 31/1963 that amended the Council of State law. The first article of this law stated, "The Council of State shall have no competence to hear requests related to matters of sovereignty. Decrees issued by the President to relieve of duty, discharge, or to dismiss, civil servants without following the disciplinary procedures shall be considered matters of sovereignty." The HAC, staffed mainly with regime loyalists, readily accepted this legislation, despite its curtailment of the Council's jurisdiction.[65]

Nonetheless, despite the limited domain for adjudication, the regime aspired to ensure tight control over the legal processes. Fearing that some activist judges might still utilize the limited adjudication space, the regime used appointment power to ensure "control from above" over all judicial institutions; a practice that all of Egypt's chief executives would embrace with varying success.

The Appointment Power

In order to control the judiciary from within, Nasser used presidential appointment authority to install loyal and politically trusted judges at the pinnacle of all judicial institutions. The pivotal positions of the PP, the president of the Court of Cassation, the president of Cairo Appeals Court, the president of Alexandria Appeals Court, the president of the Council of State and later the president of the Supreme Court, and its successor the Supreme Constitutional Court were carefully chosen to control their respective institutions, rather than representing the institutions' collective interests.[66] This might be called the hidden-hand strategy.

---

[64] Administrative Court ruling in Case 800, on April 6, 1960.

[65] HAC ruling in Case 1609, on June 29, 1963.

[66] It is important to note that in professional-bureaucratic judiciaries, senior judges have unmatched influence over junior judges and the jurisprudence of the court.

In some cases where the initial appointee was not acquiescent or compliant enough, the selected judge was replaced at the earliest occasion. For example, when the PP Muhammad Abd Al-Salam proved unyielding in some critical cases of interest to the regime (torture, corruption, etc.), he was removed from his position and transferred to the less-influential post of president of Cairo Appeals Court.[67] Later, the minister of justice worked to remove Abd Al-Salam even from this less-powerful judicial post.[68] Abd Al-Salam's successor was a particularly intriguing, if not shocking, choice. Aly Nour El-Din was a legal advisor to the president of the Republic and the president of the Administrative Prosecution Authority (*al-Niabba al-Idariyah* – a separate and usually regarded as less important part of the judiciary that prosecutes cases involving civil servants).[69] For years, Nour El-Din proved himself as a true regime loyalist. In an unprecedented decision for a judiciary that highly regards administrative divisions, President Nasser appointed him to the enormously sensitive position of public prosecutor in 1968. Later, it was revealed that Nour El-Din was a leading member of a regime-inspired secret group to infiltrate and monitor the judicial corps.[70] Nour El-Din has been the only person to assume this post from outside the ranks of the Court of Cassation or Courts of Appeal.

The appointment of Hassan al-Badawi to the highest position within the judiciary, president of the Court of Cassation, was another flagrant example of the political meddling in judicial appointments. Al-Badawi was the president of Alexandria Court of Appeal and a known regime enthusiast. By appointing him to the presidency of the Court of Cassation, the government breached a long-standing judicial practice that required prior work at the cassation level in the rank of vice-president before presiding over the court.[71] All governments under the monarchy or the republic honored this norm. This norm was never violated before or after this unprecedented appointment.

The regime also eliminated election for the HJC. The president of the Court of Cassation (2011–2012) and a leading liberal judge, Hussam

---

[67] The lack of judicial immunity for the PP and the Public Prosecution Department became an important issue in the legal political discourse. Many judges and lawyers demanded frequently that this issue be corrected. Partially, this was achieved with the new Judicial Authority Law of 1972 for members of the Public Prosecution Body and to the PP himself in 1984. See Muhammad Abd Al-Salsm, *Sanawat 'asibah: dhikriyat Na'ib 'amm* (al-Qahirah: Dar al-Shuruq, 1975), 138, 190.

[68] Ibid., 174–176.

[69] Al-Niyabah al-Idariyah al-Maktab al-Fanni, *al-Niyabah al-Idariyah 1954–2004* (al-Qahirah: al-Niyabah al-Idariyah, 2004), 19

[70] Abd Al-Salsm, *Sanawat 'asibah: dhikriyat Na'ib 'amm*, 185.

[71] Ibid., 174–181.

al-Ghiryani, illustrated the significance of the military nature of the revolutionary regime and its impact on the judiciary:

> Officers, because of the military tradition, embrace obedience and seniority.
> They became dismayed with the elected members of the High Judicial
> Council; hence, they abolished it and retained only the seniority-based
> members. Ever since the Council's membership has been based on unquali-
> fied seniority.[72]

In order to achieve tighter control over the lower-level courts, the regime
changed the selection mechanisms for the vital position of presidents of
Courts of First Instance. Traditionally, presidents of Courts of First Instance
were selected according to seniority from within the junior judges serving on
the court. These presidents were a mere first-among-equal, with little clout
over fellow judges. The regime changed this system to select presidents of
Courts of First Instance from the ranks of judges at the Courts of Appeal.
Moreover, the minister of justice commanded the authority to handpick the
presidents, with little or no review of his selection. Aided by their vast administrative powers, financial resources, and longevity in office, those presidents
were able to control the much-less-experienced junior judges. They marginalized the general assemblies of the Courts of First Instance and dominated the
general assemblies' crucial functions of assigning judges and cases to different
judicial panels.

The same was true for the Council of State. After unseating Al-Sanhuri, the
regime was keen to select a malleable replacement. The potential of legal
challenges to the RCC's decrees added to the significance of the presidency of
the Council of State. El-Said Aly el-Said, then the Council's deputy-president,
proved his loyal credentials after the attack on Al-Sanhuri. El-Said defended the
regime's assault on the Council in 1955.[73] El-Said praised the changes enacted
by Law 165 of 1955 that expanded judicial immunity to the junior members of
the Council, expanded the Council's jurisdiction on some matters, and, most
importantly, instituted a new HAC, which was empowered with the power to
review and overturn lower administrative courts' rulings. These formal positive
steps were taken to shadow the many oppressive principles in the legislation,
i.e., the purge of scores of liberal judges from the bench. Mixing reforms with
harsh measures was a frequently used regime strategy since 1952.

---

[72] Hussam al-Gheryani speech in the Judges Club's extraordinary general assembly, May 13, 2005,
quoted in *al-Quda*, September 2, 2005, 37–40.

[73] See *El-Said Aly El-Said* presidential report in the Council of State journal, *Majallat Majlis al-
Dawlah* al-Sanah 5 & 6, (Yanayir 1956): 632 and beyond.

El-Said had considerable clout as a president of the Council and the newly established HAC. Under his chairmanship and guidance, the Council became a conservative force, which favored governmental interests over citizens' and groups' rights and liberties. Judge Abd Al-Barr summarized these radical changes, stating, "The new trends of the High Administrative Court, under judge El-Said Aly El-Said's presidency, constituted a marked departure from the earlier principles established by the Administrative Court to protect citizens' rights and liberties."[74] The regime used the HAC to ensure that all its basic interests were being protected.

Furthermore, some regime loyalists within the judiciary and the legal community even advocated the idea of people's judiciary or inclusion of lay citizens in the composition of judicial circuits hearing criminal, civil, or administrative cases. The rationale was to represent the interests, ideas, and ideals of the populace and the objectives of the revolution.[75] This was a trademark feature of the socialist judicial systems in the former USSR and other communist countries. This guaranteed the Communist Party full domination of the judicial institutions. Naturally, these calls were received by a storm of criticism from professional judges, who tend to regard seniority, professional socialization, and experience highly. They argued that this could ruin the institutional nature and character of the courts, lower judicial standards, and damage citizens' respect for the judiciary.

Nevertheless, Nasser and many leading leftist regime leaders believed it was necessary to include judges in the Arab Socialist Union.[76] Ali Sabri, the Secretary General of the Socialist Union, published in the official *Al-Gomhouria* newspaper (between March 18 and 26, 1967) a series of articles that attacked the professional judiciary and demanded their inclusion in the Socialist Union to get in touch with revolutionary principles and ideals.[77]

---

[74] Abd Al-Barr, *Dawr majlis al-Dawlah al-Misri fi himayat al-huquq wa-al-hurriyat al-`ammah*, al-juz' 2, 163.

[75] See, for example, a book by Abd Al-Rahman Azzuz, *al-Qada al-sha`bi* (al-Qahirah: Dar Nahdat Misr lil-Tab` wa-al-Nashr, 1977).

[76] Founded in December 1962, the Arab Socialist Union (ASU) replaced the Nationalist Union as Egypt's sole political party. ASU's political power diminished under Sadat until it was dispended in the late 1970s.

[77] In his first article March 18, 1967, Sabri criticized both the principles of the separation of power and judges for "applying law from an upper-class perspective." In his second article dated March 19, 1967, Sabri claimed that judges because of their lack of political participation were estranged from the spirit of the people and the revolution. On the following day, March 20, 1967, Sabri continued his attack on the judiciary. He claimed that some judges expressed their

THE COURTS GO TO THE SIDELINES

The regime policies, especially after 1954, largely succeeded in silencing courts and judges. By rendering guarantees of judicial independence a farce, judges feared regime reprisal against any judge who dares to issue adverse rulings. Nonetheless, some pockets of resistance – judicial activism – continued to exist and gained some strength after 1967. As with other civil-law systems, it might be appropriate to distinguish between the behavior of the Council and the courts. I first review the Council's jurisprudence after 1954 and then move to examine the conduct of the regular courts and the Judges Club between 1952 and 1970.

The attack on Al-Sanhuri had its intended effect on the Council's judges as well as on the institution itself. Wahid Ra'fat, a prominent lawyer, law professor, and former judge at the Council of State during the 1954 episode, summarized the effect of the attack on Al-Sanhuri:

> The Council of State was immensely weakened after the assault on Al-Sanhuri; the Council started to go along with the regime instead of scrutinizing its activities. This was evident in the Council rulings, legal opinions, and legislation that it furnished to the government, which limited the Council's oversight over the regime's decisions and actions.[78]

A review of the Council of State journal, *Majallat Majlis al-Dawlah*, illustrates the fundamental transformation in the Council's judicial philosophy and professed role.[79] The journal, in early years (1950–1954), published research papers and reviews that embraced liberal ideals and ideas. The

concerns because many judges were not connected politically with the society and that some legislation was being applied against the interests of the people. On March 21, 1967, Sabri once more accused the judiciary of serving the interests of the exploiting classes [the bourgeoisie in the Marxist discourse]. In his fifth article (March 22, 1967), Sabri argued for the end of separation of power and the necessity of judges' participation in politics. On March 23, 1967, he criticized some judicial verdicts that acquitted alleged criminals on procedural or technical grounds, claiming that this would never happen if judges were connected to the masses. In his seventh article (March 24, 1967), Sabri championed the initiative to tie judges to the struggle of the masses, and put on judges' shoulders the responsibility of revolutionizing the legal codes. On March 25, 1967, Sabri yet again insisted on judges' participation in the Socialist Union, arguing that insularity from the populace is detrimental to justice. He also asserted that some judges asked to have the honor of political participation. In his last article, dated March 26, 1967, Sabri again advocated the necessity of judges' participation in the popular institutions [of the Socialist Union].

78 Ra'fat, *Fusul min Thawrat 23 Yulyu*, 187.

79 Published for the first time in 1950 and generally authored by judges and prominent law professors, *Majallat Majlis al-Dawlah* has been a clear indication of the Council's legal philosophy and jurisprudence.

journal frequently drew attention to the experiences and legislation of other administrative judiciaries in other democratic civil law European states of France, Italy, Spain, and Portugal. In addition, the Council's official views, as presented in the presidents' annual reports, were critical of the government for failing to provide the financial recourses and workforces the Council needed. The reports condemned legislation that restricted the Council's jurisdiction.

The tone and focus of *Majallat Majlis al-Dawlah* changed in the post-Al-Sanhuri's era. Published papers focused on promoting the regime's socialist policies and programs. Limited attention was given to rights and liberties. The annual presidential reports generally praised the government and Nasser himself. The reports refrained from even mildly criticizing legislation that limited its jurisdiction or infringed on its institutional independence.[80]

This "change of heart" also manifested itself in the Council's rulings and legal opinions. Al-Sanhuri's successor changed the Council's jurisprudence concerning rights, liberties, and checks and balances. While El-Said was firmly in line with the liberal views of Al-Sanhuri in his early years in the Council, he drastically "adjusted" his position to fit the interests of the military regime after 1954.[81] For instance, the established jurisprudence of the Council, during the pre-1952 era, deemed unconstitutional all legislation prohibiting judicial review of administrative decisions. The HAC under El-Said's leadership changed this judicial philosophy. The court upheld the constitutionality of Law 600/1953, which denied all courts the competence to adjudicate civil servants' appeals of dismissal orders.[82] The HAC followed the same position regarding Law 270/1956, which barred appealing the decisions of the executive branch under martial law.[83] This ruling was vital for shielding arrest and detention orders without court approval from any legal petitions for reversal or compensation. It endowed the ever-expanding security apparatus with virtual legal immunity from any adjudication.

The court reversed its stands on many rights and liberties. For example, during the liberal era, the Council ruled that it can review executive denials of citizens' right to travel. This was turned upside down after 1955. The HAC ruled the administrative decisions to grant or reject travel requests are matters

---

[80] Compilations of the first twenty-five years of the Council's reports are published in *Majallat Majlis al-Dawlah*, al-Sanah 20–25, (1975): 5–32.

[81] Faruq `Abd al-Barr mentioned that El-Said wrote the Council's landmark decision in 1948 that granted courts the power of judicial review. Furthermore, he was behind many other important rulings that affirmed many rights and liberties. See Abd Al-Barr, *Dawr majlis al-Dawlah al-Misri fi himayat al-huquq wa-al-hurriyat al-`ammah*, al-juz' 2, 151–154.

[82] HAC ruling in Case 161 on June 29, 1957.

[83] HAC ruling in Case 929 on July 13,1958.

reserved for executive judgments. The executive, on the strength of its own judgment, had the right to refuse any travel requests. The HAC presented an extremely conservative reasoning for its ruling. The court treated travel as a privilege and not a legal right. To justify its position, the court claimed the constitution did not explicitly mention travel among recognized citizens' rights.[84] By following such logic, the HAC put an end to any judicial assessment of administrative decisions concerning this fundamental personal freedom.

Moreover, despite the fact that the Council of State publicly denounced exceptional courts during the liberal era, the Council, after its domestication, ruled that both the Court of Treason and the Revolution Court were acts of sovereignty and not subject to any form of judicial review or appeal.[85]

The HAC conferred immunity on decisions by the single party (the Nationalist Union and its successor the Arab Socialist Union). The court repeatedly ruled that this organization was an "independent institution from the executive authority and other authorities. This institution performs a constitutional function." The single party became, according to the HAC's jurisprudence, a fourth power of the state, alongside the three established powers of the executive, legislative, and judicial.[86] This verdict was critically important to the regime. Single party membership was a prerequisite for membership in the parliament and other municipal councils. Successive constitutions granted the Nationalist Union and the Arab Socialist Union the right to veto candidates for mayors and governing boards of many important institutions.

However, it is important to note that not all judges or courts towed the line of the HAC. For example, Mohamed Efaat, the Council's deputy-president and long-time president of the Administrative Court, refused to change his judicial philosophy. He issued many rulings that followed the liberal jurisprudence of the Al-Sanhuri era. Nonetheless, the HAC overturned many of his decisions.[87]

As for the ordinary judiciary, between 1952 and 1967, the regime was widely successful in sidestepping the courts. Exploiting dominance over the legislative and the executive powers, the government established exceptional courts

[84] HAC ruling in Case 1555, June 6, 1956.
[85] Abd Al-Barr, *Dawr majlis al-Dawlah al-Misri fi himayat al-huquq wa-al-hurriyat al-'ammah*, al-juz' 2, 107.
[86] Sa'd 'Asfur, *al-qada al-Idari* (al-Iskandariyah: Munsha'at al-Ma'arif, 1975), 232–234.
[87] Abd Al-Barr, *Dawr majlis al-Dawlah al-Misri fi himayat al-huquq wa-al-hurriyat al-'ammah*, al-juz' 2, 176–179.

to hear cases of political or symbolic significance. Hence, the courts were not put to a decisive test.

The Judges Club's relationship with government fluctuated. The Judges Club, especially under the leadership of Mumtaz Nasar, used its publications to launch attacks against the exceptional courts that infringed on the ordinary courts' jurisdiction and to promote the principle of judicial independence. The Judges Club, especially under Nasar, was steadfast in its defense of the remaining guarantees of judicial independence. In 1963, then minister of justice Fathi Al-Sharqawi drafted legislation to tighten the Ministry of Justice's control over judges and courts. The Judges Club publicly rejected the proposed laws and even wired Nasser to register its rejection.[88] The minister managed to convince Nasser to issue Law-decree 76/1963 that dismembered the association's elected board primarily composed of ex-officio members, rather than through an election.[89] Judges responded by boycotting the appointed council and its activities. After a ministerial shuffle, in which Al-Sharqawi lost the justice portfolio, the new minister reinstated the electoral process. Judges reelected the fifteen-member board without a single change. The Judges Club continued to defend judges' corporate interests and judicial independence. This led, in 1965, to Law 43/1965, which answered some of the judges' personal and institutional demands.[90]

THE REGIME AND THE COURTS AFTER 1967 DEFEAT

After the regime established its dominance over all institutions, a new *modus vivendi* between judges and Nasser's regime emerged; as long as judges refrained from political interference, the regime seemed willing to leave judges free to adjudicate the bulk of legal disputes. The aforementioned three-point policy served the regime well until the June 1967 crushing defeat. The defeat damaged the regime's public support and control of the society. Many judges, lawyers, and other intellectuals started to question the regime's undemocratic policies. Some claimed that the lack of transparency, accountability, and the rule of law was raison d'être for the defeat. In order to quell such opposition and appease his critics, embattled Nasser issued the March 30th Declaration, which, for the first time, presented ideas about the rule of law, rights, and liberties. However, this declaration did not convince regime

---

[88] Abd Al-Mun'im, *al-Dawr al-siyasi li-Niqabat al-Muhamin, (1912–1981),* 205–206.
[89] *Al-Jarida al-Rasmiyya,* Issue 180, August 12, 1963.
[90] Mumtaz Nasar, *Ma'rakat al-'adalah fi Misr* (al-Qahirah: Dar al-Shurūk, 1974), 42–58.

critics. Judges intensified their demands for the restoration of judicial independence and the rule of law.

The Judges Club started to publicize the issue of judicial independence. A review of the Judges Club periodicals during this era (1967–1970) illustrates this idea. In the third issue of the association's journal, there is a detailed, book-length, comprehensive article entitled "Independence of the Judicial Authority." Muhammad 'Asfur, a distinguished law professor, was indirectly responding to the regime attack on judicial independence as well as launching an offensive against the regime's special Military and State Security tribunals.[91] By publishing this book, the Judges Club defied a government ban on its printing and publication.[92] This, of course, ran counter to the ideas advocated by the regime. The regime tried to enlist the support of senior judges, especially those who occupy official positions: members of the HJC, presidents of the Courts of Appeal, and presidents of First Instance Courts. These judges issued public statements defending the regime's official position. This practice would become common under Sadat and Mubarak.[93]

Judges had tacitly resisted the implementation of laws that restricted freedoms. Absent of an authoritative source of constitutional interpretations in the pre-1969 era (prior to the establishment of the Supreme Court), lower courts made constitutional interpretations themselves and refused to implement laws they found unconstitutional.[94] The regime relaxed its extensive exploitation of exceptional courts after 1967. This, coupled with the regime's wounded pride, opened the door for some confrontations over judgments that Nasser perceived as unfavorable. After 1967, courts started to issue rulings that embraced the judicial activism of the prerevolutionary era. Several decisions questioned the constitutionality of some revolutionary legislation and procedures. The courts strived to expand their domain outside the limited sphere set by the revolutionary regime. Courts issued verdicts that contradicted the regime's stated policies.

This behavioral independence far exceeded the guarantees of institutional independence that the courts enjoyed.[95] Judges were taking significant risks in

---

[91] This paper was reprinted in the July 1968 issue of *Al-Quda* and later as a book in 1969. Muhammad 'Asfur, *Istiqlal al-sultah al-qada'iyah* (al-Qahirah: Matba'at Atlas, 1969).

[92] Abd Allāh Imām, *Madhbahat al-qada'* (al-Qahirah: Maktabat Madhbūlī, 1976), 60.

[93] For more information of senior judges' behavior under Nasser see: 'Abd Allāh Imām, *Madhbahat al-qada,* 129–135.

[94] Rosberg, *Roads to the Rule of Law,* 156.

[95] On the relation between these two types of judicial review, see Peter H. Russell and David M. O'Brien, eds., *Judicial Independence in the Age of Democracy: Critical Perspectives from around the World* (Charlottesville: University Press of Virginia, 2001), 6.

delivering verdicts that offended their political masters. The regime had both legal and political power to either remove individual judges from office or to restructure the judicial institutions altogether. This liberal and courageous behavior is also an indication of the strong commitment to the rule of law, due process, and judicial autonomy.

In one case concerning alleged widespread corruption in the Ministry of Agriculture, Nasser publicly condemned a high-ranking official. To the president's dismay, the court exonerated the accused of all crimes and ordered his immediate release. Nasser became increasingly convinced that the tribunals were not committed to his political line. In another highly publicized case, known by the name of the accused Ambassador Amen Soka, the court also acquitted this senior foreign service official. In yet another case, the courts found judge Mahmoud Abd Al-Latif, who helped Nasser in his childhood, not guilty despite the grave accusations of conspiring to organize a coup against the regime.[96] Nasser responded angrily by ordering a retrial. The new circuit stunned the regime and the defense attorneys by exonerating Abd Al-Latif in the first day of the new trial. The presiding justice left the courtroom to deliver his letter of resignation to the minister of justice, stating he would not let the regime intimidate the judiciary by dismissing him.[97]

Therefore, to ensure its control over the judiciary (the last partially independent institution of the state), the regime sought to carry out a number of institutional changes:

- Separating the Public Prosecution Office from the court system and placing it within the office of the presidency.
- Mandating judges' membership in the Socialist Union. If a magistrate lost his membership in the Union, he would be dismissed from the judiciary (the same tool of control was used against members of the parliament).
- Changing courts' composition to consist of one judge and two Socialist Union members. Majority rule was to be used in all cases. This would have marginalized professional judges in favor of ordinary people, or more precisely the Socialist Union.

The Judges Club rejected out of hand these infringements on judicial independence. The club championed the calls for democratic reform and

---

[96] Later, after Nasser's death, it was claimed that Nasser had written a memo that ordered the dismissal of all judges that ruled in these cases. Ḥamādah Ḥusni, 'Abd al-Naṣir wa-al-qaḍā', 72

[97] Muhammad Abu `Alam, *Yawmiyat mustashar min dahaya madhbahat al-qada* (al-Qahirah: Akhbar al-Yawm, 1999), 80–82.

judicial independence. The regime estimated that the Judges Club became a center for anti-regime activity. The regime first tried to use the election of the Judges Club to get rid of Mumtaz Nasar and his board.[98] The officials in the Ministry of Justice, including the minister himself, publicly supported a list of regime-loyalists for the fifteen-member board. Nonetheless, judges voted to retain Nasar and all members of his board. This was a crushing defeat for the regime and the minister of justice. In order to avoid a public confrontation in a period of great national and particularly regime humiliation, the regime tried to weaken the Judges Club and the activist judges. Some regime-loyalist suggested the following plan to restore regime control:[99]

- Amending the Judicial Authority Law to change the composition of the HJC to ensure full regime control from above.
- Preventing the Judges Club from providing its services to its members by reducing government financial contribution. The plan also recommended instructing financial institutions to withhold loans to the Judges Club and to request prompt repayment of all standing loans.
- Publicly spreading information that defamed judges, especially news about trials of judges accused of corruption.[100]

The regime used the power of the purse and state-controlled media to domesticate judges. When, these measures proved lacking, the regime utilized its heavy hand to uproot the activist judges and their supporters. Nasser responded with an avalanche of presidential decrees that drastically restructured judicial institutions. Justice Sherif summarized this attack all too briefly:

> After the unfortunate result of the Six-Day War of 1967, an increasing judicial tendency to move towards democratization emerged. The political leadership at the time thought to continue its domination over the judiciary and began to express a wish to have judges enrolled in the sole political party like any other group of people. Judges argued that this step would detract from their independence, and they therefore condemned the proposal. The reaction of

---

[98] Upon graduation from the Law School in 1936, Mumtaz Nasar joined one of Egypt's best law offices. In 1942, he was admitted to the judiciary and served in different capacities until 1969. Nasar was an active member of the Judges Club Board for many years, which he served as president repeatedly from 1963 to 1969. After the Massacre of the Judiciary in 1969, Nasar worked as a lawyer and he was later elected to the People's Assembly. See Lam`i Muti`i, *Haulai al-rijal min Misr* (al-Qahirah: al-Hayah al-Misriyah al-`Ammah lil-Kitab, 1987), 182–189.

[99] Hassūnah, *23 Yūliyū– wa-'Abd al-Nasir: shahādatī*, 198–200.

[100] It was noticeable that Mubarak's regime used those exact strategies against the Judges Club and leading activist judges more than three decades after Nasser's death.

the executive to this resistance was to issue a chain of decree laws to reorganize all judicial bodies.[101]

On August 31, 1969, Nasser issued four law-decrees under the mantra of judicial reform. Those presidential decrees are better known today as the "Massacre of the Judiciary." Law-decree 81 enshrined a new Supreme Court at the pinnacle of the Egyptian judicial system. This replaced the system of "abstention control" in which each individual court practiced constitutional interpretation and periodically abstained from enforcing laws that were deemed to violate articles of the constitution. In an explanatory memorandum to Decree 81/1969, the regime did not attempt to hide the purpose of the new court when it openly declared that "It has been clear in many cases that the judgments of the judiciary are not able to join the march of development which has occurred in social and economic relations."[102] The preamble of the decree stated that the purpose of establishing the court was to "stabilize legal relationships, avoid the discrepancy in rulings, and to *enable judges to defend the Revolution and principles of the society within the boundaries of legitimacy.* "[103]

The Supreme Court consolidated the process of judicial review in trusted hands. "From 1969–1979, when the Supreme Court was in operation, it made over 300 rulings, not one of which significantly constrained the regime."[104] The Supreme Court's justices were appointed directly by the president for three-year terms. Appointed for a short term of three years, Supreme Court judges did not enjoy the life tenure (as justices in the US Supreme Court), or mandatory retirement at a certain age (a guarantee provided for all other judges). Egypt's Supreme Court was routinely stacked with pro-regime justices.[105] In the unlikely event that judicial resistance to executive policy emerged, the president could easily appoint new justices to replace the old.

---

[101] Adel Omar Sherif, "Attacks on the Judiciary: Judicial Independence – Reality or Fallacy?" in Eugene Cotran (ed.) *Yearbook of Islamic and Middle Eastern Law* Volume 6, 1999–2000 (London: Kluwer Law International, 2001), 15.

[102] Moustafa, *The Struggle for Constitutional Power*, 66.

[103] Law-decree 81/1969, *Al-Jarida al-Rasmiyya*, Issue 35, August 31, 1969.

[104] Rutherford, "The Changing Political and Legal Role of the Egyptian Supreme Constitutional Court." Paper presented at the annual meeting of the Middle East Studies Association, 1996, 13.

[105] According to Article 7 of the court law, the president had the sole authority to appoint the chief justice. The president can even disregard the age limit for his retirement. The president also appointed the deputy-chief justice and justices after gathering the opinion of the SCJP. The law also did not specify the number of the court's justices, giving the president the right to appoint additional justices when he deemed necessary. Hishām Muḥammad Fawzī, *Raqābat*

To ensure that resistance to executive power would not easily reemerge in other courts, Nasser created the Supreme Council of Judicial Bodies (SCJB), which gave the regime greater control over judicial appointments, promotions, and disciplinary action. Decree 82 empowered SCJB to "supervise all judicial bodies, coordinate between them, express opinion about issues related to them, study and propose legislation concerning advancing judicial systems."[106] The president of the republic was to preside over this council, with the minister of justice as deputy-president. The SCJB membership included a number of ex-office senior judges. The president had the authority to appoint two other members to the council, who had previously worked at judicial bodies in the capacity of at least a justice or an equivalent position. This council replaced independent judicial councils as the ultimate authority and institutional voice of those judicial organizations.[107]

Decree 83 focused on reorganization of the judicial authorities. With this law, the government acquired the power to reappoint all members of the judicial authorities to their previous positions or in other government or public-sector positions. Article 3 of this decree stated, "All those who are not reappointed are considered retired, and their retirement benefits or remuneration shall be decided according to the last salary."[108] Utilizing his legislative powers under this act, Nasser purged 189 judges including the president of the Court of Cassation, fifteen senior judges at the high court, all members of the board of the Judges Club, and many key judges and prosecutors. A review of

---

dustūrīyat al-qawānīn: dirāsah muqārinah bayna Amrīkā wa-Miṣr (al-Qahirah: Markaz al-Qahirah li-Dirāsāt Ḥuqūq al-Insān, 1999), 54–61.

[106] Law-decree 188/1952 reorganized the High Judicial Council, removing from its membership the president of Cairo's First Instance Court (an executive appointee). The same membership continued under Law 56/159; however, because this law came during unity with Syria, Council's membership increased to eleven to include Syrian judges. Nonetheless, Law-decree 74/1963, generally perceived as the first assault on the ordinarily judiciary, returned the president of Cairo's First Instance Court to the membership of the Council. However, Law 43/1965 embraced a positive change by removing the under-secretary of the Ministry of Justice, replacing him with the president of Alexandria Court of Appeal.

[107] Law-decree 82/1969, *Al-Jarida al-Rasmiyya*, Issue 35, August 31, 1969.

[108] Law-decree 81/1969, *Al-Jarida al-Rasmiyya*, Issue 35, August 31, 1969. It is important to note that judicial immunity became rather obsolete under the revolutionary regime. In addition to the two well-known purges (Council of State in 1955, and the whole court system in 1969), in a number of cases, setting judges were arrested, tortured and forced to resign their judicial posts without any consideration for judicial independence. In one case, judge 'Ali Jirishah of the Council of State was arrested in August 1965 and detained and brutalized for four months in the infamous Military Prison. He was forced to resign his judgeship and was tried and convicted before a state security court. Judge Jirishah harshly criticized the Council's leadership for asking him to resign and refusing to consider his appeal of the resignation. See Ali Jirishah, *Fi al-zinzanah* (al-Qahirah: Dar al-Shuruq, 1975).

the list of sacked judges reveals their significance. Under Sadat and Mubarak, three judges later occupied the post of minister of justice, and seven returned to assume the presidency of the Court of Cassation.

Decree 84 reorganized the administration of the Judges Club. Instead of electing all members of its governing board, the decree authorized a board composed of ex-officio members. This provided the regime with an excellent opportunity to ensure a tamed and domesticated board.[109] The goal was to transform the club from a forum representing the corporate interests of the judicial community to an instrument of regime control over the judiciary.

Those policies worked laboriously to uproot all sentiments of opposition within the judiciary and ensure regime domination of courts and judges. Nonetheless, the regime failed to change the institutional culture of the judicial corps. Judges would resume their role defending the rule of law, judicial independence, rights, and liberties after Nasser's death. Furthermore, these regime actions had grave consequences on the state-court relationship and the regime's public support after the 1967 War.

CONCLUSION

Early on, Nasser secured the support of Egypt's top judges in the Council of State and the Court of Cassation. However, in his quest for political suprem- acy, the regime sought to control all institutions, including the courts fully. Since 1954, Nasser was able to domesticate his opponents within the judiciary and dramatically increased the accountability of the court to the executive branch. Max Weber, long ago, recognized that charisma could have an adverse effect on the working of legal-bureaucratic institutions. These meas- ures had severe political costs. The regime lost all claims to legality and due process. The courts could not provide any meaningful RSFs. Nevertheless, the judiciary was not the only institution that suffered a bloody nose because of this confrontation; Nasser's regime was incurably damaged.

However, Nasser's charismatic leadership and the populist economic pol- icies were able to stabilize the political system even in the absence of legality. This depended heavily on the persona of Nasser and consequently could not be sustained after his death in 1970. Nasser's successor, President Mohamed Anwar Al-Sadat, had to find a different formula to first continue his autocratic rule and, second, distinguish himself from Nasser's commanding shadow.

---

[109] Law-decree 84/1969, *Al-Jarida al-Rasmiyya*, Issue 35, August 31, 1969.

4

The Years of Sadat

*Crisis, Regime Survival, and the Awakening
of Judicial Activism (1970–1981)*

Abd Al-Nasser and I are the last pharaohs. Did Abd Al-Nasser need laws to govern with? Or do I need laws? I put the powers that you are talking about for those who will come after us. There will be ordinarily presidents: Mohamed, Ali, and Omar ... they will need these laws to rule.

> Sadat's reaction to a question about the presidential
> massive powers under the 1971 Constitution.[1]

Most experts agree that Nasser's regime "lapsed into a period of deep political and economic crisis during the period 1968–1970."[2] Nonetheless, Nasser's enormous public appeal enabled the regime to survive. Nasser's sudden death swelled the regime's crisis to its climax. *Hilal* convincingly argued,

> Nasser dominated the Egyptian political scene for fifteen long years. His surprise departure created a 'vacuum' at the heart of the political system that cannot be easily filled by a single person or a group of individuals; particularly pertaining to the regime's relationship with the masses. Without a doubt, the legitimacy of the 1952 Revolution regime was inseparably tied to the persona of Gamal Abdel Nasser. In fact, it could be said that the source of primary regime's legitimacy was the Nasserite leadership and his achievements domestically and internationally. This unique relationship that tied the leader to the masses enabled the regime to rise above its crises and defeats.[3]

[1] Quoted in Ahmad Bahā' Al-Din, *Mu'āwarātī ma'a al-Sadat* (al-Qahirah: Dar al-Hilal, 1987), 63–64.

[2] Mahmoud Abdel-Fadil, *The Political Economy of Nasserism: A Study in Employment and Income Distribution Policies in Urban Egypt, 1952–72* (Cambridge: Cambridge University Press, 1980), 9.

[3] Ali Al-Din Hilal, Moustafa Kamel Sayed, and Ikram Badr Al-Din, *Tajribat al-dimuqratiyah fi Misr, 1970–1981* (al-Qahirah: al-Markaz al-`Arabi lil-Bahth wa-al-Nashr, 1982), 37.

Sadat endured the waning months of 1970 in the shadow of the immense national grief over Nasser's departure. However, 1971 was a crisis year for Sadat's presidency. Antagonism surrounded the new president within the regime and amongst the populace. A multitude of predicaments converged to inflate the regime's survival crisis, including the enduring national humiliation after the Six-Day War, the heightened succession struggle, and an exhaustive economic crisis with no end in sight. The defeat undermined the ideological foundations of the revolutionary regime. Arab nationalism, socialism, and above all secularism were held responsible for the creation of a corrupt and weak state that failed to defend the homeland.

When Sadat ascended to power in 1970, the Egyptian economy was already suffering. The socialist, state-controlled economy had experienced severe difficulties since the late 1960s. The inefficiency of the public sector coupled with the closure of the Suez Canal and the loss of Sinai oil revenues devastated the already struggling economy. In addition, the financially exhaustive conflict with Israel severely limited resources for economic development. After the defeat, all resources were devoted to rebuilding the army. Notwithstanding, economic resources were critical for the survival of the illiberal political system engineered by Nasser after 1954. Nasser and his colleagues embraced a particular formula for sustaining their rule. We [the revolutionaries leaders] will give you [the people] food and employment but leave politics to us. The deal was simple: providing for basic needs in exchange for the public's relinquishing its right to rule.

However, as early as the late 1960s, the state was showing signs of default on its social contract. Under an increasingly socialist economic system, where private enterprises were kept at the margin, the government had to be the principal employer of college graduates. "This commitment became explicit in 1961 when an official decree firmly established the right of every university graduate to a government job."[4] This meant "a rise in numbers [of public sector employers] from about 250,000 in 1952 to one million or more in the early 1970s."[5] Many economists, who initially supported the socialist policies and full employment, started to question its value.

By the early 1970s, the state did not muster enough resources to continue the full employment policy but dithered to shoulder the political cost to rescind it. Therefore, the official commitment to full employment remained, but its enactment was stalled for extended periods. Expectations that young

---

[4]   Abdel-Fadil, *The Political Economy of Nasserism*, 9.
[5]   Anthony McDermott, *Egypt from Nasser to Mubarak: A Flawed Revolution* (London: Croom Helm, 1988), 123.

graduates would opt for private sector positions did not materialize. The regularity of pay and security of tenure continued to make government employment popular, and the demand for the limited available positions within the colossal bureaucracy continued. Government-subsidized goods and services (food, clothes, transportation, etc.) were scarce, low quality, and poorly distributed. The prices of unsubsidized products were exceptionally high even for most of the middle class. "After the consumer boom of the early 1960s, which aroused expectations among many people who could not afford it, Egypt's extensive middle class started to feel the pinch as mass consumption was squeezed through inflation."[6]

Nasser's successor lacked the personal ties with the masses. Sadat's modest public standing during Nasser's years aggravated the regime's crisis. Sadat was perceived as a yes-man, weak, and lackluster among the leaders of the 1952 coup.[7] Sadat was the last of the Free Officers to be named vice president, and many looked upon his vice-presidential appointment with indifference. For the most part, the official positions that Sadat held, i.e., speaker of the parliament, chair of the Islamic Congress, or editor-in-chief of the official *Al-Gomhouria* newspaper, did not provide any genuine power base within the powerful state institutions (i.e., the armed forces, the security and intelligence apparatus, or the single party). Thus, Sadat "appeared before the masses as an unknown, without much weight or public appeal ... Sadat's capabilities did not reveal aptitude to rule, nor ability to fill the void of Nasser's leadership."[8]

Besides lacking Nasser's public stature among the masses, many amongst the political elite believed that Sadat was an unconvincing leader. Heikal, the long-time editor of the influential semiofficial *Al-Ahram* newspaper, a close friend and minister of information under Nasser, even implied that "Nasser deliberately avoided giving him posts which entailed making decisions affecting the country because of Sadat's abilities."[9] Therefore, at the time of Nasser's death, Sadat was, at best, first-among-equals in Egypt's governing elite. Many observers argued that he was selected to be president because all

[6]   Abdel-Fadil, *The Political Economy of Nasserism*, 112.

[7]   Zayyat argued, "Some called him 'Colonel Yes', because he would comment 'Yes' on every opinion or statement by Nasser." Muḥammad Abd Al-Salām Zayyāt, *al-Sādāt, al-qinā' wa-al-ḥaqīqah* (al-Qahirah: Jarīdat al-Ahālī, 1989), 42. The New York Times commented, a month after Nasser's death that, "Among Egyptians, el Sadat is relatively unfamiliar and the big question is how will he fill Nasser's shoes. He has no pretensions to charisma." *The New York Times*, October 27, 1970.

[8]   Anwar Muhammad, *Shuhud 'asr al-Sadat* (al-Qahirah: Dar Ayh Imm lil-Nashr wa-al-Tawzi', 1990), 12.

[9]   Joseph Finklestone, *Anwar Sadat: Visionary who Dared* (Essex: Frank Cass, 1995), 64.

other powerbrokers within the single party, the army, and the security establishment thought he was malleable and easy to sway.[10] Scores of experts at home and abroad predicted that he would keep his position as president of Egypt for a few months at best and that his regime was going to crumble and collapse.

Sadat had to establish foundations of political survival that distinguished his regime from that of his predecessor. This was no easy task as he lacked Nasser's charisma and revolutionary credentials. The struggling war economy denied any hopes of gaining public support based on entitlement or social programs for the lower classes. Sadat had two plausible alternatives to build his regime public appeal: (1) liberalize the regime, yielding to the demands of democratization, which gathered momentum after the Six-Day War and (2) acquiesce to the growing religious sentiments that also gained currency after the defeat. Sadat decided to do some of both: limited liberalization and partial Islamization.

While Sadat's Islamized discourse and policies planted essential seeds in Egypt's soil, political liberalization, however, is more of interest to this study. The regime's institutionalization and the rule-of-law discourse had a positive effect on judicial independence directly and indirectly. Directly, to gain credibility, the government strengthened the rule-of-law institutions, particularly the judiciary. Judicial institutional autonomy grew under Sadat. Indirectly, courts benefited from the atmosphere of political openness, the multiparty system, and a freer press. This context enabled the reconstitution of the judicial support structure, i.e., the bar, civil society organizations, professional syndicates, and later oppositional parties that became instrumental in defending judicial independence.

THE STRUGGLE FOR SURVIVAL AND CONTROL

In this context, Sadat faced a dual and daunting challenge: ascertaining his unqualified authority over the regime (augmenting power to avoid horizontal threats) and establishing public acceptance (building support to negate vertical threats). The two objectives seemed contradictory. Building the institutional infrastructure of authoritarianism, a prerequisite for creating widespread support, would entail limiting the vast presidential power inherited from

---

[10] This is a common practice in the Middle East and maybe elsewhere. The powerbrokers would settle on a weak president, but after a while this supposedly pale figure would prove them all wrong. A good example in this regard is Chadli Bendjedid, who was chosen as president of Algeria after its charismatic and powerful leader Houari Boumédienne.

Nasser. All policies of Sadat's regime and those of his successor could be understood in the context of the conflicting demands that those two objectives exerted on an authoritarian potentate.

Sadat's pressing priority was to ascertain his absolute control over the regime's potent institutions. Utilizing the massive presidential powers, divisions within his adversaries' camp, their lack of popular support, and the dire need for change, democracy, and liberalism, Sadat cleverly outmaneuvered his opponents. On May 15, 1971, the president ordered the arrest of many leaders of the single party, the intelligence and security services, as well several high-ranking military officers. All were accused of conspiracy to organize a coup. This event has since been known as the "Corrective Movement" and later the "Rectification Revolution'" or the "Second Revolution."[11] The power struggle heightened the regime's crisis, as Sadat purged scores of Nasser's era of top-tier politicians who occupied key positions in the government and the single party who claimed to be the guardians of Nasserism.

Sadat's commitment to a different form of survival strategy is evident in his rhetoric during and after the May 15th Revolution and the 1971 Constitution he promulgated later that year. To provide a much-needed dosage of public support for the regime, Sadat used two propaganda stunts: Islam and democracy. The two most widely used clichés were "State of Science and Piety" and "State of the Institutions."[12] The first affirmed the president's preference for an Islamic nature of the state (in sharp contrast to Nasser's secular "infidel" state). The second reflected Sadat's declared commitment to the rule of law (in contrast to the rule of personality or dictatorship under Nasser).

Alongside the rule of law, Islam was a cornerstone of Sadat's discourse. Sadat "hardly ever made a speech without mentioning the name of Allah somewhere or without beginning and ending with a citation from the Holy Book, the Word of Allah."[13] The stipulation that Islamic Jurisprudence (Shari'a) is a principal source of legislation (Article 2) was one of the most significant changes in Sadat's constitution.

---

[11] Anwar Al-Sādāt, *al-Bahth 'an al-dhāt: qissat hayātī* (al-Qahirah: al-Maktab al-Misrī al-hadīth, 1978).

[12] In Sadat's discourse, "State of Institutions" is similar to the Western idiom "government of law not of men."

[13] Raphael Israeli, "The Pervasiveness of Islam in Contemporary Arab Political Discourse: The Cases of Sadat and Arafat," in Ofer Feldman and Christ'l De Landtsheer (eds.), *Politically Speaking: A Worldwide Examination of Language Used in the Political Sphere* (Westport: Praeger, 1998), 22.

Unlike the contemporary views that put Islamization in contrast to democracy, in the 1970s, both regime survival policies were well received domestically and internationally. In Egypt, while democracy and liberalism have always been popular among the intellectuals, middle class, and university students, the religious sentiments of the rural and lower class have been traditionally strong. Similarly, Sadat's new audience in the West welcomed both Islam and political liberalization tendencies. For one thing, American and European leaders have advocated democracy and liberalism vis-à-vis totalitarianism and socialism; additionally, Islam was perceived as a fighting force against the expansion of Communism.[14]

It is important to take into account that Sadat transformed Egypt's foreign policy from nonalignment and friendship with the USSR to an alliance with the United States. In order to please his new liberal and democratic audience, Sadat was inclined to liberalize the regime to distinguish his regime from that of Colonel Nasser.[15] Hilal concurred, "The change in Egypt's foreign policy direction and the cooperation with Western states encouraged the political leadership to give an image to the outside world that Egypt enjoys political stability and democratic rule."[16] The leading Arab intellectual Fouad Zakaria maintained,

> He [Sadat] wanted to give his reign an independent zest from that of Nasser. Liberalism was forced upon him; because he changed course from the East to the West: America . . . and in order to please America, there was a necessity for some actions that might be perceived as 'liberal.'[17]

While it is difficult analytically to distinguish which of the domestic or the international considerations took precedence in Sadat's numerous political decisions, this differentiation is of secondary importance to this book. Institutionalization and Islamization as survival strategies served the regime with its domestic and international audiences. It might be plausible to say that early on, Sadat, like any other freshman ruler, was primarily concerned with establishing his authority at home before venturing abroad. Domestic

---

[14] Sadat also used his Islamization to attack Nasser's regime, the socialist policies, and his "infidel" supporters. Sadat also empowered Islamic groups within the universities to attack socialists and Nasserites who controlled all student unions. For an excellent account of Sadat's Islamized policies see Carrie Rosefsky Wickham, *Mobilizing Islam: Religion, Activism and Political Change in Egypt* (New York: Columbia University Press, 2002).

[15] Colonel Nasser was the preferred name that Western media used to highlight the military (hence undemocratic nature) of the revolutionary regime under Nasser.

[16] Ali Al-Din Hilal, Moustafa Kamel Sayed, and Ikram Badr Al-Din, *Tajribat al-dimuqratiyah fi Misr, 1970–1981*, 39.

[17] *Al-Masry Al-Youm*, May 14, 2007.

considerations took precedence over foreign policy objectives. After all, political control internally is a prerequisite for any successful international appeal. The tide changed in favor of foreign policy consideration, particularly after the enormous boost of the military success in the 1973 Yom Kippur War.

Because Sadat's rhetoric and legal reforms are of prime importance for the purpose of this work, I analyze them in detail. First, I examine Sadat's public discourse related to democracy, the rule of law, and judicial independence. Sadat's discourse divulged different core values than those of his predecessor. There was a profound emphasis on the foundations of legality and the courts' RSFs. Second, I compare Sadat's 1971 Constitution to the legal frameworks (constitutions and national charters) of the revolutionary era. The 1971 Constitution underscored rights and liberties and due process as a tool to establish a legally based political community.

Sadat's Discourse

In his intense power struggle against the remnants of Nasser's regime, Sadat's preferred slogans were "state of institutions" and the "rule of law." The president argued that antagonists did not respect the Constitution and disregarded the legal stipulations. In his first days in office, Sadat revealed his plans for democratization in Egypt. This denoted not only "his commitment to democracy but also his criticism of the previous regime."[18] Amr Shalakany, an Egyptian law professor, argued persuasively,

> In seeking to distinguish himself from Nasser, Sadat publicly committed himself to the 'rule of law' in a highly dramatic fashion. He was shown in newsreel after newsreel burning the wiretap recordings taken by Nasser's secret service, physically demolishing cell doors in an infamous political prison and, of course, reinstating the judges Nasser had fired in the 1968 'massacre.'[19]

The analysis of Sadat's public discourse reveals how distinct it was from Nasser's. Whereas social justice was the central value in Nasser's discourse, this value was rather insignificant in Sadat's discourse.[20] Social justice was only mentioned ten times in the eleven speeches, with an average of less than a yearly citation (see Figure 4.1). Sadat hardly ever contemplated justice in his

---

[18] Raphael Israeli, "*I, Egypt*": *Aspects of President Anwar Al-Sadat's Political Thought,* Jerusalem Papers on Peace Problems, (Jerusalem: Magnes Press, Hebrew University, 1981), 83.

[19] Amr Shalakany, "*I Heard It All Before*," 849.

[20] To analyze Sadat's discourse, I use his annual speech before the parliament commemorating the May 15th Revolution.

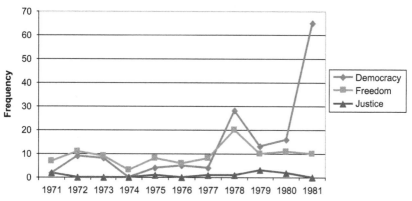

FIGURE 4.1 The frequency of democracy, freedom, and justice in Sadat's May 15 speeches (1970–1981)

discussion of Egypt's social and economic conditions. The lack of emphasis on social justice reveals Sadat's free-market political views, which stood in sharp contrast to the socialist tradition of the revolutionary regime.

Conversely, while the rule of law was hardly present in Nasser's discourse, this theme became prevalent in Sadat's speech. A concept that was mentioned only twice in Nasser's long reign was noticeably present in all but one of Sadat's speeches and messages. The rule of law was mentioned twenty-four times in the eleven speeches, with an average of more than two citations per year. In most of those citations, Sadat affirmed his commitment to the provisions of the law and the constitution. For example, in his first address after the May Revolution (May 20, 1971), the president proclaimed that the constitution must stipulate, "The state is ruled by the law as are individuals. No decision or procedure can be taken, whatever the authority issuing it, away from the oversight of the law." In his Message to the People's Assembly on the Anniversary of the Corrective Revolution, May 15, 1976, Sadat maintained, "The rule of law was realized in meaning and context . . . Governing was in the hands of state institutions and not an individual. Thus constitutional legitimacy was secured."

Freedom was mentioned a staggering 103 times and at least three times in every speech. Democracy was the highest value in Sadat's discourse. Sadat mentioned democracy 154 times, with an average of fourteen citations a year. In reference to freedom, whereas Nasser often used the concept to refer to foreign policy matters, Sadat equally focused on foreign and domestic policies.[21]

---

[21] Nonetheless, the careful review of Sadat's notion of freedom reflects two important matters: first, freedom is the will of the majority; second, the national interests restrict freedom. Sadat stated, "Freedom is the sovereignty of the majority with the minority right to express its

In the domestic domain, he usually spoke, as he did in 1971, about a free society: "We want to build a new society which we aspire for ourselves – the society of freedom and dignity." It was not surprising that one of Sadat's top lieutenants argued, "In his speeches, talks and public statements, Sadat gave priority to democracy and freedom over all other issues."[22]

Although Sadat spoke directly only a few times about judicial independence, he alluded to the concept in many speeches. The president asserted that there should be no interference with the judiciary, "The judicial family itself administers its members" (May 14, 1980 Speech) or "I never ordered an exceptional court; all offenders were sent to the ordinary courts" as in his speech before the People's Assembly and the Shura Council in May 14, 1981. Sadat, in this last speech, also, subtly criticized his predecessor's infringements on the courts, claiming that "In 1972 and early 1973 all judges [purged during the Massacre of the Judiciary] returned ... Ever since, no cynic could argue that the judiciary has not returned to its uppermost position amongst us, as it was before." An independent judiciary, in Sadat's discourse, as he did in his May 14, 1981, speech, is a guardian of rights and liberties. Judges enjoy "complete judicial immunity to establish democracy."[23]

It is evident from Sadat's discourse that the regime understood the political significance of judicial independence. The careful analysis of Sadat's rhetoric demonstrates this linkage between democracy and the rule of law and judicial independence. Sadat repeatedly criticized Nasser's regime for its undemocratic practices. Sadat argued, "The [1952] Revolution ignored the second objective – the establishment of proper democratic life altogether."[24] Sadat, also, publicly stated that his Corrective Revolution

> Established the rule of law and closed all detention centers for the first time in Egypt in forty years; asserted judicial power; founded the state of institutions; instituted safeguards that enabled citizens to know their rights and

---

divergent opinion." He also added, amid the struggle "we could not permit matters without limits and restrictions; otherwise this would mean that we leave the slogan of democracy for our enemy to use it not only against our freedom but our existence as well" (May 14, 1972). According to the president, "the exercise of our democracy should be disciplined but not restricted" (May 14, 1973).

[22] Muḥammad Abd Al-Salām Zayyāt, *al-Sādāt, al-qinā' wa-al-ḥaqīqah*, 240.

[23] In the Egyptian context, judicial immunity means secure tenure and prohibition on pursing any legal action against a judge without the prior approval of a high-ranking judicial disciplinary committee.

[24] Anwar Al-Sādāt, *Wasiyyatī*, (al-Qāhirah: al-Maktab al-Miṣrī al-ḥadīth, 1982), 12.

responsibilities and practice them in tranquility by means of proclaiming a Permanent [1971] Constitution.[25]

In addition, while Nasser never visited or addressed the judiciary or their superior councils in his eighteen-year reign, Sadat chaired the SCJB visited the Judges Club's headquarters, and addressed the judiciary in the newly created Judiciary Day. Sadat addressed judges on at least five different occasions in his eleven-year reign, about once every two years. In all these occasions, Sadat affirmed his commitment to the rule of law and his deep appreciation for judges and courts. In his meeting with the SCJP, Sadat maintained,

> All the work must be done within the framework of the rule of law, and thus you face your historical responsibility. Within this framework, we are building for our people and the coming generations, you are the guardians of the rule of the law, you are responsible for the application of the rule of law.[26]

On another occasion, the president stated, "I owe the judiciary my presence here among you in this sanctified courtroom. I say this with pride, and the entire people share with me that pride in the traditions of our judiciary."[27] In his May 14, 1978, speech, Sadat also considered the establishment of "A sound and stable constitutional structure crowned by an independent, sacred and lofty judiciary" to be one of his greatest domestic achievements. In demonstrating his appreciation for the judiciary, Sadat stated, May 14, 1980, "Throughout our long history, our judiciary has been a source of honor for us all ... Not only in Egypt but also in the whole Arab nation."

It is certain that the public emphasis on democracy, freedom, the rule of law, and the constitution served multiple ends for Sadat. First, it helped the new president gain support within the educated and most active segments of the Egyptian society. Second, it also helped with his international audience in the United States and the West in the late 1970s. Third, those slogans enabled Sadat to crush his powerful domestic antagonists that he inherited from Nasser. Sadat frequently criticized his domestic opponents whom he purged in May 1971, for their curtailment of freedom and democracy. The new regime was to restore the "true values of the July Revolution" that were

---

[25] Ibid., 15.

[26] Speech by President Anwar Al-Sadat before the meeting of the SCJP (November 26, 1975), *Speeches and Interviews by President Anwar Al-Sadat: July–December 1975*, 547.

[27] Address by President Anwar Al-Sadat to Members of the Judiciary at the Court of Cassation in Cairo, January 13, 1971, *Speeches and Interviews by President Anwar Al-Sadat: September 1970– Decmber 1971*, (Cairo: Ministry of Information, State Information Service, 1975), 135.

distorted. The Corrective Revolution of May 1971 was "a foundation for the rule of law" (May 14, 1975). The Corrective Revolution, according to Sadat's Message to the People's Assembly on the Occasion of the Corrective Revolution, May 14, 1977, was "a natural starting point of what ensued; the rule of law, the state of institutions, the provision of freedoms and the respect of the Constitution."

Therefore, Sadat's discourse revealed a strong tie between the regime's quest for survival and renewed attention to democracy, the rule of law, and judicial independence. It is important to note that even Nasser, after the 1967 defeat, started to entertain such ethics as the rule of law and democracy. Notable in this regard was the March 30th Declaration. However, Sadat's emphases were much deeper, comprehensive, and frequent. It is not the contention of this book to claim that Sadat genuinely believed in democracy or liberalism. I am arguing, instead, that he strategically used those ideals and ideas to provide the life support needed for his regime. Muḥammad Zayyat, one of Sadat's trusted advisors during this era, highlighted the rapport connecting regime survival strategy, legality, and judicial independence, stating,

> Sadat found in the term 'democracy' what he was looking for. Thus, he spoke about it, sang its praise, and raised its banner in his speech on May 14th. His speeches and talks continued and he routinely highlighted democracy, the rule of law, rights and liberties, judicial independence, state of institutions, etc.[28]

The constitution, as the highest law of the land, was evidently salient in Sadat's discourse. While Nasser rarely, if ever, referred to this supreme legal document, Sadat considered it the cornerstone of his legitimacy, citing the constitution an astounding 160 times, with an average of more than fourteen times a year. In his May 14, 1978, speech, Sadat proudly stated, "Not one day has passed without parliament and a constitution since 1971." The constitution also provided for assurances of rights and liberties. Speaking before the Constituent Assembly (CA), Sadat, in his speech on May 20, 1971, declared, "I would like the Constitution to stipulate that the law safeguards the right of every citizen to resort to justice [the judiciary]."

The 1971 Constitution

Under Nasser, constitutional frameworks lost much meaning and significance. The regime changed them at well. The 1971 Constitution restored the inviolability of the highest legal document.

---

[28] Muḥammad Abd Al-Salām Zayyāt, *al-Sādāt, al-qinā' wa-al-ḥaqīqah*, 242.

The 1971 Constitution was another strong indication of Sadat's intent to anchor his regime on institutionalized Regime Survival Functions (RSFs). On May 20, 1971, only one week after Sadat had crushed his opponents, the president authorized the writing of a new constitution. The 1971 Constitution was a "great leap forward" in the country's constitutional development. After rescinding the 1923 Constitution, Egypt was governed either by a national charter with no real legal force or by repressive temporary constitutions. In contrast to previous constitutional documents, the 1971 Constitution "included an article explicitly stating that the regime was based on the rule of law. Other articles guaranteed to Egyptians virtually all the internationally recognized political liberties and human rights."[29]

In comparison to Nasser's constitutions, the 1971 Constitution was noticeably liberal. Unlike all previous revolutionary constitutions, the 1971 Constitution clearly, repeatedly, and unequivocally reiterated the principles of democracy, the rule of law, rights, and liberties.[30] For the first time in Egyptian constitutional history, the highest legal document devoted an entire chapter – Three: Public Freedoms, Rights, and Duties – to recite in great details the fundamental rights and liberties of citizens. This lengthy chapter of twenty-four articles provided the citizenry of Egypt with a whole array of rights and liberties. In addition, what truly distinguished this constitution was "its interest in the judicial authority, and its affirmation of the rule of law and the right to litigation."[31]

Many provisions in the third chapter were comparable to the best of the world's democratic and liberal constitutions. It guaranteed a plethora of rights, including the "right to protect the private life of citizens"(Article 45), "Freedom of belief and the freedom of practicing religious rights" (Article 46), "Freedom of expression" (Article 47), "Freedom of Press and other publications"

[29] Raymond William Baker, *Sadat and After: Struggles for Egypt's Political Soul* (Cambridge: Harvard University Press, 1990), 59.

[30] In the 1956 Constitution, democracy was mentioned only twice: once in the preamble as the sixth and last objective of the society and once in the first article, which stated that Egypt is "a democratic republic." Rights and liberties were generally on the periphery of the constitution, and when it was discussed, as in article six, it was stated as a gift of the state rather than natural inalienable rights. Article six stated, "The state guarantees freedom, security, tranquility, and equality of opportunity for all Egyptians." The temporary constitution of 1958, issued upon the unity with Syria, also paid lip service to democracy as well. Democracy was again only mentioned once in describing the nature of the state. The 1964 Constitution was not different. Democracy was only mentioned once in article one, and twice in the preamble arguing that the socialist economy is the enabler of "social democracy ... the door to political democracy."

[31] Abd Al-Ghani Basyuni ʿAbd Allah, *Mabda al-musawah amama al-qada wa-kafalat haqq al-taqadi* (al-Iskandariyah: Munshaat al-Maʿarif, 1983), 135.

(Article 48), "Freedom of peaceful and unarmed private assembly, without the need for prior notice" (Article 54), "Universal suffrage, as well as the right to form civil Associations" (Article 55), "The right to litigation for all legal disputes" (Articles 68).

The 1971 Constitution also emphasized equality before the law. Article 40 states "All citizens are equal before the law." In addition, the constitution repeatedly stressed that the rule of law is the basis of the state, and the state is entirely subject to the law. Sharqawī, an Egyptian law professor, argued that the most important aspect of the 1971 Constitution was to deem any violation of public rights and liberties guaranteed by the constitution "criminal and civil offense[s] not subject to the statutes of limitations."[32]

Additionally, for the first time in Egypt's legal history, the constitution included a new chapter titled the "Rule of Law". This chapter affirmed that all government institutions would abide by the law. Article 64 was unequivocal in this commitment: "The rule of law is the basis of state rule." Article 65 was particularly interesting in its blunt linkage of citizens' rights to judicial independence. It stated, "The state shall be subject to the law. The independence and immunity of the judicature are two basic guarantees to safeguard rights and liberties." Article 41 empowered the judiciary to protect citizens' rights and freedoms, especially against abuses by the security forces:

> Personal freedom is a natural right not subject to violation except in cases of *flagrante delicto*. No person may be arrested, inspected, detained or have his freedom restricted in any way or be prevented from free movement except by an order necessitated by investigations and the preservation of public security. This order shall be given by a competent judge or a public prosecutor in accordance with the provisions of the law.

The 1971 Constitution's recognition of the rights and liberties of individuals and groups and its ties to the judiciary was an attempt to establish a legal-based political authority. Nevertheless, it is important to note that Sadat did not intend to create a liberal political system. His purpose was to use the courts to provide the much-needed RSFs without relinquishing his absolute presidential power. Therefore, many of the Nasser era's illiberal institutions and practices were integrated into the constitution; the single-party system persisted, and the government maintained its domination of the press, labor unions, and professional syndicates.

---

[32] This meant that any human rights violation could be prosecuted regardless of the time passed since it occurred. Su'ād Sharqāwī, *Nisbīyat al-ḥurrīyāt al-'āmmah wa-in'ikāsātuhā 'alá al-tanẓīm al-qānūnī* (al-Qāhirah: Dār al-Nahḍah al-'Arabīyah, 1979), 143.

Sadat wanted the constitution to reflect an image rather than the substance of a democratic system.[33] Rutherford convincingly argued that one could understand the constitution as a device by which "the presidency copes with defeat and succession."[34] There is evidence that Sadat pressured the CA directly and indirectly to expand presidential power.[35] Fouad Srag El-Din, founder and former president of New Wafd Party, argued, "when President Sadat commissioned a Constituent Assembly for the 1971 Constitution, he did not accept the Assembly's views and added many articles without its consent, e.g., the famous Article 74 which he used in the September 1981 detention decisions.[36] When the Assembly rejected this article, Sadat added it and other provisions without the Constituent Assembly's consent and even without its knowledge."[37]

Regardless, Sadat undertook a number of reforms to carry favor with judges and to show the public that his regime was different from his predecessor. This included reinstituting judges that had been dismissed by Nasser in the 1969 Massacre of the Judiciary, forbidding the use of wiretaps and confiscation of land without a court order, and a new law for the judiciary. This reflected "a change of heart" in the regime's attitudes toward the courts.

THE JUDICIARY AND THE REGIME: FROM PARIAH TO PARTNER

Sadat's rivals were in command of the armed forces, the Arab Socialist Union (the single-party), the security apparatus and the intelligence establishment. Sadat needed to explore alternative sources of political power. A mixture of institutions surfaced; at the forefront were the parliament (of which Sadat was

---

[33] After all, many statements indicate that Sadat was involved in the massacre of the judiciary. Isam Hassunah, minister of justice from 1965–1968, testified that then-vice-president Sadat presided over the committee that advised Nasser on Law-decrees 1603 and 1605/1969 that sacked scores of judges. Nevertheless, Sadat later claimed that he did not support these measures in any way, maintaining that upon assuming power, he reinstated all judges to their positions without a delay. Hāmid Ahmad Yūsuf, 'Abd al-Nāsir wa-aqzām al-sultah (al-Iskandarīyah: Dar al-Huda lil-Matbu'at, 1989), 106–107, Mahmud Jami', 'Araftu al-Sadat: nasf qarn min khafaya al-Sadat wa-al-Ikhwan (al-Qahirah: al-Maktub al-Misri al-Hadith, 1998), 72, and Isam Hassūnah, 23 Yūliyū– wa-'Abd al-Nasir: shahādatī, 207.

[34] Rutherford, *The Struggle for Constitutionalism in Egypt*, 251.

[35] Personal interview with Ibrahim Darwish, a constitutional law professor and member of the 1971 Constitutional Drafting Committee, June 16, 2006.

[36] Article 74 reads, "If any danger threatens the national unity or the safety of the motherland or obstructs the constitutional role of the State institutions, the President of the Republic shall take urgent measures to face this danger, direct a statement to the people and conduct a referendum on those measures within sixty days of their adoption."

[37] Muhammad, *Shuhud 'asr al-Sadat*, 38–39.

speaker for many years), the press, especially the influential *Al-Ahram* newspaper (where Sadat's friend and ally Heikal was editor-in-chief), and the
judiciary (where many members were dismayed by Sadat's archrival Ali Sabri's
vicious public assaults on their institution).

Nonetheless, the president sought to create (reconfigure) institutions
needed for his political survival without relinquishing absolute control. Sadat
perceived the judiciary as a promising territory for gaining support because it
was deeply weakened under Nasser. Sadat's personal experience with the
judicial system prior to 1952 had a role in this stance.[38] In 1946, Sadat was
brought before a criminal court charged with participating in assignations of
pro-British politicians. The prosecution and the judges were sympathetic to
his nationalistic aspirations. Sadat later duly praised them stating,

> In this very same auditorium, 23 years ago I was sitting in this accused section
> on the left and on this platform were seated the judges of Egypt, the
> conscience of Egypt, and the spirit of Egypt ... In spite of all other forces,
> the Egyptian judiciary pronounced its word, the words of justice, and
> freedom ... I shall always remain indebted to our judicial family and shall
> remain proud of our Egyptian judiciary throughout the ages.[39]

The judiciary was a willing, seemly reliable, and credible partner in Sadat's
venture to create an institutional base for his regime and distinguish it from
Nasser's. Judges also lent their support during the decisive days of mid-May
1971. On May 14, 1971, Sadat addressed a judicial delegation that came to
express support at this critical juncture. In a brief speech, Sadat struck the right
tone, stating, "I pledge to you and the people through you, that law will
prevail, the Revolution will be codified, no measures will be taken, except
through the law."[40] Understandably, the delegation responded favorably and
granted Sadat a loud ovation, which was widely reported in the regime-
controlled press. The judiciary "effectively lent its considerable public stature
to the cause of Sadat in this pivotal moment, believing that he offered the
better prospect for strengthening the rule of law."[41] Others within the legal
community shared the same belief. In addition to hosting and addressing a

[38] Anwar Sadat, *In Search for Identity: An Autobiography*, (New York: Harper and Row, 1978).
[39] Speech by President Anwar Al-Sadat before the meeting of the SCJP, (November 26, 1975).
    Speeches and Interviews by President Anwar Al-Sadat: July -December 1975, (Cairo: Ministry of
    Information, State Information Service, 1980), 549–550. He repeated the same meaning in
    many different public speeches.
[40] Speech by Sadat to the Delegation of the Judiciary, May 14, 1971, quoted in *Speeches and
    Interviews by President Anwar Al-Sadat: September 1970–Decmber 1971*, (Cairo: Ministry of
    Information, State Information Service, 1975), 301.
[41] Rutherford, *The Struggle for Constitutionalism in Egypt*, 271.

judicial delegation on this pivotal day, the only other delegation that Sadat received was from the bar. It is worth noting that among all sectors of the society, Sadat was eager to command support from members of the legal community, which traditionally has been liberal and not particularly gracious to Nasser's illiberal policies. The partnership between the legal community in general and the judicial corps particularly and the new regime was expected to influence the government's perception of and appreciation for the role the judiciary plays in the political sphere.

In sum, Sadat was in dire need for a survival stratagem for his regime. In addition to religious gestures, the president embraced elements of liberalism, democracy, and the rule of law. Sadat also empowered institutions that were not tainted by strong ties to his adversaries. These policies strengthened the judicial institutions as an engine to protect rights and liberties. While some empowerment of the institutional independence of the judiciary occurred, the state-court relation retained the stamp of the revolutionary regime's suppressive policies. Sadat's era, after all, was of a transitional nature. The most significant push for judicial independence took place during the early years of a new regime, where the struggle for survival was at its peak. Setbacks would occur later as the regime felt more confident in its hegemony and domination. The same story would repeat itself decades later under Mubarak albeit with different outcomes.

SADAT AND THE JUDICIARY

In the first few months of his reign in 1970, Sadat's judicial politics seemed to offer little variance from Nasser's. Sadat used an exceptional court, the Revolution Court, to convict his adversaries during the May 1971 struggle. Sadat personally designated members of the courts, which included the speaker of the Parliament, a presidential advisor, and the chief justice of the Supreme Court. When the Public Prosecutor (PP) indicated lack of evidence to convict the accused, Sadat ordered the prosecution responsibility to be transferred to the newly appointed and politically reliable Socialist Public Prosecutor (SPP).[42] Sadat was able to impose preferred verdicts on his rivals. This outcome convinced the president that it was possible to achieve his desired ends through law and courts.[43] Regardless, the use of exceptional courts was not as widespread or commonplace as under Nasser. With a few

---

[42] Imam, *Inqilab al-Sadat: ahdath Mayu 1971*, 291.
[43] Initially Sadat wanted a death sentence against his adversaries, but faced with resistance from some members of the exceptional court and the military court, Sadat pledged to amend the

limited exceptions, during Sadat's early years in power, the regular court systems adjudicated the bulk of the critical legal disputes.

This section focuses on the state-court interactions and is divided into two main parts. The first outlines the linkage between the regime's struggle for survival and the restoration of elements of judicial independence and consequently judicial activism. The second part investigates the regime's behavior and courts' responses to the de-liberalizing and repressive measures enacted by the regime after Sadat solidified his grip on power and consolidated his political authority after the 1973 "victory" and his newly established international prominence.

THE EARLY YEARS: THE STRUGGLE FOR SURVIVAL AND THE EXPANSION OF THE JUDICIAL ROLE

After the Corrective Movement, Sadat became the master of the house and endeavored to consolidate his power. The rule of law became an essential foundation of his authority. As legality and the rule of law turned into a cornerstone of the regime rhetoric, judicialization became feasible.

With the aim of appeasing the judicial corps and gaining favor with the public opinion, Sadat reinstated some of the judges purged during the Massacre of the Judiciary. In December 1971, Sadat issued Law-decree 85/1971 that reappointed some of the judges to their previous positions. A careful reading of this law leaves no doubt that Sadat used it as a gesture of his regime's renewed commitment to the rule of law and judicial independence as a foundation for its legitimacy. Sadat wasted no time in capitalizing on this, Hassūnah argued, "After he defeated his domestic enemies on May 15th, Sadat boasted that he was the president that restored dignity to the judiciary, highlighting this action as one of his national achievements."[44]

Nonetheless, this decree ignored forty-six of the leading judges purged in 1969. Those excluded included Mumtaz Nasar (the president of the Judges Club) and Yahia Al-Rifai (a prominent board member of the Judges Club), in addition to scores of judges of the Council of State, the Administrative Prosecution Authority, and State (Government) Cases Body. It is entirely plausible to argue that Sadat did not want to reinstate the most active judges.

---

verdict to a life sentence if the court issued a death sentence. Zayyāt, *al-Sādāt, al-qinā' wa-al-ḥ aqīqah*, 275.

[44] Hassūnah, *23 Yūliyū– wa-'Abd al-Nasir: shahādatī*, 207.

In this occasion and many others, Sadat wanted to build an image of liberalism and the rule of law at a minimum political cost.

However, after the proclamation of the law, the Court of Cassation issued a landmark ruling that scrapped Law-decree 83/1969 and ordered the reinstatement of all judges.[45] When faced with a litmus test for its rule of law rhetoric, the regime acquiesced. Law 43/1973 was drafted to mandate the return of all judges who did not reach the mandatory age of retirement. Al-Bishri authoritatively confirmed the rational calculations of the regime arguing, "The sacked judges returned after procrastination and postponement."[46]

The constitutional emphases on the judiciary were rather illuminating. Sadat's constitution is noticeably different from its ancestors under the republic or the monarch. While previous constitutions referred to courts and the judicial system, these mentions were general, succinct, and brief. Conversely, the 1971 Constitution shed considerable light on the judiciary; of the original 193 articles stipulated in the 1971 Constitution a staggering fifty-seven articles (about 30 percent) were either directly related to the judiciary or linked to citizens' rights and liberties, hence, indirectly associated with courts as the guarantor of those rights. Part Four of chapter five of the constitution, "The Judicial Authority," included nine noticeably long articles and is entirely devoted to matters related to the administration of justice. This is critical because

> Written constitutions are also symbolically costly and, as a result, can serve as signals of the actual intentions of the rulers. Beyond their role in establishing institutions, constitutions are "billboards" that can emit communicative signals of government policy (Yu 2010). They play this function because they are politically encumbering. Constitutions are typically, though not always, more entrenched than ordinary law, which means they are also more costly to change. Even if not manifestly are "hallowed vessels" and adorned with political and ceremonial weight. Drafting a constitution consumes significant

---

[45] Yahia Al-Rifai, a leading board member of the Judges Club and one of the judges purged during the Massacre, filed a lawsuit against the Ministry of Justice and the president of the Republic before Court of Cassation's Circuit on Judges' Affairs. Despite all the harassment of the security services under Nasser, Al-Rifai insisted on continuing his legal challenge of the Massacre's legislation. The court quashed the law and ordered his return to the judicial corps. Later, Al-Rifai became a vice president of the Court of Cassation and the president of Judges Club. Those who follow his ideals on judicial independence and politically active courts are now known as *Al-Rifais*. See Yahia Al-Rifai, *Sh'wan regal al-quda'*, (al-Qahirah: Nadi al-Quda, 1991), and a personal interview with Yahia Al-Rifai, April 5, 2006.

[46] Tariq al-Bishrī, "al-Qaḍā' al-Miṣrī bayna al-istiqlāl wa-al-iḥtiwā'" in 'Alā' Abū Zayd and Hibah Ra'ūf 'Izzat (eds.), *al-Muwāṭanah al-Miṣrīyah wa-mustaqbal al-dīmuqrāṭīyah: ru'á jadīdah li-'ālam mutaghayyir* (al-Qahirah: Maktabat al-Shurūq al-Dawlīyah: 2005), 633.

political energy on the part of the governing elite and provides a repository of regime rhetoric. The costly nature of constitution making supports the idea that a constitution can be credible signal of political intentions, even for autocrats.[47]

The examination of the drafting subcommittee on the judiciary deliberations regarding the judicial authority is illuminating. Most subcommittee's members on the political system were judges, lawyers, or law professors. Arguably, most of them were against the encroachment on judicial independence under the revolutionary regime, notably the "Massacre of the Judiciary." The majority of members believed an independent judiciary was a prerequisite for the protection of rights and liberties. Justice Badawi Hamouda, then chief justice of the Supreme Court, stated that an independent judiciary was "indispensable to individuals' rights."[48] The committee put forward several proposals to strengthen judicial independence:[49]

- Constitutionally mandated legal immunity for all judges.
- Independent Supreme Constitutional Court (SCC) to replace the executive-dominated Supreme Court.
- Prohibition against assigning sitting judges to extrajudicial positions in the executive branch.[50]
- Increasing judicial salaries to provide financial security.
- Legal penalties for failure to implement court orders.
- Closure of exceptional courts and a ban on executive's authority to abolish such court.[51]

The 1971 Constitution reflected many of these paragons and established three crucial new principles: for the judiciary in general, the Council of State, and the SCC. The constitution declared that the judiciary is a full-fledged independent authority of the state. It stood on equal footing with the other two branches. Previous constitutions spoke of independent judges, rather than the

---

[47] Zachary Elkins, Tom Ginsburg, and James Melton, "The Content of Authoritarian Constitutions," in Tom Ginsburg and Alberto Simpser (eds.), *Constitutions in Authoritarian Regimes* (New York: Cambridge University Press, 2014), 148–149.

[48] Meeting No. 12, al-Legna al-Tahdeereyya li Wada'a Mashrua'a al-Dustur, Legnat Nitham al-Hukm (al-Qahirah: majlis al-Shaab, no date), 23.

[49] Meeting No. 13, al-Legna al-Tahdeereyya li Wada'a Mashrua'a al-Dustur, Legnat Nitham al-Hukm (al-Qahirah: majlis al-Shaab, no date), 5–12.

[50] The 1971 Constitution omission of this proposal reveals the regime's comprehension of the power the executive yield over judges through seconding to lucrative advisory positions. This provision was included in the 2012 Constitution.

[51] The 1971 Constitution shunned this demand and empowered the legislature to create exceptional courts.

independent judiciary.[52] Article 165 affirmed the institutional independence of the judiciary, declaring, "The Judicial Authority shall be independent."

The constitution mandated full judicial immunity for all judges. Previous constitutions, including the 1923 Constitution, delegated the provisions of judicial immunity to statutory legislation, which limited protection to senior judges. Article 166 guaranteed the independence of all individual judges, proclaiming, "Judges shall be independent, subject to no other authority but the law. No authority may intervene in judicial trials or the affairs of justice." This independence and immunity were further confirmed in Article 168 that stated, "The status of judges shall be irrevocable."[53]

The constitution cemented the Council of State's position as a constitutionally mandated and independent judicial institution. The Council was endowed with exclusive jurisdiction over all administrative litigation. Article 172 stated unmistakably, "The Council of State shall be an independent judicial organization competent to take decisions in administrative disputes and disciplinary cases." Previous constitutions did not include any provisions related to the administrative judiciary, leaving the Council consistently at the mercy of the executive-controlled legislature. A former dean of Alexandria Law School argued, "This is a safeguard and a constitutional guarantee of the Council's existence and independence, so legislation cannot rescind it without amending the Constitution itself."[54] Hence, the fear of dismantling the Council with legislation "became a fallacious weapon of the past."[55]

In addition to safeguarding its independence, the constitution expanded the possibilities of judicialization. It mandated that all administrative decisions and actions be subject to the Council's review. Article 68 maintained, "Any provision in legislation stipulating the immunity of any act or administrative decision from the control of the judicature shall be prohibited." All executive actions became a subject of judicial oversight, a marked difference from the Nasserite era. The notable constitutional scholar Yahia Al-Jamal asserted,

---

[52] In addition, some leftist ideologues had claimed during Nasser's era that the judiciary is not an independent institution and is subject to the control of the single party and the executive. Many articles written by Ali Sabri, the Secretary-General of the Arab Socialist Union in *Al-Gomhuria* newspaper; quoted in Chapter 3.

[53] According to the constitution, judges cannot be removed from office or deprived of their legal protection except by a disciplinary committee of most senior judges. The composition of this committee and the irrevocability of its decisions will be a highly contested political issue under Mubarak.

[54] Abd Allah, *Mabda al-musawah amama al-qada wa-kafalat haqq al-taqadi*, 137.

[55] Abd Al-Barr, *Dawr majlis al-Dawlah al-Misri fi himayat al-huquq wa-al-hurriyat al-`ammah*, al-juz' 3, 1759.

To understand the real value of this critical article, it suffices to recall the numerous rulings of the administrative judiciary and the Supreme Court after the proclamation of the Constitution in cases related to dismissing civil servants and prohibiting them from seeking judicial remedy . . . on the pretext that those actions are acts of sovereignty.[56]

All these changes were necessary for the judiciary to be taken seriously by the public and particularly the opposition, and hence able to perform the RSFs. As for the SCC, the constitution established, for the first time, a high court empowered with judicial review. The SCC had the exclusive prerogative of judicial review and was composed exclusively of legalists (judges, lawyers, and law professors). Article 174 stated, "The Supreme Constitutional Court shall be an independent judicial body." The constitution granted the SCC the exclusive competence to "undertake the judicial control in respect of the constitutionality of the laws and regulations and shall undertake the interpretation of the legislative texts in the manner prescribed by law" (Article 175). Moreover, Article 177 assured the independence of the SCC's justices, stating, "The status of the members of the Supreme Constitutional Court shall be irrevocable. The Court shall call to account its members, in the manner prescribed by law." All these provisions were significant improvements in comparison to the statute that established the Supreme Court in 1969.[57]

Despite all these reforms "The 1971 Constitution was not a clean break with Egypt's authoritarian past. Rather, it signified a transition point: significant opportunities for LC [liberal constitutionalism] were created in the document, but many of the old institutions and attitudes persisted."[58] The constitution kept the SCJP to ensure executive control over judicial affairs. It also created the new position of SPP, "responsible for taking the measures which secure the people's rights, the safety of the society and its political regime" (Article 179). This position was mandated despite the fierce opposition within the CA. Several members rejected such idea, arguing that the SPP would be "detrimental to the rule of law," would constitute the formation of an

---

[56] Yaḥyá Jamal, *al-Qānūn al-dustūrī: maʿa muqaddimah fī dirāsat al-mabādiʾ al-dustūrīyah al-ʾāmmah* (al-Qahirah: Dārr al-Nahḍah al-ʿArabīyah, 1995), 191.

[57] The drafting committee of the constitution was keen to state clearly and unequivocally the judicial and independent nature of the SCC, fearing that the government using its rubberstamp legislature might pack the court with its political appointees from outside the legal profession. A fear that did materialize later in many politically sensitive courts: for example, Law 40/1977 about political parties. See Aʿmāl al-taḥdīrīyah la Dustūr 1971, session No 15 in 29/6/1971, (al-Qahirah: al-Matbaʿah al-Amiriyah, no date), 35–75.

[58] Rutherford, *The Struggle for Constitutionalism in Egypt*, 219.

"exceptional judicial body," and would contradict the committee's decision to outlaw all judicial bodies that were not an integral part of the court system. In the end, the committee opted for not including the SPP in the constitution. Nonetheless, Article 179 was added to the end of Sadat's request.[59]

The constitution included provisions on the participation of lay members in judicial activities. Lay involvement in trials is an idea that most professional judges, lawyers, and law professors rejected out of hand; Article 170 stated, "The people shall contribute to maintaining justice."[60] In addition, the constitution enshrined exceptional courts. Article 171 affirmed the position of the State Security Courts. Furthermore, the constitution continued the revolutionary habit of a constitutionally mandated military judiciary. Article 183: "The law shall organize a military judicature; prescribe its competencies within the limits of the principles prescribed by the Constitution."

The minutes of the CA leave no doubt that the regime wanted initially to create a politically subservient SCC. The original proposal stated that the president of the Republic would appoint the chief justice of the court and one-third of the judges, the People's Assembly (parliament) would select another third, and the SCJB would name the final third.[61] All judges were to serve a six-year term subject to renewal by the appointing body.[62] This proposal would have created a more independent court than Nasser's Supreme Court. However, because of the executive's domination of the legislature and the SCJB, this plan could enable the regime to tightly control the SCC and negate any prospects for an independent-liberal judicialization. The overall assessment of the 1971 Constitution affirms the notion of trying to attain conflicting goals of reflecting a commitment to the rule of law (a prerequisite for the institutionalized regime) and control over the political process (a necessary condition for the imperial presidency).

---

[59] Ibrāhīm 'Alī Ṣāliḥ, *al-Wajīz fī sharḥ qānūn al-Mudda'ī al-'Āmm al-Ishtirākī* (al-Qahirah: 'Ālam al-Kutub 1986), 57.

[60] In the Egyptian context, popular contribution to the maintaining justice includes in addition to regular jury system, the appointment of public dignitaries to adjudicate particular cases alongside professional judges. The terminology "public dignitaries" is used in the Egyptian legal discourse to refer to individuals who serve in special courts or committees that are not members of the judiciary. This includes the Courts of Values, the Political Parties Court, as well as other semijudicial committees such as the Presidential Election Committee or the Parliamentary election Committee.

[61] The original ideas reflect the regime's intention to create a politically reliable institution, not an independent court.

[62] Meeting No. 15, al-Legna al-Tahdeereyya li Wada'a Mashrua'a al-Dustur, Legnat Nitham al-Hukm (al-Qahirah: Majlis al-Shaab, no date), 50–53.

As with the 1971 Constitution, legislations related to the judiciary under Sadat sought to attain the support of judges and reflect an image of the rule of law without forfeiting the regime's control. Many legislations enhanced judicial independence but not without limits or setbacks. Some provisions strengthened the independence, autonomy, and role of the courts while others maintained elements of regime control over the judicial institutions and its personnel. Article 67 of Law-decree 46/1972 (generally known today as the Law of Judicial Authority) mandated, for the first time, full immunity for all judges, stating "Judges of the Court of Cassation and Courts of Appeal, as well as presidents and magistrates of Courts of First Instance cannot be removed." For the first time in Egypt's judicial history, all members of the judiciary enjoyed legal immunity. Law 47/1972 provided all the Council of State's judges, except those at the entry level, with the same assurance. This legislation also removed the provision that Law-decree 27/1967 added which subjected the Council to the oversight of the Ministry of Justice. The preamble of Law 50/1973, which amended some provisions of Law-decree 47/1972, proclaimed

> The Council of State is not like any other judicial authority . . . The Council is the adjudicator of administrative disputes between the individual and the administration, and it is the guarantor of individual liberties and the guardian of public rights . . . therefore it is rather illogical that the Council is subject to the Ministry of Justice or under its oversight.[63]

The regime put an end to the much-despised administrative sequestration. Consequently, Law 34/1971 prohibited imposing sequestration on individuals without a court order. A newly established court, the Court of Sequestration, was empowered to hear sequestration cases inherited from Nasser's era as well as any new sequestration petitions filed by the SPP. The Court of Sequestration was staffed by a presidential decree, with a vice president drawn from the Court of Cassation as president and three judges from Courts of Appeal and three citizens chosen from a list prepared by the minister of justice.[64] The Court of Sequestration was another exceptional tribunal; it was, nonetheless, a step forward in the early 1970s, since sequestration was not subject to any form of judicial review under the previous regime.

---

[63] Majlis Al-Shaʿb, al-Lajnah al-Tashrīʿīyah, *al-Qawanin al-asasiyah al-mukammilah lil-dustur: maʿa mudhakkirathā al-idahīyah wa-taqarir Lajnat al-Shuʿūn al-Tashriʿiyah wa-munaqashat al-majlis*, al-juzʾ 2 (al-Qahirah: al-Hayʾah al- ʿĀmmah li-Shuʿūn al-Maṭābiʾ al-Amīrīyah, 1974), 190.

[64] ʿAlī Ṣāliḥ, *al-Wajīz fī sharḥ qānūn al-Muddaʿī al-ʿĀmm al-Ishtirākī*, 179.

Other legislation restored courts' jurisdiction over many legal matters. For instance, the regime annulled Law 119/1964 and Law 50/1965 regarding state security. This law was particularly notorious in its infringements on citizens' rights. It authorized the president of the Republic without court orders to detain people and to impose administrative sequestration on funds and properties of citizens deemed working against the national interests. None of these actions had been subject to any form of judicial review.[65] Law 37/1972 prohibited administrative incarceration except under the state of emergency and speeded the process of judicial review of detention orders.[66]

Nonetheless, Sadat refused to reinstate the High Judicial Council (HJC). The executive-dominated SCJP continued to control judicial affairs. Al-Bishri stated, "Those statutes maintained the hegemony of the Minister of Justice over judicial bodies through the SCJP, and preserved the Ministry of Justice's operational role and oversight over judges and courts."[67] The crucial and politically sensitive position of PP was to be a political appointee. The PP and other members of the PPD did not enjoy immunity and could be removed at will. This provision was to ensure political control over the prosecution department through managing its personnel.[68] Sadat dismissed Nasser's PP Ali Noor El-Din, who allegedly conspired against him, and handpicked his successor.[69] The new PP was a close friend of the president. Nonetheless, when he adhered to due process in the prosecution of Sadat's adversaries in 1971, the case was removed from his jurisdiction and transferred to the politically reliable SPP.[70]

The legislation affirmed the minister of justice's control over the crucial Judicial Inspection Department (JID).[71] In addition to control over the JID,

---

[65] Husni Darwish Abd Al-Hamīd, *al-Qaḍā' hisn al-hurriyat* (al-Qahirah: Dar al-Maʿārif, 1986), 69–70.

[66] Ibid., 70–72.

[67] Al-Bishrī, "*al-Qaḍā' al-Miṣrī bayna al-istiqlāl wa-al-iḥtiwā*," 633.

[68] During the deliberations concerning this law in the People's Assembly, some members criticized the lack of immunity for the prosecutors, demanding that they enjoy the same immunity all judges enjoy under the proposed legislation. The minister of justice objected to any change, arguing that is provision has been present in all judicial authority legislation. See Majlis Al-Shaʿb, *al-Qawanin al-asasiyah al-mukammilah lil-dustur*, 105–117.

[69] Imam, *Inqilab al-Sadat: ahdath Mayu 1971*, 195.

[70] Muḥammad Abd Al-Salām Zayyāt, *Miṣr ilá ayn: qirā'āt wa-khawāṭir fī al-dustūr al-dā'im 1971*, (al-Qāhirah: Dār al-Mustaqbal al-ʿArabī, 1986), 270.

[71] The Judicial Inspection Department (JID) is arguably the most influential department within the Ministry of Justice. Its duties include reviewing, evaluating, and recommending promotion or discipline procedures. Executive control through the minister of justice over this powerful department is a subject of fierce critique of advocates of judicial independence. Repeatedly, executive influence over the JID proves vital for pressuring judges.

the executive branch continued to command extensive powers that could be exploited to restrict the independence of judges. The minister of justice maintained his control over a whole array of important powers including nominating judges to the Court of Cassation, provisionally appointing Court of Appeals judges to the Court of Cassation, or reassigning them to other appellate courts, supervising all courts and judges. The minister can reprimand junior judges and initiate disciplinary actions against all judges. These broad powers enabled the minister of justice to influence members of the judiciary.

Additionally, the regime postponed the establishment of the constitutionally mandated SCC. For eight long years, the regime continued to exploit the subservient and politically reliable Supreme Court. The government used the Supreme Court to circumvent unfavorable and politically sensitive judicial verdicts from both the courts of general jurisdiction and the Council of State. One common practice was to ask for a legal interpretation from the SC to avoid compliance with rulings that the regime perceived as detrimental to its interests. This was a legal maneuver to ensure a favorable decision without the public appearance of noncompliance with judicial rulings under Sadat, Mubarak, and Sisi.[72]

The regime, also, resisted reinstating the elected board of the Judges Club. The government only complied under intense pressure and after much delay. Sadat's successive ministers of justice followed in Nasser's footsteps in trying to control the club through influencing its elections, especially in the second half of the 1970s.

Nevertheless, Sadat's approach to swaying the judiciary was considerably different from his predecessor. Sadat never sacked judges, publicly attacked the judiciary, or infringed on judicial immunity. All these changes were necessary for the ability courts to provide the needed RSFs. During Sadat's reign "a new approach emerged that depended on legal and financial

---

[72] In one case that involved the critical MP Kamal El-din Hussein, who was expelled from the People's Assembly for his fierce criticism of Sadat's policy and tried to regain his seat, the minister of justice asked the SC for its legal opinion on the legality of his standing. The government sought to preempt a verdict from the Administrative Court that was highly anticipated to grant Hussein the ability to run. The SC issued a legal opinion that favored the regime's position, denying Hussein the right to stand in the election. Faced with a legally binding opinion, the Administrative Court refused to continue its adjudication and refused to hear the case. Mr. Hussein appealed to the HAC. The HAC reversed the decision and censured the government for the misuse of its authority. The court also demanded the enactment of the constitutional provision and the establishment of the Supreme Constitutional Court. Faruq Abd Al-Barr, *Dawr majlis al-Dawlah al-Misri fi himayat al-huquq wa-al-hurriyat al-`ammah*, al-juz' 3 (al-Qahirah: Matabi` Sijill al-`Arab, 1998), 188–191.

resources to control. These mechanisms proved to be more effective and less provocative."[73] Sadat's regime used economic incentives to sway judges in critical positions. As salaries did not increase to match the high inflation, the government used the extrajudicial appointment to exert a subtle influence on judges. These extrajudicial assignments facilitated empathy for the administration. It could influence how judges, especially in the administrative judiciary decide cases in which the government was a party.[74] Sadat also expanded the practice of appointing judges to executive and legislative positions to show the regime's appreciation for their loyalty. In his 1980 Judiciary Day Speech, Sadat conferred the highest national award on a senior justice and appointed him and another colleague to the Shura Council as "representatives of the judicial family."[75]

The Courts Seize the Opportunity

Judicial activism is expected to flourish provided that some judges have liberal orientations, the legal system offers guarantees of rights and liberties, and the political system is sufficiently open to enable the judicial support structures to provide a political shield for the politically active judges. These conditions emerged to some extent under Sadat's presidency; therefore, some judges endeavored to expand judicialization (further their institutional power) against the immediate interests of the executive. These rulings enhanced the credibility of the courts and hence its ability to perform plausible RSFs. The regime traded in some control over the populace in exchange for the more durable reign.

Courts and judges benefited from the expansion of judicial independence and limited liberalization of the political system. Nasser's reign did not drastically change the judicial culture. While some judges came to identify with the interests of the state, most judges maintained their commitment to liberal ideology. The insular nature of the judicial profession coupled with the relatively small membership in the court system facilitated the preservation of judges' liberalism.[76] Rutherford maintained,

---

[73] Ibid., 202.

[74] Ibid., 202–204.

[75] Speech by President Anwar Al-Sadat in the Judiciary Day, October 11, 1980.

[76] An indication of the resiliency of institutional culture is the type of discourse used within the judicial community; as a senior judge once notice, "even though the Revolution, in its early months, disregarded the use of civilian titles 'Bek and Pasha,' judges continued to use it. Junior judges would affix the title 'Bek' to their names and judges would affix the title 'Pasha'." Muhammad Sa'id `Ashmawi, `Alá minassat al-qada (al-Qahirah: Dar al-Hilal, 2000), 7. The

There were only 700 active judges during the Nasser period. Most of them graduated from either Cairo University Law School or Alexandria University Law School. They came from similar social and economic backgrounds, and participated in the same social circles. They also regularly interacted at the monthly meeting of the Judges Club in Cairo, where they discussed the direction of government policy and the role of the judiciary.[77]

In fact, courts started to revitalize their role in politically sensitive cases after the 1967 defeat. However, a significant expansion took place after Nasser's death. Benefiting from the sympathetic views of Sadat and building on his rhetoric, the courts started to issue politically sensitive rulings as early as 1972. The judiciary started, even as early as 1971, to expand its protection of rights and liberties and worked to put limits on the vast executive powers. Baker evaluated the attitude and impact of the judiciary during Sadat's era:

> In the Sadat years, the Egyptian judiciary buttressed the liberal consciousness by demonstrating autonomy in the face of the regime's attempt to use the courts to enforce its will by "legal" rather than administrative means. The judges acted in such a way as to preserve the liberal heritage of legality and constitutionality ... Despite the regime's effort, the lawyers and judges ensured that the courts remained a sanctuary for liberal values and practices such as free speech, legitimate political discourse, and an independent judicial system.[78]

One noteworthy contribution was limiting the power of exceptional courts under the state of emergency. Egypt was under the state of emergency and, for all but a few months since 1967, the ESSC was prevalent in the litigation process.[79] The judiciary narrowly defined the ESSC's jurisdiction. In a number of cases, the Court of Cassation ruled that regular courts' jurisdiction is the norm. The court maintained that cases that fell within the ESSC's jurisdiction might be adjudicated before the regular judiciary as long as the legislature did not grant these special tribunals exclusive jurisdiction. In

---

common use of those titles until the present day reflects the power of vocational socialization within a bureaucratic judiciary. Junior members, the greatest majority were born after the 1952 Revolution, commonly suffix those titles to their names and use to address fellow judges.

[77] Rutherford, *The Struggle for Constitutionalism in Egypt*, 303–304.

[78] Baker, *Sadat and After*, 63.

[79] The state of emergency is yet another example of the French legal influence on Egypt's constitution. It gives the executive branch overwhelming power and limits the power of the legislative and judicial branches.

addition, the Court of Cassation ruled that the ESSC's jurisdiction is set by law and could not be expanded by executive orders.[80]

The courts addressed the abuses of rights and liberties under Nasser.[81] In a much-publicized case that involved a former judge of the Council of State who was stripped of his judicial immunity, imprisoned, and tortured on accusations of membership in the Muslim Brotherhood, the court ordered a large restitution. The verdict also harshly condemned Nasser's regime for its appalling violations of human rights.[82]

In many politically sensitive cases, the courts defied the regime and stood by the defendants' legal rights and due process. The ruling in the highly publicized 18–19 January case was a major setback for the regime.[83] The court refuted the PPD's claims that the demonstrations were premeditated. The court reasoned instead that the public was spontaneously reacting to the price increases. The court ruled out most of the evidence and testimonies presented by the State Security Department and their eyewitnesses. In the end, the court acquitted most of the 176 defendants and sentenced only 19 for between 1 and 3 years (most was time already served).[84] Therefore, it was argued, "The percentage of acquittals for those charged with political crimes was consistently high at all levels of the judiciary, including the State Security Courts appointed by presidential decree."[85]

The Council of State's jurisprudence also bounced back from its timid nature during the revolutionary era. Although the HAC was created to tightly control the Council's case law in such a manner to defer to the executive

---

[80] Court of Cassation ruling in Case No. 1920, April 12, 1976.

[81] The judiciary was aided in its quest to prosecute torture cases by a provision in the 1971 Constitution that waived all time restrictions for filing cases involving violations of human rights. In addition, the courts started to rely on international human right conventions, especially the Universal Declaration of Human Rights. This became critically important in later stages. Maḥmūd Riḍā Abū Qamar, *al-Qaḍā' wa-al-wāqi' al-siyāsī: dirāsah taṭbīqīyah 'alá al-qaḍā' ayn al-idārī wa-al-dustūrī fī Miṣr* (al-Qāhirah: Jāmi'at 'Ayn Shams, Kullīyat al-Ḥuqūq, 1995), 111–113.

[82] The verdict includes a devastating attack on the Nasserite regime's record on rights and liberties. The full manuscript of this historic ruling is quoted in Ali Jirishah, *Fi al-zinzanah,* 119–156.

[83] After the government announced a sharp increase in many basic food necessities, a huge wave of demonstrations stormed through most major cities. The police could not quell the demonstrators. Sadat had to order the army to intervene to enforce martial law, and the price increases were repealed. Sadat felt personally insulted and publicly claimed that communists and anarchists inspired and incited the massive civil unrest and the security establishment was mobilized to provide evidence to convict the defendants.

[84] The full verdict is quoted in Husayn 'Abd al-Rāziq, *Miṣr fī 18 wa-19 Yanāyir: dirāsah siyāsīyah wathā'iqiyah* (al-Qāhirah: Shuhdī, 1985), 299–390.

[85] Raymond William Baker, *Sadat and After,* 63.

branch, all this changed after Nasser's death. Abd Al-Barr argued, "The Council of State re-emerged to try to restore its old and great tradition in defense of liberty, democracy, and justice in Egypt."[86]

The largely timid Supreme Court took a more liberal stand on a number of issues. The court ruled in late 1971 "Article 68 of the Constitution proclaimed that the right to adjudication is an inalienable right for all people, and every citizen is entitled to appeal to his ordinary judge."[87] The court also ruled that with the single exception of matters of sovereignty, all final administrative decisions are subject to judicial review.[88] The Supreme Court, nonetheless, deemed constitutional a plethora of highly controversial legislation that many judges and law professors considered unconstitutional. For example, the court upheld Law-decree 48/1967 that exempted all the Revolution Court's rulings from any judicial review.[89] In addition, the Supreme Court acquiesced to the regime and issued an explanatory opinion that reversed the Council of State's verdict permitting a hardliner opposition candidate to run for a parliamentary seat. The urgency and speed with which the court issued its decision leave no doubt that it was a political rather than a legal decision.[90] Furthermore, the court provided an advisory opinion that permitted the legislature to slash a cluster of cases from the domains of the courts and the Council of State and delegate the adjudication process to other institutions.[91]

Judges continued their struggle for more guarantees of judicial independence. The reestablishment of the HJC and the rescinding of the executive-dominated SCJP was an institutional goal. General assemblies of the courts, Cassation, Appeals, and First Instance, as well as the Judges Club, repeatedly and forcibly demanded the return of the Council. In 1974, the Court of Cassation's General Assembly stated, "This restoration is a confirmation of the independence of the judicial authority mandated by article 165 of the Constitution."[92] Mumtaz Nasar, a former president of the Judges Club turned politician, argued for the return of the HJC, the end of all exceptional courts, full independence, and immunity for judges and prosecutors. The same

[86] Faruq Abd Al-Barr, *Dawr majlis al-Dawlah al-Misri fi himayat al-huquq wa-al-hurriyat al-'ammah*, al-juz' 3, 4.

[87] Supreme Court, Case No. 2 of the First Judicial Year, November 6, 1971.

[88] Ibid.

[89] Supreme Court, Case No. 8 of the Fifth Judicial Year, March 3, 1976.

[90] Su'ād Sharqāwī and Abd Allāh Nāṣif, *Nuẓum al-intikhabāt fī al-ʿālam wa-fī Miṣr* (al-Qahirah: Dar al-Nahḍah al-ʿArabīyah, 1994), 212–215.

[91] Supreme Court's Interpretive Decision No 15 of the Eighth Judicial Year, January 4, 1987.

[92] Yahia Al-Rifai, *qudah ʿdiʾd al-astbdad* (al-Qahirah: al-Maktab al-Miṣrī al-Ḥadīth, no date), 143–163.

demands were echoed at the Council of State. Administrative judges demanded the establishment of a special council with exclusive jurisdiction over appointment, transfer, and promotion.[93]

THE REGIME IN LATE 1970S: DELIBERALIZATION AND LIMITING OF THE JUDICIAL ROLE

After the Yom Kippur War and the Egypt–Israel Peace Treaty, Sadat concluded that he could enshrine his regime survival on the military achievements, foreign policy accomplishments, and the improvements in the standards of living that were supposed to accompany it.[94] By the late 1970s and especially after the events of January 17 and 18, 1977, Sadat determined that managed political liberalism went too far.

In addition, while the institutionalized survival strategy provided favorable conditions for judicial independence and empowerment of the judicial role, the regime continued its domination of the political system. The executive near-monopoly control over the lawmaking machine thwarted the courts. The regime was able to rush through legislation that established exceptional courts and slashed parts of the regular courts' jurisdiction. Regardless, and contrary to Nasser, the government tried to disguise these illiberal policies through combining them with liberal measures; "The government timed issuance of the Law of Shameful Conduct to coincide with the termination of the state of emergency in effect since Sadat had taken power in 1970. The President announced both measures as part of the official liberalization."[95]

The Judges Club and the general assemblies of most courts, the Council of State and the bar were steadfast in their opposition to the wave of deliberalizing legislation. When the regime declared its intentions to issue a new law to subdue its opponents in 1979, the Judges Club, the Court of Cassation, the Council of State, the Bar Association, and law schools condemned the government proposals. The Judges Club led the opposition to the new legislation. With the intention of silencing the judiciary, the regime lobbied heavily against the liberal judges on the board and promised financial benefits if government loyalists were elected in the association's 1980

---

[93] Nasar, *Ma'rakat al-'adalah fi Misr*, 141–148.

[94] In Egypt, the October or Ramadan War is portrayed as a great historical victory. Sadat and Mubarak exploited the war to garner public support based on their role in this battle that ended the national humiliation since the Six-Day War. In addition, the regime-controlled media publicized Sadat's elevated international standing notably after Sadat shared with the Israeli Prime Minister Menachem Begin the 1978 Noble Peace Prize.

[95] Baker, *Sadat and After*, 47.

elections. In the absence of a clear threat to their institutional autonomy, some judges wanted to enhance relations with the executive to further material well-being.

The government's intense pressure succeeded, and some of its supporters were elected to the board, changing its composition and political orientation. The regime seized the opportunity and rushed through a series of de-liberalization acts was enacted through the ever-submissive People's Assembly. This included Law 33/1978 on the Protection of the Domestic Front and Social Tranquility,[96] Law Protecting Values from Shame (commonly known as the Law of Shame or the Law of Shameful Conduct),[97] law regarding the establishment of State Security Courts that Sadat issued five days after the end of the state of emergency, as well as other legislation that granted extensive powers to the security forces,[98] and Law 95/1980 in regard to the Socialist Public Prosecution.

Law 36/1979 regarding political parties gave the regime-controlled Political Parties Committee vast powers over party establishment, organization, and internal affairs. Initially, decisions rendered by the Political Parties Committee were appealed before the Court of Administrative Judiciary. The court's liberal rulings strengthened the party system. In response, the government amended the law. Law 36/1979 installed a new exceptional court, the Parties Court, to adjudicate legal disputes related to political parties. The law mandated that all cases related to political parties are to be heard before the first circuit of the HAC. This circuit composition included lay members appointed by an executive decree.

In addition, the first article of the Protection of the Domestic Front and Social Tranquility Law provided for sanctions against those who disputed the principles of the July Revolution or the May Revolution.[99] All civil servants and candidates for public offices had to abide by these vague principles. The SPP could dismiss any candidate accused of violating these principles. Individuals who "contributed to the corruption of political life before the July revolution" were completely stripped of their "political rights," including the right to participate in elections or political parties.

---

[96] *Al-Jarida Al-Rasmiyya*, Issue 22 II, June 3, 1978.

[97] This law decree prohibited a wide group of people to own, manage or edit any publication, including "Those outlawed from political activities; those forbidden from establishing political parties; those who preach atheism; those convicted by the Court of Protecting Values from Shame and the Superior Court of Values." Naseer H. Aruri, "Disaster Area: Human Rights in the Arab World," *MERIP Middle East Report* 149, (November–December 1987): 12.

[98] Al-Rifai, *Sh'wan regal al-quda*, 147–150.

[99] *Al-Jarida Al-Rasmiyya*, Issue 22, June 3, 1978.

Sadat drew on exceptional courts to subdue the fierce opposition that emerged by late 1970s. "The Law of Shame allowed the punishment of any act contrary to morality, as defined by the regime. As a catch-all, it applied to the dissemination of 'immoral' messages as much as to public criticism of religious values."[100] Mustafa Marei, a former president of the bar and the dean of Egyptian lawyers, spoke in length criticizing provisions of the law, arguing, "presumably, they aim to protect society from shameful conduct, but in reality, they seek to shield the regime from criticism."[101] Those who were accused of such crimes appeared before a special court, the Court of Ethics.[102] The Court of Ethics became the only venue to appeal measures taken by the executive against the press. Without a doubt, "The provision in the law for a special Court of Ethics weakened the independence of the courts."[103]

Sadat became intolerant of the expansion of the judicial role. He, therefore, revisited some of Nasser's methods to limit judicial activism. Sadat wanted to exempt emergency measures according to Article 74 of the constitution from the Council of State oversight. In 1981, Sadat issued Law-decree 154. The first article endowed the Court of Ethics with exclusive authority to review petitions from individuals affected by actions made under Article 74. Wahid Ra'fat contended convincingly, "The intent was to prevent the administrative judiciary in the Council of State from reviewing those appeals."[104]

Only five days after the termination of the state of emergency, the regime issued Law 105/1980 that established the Permanent State Security Courts (PSSC). As a notable senior judge accurately argued, this legislation was "a wicked attempt to normalize exceptional circumstances."[105] The law permitted the president to add two senior officers to the courts' composition. A presidential decree appointed judges (civilian and military) after conferring

---

[100] Eberhard Kienle, *Grand Delusion: Democracy and Economic Reform in Egypt* (London: I. B. Tauris & Company, 2001), 20.

[101] Quoted in Ibid., 48.

[102] The Court of Ethics had two levels. The (ordinary) Court of Ethics was composed of seven members, with a vice president from the Court of Cassation as president and three judges from the Court of Cassation or the Courts of Appeal and three public dignitaries. The High Court of Ethics was a nine-member court, under the leadership of a vice president from the Court of Cassation and four judges from the Court of Cassation or the Courts of Appeal and four public dignitaries. Article 27 of Law Number 95 (1980), known as the Law of Shame. *Al-Jarida Al-Rasmiyya*, Issue 20, 15 May 1980.

[103] Baker, *Sadat and After*, 49.

[104] Wahid Ra'fat, *Dirāsāt fī ba'd al-qawānīn al-munazzimah lil-hurrīyāt* (al-Iskandarīyah: Munsha'at al-Ma'ārif, 1981), 203.

[105] Sirrī Ṣiyām, "al-Qaḍā' al-Tabī'ī al-Musāwāh amāma al-qaḍā" in *al-Musāwāh amāma al-qaḍā'* ed., Badr Minyāwī (al-Qāhirah: al-Markaz al-Qawmī lil-Buḥūth al-Ijtimā'īyah wa-al-Jinā'īyah, 1991), 130.

with the minister of justice and the minister of defense respectively. Moreover, according to Article 12 of the abovementioned law, verdicts issued by the PSSC could not be appealed and become final only after the president of the Republic approves the verdict. The president commanded the authority to pardon, shorten the sentence, or even order a new trial before another circuit.

According to the law, a person may simultaneously be tried before PSSC and Courts of Ethics on similar indictments in the former for criminal offenses and in the latter for the financial assets associated with those offenses. The Courts of Ethics had the authority to confiscate economic gains obtained under indictable crimes and may add prison terms to those ordered out by PSSC. If the Courts of Ethics and PSSC reach contradictory verdicts, the defendant may appeal to the president for a pardon.

Law 95/1980 regulated the affairs of the SPP. The SPP had the exclusive jurisdiction to prosecute a number of offenses before the Court of Ethics. The SPP was appointed by a presidential decree and can be removed by a vote of no confidence from a majority in the People's Assembly. In addition, the tenure of the SPP ended with the conclusion of the People's Assembly legislative session or its dissolution.[106] All these provisions put the SPP under the mercy of the regime.

Judges Continue the Struggle

After those oppressive laws passed, the Council of State struggled to limit their effect. When the regime used the provisions of Law 33/1978 on the Protection the Domestic Front and Social Tranquility to purge opposition members of the People's Assembly, the Administrative Courts narrowly defined the legislation and put the burden of proof on the government. The Council limited

---

[106] In response to the storm of criticism from the bar, the Judges Club, general assemblies of different courts and the Council of State's General Assembly, the People's Assembly's Committee on Legislative, and Constitutional Affairs' report on the Law of Shame argued, "Undoubtedly, the notion of normal judiciary is established on the principles of judicial independence and judicial impartiality ... Following this logic, legal jurists in Egypt concurred that normal judiciary is founded on three foundations: a) The legislation establishes a court and delineates its jurisdiction ... b) The court and its jurisdiction must be established before the crime ... c) The court has to be permanent. Indisputably, those three principles are present in the two degrees of the Court of Values. This proposed bill will be the legislation to establish this court, this legislation is going to cover only acts that occur after its enactment, and the Court of Values is a permanent court not related to a specific epoch or emergency conditions." See Alī Ṣāliḥ, *al-Wajīz fī sharḥ qānūn al-Muddaʿī al-ʿĀmm al-Ishtirākī*, 434–435.

the application of the oppressive provisions in the law to the fewest number of people.[107]

The struggle over the establishment of the SCC, during the 1978–1979 period, is an example of the revival of the political role of the legal profession, especially judges and lawyers. It is also indicative of the linkage between the regime's actions and rhetoric, on the one hand, and judicial independence and judicial activism on the other.

The establishment of the SCC in 1979 is illustrative of the regime's effort to reflect a façade of institutionalism while maintaining firm executive control over the state, the law, and the courts. Article 174 of the 1971 Constitution mandated the establishment of the SCC. The regime deliberately procrastinated in establishing this body during most of the 1970s.

The domestic and international scene changed, and by the end of 1970s, the regime was under fire domestically and internationally for its de-liberalization policies and legislation.[108] Sadat was eager for a liberalization gesture, preferably with a minimal political cost. Rutherford, in his excellent discussion of the establishment of the SCC, quoted then Speaker of the People's Assembly, Sufi Abu Talab, who maintained that in response to the sharp criticism domestically and internationally, Sadat was eager to

> Counter this increasing criticism by demonstrating his commitment to democratic, liberal principles . . . Sadat had four types of liberalizing gesturers available to him in 1979: grant greater freedom to political parties; expand freedom of the press, hold freer elections; or, undertake judicial reform, including establishment of constitutional court. Of these options, a consti-tutional court was the least threatening to the regime and was the easiest for Sadat to control.[109]

---

[107] Abd Al-Barr, *Dawr majlis al-Dawlah al-Misri fi himayat al-huquq wa-al-hurriyat al-`amah*, al-juz' 3, 75–77.

[108] It seems that the SCC was fortunate because Sadat was preoccupied at the time of the drafting of the law with his major foreign policy initiative, i.e., the Egyptian-Israeli peace process. Therefore, he delegated this issue to his minister of justice, Mamdouh Attia. Attia is an exceptional official. He was the minister of justice under Sadat (1977–1978) and the first SCC chief justice (1979–1982), and again minister of justice under Mubarak (1982–1986). He is the only person since 1952 to hold the office of minister of justice under two presidents and to move in and out of the post. Attia, a former senior judge, used this authority to advance an interest in building a robust constitutional court. He had served on the SCC's predecessor court, the Supreme Court, in the early 1970s, and was frustrated by its lack of independence. Attia was eager to transform it into a capable institution for advancing the rule of law. It seems that Attia had his eye on the SCC's chief justice post as he later accepted presidential appointment as the SCC's first chief justice. `Ammar `Ali Hasan, *Wizarat al-`Adl* (al-Qahirah: Markaz al-Dirasat al-Siyasiyah wa-al-Istiratijiyah, 2003), 155–156.

[109] Rutherford, *The Struggle for Constitutionalism in Egypt*, 312.

The establishment of the SCC was, from the regime's calculations, a tool to enhance its domestic and international standing with a minimum political cost. The proposed legislation was to create a mostly politically subordinate court. It stated that the court is an "independent entity" omitting the adjective "judicial." SCC members were to be appointed by a presidential decree after being nominated by the minister of justice and confirmed by the People's Assembly. Judges were to be appointed for a five-year term. The government could appeal to the SCC any verdict by the Council of State or the ordinary courts. The SCC would have the competence to suspend or invalidate any judicial ruling by any court, including the two top courts; the Court of Cassation and the HAC.[110]

The legal community was particularly furious over the proposed law. The general assembly of the Judges Club protested the proposed law and argued that this legislation is "a substantial setback to the principles of freedom, democracy, and the rule of law that the people started to enjoy after an extended period of suffering and agony. It violates the principle of separation of powers among the executive, legislative, and judicial authorities. It also includes numerous major infringements on the provisions of the constitution and judicial independence."[111] The general assembly of the Council of State followed suit and harshly criticized the proposed legislation and denied that its legislative section had ever approved such a draft. The general assembly formally requested the government to withdraw this legislation.[112] The Bar Association's general assembly condemned the proposed legislation as "a threat to the rule of law."[113] In the end, faced with unexpected uproar, the government yielded and the legislation that established the SCC provided the court and its members with a wide range of guarantees for its independence and autonomy (appointment, disciplining, and finance).

Despite this step, the Speaker of the House during this era later maintained that Sadat "believed that the SCC would constrain only the legislature and the Cabinet. He did not expect that it would dare to challenge presidential power."[114] Yahiya al-Jamal, minister of administrative affairs in 1978–1979, stated, "Sadat probably wasn't aware that he was creating such a strong Court. If he had been, he would never have approved it."[115] This sharply contradicts the story presented by Mustapha regarding the establishment of the SCC as a

---

[110] Jamal, *al-Qānūn al-dustūrī*, 299–300.
[111] Quoted in al-Muḥāmāh 58, no. 1–2, (January-February 1978): 181.
[112] Ibid., 183–193.
[113] Ibid., 176–180.
[114] Rutherford, *The Struggle for Constitutionalism in Egypt*, 315–316.
[115] Quoted in Ibid., 314.

guarantee for foreign investment. Sadat's de-liberalizing efforts came to an end with his assentation on October 6, 1981. The relationship between generals and judges would take another tern under Sadat's handpicked successor, Mubarak.

CONCLUSION

Sadat longed to stabilize his regime by raising the banners of law, democracy, and judicial independence. This coupled with the reservoir of legal liberalism and political activism within the judicial corps provided a hospitable environment for liberal judicialization. Nonetheless, the legacy of revolutionary-populist rule inherited from the Nasserite era along with the structural malfunctions of the First Republic limited active and liberal judicial behavior.

The Sadat era, therefore, is best conceived as a transitional bridge between two periods. Revolutionary, when judicial independence was at a minimum and hence judicial activism was limited, and the postrevolutionary, when the changed political realities allowed for expanded judicialization. This was more than what Sadat bargained for. The regime started to restrict judicialization and assert control. In doing so, Sadat undermined his survival strategy and contributed to the public anger toward his government.

By the late 1970s, Sadat's regime was in profound economic, social, and political crisis. The high hopes of economic prosperity and political liberalization, which the government inspired and publicized, had faded away. The economic liberalization was a catastrophic failure. By the end of the decade, hyperinflation skyrocketed and corruption mounted. The gap between the rich and the poor multiplied, and a tiny fraction of high-ranking bureaucrats and shady entrepreneurs amassed vast fortunes at the expense of the people. "The excesses of the *infitah* served to discredit economic liberalization among broad sectors of the population."[116]

The domestic political front did not fare better. By 1977, the cycle of openness and repression made a full swing. The managed political liberalization had not only come to a halt, but the regime started implementing a whole array of repressive measures. The 1979 parliamentary election was rigged. The Political Parties Law was changed to ensure ultimate government domination over the political process. The constitution was amended to allow Sadat to run for a third term. Besides, religious tensions and sometimes-violent confrontations between Muslims and Copts (Egyptian Christians) became widespread

---

[116] Robert Springborg, *Mubarak's Egypt: Fragmentation of the Political Order* (Boulder: Westview Press, 1989), 5.

in parts of Cairo and Upper Egypt. Sadat used Article 74 of the constitution to order the arrest of hundreds of the Egyptian political and cultural elite. The individuals arrested in September 1981 were a "who's who" of Egyptian society, including political leaders from the right and the left, Islamists, notable intellectuals, journalists, academics, and human rights activists. The patriarch of Alexandria, the spiritual head of the millions of Christian Egyptians, was placed under house arrest.

Or, on the regional side, the regime was isolated from its natural allies in the Arab world. Most Arab nations severed diplomatic, economic, and political ties with Egypt after Sadat signed a separate peace treaty with Israel. The economic and political benefits that Egypt had gained after its alliance with Uncle Sam did not outweigh the costs of forgoing the Arabs petrodollars.

5

Judicial Politics under Mubarak

Judges and the Fall of the Pharaoh (1981–2011)

Our future depends on the position of judges. If they insist on their noble struggle for liberty and democracy, the regime will not be able to continue to humiliate, suppress, and siphon off the Egyptian people. Judges, today, lead the nation and speak on behalf of the entire Egyptian people ... Our duty as Egyptians is to stand by them and support them with all our power.

> – Alaa Al-Aswany, the renowned Egyptian novelist during
> the Judicial Intifada of 2005–2006.[1]

Mohamed Hosny Mubarak was the fourth officer to assume Egypt's presidency. The air force general became president shortly after Sadat's assassination in October 1981. Mubarak was both similar and different from his predecessors. The similarity came from wearing the same military uniform that both Sadat and Nasser once wore. However, Mubarak was not a member of the Free Officers, who ruled Egypt since the 1952 army takeover. Nasser and Sadat used these revolutionary credentials to legitimize their rule with varying degrees of success. Mubarak could not do the same. He had no connection to the revolutionary change.

Mubarak's ascent to power on the eve of Sadat's assassination seemed more of a challenge than an opportunity. Sadat's assassination was a landmark event in Egypt's modern history. The militants considered assassinating the president the first step in their grandiose plan to carry out a revolution that would lead to an Islamic state. The regime that Mubarak inherited faced severe difficulties at all levels.

What is more, very little about the new president's personality or record could help mitigate the acute legitimacy crisis. Mubarak, who is "not a

---

[1] Quoted in Sharīf Yūnus, *Istiqlāl al-qaḍā* (al-Qāhirah: Markaz al-Qāhirah li-Dirāsāt Ḥuqūq al-Insān, 2007), 78.

charismatic figure, nor even one who appears comfortable in a political environment,"[2] had to ease the domestic tension and strengthen the regime's survival prospects. Therefore,

> On succeeding to the presidency after Sadat's assassination, Mubarak immediately adopted a low-key, conciliatory tone. He released political prisoners who had been rounded up by Sadat in the months preceding his death, and reinvigorated the process of political liberalization that had been launched in 1976 but aborted by Sadat in 1978–1979.[3]

While Sadat used two different legitimation devices, Islam and democracy, Mubarak's did not have the same latitude. Using Islam to garner political support was difficult. For one thing, militant Islamists, who assassinated Mubarak's predecessor, launched a terror campaign and tried to overthrow the regime.[4] Additionally, the peace treaty with Israel, a commitment that Mubarak could not afford to breach, negated any appeal for the religious legitimization of the regime.

Mubarak's options, therefore, were limited. The absence of charisma, healthy economy, financial revenues, influential regional role, appeal to religion, and adequate capacity to repress the society through naked force presented a dilemma for a less-than-skillful politician.[5] Institutionalization seemed to be the most suitable alternative. After all, Sadat used it before. It carried little political cost and was compatible with the regime's foreign policy and structure of allies. Furthermore, the appeal to legality was attuned to Mubarak's inclinations. As with Sadat before him, Mubarak's personal experience influenced his thinking. Mubarak's respect for the judiciary is at least partially driven by his personal appreciation for Abd al-Aziz Pasha Fahmi. This great judge was the most prominent figure in Mubarak's small village of Kafr al-Moselha. The Pasha, as the villagers used to call him, provided

---

[2]   Springborg, *Mubarak's Egypt: Fragmentation of the Political Order*, 24.

[3]   Ibid., 23.

[4]   The expansion of political Islam could be at least partially attributed to Sadat himself, who thought to use religion to battle Nasserites and socialists. In addition, the support of the petro-dollar rich Gulf countries, the success of the Iranian Revolution, and the Western support to the *Mujahidin* in Afghanistan all revived political Islam as a viable alternative to the failing secular regimes in the Arab world.

[5]   The January 17–18, 1977 uprising proved the domestic security forces lacking. The regime had to order martial law and bring in the army to quell the popular violent protests. The assassination of Sadat in an army parade and by some army officers wounded the pride of the armed forces. Moreover, Sadat's murder ignited a plot to violently overthrow the regime that included numerous brutal attacks on security forces' headquarters in various Egyptian cities and towns.

financial support for students of needy families. Besides, Mubarak's father was a junior court clerk at a local court.[6] Mubarak grew up in an environment where judges assumed great authority and respect.

The regime's bid for political survival, based on the courts provided Regime Survival Functions (RSFs), manifested itself in official discourse and legislation related to the courts. Mubarak was to expand, at least early on, the rule of law, democracy, and judicial independence discourse inherited from Sadat. Mubarak enhanced the guarantees of judicial independence instituted by the previous regime, but in the same vein sought to devise informal control mechanisms to influence the judiciary. I first shed light on Mubarak's discourse, highlighting the similarities with and differences from his predecessors, and then move to investigate the changes in legislation related to various judicial institutions.

MUBARAK'S DISCOURSE: THE EMPHASIS ON LEGALITY

The analysis of Mubarak's public discourse, as detailed in his speeches inaugurating the opening sessions of the parliament, shows unmistakable similarities with Sadat (at least until the beginning of his six terms in office). As with his predecessor and unlike Nasser, justice (distributive: social and economic) is somewhat marginal in Mubarak's discourse (see Figure 5.1). Justice was utterly absent in seven speeches. Furthermore, except for 2007, in which this principle was mentioned a staggering twenty times, the average recurrence of justice was less than four yearly citations.[7] This is not surprising as Mubarak continued and deepened Sadat's free-market approach. On the contrary, freedom received much more attention in Mubarak's discourse. Except in 1982, 2009, and 2010, Mubarak mentioned freedom at least twice in every speech, with an average of 7.5 citations per speech. As with Sadat, democracy was the highest value in Mubarak's discourse. Mubarak mentioned democracy a staggering 373 times, with an average of 12.4 citations a year.

What's more, as with Sadat, the rule of law emerged as an essential principle in Mubarak's discourse. This concept was mentioned in most of the speeches at least once. Figure 5.2 puts the three presidents' emphasis on the rule of law in a comparative light. A concept, mentioned only twice during

---

[6] Abu `Alam, *Yawmiyat mustashar min dahaya madhbahat al-qada*, 135–137.

[7] Independent estimates put those who live below the poverty line in Egypt at 52 percent. The economic crisis and the gap between the rich and the poor reached an acute level in 2007, forcing Mubarak to publicly acknowledge the problem and to promise immediate government policies to deal with it.

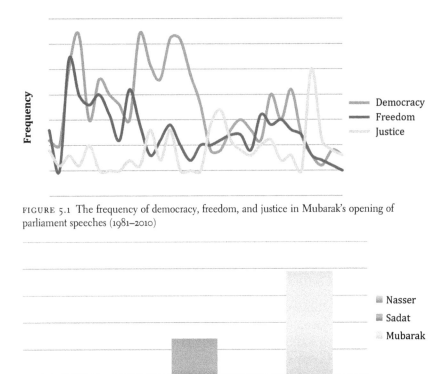

FIGURE 5.1 The frequency of democracy, freedom, and justice in Mubarak's opening of parliament speeches (1981–2010)

FIGURE 5.2 The aggregate number of "rule of law" mentions in presidential discourse (1954–2010)

Nasser's long reign, was cited twenty-four times in Sadat's speeches and was referenced forty-eight times under Mubarak.

The regime, following in Sadat's footsteps, wanted to link the rule of law to the courts. Mubarak emphasized this in his 2003 speech, asserting

> Our choice to designate the rule of law as a leading method for national and executive work has enhanced the political and democratic reforms and strengthened the state of institutions. Our reliance on an independent and impartial judiciary, which has guaranteed justice and equality and enriched our democratic experience through their full oversight of the elections.

The focus on the judiciary and the related RSFs is evident under Mubarak. The president spoke of constitutional legitimacy in 1994 and 2005. In the 2005 speech, he maintained,

> We have succeeded in the previous phase in establishing the required institutional framework for any democratic system: a constitution that provides for

the structures, institutions and foundations of a modern state that protects the fundamental rights and freedoms of citizens; *a constitutional court within a judiciary that guarantees the rule of law*; a multi-party system; freedom of the press and media; and other necessities of any well-grounded and effective democratic system.

Mubarak also devoted considerable attention to highlighting the independence of the Egyptian judiciary, a prerequisite for the courts to be able to provide the much-needed RSFs. For instance, in his 1989 address, he asserted, "we have strongly insisted on the ultimate respect for judicial independence, as a refuge for every aggrieved, an asylum to dispense justice, and an arbitrator among citizens and between them and all governing institutions." In his 1999 address, Mubarak declared, "We firmly believe that the independence of the judicial authority is one of the most important mainstays of governing in Egypt. The state provides all forms of support for such independence that the judiciary rightly deserves. It [the judiciary] is a source of pride for every Egyptian." Mubarak consistently underscored the privileged place and elevated role the judiciary has played in service of the state and citizenry. In 1996, the president argued,

> Judges, the guardians of justice, devoted their lives to uphold righteousness, affirm justice, and enforce the law; they instituted with their impartiality and dedication a formidable Egyptian fortress, which we applaud and acclaim. For this reason, we do not spare any effort to strengthen this great institution and provide it with resources that enable it to perform its mission in service of the society in the best of all fashions.

In the following year (1997), the president reiterated the same message:

> We utterly revere the elevated stature of our judiciary that articulates the conscience of the nation, safeguards justice and rights for all members of the community, strong or weak, rich or poor alike without distinction. This prominent institution has performed its duty with all loyalty and allegiance to the nation and presented Egypt with pioneering generations of excellent judges, who have played an honorable role in the service of the people.

Because the judiciary has performed a vital and dignified function, Mubarak, in his 2000 speech, argued that the regime was "keen to further its independence, and place it in a noble place to advance the rule of law." The same tone was echoed the following year (2001): "Greetings to Egypt's lofty judiciary, which provided with its fairness and independence, all the support to maintain security and stability of the homeland where the rule of law prevails, and the people enjoy freedom, equality, and justice."

Like Sadat and unlike Nasser, Mubarak visited the Judges Club, the Council of State, the Court of Cassation, and the Supreme Constitutional Court (SCC). He delivered the inaugural address at the First Justice Conference. In this speech, Mubarak stated, "The respect for the high bench ... is the primary responsibility and commitment of the ruler." Mubarak additionally affirmed his commitments to the rule of law, contending, "I have committed, since the first day I assumed responsibility, to wait for judicial verdicts in all matters appropriate for adjudication. I hereby assert the respect of all state institutions of courts' rulings, and we will enforce these judgments in letter and essence."

This emphasis on judicial independence and the rule of law served the regime's quest for political acceptance at home and abroad. The regime strategically used judicial oversight of the election to rebuff calls for international monitoring of the electoral process. Mubarak maintained in his 1995 speech, "As a sign of respect for our independent and impartial judiciary, in their presence, there should not be other domestic or international supervising entity." In 1999, he repeated the same idea: "I promise that the coming election will be clean, impartial, and completely subject to full judicial oversight." In his 2000 speech, Mubarak maintained, "I congratulate members of the Assembly, who won the confidence of the masses in an untainted electoral competition: the first [election] in Egypt's history to be conducted under full judicial oversight at all levels."

Much of this has changed in Mubarak's six terms. The constant emphasis on democracy (fourteen mentions per speech 1981–2005) receded. Mubarak only spoke of democracy a little more than three times since 2006. In 2008, it was absent except for a brief mention of "democracy in international interactions among developed and developing nations." The emphasis on freedom plummeted as well, from more than eight citations per-speech between 1981 and 2005 to just over two mentions since 2006. Emphases on justice, on the other hand, grew from about three citations during Mubarak's first twenty-five years to eight during his last term. Nevertheless, justice mostly had the modifier social before it. The prominence of social justice in Mubarak's discourse revealed much resemblance to Nasser's and a sharp departure from Sadat's. Furthermore, the post-2005 speeches exhibited much less emphasis on the rule of law. Between 2008 and 2010, Mubarak mentioned it only once, another sharp departure from the frequent mentions in the pre-2005 speeches. This was an indication of a "change of heart" for the regime. It also signaled a deliberate effort to limit political rights and judicial activism.

THE EXPANSION OF JUDICIAL INSTITUTIONAL INDEPENDENCE

For a quarter century, Mubarak refrained from amending the 1971 Constitution. This was auspicious for the courts, as the 1971 Constitution provided for many guarantees of judicial independence. Furthermore, to enable the courts to perform the critical RSFs, Mubarak agreed to amend the Judicial Authority Law and the Council of State legislation to provide for more guarantees of judicial independence. The vital amendments to the existing laws were enacted fewer than three years after Mubarak's ascendency to the presidency. This further confirms the tie between judicial independence and the regime's quest for political survival. The 1984 amendments of both the Law of Judicial Authority and the Council of State Law enhanced the guarantees of judicial institutional independence, a prerequisite for the courts to provide the RSFs.

Since Nasser abolished the HJC, judges fought to restore the Council. After all, judicial autonomy is one of the very few causes that all judges support. The judges' dedicated efforts almost paid off during Sadat's waning years in office. After Sadat's death and with the political openness at the beginning of Mubarak's era, judges forcefully and publically reinstated their demand.

The minister of justice, Mamdouh Attia, however, was steadfast in his opposition to changes that would limit his political power over the judiciary. When the Judges Club sent a memo to the cabinet making a case for the proposed amendments, Attia responded with a counter-memo that opposed it.[8] The Judges Club had no alternative but to go public with its demands, and the association's secretary general, the unwavering Yahia Al-Rifai, wrote a comprehensive response in *al-Ahram* (Egypt's most read newspaper at the time). The "going public" strategy put Mubarak to the test. The regime yielded to pressure but tried to limit substantial concessions. The government proposal reinstated the HJC and granted legal immunity to members of the Prosecution Department, but it kept much of the minister of justice's powers intact. These prerogatives included his control over the Judicial Inspection Department (JID), budget and finance, the appointment of presidents of Courts of First Instance, and many other matters related to the day-to-day work of the courts.

Nevertheless, after two decades of continuous struggle, judges were able to reestablish the HJC. The preamble of Law 35/1988 affirmed the inseparable

---

[8]   All correspondence published in Al-Rifai, *tashriat al-soltah*, 642–650.

link between the HJC and judicial independence, stating, "To augment judicial autonomy proclaimed in articles 165 and 166 of the Constitution, a High Judicial Council staffed with members of the judiciary itself to manage judicial affairs will be established."[9]

In addition to the reinstatement of the HJC, the debate over the Public Prosecutor's (PP) security of tenure was particularly impressive. While the government's initial proposal consented to the security of tenure for the entire PPD, it nevertheless denied the PP himself this critical legal guarantee, keeping the government's prerogative to replace or transfer him at will. Because the PP maintained administrative and supervisory authority over the entire PPD members, the government wanted to keep its power over the officeholder. The Alexandria Judges Club's extraordinary general assembly led the charge against this infringement. The club convincingly argued that it is unreasonable that the head of the prosecution department would not enjoy a legal guarantee that his staff enjoys.[10]

The judges had to reach out to the pinnacle of the political system to secure the recognition of their cause. Farid Fahmi al-Gazirli, then chairman of the Alexandria Judges Club, seized the opportunity of an exclusive audience with Mubarak. Using the army lingo that the president understood well, al-Gazirli argued, "It is ludicrous that the general will have less legal rights than his soldiers in the field."[11] Adel Qorah, former president of the Court of Cassation and a member of the committee that drafted the law, acknowledged, "due to the political sensitivity of this issue the Minister of Justice had to obtain presidential consent to grant the public prosecutor the security of tenure."[12]

Unsurprisingly, judges and the rest of the legal community perceived those amendments as steps in the right direction. The reestablishment of the HJC was a matter of institutional autonomy as well as a symbol of the judges' professional pride. The security of tenure for the entire PPD had long been among the main demands that liberal judges championed under Sadat and Mubarak. The regime, nevertheless, was unwavering in maintaining its discretion to appoint the PP.

The Council of State's institutional independence as well received a significant boost in these early years of Mubarak's presidency. The regime

---

[9] *Al-Jarida al-Rasmiyya*, Issue 14, March 31, 1984.
[10] The Alexandria branch of the Judges Club is historically known for its strong, liberal, and independent stands. In 2005, this branch led the effort to amend the Law of Political Participation and the Law of Judicial Authority. Many of the leading liberal judges in the Judges Club and the Court of Cassation have been members of the Alexandria Judges Club.
[11] Personal interview with Hussam al-Ghariani, May 12, 2006.
[12] Personal interview with Adel Qorah, February 25, 2006.

issued Law 136/1984, which instituted many reforms demanded by administrative judges. The first article was particularly significant stating, "The Council of State is an independent judicial authority," omitting the provision "attached to the Minister of Justice," hence, removing the minister of justice's influence over the Council.

Another particularly noteworthy amendment was related to Article 83. The Council's president would be appointed after consulting with a special general assembly composed of all senior judges. In practice, this meant that the most senior vice president would be elevated. This significantly strengthened the Council's independence. Before this legislation, the executive had the latitude to choose any of the Council's vice presidents, requiring only the advisory opinion of the executive-dominated SCJB. Another amendment mandated the approval of the Council's general assembly for the appointment of vice and deputy presidents.

Furthermore, the Special Council for Administrative Affairs (SCAA), composed of the Council's seven most senior judges, now commanded the sole responsibility to appoint all other Council members. SCAA, in lieu of the SCJB, was granted exclusive authority over discipline, promotion, and assignment of judges. Another amendment expanded the security of tenure to all members of the Council, except those at the entry level. The law mandated for the first time that members of the Council "enjoy all the guarantees enjoyed by judges [legal immunity and security of tenure]." Furthermore, Article 111 also granted the Council's president, with the approval of the SCAA, the authority to organize health and social services for the Council's members. These amendments made the Council the most independent institution in the Egyptian judiciary, a decision that Mubarak would later regret

THE REGIME AND THE JUDICIARY

Mubarak faced a conundrum. On the one hand, he worked to highlight the legal-institutional foundations, which required instituting checks and balances, limiting the vast presidential power, empowering the judicial institutions, and enhancing the power of the parliament. On the other hand, the president maintained the age-long tradition of a heavily centralized political system. As with Sadat, Mubarak wanted to depict an image of liberalism and democracy to serve his interests at home and abroad while adequately maintaining the imperial presidency.

Courts and judges as well as other political actors seized on the regime's dire need for their RSFs to enhance their institutional independence, expand judicialization, and further political rights and liberties. The courts' "liberal" jurisprudence won them new allies in the civil society and among the masses. In this section, I first sketch a brief description and appraisal of the Council of State. Then, I move to the courts of general jurisdiction and end with the SCC.

THE COURTS EXPAND ITS POLITICAL ROLE

The Council of State

Throughout Mubarak's reign, the Council of State expanded its role defending civil and political rights. Hill affirmed the pivotal role of the Council: "although constitutional questions now are submitted to the Constitutional Court, issues concerning civil rights are still usually taken to the *Majlis al-dawla* (Council of State) by virtue of its continuing function as protector of citizens from arbitrary and unwarranted government actions."[13] The Council's role was critical in many issues related to civil and political rights. However, consistent with the central questions of this work, I focus only on rulings related to the fundamental regime interests, particularly in relation to structuring civil and political participation and controlling the political contestation process.

During Mubarak's years, the Council was the only feasible path to establish opposition parties. The Law of Political Participation required the approval of the government-appointed Political Parties Committee (PPC) to grant political parties the necessary license.[14] The PPC routinely rejected applications for new political parties that might pose any threat to the ruling National Democratic Party (NDP). The only alternative was to appeal the PPC decisions to the Council of State.[15] Almost all major opposition parties were granted licenses to operate through the Council's rulings.

[13] Enid Hill, *"Al-Sanhuri and Islamic Law"* Cairo Papers in Social Science (Cairo: American University in Cairo, 1987), 100.

[14] The Parties' Court within the Council, which adjudicated legal disputes related to political parties, was of mixed composition. In addition to the Council's president and other senior judges of the first circuit of the HAC, there are an equivalent number of public dignitaries. While the rulings, as others from other courts in Egypt, do not reveal the individual votes of each member, it is safe to assume that those public dignitaries appointed by the minister of justice had been more conservative and restrictive in their votes especially regarding viable political parties that might pose a threat to the domination of the ruling National Democratic Party (NDP). After the January 2011 Revolution, all non-judicial members were removed from the composition of the court.

[15] According to a survey of the Political Parties Committtee's (PPC) decisions from 1977 until the end of 2002, the committee reviewed forty-nine applications to establish new political parties.

Furthermore, the Council of State's rulings strengthened opposition parties. Sadat and Mubarak used the multiparty structure to reflect an image of liberalism without giving these parties any real opportunity to gain power. In December 1983, the Council ruled that political parties had the right to hold public meetings anywhere in the country. This decision expanded the operational capacities of opposition parties. The administrative courts defended the right to hold public meetings for political purposes. These rulings were critical in granting opposition parties the ability to organize mass gatherings.[16] Furthermore, the Council, in April 1984, ruled that political parties had the right to communicate their programs through state-owned media, especially television. Consequently, in the 1984 legislative elections, each recognized political party was granted free TV airtime. The same practice continued in the 1987 election and was expanded to provide free airtime on the radio.[17]

In addition to these rulings, the administrative courts upheld the freedom of expression. The Council ruled that it has the power to examine administrative decisions denying citizens and groups their right to hold mass demonstrations. In one ruling, for example, the court discredited the security forces' justifications for the refusal to issue the proper permit for a rally in front of the presidential palace.[18]

The Council furthermore affirmed citizens' unqualified right to seek judicial remedies for administrative infringements on their rights and liberties. In one case, in which the Southern Cairo Court's refused to allow the plaintiff to file a lawsuit, the administrative court condemned this decision as a flagrant transgression on a constitutional right, stating,

> The clerk of the courts cannot refrain from filing any proceedings that citizens may request. This refusal eliminates without justification and any basis of law, the constitutional assurance of the rule of law that is the right to appeal to courts.[19]

The PPC rejected more than 90 percent of these applications and only approved a handful. Riḍā Muḥammad Hilāl, "mawqif Lajnat shu'ūn al-aḥzāb min Ṭalabāt ta'sīs al-aḥzāb al-ṣ aghīrah," in ʿAmr Hashim (ed.), *al-Ahzab al-saghirah wa-al-nizam al-hizbi fi Misr* (al-Qahirah: Markaz al-Dirasat al-Siyasiyah wa-al-Istiratijiyah, 2003), 170.

[16] For example Ruling No. 5094 of Year 36, issued in September 5, 1982, and Ruling No. 7131 of Year 36, issued on August 31, 1989.

[17] Gamal Zahran, "al-dawr al-siyāsī lal-qaḍa' al-Miṣrī fī ṣun' al-qarār," in Alī al-Dīn Hilāl (ed.), *Al-Niẓām al-siyāsī al-Miṣrī: al-taghayyur wa-al-istimrār* (al-Qahirah: Maktabat al-Nahḍah al-Miṣrīyah, 1988), 237.

[18] Ruling No. 4525 of Judicial Year 39, issued June 15, 1985.

[19] Magdi al-Jarihi, *Majlis al-Dawlah (Qadai al-mashrū'īyah): al-musāwāh wa-al-ḥurrīyah* (al-Qahirah: Dar el-Tahrir, 2006), 188–189.

The Council championed the freedom of the press. It ruled that freedom of the media is one of the public freedoms guaranteed by the constitution. The administrative courts reversed executive orders to close down a newspaper, refuting the government's justifications in this regard.[20] The Council argued, "Freedom of the press, as one of the manifestations of freedom of speech, ought not to be restricted."[21] The administrative courts' consistency in upholding the freedom of the press cut across the ideological divide, as the Council of State repeatedly ruled in favor of liberals, leftists, Nasserites, and Islamists.

Additionally, the Council in 1987 invalidated a presidential decree that allowed transferring civilians accused of politically motivated crimes to the military courts.[22] The government responded by returning the cases to the civilian courts, which provide far greater legal guarantees to defendants.[23] Consequently, the High State Security Court (HSSC) acquitted all the defendants. In the ruling, the HSSC scrapped the evidence presented by the security establishment and condemned it for torture.[24]

The administrative court affirmed the constitutional right of freedom of movement to political dissidents. In one famous case, where the security apparatus restricted Sheikh Omar Abdel-Rahman's freedom of movement, the court quashed the Ministry of Interior's decision and permitted Abdel-Rahman to move freely inside Egypt.[25] The court condemned the decree, declaring "This decision violates one of the personal freedoms, guaranteed by the Constitution to the plaintiff."[26] In another case, the court ruled that criticizing the regime did not justify a decision to deny the claimant his right to travel.[27] The courts, in congruence with their liberal era's jurisprudence, ruled that membership in an organization with militant ideas does not warrant

[20] Abd al-Ḥamīd, *al-Qaḍā' hisn al-hurriyat*, 133–134.

[21] Ruling No. 4828 of Judicial Year 53 on December 14, 1999.

[22] The reasoning of the Council was very similar to the US Supreme Court's decision in *Ex Parte Milligan*, (1866).

[23] Zahran, "*al-dawr al-siyāsī lal-qaḍa' al-Miṣrī fi ṣun' al-qarār*," 237.

[24] Abdullah Salah, "al-dawr al-siyāsī lal-qaḍa' al-Miṣrī," in Muḥammad Ṣafī al-Dīn Kharbūsh (ed.), *al-Taṭawwur al-siyāsī fī Miṣr, 1982–1992* (al-Qāhirah: Jāmiʿat al-Qāhirah, Kullīyat al-Iqtiṣād wa-al-'Ulūm al-Siyāsīyah, Markaz al-Buḥūth wa-al-Dirāsāt al-Siyāsīyah, 1994), 219–220.

[25] Omar Abdel-Rahman, sometimes referred to as the blind sheikh, was the spiritual leader of Al-Gamaʿa al-Islamiyya (The Islamic Group), a militant Islamist movement in Egypt. Abdel-Rahman spent three years in Egyptian jails where he was severely tortured as he awaited trial on charges of issuing a *fatwa* resulting in the 1981 assassination of Sadat by Egyptian Islamic Jihad. He then moved to Afghanistan and the United States, where he was convicted of "seditious conspiracy" after the World Trade Center 1993 bombings.

[26] `Abd al-Barr, *Dawr majlis al-Dawlah al-Misri fi himayat al-huquq wa-al-hurriyat al-`ammah*, al-juz' 3, 480–481.

[27] Ibid., 510–511.

declaring a person a security threat as long as he did not personally commit an act of violence.[28]

The administrative courts consistently affirmed their competence to review presidential decrees detaining political dissidents.[29] On numerous occasions, the administrative courts dismissed the security justifications for decisions and ordered the immediate release of detainees. In many other rulings, the courts ordered compensation for the time spent in detention.[30] Besides, the Council of State mandated the dismissal of police officers convicted of torture.[31]

The Council's rulings and opinions directly expanded judicialization. The Council issued an opinion requiring the executive to apply any of the SCC's verdicts to any party in the same legal position, not just those who brought the lawsuit resulting in the ruling.[32] On other occasions, the administrative court ordered the suspension of the minister of work force's orders to organize the labor unions' elections because it did not adhere to the principle of judicial oversight of the vote as mandated by the SCC.[33]

Finally, the indirect influence of the Council was as crucial as its rulings. The Council has been the gateway for transferring a plethora of landmark cases to the SCC.[34] This was critical for two reasons. The SCC exclusively commands the power of judicial review, but citizens cannot appeal directly to the Court; second, transferring any politically sensitive case meant it would come before the public and would receive considerable media attention. While the SCC did not always rule all legislations transferred from the Council unconstitutional, it invalidated many, including

- Law 50/1982, which entrusted the Emergency State Security Courts (ESSC) with the power to review presidential orders to detain individuals under the state of emergency.
- Law 40/1977, which severely restricted individuals' ability to establish political parties.
- Law 33/1978, which stripped many prominent opposition leaders of their political rights.

[28] Ibid., 527–528.
[29] Abd al-Ḥamīd, *al-Qaḍā' hisn al-hurriyat*, 122–123.
[30] Ibid., 123–128.
[31] *Al-Masry al-Youm*, November 7, 2006.
[32] *Al-Ahram*, November 22, 2005.
[33] *Masrawy*, November 2, 2006.
[34] In addition, most Supreme Constitutional Court (SCC) justices and chief justices during its active-liberal era (until 2000) came from the ranks of the administrative judiciary and their legal reasoning shows the influence of the Council of State's professional socialization.

- Law 38/1972 and Law 114/1983, which denied citizens who did not belong to a recognized political party the right to contest elections.

Under Mubarak, the administrative courts demonstrated a strong commitment to their liberal institutional heritage of the prerevolutionary era. The Council defended the political and civil rights of individuals and groups in different walks of life. It stood up to the regime's effort to limit political activism. The administrative courts were steadfast in their support of civil and political rights. The courts' jurisprudence is very similar to its liberal era jurisprudence. What is noticeable is the difference in the jurisprudence between the administrative courts and the High Administrative Court (HAC). In many cases related to rights and liberties of individuals and groups, the HAC was considerably more conservative in comparison to the lower administrative courts. In many occasions, the HAC leaned toward responsibility over liberty and defended public interest over individual rights. It could be argued that the regime, through lucrative extrajudicial assignments, was able to attract support from some senior judges at the pinnacle of the Council. Through them and the HAC's appellate power, the regime was somehow able to check the liberal-activist judges on lower courts.

The Courts

Many judges on the civil and criminal circuits have issued rulings that strengthened the principles of the rule of law, fair trial, and due process. The Court of Cassation is the clearest example of a consistent and continuous commitment to those principles. The court, because of its remarkable institutional independence and efficacious general assembly, has on many occasions successfully, withstood the regime's pressure to influence its adjudication.[35] In this, the Court of Cassation stands in sharp contrast to other lower courts in which the regime has been able to exert considerable influence.

---

[35] The Court of Cassation is, perhaps, Egypt's most independent court. While the law mandates two nominating authorities: The court's general assembly and the minister of justice, in reality, the Court of Cassation's general assembly, is the gateway to the high bench. The accepted practice under Mubarak is that the minister of judge would nominate two judges only. In order to increase the religious diversity in the court, in most cases, those judges have been Christians. The rest of the nominees are left to the court's general assembly. Because liberal judges tend to have such a strong voice in the general assembly, the court is a self-perpetuating body. Unlike the general assemblies of some lower courts, which the regime was able to domesticate, the Court of Cassation's general assembly is also influential and carefully guards its institutional prerogatives. Personal interview with Yahia Al-Rifai, April 5, 2006.

The liberal jurisprudence of the court manifested itself in countless rulings. The Court of Cassation ruled police officers did not have the authority to search citizens only because of their presence in a high-crime neighborhood. The court held this search to be a violation of individuals' freedom. Hence, all pieces of evidence obtained after this illegal search were deemed inadmissible.[36] In another ruling, the court denied police officers the authority to stop and search vehicles without reasonable cause.[37] Similarly, the Court of Cassation ruled that even under a state of emergency, the security services did not have the authority to monitor citizens' communications.[38] Limiting the power of the security apparatus was critical to protecting rights and liberties, particularly of opposition activists.

Furthermore, the Court of Cassation overturned the convictions of many political decadents. Notable among them was the Egyptian academic and human rights activist Saad El-Din Ibrahim. This Court of Cassation invalidated the State Security Court's rulings against him twice. In the first instance, the court ordered a retrial, but this time it ruled on the merits of the case itself.[39]

The Court of Cassation was also instrumental in protecting judges from executive infringements. The court exempted judges from the oversight of the Administrative Control Authority (ACA).[40] The court stated, "Members of the judicial authority are not public employees of the government."[41] Hence, they could not be subjected to the authority of the ACA.

The Courts of Appeal had a decisive role in defending citizens' rights. Cairo Appeals Court quashed an SSPD's decision to put Issam al-Irian and Mohamed Mursi (two prominent leaders of the Muslim Brotherhood) under house arrest.[42] What was surprising is the fact that some ESSC rulings contributed to the advancement of civil and political rights. In 1985, during the al-Jihad Trial, the court withstood the regime's pressure for stiff sentences, and the verdicts were light. Sheikh Omar Abd al-Rahman was acquitted, and the

---

[36] *Akhbar El-Youm*, July 22, 2006.

[37] Court of Cassation ruling No. 16412 of the 68 Judicial Year, issued May 14, 2001.

[38] Court of Cassation ruling No. 8792 of the 72 Judicial Year, issued September 25, 2002.

[39] The Egyptian law sanctions the Court of Cassation to rule on the merits of a case itself, if it accepted the appeal for a second time. *Asharq al-Awsat*, March 19, 2003.

[40] The Administrative Control Authority (ACA) was established in 1964 as an independent organization affiliated with the prime minister. The ACA is responsible for detecting as well as fighting corruption in the government, public business sectors, and the private sector accomplishing public work. Most of its staff and leadership generally come from the army or the police.

[41] Court of Cassation ruling No. 8792 of the 72 Judicial Year, issued September 25, 2002.

[42] *Al-Mesryoon*, October 10, 2006.

court condemned the torture that the security forces inflicted on the detainees.[43] Again, in 1986, the Cairo ESSC cleared many defendants because of their leadership roles in organizing strikes. To circumvent the Emergency Law in effect at that time, the court cited Egypt's signature on the International Covenant on Economic, Social and Cultural Rights to provide a legal justification for the right to strike even under a state of emergency.[44] The regime sought to deny workers the ability of collective action against the waves of privatization and growing chronic unemployment.

The HSSC twice cleared the leading Muslim Brotherhood member Hassan Hayouan of allegations of acquiring 400 automatic guns to disrupt the electoral process in Sharquia Governorate. Hayoun was acquitted initially, but the SSPD petitioned the Office of State Security Affairs (OSSA) (part of the presidency office) to repeal the ruling and order a retrial.[45]

While the courts' direct (on-the-bench) political role was impressive under Mubarak, judges' indirect (off-the-bench) role is no less politically significant. The Judges Club utilized several tools to achieve its objectives. This included proposing new legislation; hosting conferences and seminars on political and legal matters; convening the Club's general assembly; writing official communiqués to the presidency, the minister of justice, and the HJC; publicizing relevant points in the Club's publications and public statements; and forming specialized committees to follow up on significant issues.

The Judges Club's efforts were the *raison d'être* for the resurrection of the HJC in 1984. The Judges Club, as early as 1986, spearheaded the calls for full judicial oversight of the electoral process. The association's general assembly issued a statement (November 13, 1986) that unequivocally highlighted the judges' awareness of the regime's use of the judiciary to provide needed RSFs. "In order to augment the confidence in the electoral procedures, the executive authority and various mass media networks repeatedly stated that elections were conducted under the oversight of judges. This is because they realize the public's faith in judges' impartiality and integrity." The statement called on the regime either guarantee full judicial oversight or relieve judges of this duty.[46] This was

---

[43] In 1984, the regime's distrust of the courts led to an "eye-grabbing event: the security services eavesdropped on the State Security Court's deliberations on the al-Jihad Trial." Abū Qamar, *al-Qaḍā' wa-al-wāqi' al-siyāsī: dirāsah taṭbīqīyah 'alá al-qaḍā' ayn al-idārī wa-al-dustūrī fī Miṣr*, 100.

[44] Case No. 4190 of year 1986 Azbakia, published in *Akhbar al-Muḥāmāh* 8, (July 1987): 11–13.

[45] *Al-Masry al-Youm*, November 13, 2006.

[46] Quoted in Atef Shahat, "dor Nadi al-qudah fi ta'ziz istqlal alquda wa al'ashalh alsiasi," in Nabil Abdel Fattah (ed.), *dwar al-qudah fi al-aslah al-siasi* (al-Qāhirah: Markaz al-Qāhirah li-Dirāsāt Ḥuqūq al-Insān, 2006), 371.

an early sign that most judges are reluctant to perform tasks that could hinder their professionalism and social status.

The Judges Club organized the first (and until now the only) Justice Conference in April 1986. The conference, which was attended by all prominent judges, law professors, and legal scholars, was inaugurated by a presidential address. The conference focused on strengthening judicial independence and facilitating the adjudication process. The first Justice Conference stipulated a roadmap for comprehensive judicial reform. This included the separation of prosecution and indictment powers, establishing judicial police to enforce rulings, rescinding all exceptional courts and limiting the jurisdiction of military tribunals to armed forces personnel. It called for restructuring the judicial oversight of the elections to ensure full judicial control over the electoral processes as well as the legal appeals related to it.[47]

The regime's response to these demands was not particularly warm. Liberal judges ventured into treacherous territory, at least from the regime's perspective, when they forcibly demanded an end to emergency law. In fact, the president of the Judges Club infuriated Mubarak when he concluded his speech during the opening session by calling for an end to the state of emergency.[48] Al-Rifai and other pro-reform judges argued that this call to return to the normality was behind the Ministry of Justice's relentless effort to remove the association's liberal board.[49]

The Supreme Constitutional Court

The Supreme Constitutional Court, established in the waning years of the Sadat's presidency, came to full bloom in the 1990s under the commanding stewardship of Chief Justice Awad Al-Morr. Sadat allowed justices on the subservient Supreme Court to serve until they reached the mandatory age of retirement. Thus, during the 1980s, the SCC's jurisprudence was not drastically different from its antecedent. Nevertheless, when new justices replaced the retired old guard, the SCC's role expanded impressively. The court's liberal-activist jurisprudence, despite being self-restrained in certain sensitive matters, provided significant constitutional guarantees for rights and liberties.

---

[47] Nadi al-Quda, *Mu'tamar al-'Adālah al-Awwal, 1986: al-Wathā'iq al-asāsīyah: wathā'iq al-jalsatayn, al-iftitāḥīyah wa-al-khitāmīyah* (al-Qahirah: Nadi al-Quda, 1986), 32–53.

[48] Ibid., 18.

[49] Personal interview with Yahia Al-Rifai, April 5, 2006.

The SCC declared numerous legislation unconstitutional. A number of these rulings had far-reaching effects on Egyptian society and politics. In the following paragraphs, I discuss, briefly, a number of critical judgments in two essential domains: freedom of expression and freedom of association.

The court's adjudication posited that freedom of expression is the cornerstone of every democratic system. It must not be restricted by any means. Accordingly, any legislative restrictions that unacceptably constrain the constitutionally protected freedom of expression are unconstitutional. For instance, in 1993, the SCC affirmed the right to express bona fide criticism of public officials.[50] The court also, in 1995, ruled that the presidents of political parties were not criminally liable for news or commentary published in the parties' newspapers. This was particularly important for protecting dissent and critical opinions published in political parties' newspapers from the government's efforts to crack down on criticism.[51]

The court conjoined freedom of expression to freedom of association. The SCC expanded the right of association for citizens, labor unions, professional syndicates, nongovernmental organizations, and political parties. Consistently, the SCC defended citizens' rights to participate in politics. For instance, in 1986, the SCC scrapped Article 4 of the Protection of the Internal Front and Social Peace Law, which denied nearly all prominent politicians of the pre-1952 regime their political rights indefinitely.[52] Furthermore, the court twice voided the electoral laws on the premise that these electoral rules discriminated against citizens who did not belong to "recognized" parties. The SCC affirmed any citizen legal right to contest elections as an independent candidate. This was critical taking into consideration the regime's grip over political parties. These two historic rulings struck hard at the regime's control of the electoral process. The rulings enabled Islamist candidates, the only credible contender from the regime's perspective, to run and win parliamentary seats. Additionally, these rulings forced Mubarak to dissolve parliament and call for early elections.[53]

In many rulings, the SCC shielded the institutional independence of labor and professional syndicates.[54] Particularly pertinent to this study is the court's

---

[50] Case No. 37 for the 11th Judicial Year, Decided February 6, 1993.
[51] Case No. 25 for the 16th Judicial Year, Decided July 3, 1995.
[52] Case No. 56 of 6th Judicial Year, decided June 31, 1986.
[53] Case No. 131 for the Sixth SCC Judicial Year, decided April 16, 1987 and Case No. 37 of the Ninth SCC Judicial Year, Decided May 19, 1990.
[54] Case No. 6 for the 15th Judicial Year, decided on April 15, 1995, which ruled unconstitutional legislation limiting the right of members of professional syndicates to serve on the board of a workers' syndicate.

position on the bar. The bar has been at the forefront of the struggle for democracy and liberalism. Therefore, successive regimes tried to control its leadership. A fierce confrontation with Sadat ended with legislation (Law 125/ 1981) that sacked the association's elected board. Mubarak sought to ease tension and amended the law but sought to preserve the regime's sway in selecting the bar governing board. The SCC ruled this legislation unconstitutional. The SCC criticized the government for improperly seizing the prerogatives of the bar's general assembly, "a prerogative that no authority can undermine under the provisions of freedom of association."[55]

The court also defended civil society organizations against government oppression. For instance, in 2000, the SCC deemed the widely criticized law on Private Associations and Institutions (Law No. 153 of 1999) unconstitutional, arguing that this law "imposed a wide range of restrictions on the NGOs and grants authorities far-reaching control of their activities."

Furthermore, the SCC played a critical role in expanding the institutional independence of the courts and the Council of State. Article 104 of the Council of State Law and Article 38 of the Judicial Authority Law exempted HJC and the SCAA's decisions regarding the transfer and seconding of judges from any judicial review. The SCC found those provisions unconstitutional. The ruling granted judges the right to appeal these decisions to the Court of Cassation and the HAC. The court also affirmed the independence of judges' associations. The SCC decreed that such associations, because they represent the interests of a constitutionally mandated independent authority, could not be subjected to the oversight of the executive branch.

During the 1990s, the SCC's liberal jurisprudence cultivated public respect and support among the intellectuals. On the other hand, the SCC sought not to alienate the dominant executive branch. This approach manifests itself in many rulings that served the regime's fundamental interests.

For instance, the SCC deemed constitutional legislation that permitted the Mubarak to transfer civilians to military courts. In 1992, an administrative court issued a ruling that limited presidential authority to transfer cases involving civilians to military courts.[56] This was a bold legal challenge to the regime's authority.[57] The regime sought to circumvent the ruling by

---

[55] Abd al-Ḥafīz, "kayfa tas'á al-aḥzāb wa al-Niqābāt litawẓīf al-qaḍā' li-ṣāliḥa," in `Abd al-Fattāh, (ed.), *al-Quḍāh wa-al-iṣlāḥ al-siyāsī*, 415.

[56] Administrative Court Ruling No. 763 of Judicial Year 47 issued on December 8, 1992.

[57] In order to mitigate the public effect of the ruling, the regime media launched a smear campaign against the Administrative Court and the judges who issued the ruling. *al-Gomhuria* December 10, 1992, and *el-Akhbar* December 13, 1992. Using the regime-controlled media to attack unfriendly judges and courts is a common practice under Mubarak.

asking the SCC to issue an explanatory opinion. The SCC issued its opinion on January 30, 1993, which granted the president, under a state of emergency, the authority to transfer sets of cases as well as particular individuals to military tribunals. The HAC had no alternative but to abide by the judgment of the country's highest court.[58]

The court also served the regime by condoning some unpopular economic policies, especially privatization. The 1971 Constitution was prepared and promulgated at a time when Egypt was officially "socialist." The socialist economic language remained even after Sadat embarked on his free-market reforms. The court granted the capitalist-oriented regime a favor by affirming the constitutionality of the privatization laws.[59] Brown summarized the political nature of the SCC's adjudication during this era arguing, "It is difficult to escape the conclusion that the Court carefully judged not only the cases before it but also what the broader political context would permit."[60]

THE REGIME AND THE COURTS: THE HIDDEN-HAND STRATEGIES

Mubarak's relationship with the judiciary is complex and multifaceted. The regime fully understood the need to maintain the perception of independent courts for the bench to be able to perform the critical RSFs needed for regime survival. Nonetheless, Mubarak wanted to keep judges at bay. As with Sadat, this conundrum of autonomy and control characterized the state-court interaction under Mubarak. Courts and judges, for corporate and ideological reasons, aspired to move toward full judicial independence and expanded judicialization. The regime, on the other hand, distinguished between a limited degree of judicialization required for political survival and transformative judicialization that could threaten authoritarian rule. The first was desirable, the latter unacceptable.

The regime wanted to walk the thin line between overt control, which the government considered to be counterproductive, and lack of sway, which might be devastating for the interests of the potentate. Mubarak's lieutenants

---

[58] `Abd al-Barr, *Dawr majlis al-Dawlah al-Misri fi himayat al-huquq wa-al-hurriyat al-`ammah*, al-juz' 3, 191–193.

[59] An example of this trend is the court rulings in Case No. 17 of the 14th SCC judicial year and Case No. 300 of the 16th SCC judicial year. In both cases, the court rendered privatization to be constitutional. Hishām Muḥammad Fawzī, *Raqābat dustūrīyat al-qawānīn: dirāsah muqārinah bayna Amrīkā wa-Miṣr* (al-Qāhirah: Markaz al-Qāhirah li-Dirāsāt Ḥuqūq al-Insān, 1999), 204–206.

[60] Nathan J. Brown, *"Reining in the Executive: What Can the Judiciary Do?"* The Role of Judges in Political Reform in Egypt and the Arab World Conference, Cairo (April 1–3, 2006): 6.

in the Ministry of Justice, the security apparatus, and the presidential administration devised several tactics to influence the judiciary without appearing to infringe on judicial independence. Particularly significant among those tactics were the strategic use of appointments, the power of the purse, and its legislative majority.

Political Appointment Power

In keeping with the bureaucratic character of civil law judiciaries, many senior positions within the judicial system, such as the presidents of the Court of Cassation, Courts of Appeal, and the Council of State, were based on seniority. Mubarak respected the seniority system but thought to use it to his advantage.

Seniority is determined by the date of joining the service and the placement within the appointed list. Rank is a function of the judges' grades in law school. Hence, public records unquestionably reveal which judge is expected to assume a specific position if he continues to advance satisfactorily.[61] In most cases, the most senior vice president who did not reach the mandatory age of retirement would be appointed. As for the Courts of Appeal, the law mandates that the most senior sitting judge would assume the presidency of the Cairo's Court of Appeal, while the second most senior justice would chair the Alexandria's Court.

In general, the regime tried to navigate its way without disrupting the highly regarded seniority system. The incident of Judge Tariq al-Bishri is revealing. Al-Bishri was due to assume the presidency of the Council of State. His liberal jurisprudence and forceful personality made him less than an "ideal" candidate from the regime's perspective. Mubarak was not willing to openly disregard seniority and upset judges. The solution was to persuade the only more senior judge to forsake a lucrative position in the Gulf and return to Egypt to take command of the Council. By doing so, the regime maintained an image of respect for the law and the recognized norms without sacrificing its control mechanisms. When asked about this incident, al-Bishri's response was bitter but respectful: "No comment."[62]

---

[61] It was no wonder that a vice president at the Court of Cassation mentioned during our conversation that he is going to chair the High Judicial Council (HJC) in 2018. Another fairly young administrative prosecutor stated that his seniority would allow him to join the Administrative Prosecution Authority's (APA) Special Council in 2040. Evidently, the regime was aware of such expected advancement and sought to "conscript" those expected senior judges to its forces.

[62] Personal interview with Tariq al-Bishri, May 6, 2006.

This appointment power, coupled with the traditional respect and authority that senior judges command, facilitated the regime's interests within the judiciary. Brown argued, "Even judicial councils that are formally independent might do the executive a favor by concentrating collective judicial power in a few hands. In such a case, it no longer becomes necessary to co-opt each judge; a few senior judges at the apex of the system might be sufficient."[63] These senior judges could sway colleagues and subordinates to accommodate the regime's interests.

On the other hand, the regime took full advantage of the presidential prerogative to appoint central positions in the court system, especially the PP and his deputies. The PPD had been empowered since 1951 not only with investigating misdemeanors and felonies but also prosecuting (or refraining from indicting) those cases. Besides, the PPD has the sole authority to inspect jails and other detention facilities.[64] This PP can influence the prosecutors directly (he has the authority to reprimand all public prosecutors) or indirectly (through transfer to remote districts). This authority is particularly valuable in handling politically sensitive matters: public demonstrations, torture, and political opposition, particularly Islamists.

In his first decade in office and in accordance with the regime's effort to build the rule of law image, the public prosecutors were chosen from amongst the ranks of senior prosecutors and judges. This changed dramatically in the 1990s when Mubarak became confident of his grip over the polity. The appointment of Ragaa al-Arabi as the PP in 1991 was met by a storm of criticism. Al-Arabi was appointed on the background of his previous service at the State Security Prosecution Department (SSPD). The SSPD is an office of the PPD empowered to prosecute politically sensitive cases. To promote al-Arabi to this crucial position, Mubarak's surpassed many senior judges. The same happened in 2000 with his successor, Maher Abd al-Wahid, who served for an extended period as an assistant to the Minister of Justice.[65]

---

[63] Brown, "Reining in the Executive," 137–138.

[64] The official edicts of the Public Prosecution Office had clearly chosen to limit the authority of public prosecutors to inspect detention facilities. Human rights activists argued that this lack of oversight encourages security services to continue their human rights abuses. In response to a report by the *Sawasya* Center for Human Rights and Anti-Discrimination that detailed systematic abuses in detention facilities, and after a series of high-profile and embarrassing torture cases, the Public Prosecutor had to issue a public statement recognizing the problem and vowing that the Prosecution Office would continue its periodic inspection of all detention facilities.

[65] Abd Allāh Khalīl, "al-nā'ib al-'āmm: bayna al-sulṭah al-qaḍā'īyah wa al-sulṭah al-tanfīdhīyah," in ʿAbd al-Fattāḥ (ed.), *al-Quḍāh wa-al-iṣlāḥ al-siyāsī*, 125.

TABLE 5.1 *Details the professional career of the Public Prosecutor Abd al-Majed Mahmoud*

Year	Position
1985–1991	District-Attorney
1991–1992	First District-Attorney
1992–1993	President in Cairo Court of Appeal
1993–1996	Deputy-director, PPD Inspection Department
1996–1999	Assistant Public Prosecutor, Cairo Appeals Prosecution
1999–2006	Deputy Public Prosecutor and Director of the PPD Inspection Department
2006–2012 (2013)	Public Prosecutor

Abd al-Wahid's successor Abd al-Majed Mahmoud is another illuminating example of the nature of political appointment (see Table 5.1). Mahmoud joined the judiciary in the late 1960s and served within the PPD. The following table shows his judicial functions since that service. In about forty years of service, Mahmoud sat on the bench as a judge for a few years. Since 1985, he has been a sitting judge for only a single year (1992–1993).

Mubarak repeatedly used the PPD to realize two related goals. First, publicly highlighting its "judiciality" and impartiality, the regime delegated embarrassing incidents or scandals to this office. This delegation worked as a buffer against opposition demands for independent investigations. Second, the absolute authority of the PP and his associates ensured that "political" cases were handled in such a way that benefited the regime. Human rights activists claimed that public prosecutors, particularly the SSPD, abused their power of pre-trial detention to detain opposition members, mostly from the Muslim Brotherhood. A former prosecutor narrated his experience with a politically sensitive case as follows:

> The Public Prosecutor's directives have been to detain all individuals accused of marching and endangering public safety for four days. This was perceived as deterrence for them and others from engaging in such actions in the future. Some students, accused of such offenses, were brought before me. There was no evidence, and I did not think they committed any crime; hence, I ordered their immediate release. The very next day, I was summoned to the District Attorney's office. The DA, my superior, irately asked why did I, despite the PP's directives, released those students? I stated my position, and he was not persuaded, asserting that I should abide by the PP's directives. I argued with him and explicitly indicated that I would follow

my professional judgment. After this incident, he stopped assigning such cases to me.[66]

The regime created the SSPD in order to mitigate the influence of the independent and courageous prosecutors.[67] The SSPD was staffed with highly trusted prosecutors who received lucrative incentives: generous financial remuneration, ample opportunities for professional development, and career prospects inside and outside the judicial institution.[68] A notable Egyptian law professor contended,

> The SSPD was pressured to provide a legal façade for many of the State Security's measures against opposition political forces … Furthermore, the PPD deserted its duty to inspect prisons that include political prisoners, even though the law requires it to examine these facilities at least once a month.[69]

Some public prosecutors and judges proved their loyalty to the regime by handling embarrassing cases.[70] Usually, those were chosen to fill the critical positions within the PPD's Inspection Department (PPDID), and the Courts of First Instance. Besides using the powers of the PP, the regime utilized the minister of justice's appointment power to select "reliable" judges to preside over the Courts of First Instance and many critical posts within the Ministry of Justice's hierarchy, particularly the powerful JID.[71]

In addition to commanding significant financial and administrative resources, presidents of the Courts of First Instance have considerable seniority and experience in comparison to the junior judges on the court.[72] In many

---

[66] Personal interview with a judge at Banī Suwayf Court of First Instance, Cairo, March 3, 2006.

[67] The State Security Prosecution was established by ministerial decree in 1952. It has jurisdiction to prosecute cases related to military felonies, state security crimes, as well as newspapers and press-related offenses.

[68] Ragaa Al-Arabi, a former PP, and former Giza governor Maher al-Gendi are but a few examples of judges who served at the State Security Prosecution Department and were later rewarded with well-paid posts within the judiciary and outside it.

[69] Abū Qamar, *al-Qaḍā' wa-al-wāqi' al-siyāsī: dirāsah taṭbīqīyah 'alá al-qaḍā' ayn al-idārī wa-al-dustūrī fī Miṣr*, 154.

[70] Sameh al-Kashef is a good example. After helping the regime with an exceptionally troubling case, El-Kashef joined the critical Judicial Inspection Department (JID) where he served as deputy-director. He was also chosen as the official spokesperson for the 2005 Higher Election Commission, entrusted with supervising all legislative elections in Egypt. Hamadah Imam, *al-Jins al-siyasi: al-'alaqah al-khafiyah bayna al-sultah wa-al-sihafah wa-al-fannanat* (al-Jīzah: Madbuli al-Saghir, 2002), 174.

[71] The Judicial Inspection Department controls the transfer (to different geographical locations) and seconding (to the Ministry of Justice, exceptional courts, and extrajudicial assignments of judges).

[72] These senior judges also can recommend judges to lucrative positions in "specialized courts" where compensation is higher, and the workload is considerably lighter. One junior judge maintained that the president of Northern Cairo First Instance Court hinted to the prospect of

occasions, the hand-picked presidents of these courts were able to subdue the courts' general assemblies. These arrangements hindered the "individual autonomy" of junior judges to make independent decisions without someone looking over their shoulders or giving them direct instructions or hints of desired behavior.[73]

This power was used to serve the regime's interests from behind the scenes. On the pretext that there are many minor administrative details that the courts' general assemblies have no aptitude for, the standard practice has been for the general assembly to grant its president the authority to second judges to extrajudicial missions, amend case assignments, and issue search and surveillance warrants. The minister of justice also had a freehand in appointing the director and members of JID. Because of its essential role in matters of promotion, transfer, secondment, and foreign assignment, the JID could be used as a political tool against activist judges.[74]

The Power of the Purse

While presidential appointment prerogatives were used to the fullest to install friendly judges in crucial positions, the regime developed alternative sets of tools to influence judges in critical offices or those judges expected to assume leadership roles in the future. Mubarak's regime became superbly skilled in attracting support from those who would be in leading positions in various judicial institutions. Judge al-Khodiry maintained,

> The government had tried using force and intimidation against judges in 1969 and did not succeed. It came out of this battle with disgrace, and humiliation and judges returned more powerful than they were. Now the government is trying enticement, hoping it would be more successful and less troubling.[75]

such appointments as he was trying to convince a junior judge of the merits of taking "state interests" into account. An interview with a judge at Northern Cairo First Instance Court, January 5, 2011.

[73] Fiss argued that the individual autonomy of a judge would be violated by the exercise of power by one judge (or by a group of judges) over another judge to mandate a decision that, in estimation of the subordinate judge, is not required by precedent or by reasonable interpretation of substantive or procedural rules of law. Owen M. Fiss, "The Right Degree of Independence," 55–56.

[74] The JID was used during the 2005–2007 judicial–executive clashes to exert pressure on liberal judges. Many junior liberal judges related in personal interviews that JID inspectors visited them with much higher frequency than other judges.

[75] *Al-Masry al-Youm*, May 25, 2007.

The regime used its monopoly over the "purse" to attract support from judges in different forms: seconding judges to extrajudicial positions with considerable financial benefits,[76] recruiting relatives of influential judges to serve within the ranks of the executive or the legislature, rewarding loyal judges with high-income positions upon reaching the mandatory age of retirement. The government also utilized the Ministry of Justice's resources to favor some judges and public prosecutors.[77]

Financial benefits in a Third World nation such as Egypt are critical for keeping up with the rising cost of living. While judicial remuneration is generally among the best pay scales in the country, it is still not sufficient to cover the expenses of a middle-class family. Due to inflation and rising prices, the government granted judges numerous allowances. The government was aware of judges' financial problems and used them for its benefit. A number of judges interviewed believe that the government has structured salaries in a way to make them ever more dependent upon the plethora of supplementary incomes.

Seconding judges to extrajudicial assignments within the Ministry of Justice or other government ministries and public companies was not an innovative practice: Nasser and Sadat used it before. However, this praxis became a well-known trademark during Mubarak's reign for many reasons. First, the method became widespread, especially among Council of State members. Unofficial estimates and personal inquiries indicated that every member of the administrative judiciary served at least once outside the Council. Second, financial rewards for this extrajudicial service have become considerable. In many instances, a judge received a much more generous remuneration from his extrajudicial work than from his official salary and benefits.

From the regime's perspective, seconding serves three interrelated objectives. First, it was used as a laboratory for testing judges' resolve; especially those who are expected, according to seniority, to hold critical posts. Those judges who proved loyal and committed to the regime's political line continued to serve off the bench for many years or until seniority permits them to hold critical positions within the judicial hierarchy. Those senior

---

[76] Seconding in the Egyptian judicial and political discourse refers to the process by which the government appoints judges to perform legal functions in different state and public-sector institutions.

[77] Yahi al-Rafai, *mulḥaq Istiqlāl al-qaḍā' wa-miḥnat al-intikhābāt* (al-Qahirah: al-Maktab al-Miṣrī al-Ḥadīth, 2004), 22–23.

prosecutors who proved their loyalty usually staff many critical positions especially OSSA. The OSSA had the authority to sanction the rulings of ESSC.[78]

Second, seconding was used to reward (and punish) specific actions. In the absence of any objective criteria for seconding judges, secondment could be an instrument to reward some and castigate others according to the wishes of the executive authority. Hussam al-Ghiryani, who according to seniority was expected to be the president of the Court of Cassation, was seconded to the Ministry of Justice. After proving unwavering in his commitment to justice and judicial independence, his appointment was not extended, and he has not served off the bench since.[79]

Third, seconding was used as a means to change judges' attitudes and perceptions vis-à-vis the executive and its interests. Several scholars argued that these professional ties create a special affinity with the executive branch. That is similar to what Fiss dubs "cultural ties" that "could cause the judge to identify with one party more than the other."[80] After all,

> Secondment for long stretches of time trains the judges on thinking of judicial affairs with the executive branch's eyes, and they [judges] come back after this indoctrination to hold high-ranking positions (such as Public Prosecutor or Minister of Justice) that can hinder judicial independence. Also, this secondment and the accompanying privileges foster a mindset that considers executive posts superior to the judicial bench.[81]

There has been a lively debate among the judicial community about the effect of this extrajudicial work on the judges' impartiality, public trust, and even their ability to perform their original duties. Some senior judges, within both the courts and administrative judiciary, claimed that serving "off-the-bench" did not affect their jurisprudence. Jamal Dahroug, first vice president of the Council of State (retired in 2006), stated, "That is entirely not true. Serving as government advisor did not affect my rulings."[82] Most judges, however, agreed that serving off the bench is counterproductive. "I am principally against working outside the Council. It affects the impartiality of the bench. I only served for a brief period and under strict conditions and on a

---

[78] Abd Allāh Khalīl, "al-nā'ib al-'āmm bin al-sulṭah al-qaḍā'īyah wa al-sulṭah al-tanfīdhīyah," in *dwar al-qudah fī al-aslah al-siasi*, 129.

[79] Personal interview with Hussam al-Ghiryani, April 2, 2006.

[80] Fiss, *"The Right Degree of Independence,"* 5.

[81] Yūnus, *Istiqlāl al-qaḍā*, 31.

[82] Personal with Jamal Dahroug, December 17, 2005.

national mission," said a Council's junior vice president.[83] A notable law professor and lawyer maintained in this regard, "Seconding Council of State's judges to government offices or public-sector corporations reshapes their incentive structure and makes them cater to administrative agencies rather than do justice to citizens."[84] He added,

> Seconding some judges to the governorates [Egypt's territorial administrative divisions], local governments, and to the People's Assembly, all this affects judicial independence. This means that the state uses a 'carrot and stick' policy. Add to this the appointment of some justices after retirement to be mayors of cities or assistant-governors ... judges are human.[85]

Mahmoud Mekki linked seconding to corruption: "Look for the names of judges who were condemned for rigging and manipulating elections, and you will find that those are the select few that enjoy the spoils of secondment."[86] Even judges who defend the necessity for the secondment of judges argue, "A most considerable majority of judges are against secondment, and they only accept it under the pressure of living standards and financial obligations."[87]

Another way the regime used its control over financial resources to influence judges was by appointing some senior judges to lucrative government positions. Pro-regime judges had a quota, usually two or three, in the positions of governors. For instance, former Council vice president Yahia Abd El-Magid and former Judge Adly Hussein served as a governor of Sharkia and Kalyobiya Governorates respectively. In addition, former president of the Council of State Godat al-Malt headed the influential General Authority of Accounting. These judges joined an extended list of loyal judges that the regime rewarded for their service in the past. This list included Ali Abd-al-Shakur, former president of the Southern Cairo Court of First Instance, who was responsible for running the affairs of many professional syndicates, was awarded the position of governor of Kfor El-Sheikh. Other examples included the former judges and later minister of justice Mahmoud Abu El-Lil, who served as governor of many governorates, as well as Maher al-Gindi, a former high-ranking member of the SSPD, who served as governor of Giza.

---

[83] Personal interview with Judge Mahmoud Abd Altif, vice president of the Council of State, December 17, 2005.

[84] Ahmad Subhi Mansur, ed., *Dawr al-qada fi da`m thaqafat al-mujtama` al-madani: halaqat niqashiyah* (Al-Qahirah: Markaz Ibn Khaldun lil-Dirasat al-Inmaiyah, 1997), 59.

[85] Ibid. 56.

[86] *Al-Masry al-Youm*, May 25, 2007.

[87] Ibid.

The regime also provided considerable benefits for judges serving in critical positions, including official cars, government residences, subsidized land, and housing, etc. Former Judges Club president Al-Rafai wrote,

> It's a norm nowadays that members of the PPD – especially the SSPD, Presidents of Courts of First Instances and members of the JID receive preferential financial treatment in direct opposition to Article 68 of the Judicial Authority Law. This is a colossal and disastrous intrusion on judicial independence.[88]

Furthermore, high-ranking judges received considerable financial benefits through their participation in government-assigned arbitrations and other legal consultations.[89] Additionally, members of the HJC, the SCAA, and their counterparts in the APA and SCA received generous remuneration for putting their respective councils' stamps of approval on the executive branch's discretionary assignments of judges to various electoral processes. Former Council of State's president Amin al-Mahdi was reported to have sent back to the Ministry of Justice a check for of 100,000 EGP. The Ministry of Justice gave this astounding amount, equivalent at that time to about $30,000, to each president of the various judicial authorities during the 2,000 parliamentary elections.[90]

Another technique the regime used was appointing or withholding appointment for family members of some senior justices to influence their decisions. For instance, the government offered lucrative positions to the sons of judges in the upper echelon of the judicial hierarchy, who could not be seconded. These politically motivated appointments functioned as an indirect reward for senior justices. For example, Khaled Siri Siyam was appointed deputy-chairman and later chairman of the Capital Market Authority, a highly lucrative position. Before this, Siyam served as the legal advisor to the minister of finance.[91] Siyam was the son of Siri Siyam, president of the HJC 2010–2011. Another example of these practices in the past was the son of the then-president of the Court of Cassation, Ahmed Shawqi al-Miliji, who was

---

[88] *Al-Ahram*, January 19, 1984.
[89] For instance, both Sayd Nofel, then the president of the Council of State and Jamal Dahroug, the first vice president of the Council and the former member of the Supreme Presidential Election Committee, have served on the Trade Arbitration Authority. *Al-Ahram*, October 24, 2006.
[90] Sayyid Ismāʿīl Dayf Allāh, *Nazāhat al-intikhābāt wa-istiqlāl al-qaḍāʾ* (al-Qahirah: Markaz al-Qahirah li-Dirāsāt Ḥuqūq al-Insān, 2000), 214.
[91] *Al-Ahram*, February 22, 2008.

appointed as a legal advisor to the speaker of the People's Assembly.[92] Those examples were only the tip of the iceberg, as many such appointments were not reported. The appointment of female judges in 2007 and 2008 was another indication of the regime's use of appointment power to reward loyal judges. Most of the female judges were daughters of prominent judges, serving and retired.[93]

Legislative Control

In addition to utilizing its appointment power and financial resources, the regime used its hegemony over the legislative machinery to issue laws to impel the courts and shape its adjudication. This has taken different forms: chief among them was removing politically sensitive legal affairs from courts' jurisdiction, manipulating the retirement age for political objectives, and extending the judicial domain to include matters not typically related to the adjudication functions.

Limiting the Courts' Jurisdiction

While Mubarak, keeping with his court-based survival strategy, did not establish new exceptional courts, the government continued to utilize the Sadat's era exceptional courts. The regime used its overwhelming legislative majority to draft legislation that limited the jurisdiction of regular courts. Vice president of the Court of Cassation Hisham El-Bastawissi, a leading figure in the reform camp, argued,

> The reason behind establishing any exceptional courts is the inability of the despotic state to control the judiciary. Hence, it creates exceptional courts. Had it managed to control the bench and make it malleable to its will, it would not need to establish military courts. But because the judiciary in Egypt strives to keep its independence and does not yield to the executive branch's attempts to manipulate it or contain it, the creation of exceptional tribunals was a solution the government found to free itself from unwelcome judicial rulings.[94]

Nonetheless, in contrast to Nasser's regime, Mubarak was aware of the adverse effect these exceptional tribunals exert on the ability of the judiciary

---

[92] Many prominent writers argued that this might have influenced al-Miliji's position in the famous case of the administrative Courts' rulings for opposition candidates. *Al-Wafd*, July 11, 1989.

[93] *Al-Masry al-Youm*, March 15, 2007.

[94] *Al-Karama*, July 5, 2007.

to perform the RSFs. Thus, those exceptional legal avenues were saved for the most severe political enemies: militant Islamists in the 1980s and early 1990s and the Muslim Brotherhood since and did not extend in general to the secular opposition.

Another manifestation of limiting the jurisdictional domain of influence was related to the SCC. The regime enacted legislation to restrict the jurisdiction of the SCC. In the 1990s, the court ruled unconstitutional some tax laws. The SCC's docket included many other cases of a similar nature, and the court was expected to rule in favor of the plaintiffs.[95] The regime's response was to use its legislative arsenal to amend the SCC's law. Moustafa explained,

> Mubarak issued a presidential decree that restricted retroactive compensation claims as the result of SCC taxation rulings to the party initiating the constitutional petition. All other citizens were effectively denied the right to retroactive compensation for the same unconstitutional legislation.[96]

The Retirement Age

The regime repeatedly used the NDP's clear majority in the People's Assembly to change judges' retirement age for political reasons. The government, because of its dependence on the pivotal role of the various high judicial councils, had repeatedly sought to increase the retirement age to keep loyal supporters on the top of the various judicial institutions. Also, the government used the retirement age to keep trusted judges at the pinnacle of the different judicial institutions. This legislative tool was used to lure support from senior judges approaching the mandatory age of retirement. The government's mere hint to increase the retirement age could act as an incentive for senior judges to tow the government's line.

In a single decade, between 1993 and 2003 the law was changed on three different occasions.

- Law-Decree 183/1993 increased the retirement age from 60 to 64.
- Law 3/2002 raised the retirement age from 64 to 66.
- Law-Decree 159/2003 increased the retirement age from 66 to 68.[97]

---

[95] The SCC's tax rulings came at the worst possible time for the regime. They coincided with the aftermath of the Luxor Massacre of November 1997. This brutal attack against tourists sharply decreased the number of foreign tourists coming to Egypt. Tourism is among Egypt's top sources of foreign currency. In addition to draining the coffers of the regime, Mubarak had to channel massive funds to the security forces and its war against violent Islamic groups. Therefore, a case could be made that the rulings were related to fundamental regime interests.

[96] Moustafa, *The Struggle for Constitutional Power*, 179.

[97] In 2007, the mandatory age of retirement was increased again to seventy years.

Overburdening the Courts

By delegating many non-judicial responsibilities to the courts, the regime used the court to achieve several political objectives. An excellent example of this strategy was the Democratic Guarantees of Professional Syndicates Law, (Law 100/1993). The government by the early 1990s had become increasingly apprehensive of the Muslim Brotherhood's control over many powerful professional syndicates, i.e., the bar, the Egyptian Medical Association, and the Egyptian Engineers Association. This legislation required a one-third quorum of members for the election of syndicates' officers to be valid. This was an exceptionally high threshold in a country where turnout has been meager. If the turnout did not reach this threshold, a judicial commission chaired by a senior judge and four judges and four members of the syndicate was entrusted with all the powers of the syndicate's board of directors. In this case, the regime kept the courts busy with missions outside the scope of the judicial mandate and did not appear to be hindering the democratic process. In fact, "the judiciary will appear before the masses and the intellectuals as the obstacle to democracy in the syndicates."[98]

JUDICIALIZATION OF POLITICS IN THE THIRD MILLENNIA

Between 1981 and 2000, both the regime and judges used available resources to expand their political influence. Judges eager to extend their authority and political role capitalized on the regime's reliance on their RSFs. Judges used the available resources in an effort to transform a "sham constitution into a strong one." The regime, on the other hand, used its massive advantage in the realm of appointment, financial resources, and legislative majority to restrain the process of judicialization. Neither judges nor the regime have been able to achieve every objective they desire. The courts pushed judicialization beyond what the regime initially wanted, and the government sought to push back without undermining its survival strategy.

The new millennia ushered a historical milestone in the executive–judicial relationship. The regime's objectives and calculations started to change with the grooming of Gamal Mubarak. The First Family's appraisal of the role the judiciary played to further regime survival was overshadowed by the suspicion of the negative impact judicialization might have on the succession process.

---

[98] `Abd al-Barr, *Dawr majlis al-Dawlah al-Misri fi himayat al-huquq wa-al-hurriyat al-`ammah*, al-juz' 3, 356–357.

This new stance became indeed evident from the regime's perspective when the SCC ruled the parliamentary electoral law unconstitutional.[99]

The 1971 Constitution enshrined a noteworthy procedure of mandating judicial oversight of elections. For three decades, Sadat and Mubarak negated this provision through a complex set of legal and political maneuvers and managed to keep judicial oversight superficial. In 2000, the SCC rendered a landmark ruling requiring full judicial oversight of all polling locations. This principle was later dubbed "One Judge, One Box." The decision affirmed the high stakes in judicial politics in Egypt. It dealt a significant blow to the managed liberalization program of Sadat and Mubarak.[100] Judges' oversight of the electoral contests would limit the ability of the security apparatus to determine electoral results. This oversight could potentially end the NDP's domination of the elected offices, including the presidency.

The SCC was conscious of its delicate position as a liberal-reformer agent of the rule of law within an authoritarian context. The court, knowing the impact of its decision, sought to minimize its effect by validating numerous laws enacted by the previous "illegitimate" legislatures. This ruling confirmed the proposition that members of the SCC were interpreting the law "politic-ally" by trying to advance the process of democratization and the rule of law incrementally. The following day's newspapers perfectly reflected this. The front page of the state-owned al-Ahram newspaper reported, "The Supreme Constitutional Court's Ruling Affirms the Constitutionality of all Legislations Enacted by the Parliament." The leading opposition newspaper al-Wafd ran an enormous headline on the front page declaring "The People's Assembly . . . Illegitimate!!"

Mubarak, tied to his rhetoric on legality, had little room to maneuver. The president taking into consideration the significance of the court's RSFs for the survival of his regime, had a measured response. This approach is very different from the strategy employed by Nasser in the 1950s and 1960s. It was also different from the method used by Sisi later, and other authoritarian leaders when faced with adversary rulings. Shetreet, for example, underscores the experience of Ecuador's Constitutional Court wherein 2007; all nine judges were removed following an unpopular decision. "The removal was

---

[99] The SCC's ruling concerning Article 24 of Egypt's Law of Political Participation (73/1956), which governs the monitoring of parliamentary elections.

[100] For an insider and detailed account of the regime's rigging techniques, see Mahmoud Qatri, *Tazwīr Dawlah: shihādāt. al-istibdād wa-tazwīr al-intikhābāt* (al-Jīzah: Markaz al-Mustaqbal al-Miṣrī, 2005).

executed by a congressional vote lacking any legal basis. According to Ecuadorian law, the Constitutional Court's judges are removable only by impeachment. Still, this was the third time in three years that judges were removed by Congress."[101]

The regime had at least to appear in compliance with the ruling. Bold confrontation with the SCC or non-implementation of the verdict could ruin the regime's survival strategy. Nonetheless, in keeping with the conundrum of survival and control, the administration tried to minimize the net political effect of the ruling. The president publicly announced that the government would comply with the high-court decision. The state-controlled media celebrated this as a clear sign of Mubarak's commitment to the rule of law and respect for the judiciary. However, behind the scenes, Mubarak's protégés instituted several practical mechanisms to ensure a degree of control over the electoral processes. This minimal or legalistic compliance meant that a member of the judiciary would supervise each polling station, as the ruling mandates. Nevertheless, the regime expanded the definition of "members of the judiciary" to include the administrative prosecutors and members of the SCA. The executive branch, represented by the minister of justice, also maintained control over assigning judges to the specific electoral districts, determining their compensation, and decreeing the procedures judges applied in their administration of the election.

Nonetheless, the 2000 parliamentary election was a historical event. No bureaucratic intrusions were sufficient to maintain the NDP's political supremacy. The ruling party lost its majority (72 percent in the previous assembly). Out of the 444 elected seats in the People's Assembly, the NDP managed to win only 172 seats or 38 percent and was only rescued after 216 "pro-NDP" independent candidates joined the party after the election, giving it a substantial majority.[102] The dismal performance of the NDP, coupled with the strong showing of the Muslim Brotherhood candidates, forced the regime for the first time to use its heavy hand. Security forces blocked voters in many opposition strongholds. The election was rightly described as "Cracks in

---

[101] Shimon Shetreet, "Creating a Culture of Judicial Independence," in Shimon Shetreet and Christopher Forsyth (eds.), *The Culture of Judicial Independence: Conceptual Foundations and Practical Challenges*, 24.

[102] In previous elections, NDP's nomination was generally sufficient to secure a parliamentary seat. However, many members of the ruling party, encouraged by the increased guarantees of fairness with judicial oversight, challenged the ruling party's official candidates. After its abysmal showing at the booth, the ruling party had no alternative but to try to incorporate those "pro-NDP" candidates. Pro-NDP candidates were NDP members that were not nominated by the party and ran as independent candidates.

Egypt's Electoral Engineering."[103] The NDP seemed to be on the same declining path that the PRI in Mexico went through. Genuine political change, while far on the horizon, was possible for the first time since the foundation of the republic.

These developments forced the regime to reconsider its approach to the SCC. The perception of the SCC, and for that matter all courts, moved from a partner to pariah. Limiting the SCC's activism became a primary objective. Again, Mubarak wanted to "contain" the court without completely forgoing his appeal to legality and the rule of law. Thus, instead of dismissing justices or amending the courts' legislation to limit its jurisdiction or change its mandate, as many authoritarian rulers would have done, Mubarak waited for the opportunity to achieve his objectives with minimal political cost. He had an ample opportunity when the SCC Chief Justice M. Wali al-Din Galal retired in August 2001.[104] Mubarak's court packing plan was simple: appoint a trusted chief justice and use him to fill the SCC with highly trusted justices.

As with other Egyptian courts, the established norm in the SCC was strict seniority. The position of chief justice went to the most senior member of the court, making it virtually a self-perpetuating body. This seniority-based method made possible a remarkable degree of independence and activism. To rein in the court, Mubarak used his appointment power to bring in a series of chief justices who were closely aligned with the presidency. The first such figure, Fathi Naguib, was widely perceived as a pro-regime figure. Naturally, the appointment of Chief Justice Naguib, an outsider, was met with some muffled resentment from the SCC's justices, who justifiably perceived it as a breach of an established norm. Mustafa nicely summarized the public reaction to this move, stating

> Opposition parties, the human rights community, and legal scholars were stunned by the announcement. Not only had Fathi Naguib proved his loyalty to the regime over the years, but he was the very same person who had drafted the vast majority of the regime's illiberal legislation over the previous decade, including the oppressive law 153/1999 that the SCC had struck down only months earlier. Moreover, by selecting a Chief Justice from outside of the justices sitting on the Supreme Constitutional Court, Mubarak also broke a strong norm that had developed over the previous two decades.[105]

---

[103] Vickie Langohr, "Cracks in Egypt's Electoral Engineering: The 2000 Vote," *Middle East Report Online*, 7 November 2000.

[104] Up until 2011, the SCC law empowered the president with the exclusive progrative to appoint the SCC chief justice without any input from the court or the legislature.

[105] Mustafa, *The Struggle for Constitutional Power*, 199.

However, Naguib was a cleverly calculated choice. After all, Naguib was a respected jurist and as the president of the Court of Cassation was Egypt's most senior judge. Besides, Naguib's tactful persona lessened the opposition to his appointment. By breaking the norm, Mubarak restored his latitude in appointing trusted political allies to this critical post. This appointment power would prove to be a precious political asset, especially after the SCC's chief justice was selected to chair of the powerful Supreme Presidential Election Committee (SPEC).

What was noticeable was the inability or unwillingness of the SCC to protest or challenge this appointment. The spineless nature of the court became apparent in the lack of action against this clear executive infringement on judicial independence. Activist and lawyer Essam e-Islamboli petitioned the administrative court to invalidate the presidential decree appointing a chief justice from outside the SCC; the court transferred the case to the SCC. The SCC first waited four long years before reviewing the case and then a year later dismissed it on procedural grounds.[106]

Upon assuming office, Naguib announced that he would increase the number of justices. In doing so, the regime took advantage of the fact that neither the 1971 Constitution nor the SCC law set the court's membership. However, the established practice since 1979 set the number of justices at nine.[107] Naguib increased the number of justices dramatically to fifteen. The recruits came mostly from the Courts of Cassation and the appeals courts. This new recruitment method broke another established norm of recruiting the SCC's justices predominantly from the Council of State. The Council's judges are typically more inclined to restrict government authority. However, to obscure these actions, Naguib nominated the first female SCC justice, the nationalist lawyer Tahani Al-Gibali. Her appointment was celebrated in state-controlled media as a milestone of gender equality.

With the appointment of Naguib and the subsequent backing of the court, the regime was assured that the SCC's activism era had ended.[108] The SCC under Chief Justice Naguib took a conservative stance. First, the SCC

---

[106] Case No. 1 of the 28th Judicial Year, issued June 10, 2007.

[107] There was no work-related justification for the increase in the SCC's membership. The court has performed its functions fully with nine members on the bench. Personal interview with a deputy chief jusruce of the SCC, March 13, 2018.

[108] Although he is theoretically merely *primus inter pares*, the chief judge has considerable administrative power in managing the court's docket, assigning the court's opinion writing, and, most notably, nominating judges to the court. The SCC law specifies that members of the court are appointed by presidential decree from among two candidates, one is chosen by the general assembly of the court and the other by the chief judge.

accepted the idea of an abstract review. This proposal, which was rejected under Al-Morr, stripped the SCC of its judicial review power in favor of a more advisory role before the drafting of legislation.[109] Naguib also affirmed his commitment to an apolitical court.[110] Naguib's court did not trouble the regime with any significant ruling. The most critical SCC ruling under his leadership was to exempt the People's Assembly decision on presidential nomination from any judicial revision. Naguib criticized the SCC's prior activism. Mustafa quoted him:

> They [SCC's justices] were issuing rulings that were bombs in order to win the support of the opposition parties. They were very pleased with the rulings, but the rulings were not in the interest of the country. This needed to be corrected. Now the president [Mubarak] can be assured that the court will make rulings that are in the interest of the country and yet still maintain its independence.[111]

Foreseeing Naguib's reaching the age of retirement in 2004, the regime debated extending the mandatory retirement age of all judges to sixty-eight (he was born in 1938). However, in August 2003 Naguib passed away. Once more, another trusted regime loyalist was chosen to replace him. Mubarak's choice was Mamdouh Marra – then-president of the Cairo Court of Appeal. Again, appointing an enormously senior judge reflected the regime's awareness of the crucial role seniority plays within a bureaucratic judiciary.[112] Marra, like Naguib, was a dutiful regime loyalist.[113] He, like his predecessor, worked for many years within the ranks of the Ministry of Justice and presided over the all-important JID.[114] This was the very same position that Naguib held before assuming the presidency of the Court of Cassation.

Under Marra, the SCC's domestication advanced even further. The court became a primary political instrument to subdue the activism of other courts. For instance, the SCC included members of the APA and the SCA within

---

[109] Naguib's comments during a meeting with the editors-in-chief of some major Egyptian newspapers. *Al-Ahram*, January 14, 2003.

[110] Interview with Naguib in *al-Ahram*, November 9, 2002.

[111] Moustafa, *The Struggle for Constitutional Power*, 201.

[112] Gamal Dahroug, then the Council of State's first vice president, stated, "Seniority is sacred (he repeated it 3 times). Seniority is the heart of our legal system. Without seniority, our institutions cannot function." Personal interview with Gamal Dahroug, December 17, 2005.

[113] During his tenure in the JID, Marra' issued a memorandum that directed all judges to submit to the JID any cases in which a celebrity or a high-ranking official was implicated. This memorandum had created an outcry among many judges who perceived it as a flagrant infringement on their judicial independence. This is at the heart of Fiss' second concept of judicial independence: individual autonomy.

[114] *Al-Ahram*, August 27, 2003.

members of the judicial authorities empowered to supervise elections.[115] Marra reached the mandatory age of retirement in 2006. He was replaced by the PP Maher Abd al-Wahid. After Abd al-Wahid's retirement in 2009, Mubarak's choice was no other than the president of Southern Cairo Court of First Instance Farouk Sultan. Sultan who was neither a senior judge nor versed in constitutional law was appointed on his background as a regime's devotee. Sultan spent most of his professional life in military courts and state security courts. He was accused of undermining the bar and other candidates in his capacity as superintendent of their elections. It was clear that his appointment was meant to place a highly trusted ally at the helm of the SCC and SPEC in advance of the anticipated 2011 presidential elections. This continued a pattern of political appointments to that position in a manner that has sidelined the SCC.

Still, when the regime grew confident that the SCC was neutralized, another avenue for judicial activism opened. This is another substantiation of the need to study the political role of the courts within a single analytical framework. The pessimistic conclusion advanced by Moustafa, while technically correct on his assessment of the SCC, is inaccurate if we include all of Egypt's courts.

The Judges Club, which had fallen under the pro-regime leadership of Moqbel Shaker since 1991, changed hands. In 2001, the reformer Zakaria Abd Al-Aziz surprisingly defeated the three-term president Shaker. However, Abd al-Aziz's triumph was limited, as Shaker's faction of quintessential pro-regime judges maintained their majority on the board and sought to curtail the activism that the new president vowed to embrace. The regime convinced the president of Court of Cassation, in his capacity as the president of the club's general assembly, to order an early election, hoping that heavy regime lobbying would reinstate Shaker as president.

---

[115] Al-Ghiryani infuriated the regime by issuing a ruling invalidating the 2000 parliamentary election results in the East Cairo district of Zeitoun. This was terribly embarrassing for the regime, as the MP for this district was no other than Zakaria Azmy, Mubarak's long-time chief of staff and a prominent NDP leader. The court reasoned that some of those who supervised the Al-Zeitoun district were not members of the judiciary, but rather members of the State Cases Authority and the APA, two authorities affiliated with the Ministry of Judge. Hence, the election in this district did not meet the requirements of full judicial oversight mandated by the constitution and the SCC. The regime responded by launching a campaign affirming the judicial credentials of these authorities. When this media campaign proved lacking in silencing the court, the regime enlisted the support of the SCC. The regime asked the SCC to provide its explanatory opinion of the definition of judicial authorities. The SCC, now under the pro-regime leadership, sided with the government and declared that members of these two authorities are indeed within the definition of members of the judicial authorities mandated to supervise elections. *Majallat al-Quḍāh*, March 12, 2004, 18–19 and 55–61.

This meddling infuriated many on-the-fence judges, who perceived the early election decision as a blatant intrusion on judicial affairs and an assault on judicial independence. Judges, historically, have been particularly sensitive about such interferences. With turnout approaching 50 percent for the first time in the association's history; Abd Al-Aziz not only triumphed over Shaker, but his *Change and Renewal* list won every seat on the board. This major electoral upset instituted, for the first time in a decade, a robust pro-reform board. This would prove instrumental in the court–executive clashes in the years to come.[116]

Naturally, the pro-reform board under Abd al-Aziz's strong leadership portended an amplified political profile for the Judges Club. It also insinuated more vocal demands for a new judiciary law. The regime tried to preempt the club's activism by demanding its compliance with Law 84/2002, i.e., answer to the Ministry of Social Affairs. Judges were steadfast and utterly refused to comply with such law.[117] Abd al-Aziz was successful in framing government demands as an assault on judicial independence and himself as the champion of the cause. This ensured widespread support among the judicial corps and will prove instrumental in future confrontations with the regime.

After foiling the regime's plan, the association defeated another attempt spearheaded by the Court of Cassation's president Fathy Khalifa. Khalifa sought to place the association under the auspices of the HJC. The club's general assembly convened to discuss the matter, which was marked by escalating tension with Khalifa apparently on the losing side of the debate. The HJC responded by reprimanding Hussam al-Ghiryani and Ahmed Mekki, the most senior judges in the reform camp who spearheaded the defense of the association's institutional independence.[118] Then, on March

---

[116] This activism was not confined to judicial politics or even broader domestic affairs, but it transcended to regional and international relations. In March 2003, in an unusually bold move, the Judges Club issued a high-profile statement against the United States invasion of Iraq.

[117] In 1991, the pro-reform board drafted a new Law of Judicial Authority to achieve more guarantees of judicial independence. The regime counterattacked by supporting Shaker to the presidency, which he won over the pro-reform candidate. To the dismay of many independent judges, under Shaker, the proposed law technically went into a state of hibernation. The club's monthly magazine nearly disappeared between 1991 and 2001. The editors, on the other hand, dedicated the quarterly magazine to legal studies only in addition to some editorial comments. Those editorial comments reveal little interest in emphasizing judicial independence or judicial activism in favor of more conciliatory appraisal of the regime and accentuation on the privileges and preferential financial treatment that the regime bestowed on judges.

[118] Mohamed Hussam al-Ghiryani and Ahmed Mekki, were considered the godfathers of the 2005 independent movement within the judiciary. Both former judges were disciples of the al-Rafai pro-reform liberal wing within the Court of Cassation and the Judges Club.

12, 2004, 3,000 judges convened for another extraordinary general assembly to protest the HJC's actions against al-Ghiryani and Mekki.

The Judges Club's active role was aided by the success of the pro-reform camp in Alexandria Judges Club's elections. This Alexandria Judges Club was historically known for its firm positions in defense of judicial independence and a liberal-activist judicial role. During the 1990s, it became lackluster under the leadership of one of the regime collaborators, Ezzat 'Agwa. In April 2004, hardline reformer Mahmoud Rida al-Khodiry crushed 'Agwa's massive electoral machine and won the chairmanship of the club. Al-Khodiry electoral triumph would soon pay dividends in furthering judicial activism. Exactly one year later, the pro-reform Alexandria Judges Club convened a general assembly that sparked judicial action for full electoral oversight, and, for the first time, judges floated the idea of an election boycott.[119]

The Judges Club picked up on its Alexandria affiliate's ideas and convened a general assembly on May 13, 2005. This action could not have come at a worse time for the regime; Mubarak had previously announced a constitutional amendment to allow multiple candidates to compete in the 2005 presidential elections.[120] This amendment to the presidential election procedures was tied to the international pressure on Egypt to accelerate the stagnated political reform. In his speech at the Twentieth Anniversary of the National Endowment for Democracy, President George W. Bush maintained, "The great and proud nation of Egypt has shown the way toward peace in the Middle East, and now should show the way toward democracy in the Middle East." Officials in Egypt had initially thought that Bush's "Forward Strategy for Freedom in the Middle East" would wither away. The US president

---

[119] Al-Khodiry represented the strong activist wing within the reform camp. He had his webpage, frequently wrote in independent and opposition parties' newspapers, appeared on TV (independent stations, of course), and attended lectures, seminars, and conferences. He linked the struggle for judicial independence to the overall crusade for democracy, arguing, "Mistaken are those who think that the fight for judicial independence is going to be settled after amending the Law of Judicial Authority . . . The proclamation of this amendment is only a fraction of the battle for the independence of Egyptian people will in change and reform. The Egyptian people struggle to have a robust judicial authority that can furnish its part in reform and change. In fact, what moves the positions of judges, as part of the Egyptian people that yearns for genuine freedom and democracy, is that Egypt would attain, in addition to a powerful judicial authority capable of performing its obligation to safeguard freedoms, a real legislative authority that can perform its role in drafting legislation apart from the hegemony and control of the executive authority." *Al-Masry al-Youm*, June 15, 2006.

[120] Under the 1971 Constitution, parliament, which was dominated by Mubarak's NDP, was to nominate one candidate, and Egyptians vote "yes" or "no" in a presidential referendum. Opposition has long demanded a multicandidate and competitive presidential election to replace the meaningless referendums.

proved them wrong, and in his 2004 State of the Union Address, reiterated his administration's commitment to democratizing the Middle East forcibly:

> As long as the Middle East remains a place of tyranny and despair and anger, it will continue to produce men and movements that threaten the safety of America and our friends. So America is pursuing a forward strategy of freedom in the greater Middle East. We will challenge the enemies of reform, confront the allies of terror, and expect a higher standard from our friend.

Many seasoned observers of American–Egyptian relations noticed the strained relationship between the two governments. American officials were increasingly exerting pressure on Egypt to show signs of substantive political reform.[121] Mubarak's regime, which depended on its strategic alliance with the United States, had to demonstrate adherence to the new trend in US foreign policy. This dependency explains Mubarak's decision to change presidential elections procedures after twenty-four years in office.

A managed and predetermined presidential election seemed like a good idea to demonstrate apparent democratization without surrendering political power. To ensure control, the regime established the SPEC. The SPEC's composition was another example of using the judiciary to legitimize regime domination. The ten-member commission was presided over by the chief justice of the SCC and included four other ex-officio judges. The rest of the commission was made up of five independent public figures: three selected by the People's Assembly and two selected by the Shura Council. The regime's media repeatedly emphasized the judicial nature of the commission, even though half of the SPEC's members were political appointees. Here again, the regime made sure to use reliable judges as smokescreens for its control of the political process. Mubarak needed the legitimation stamp that judicial oversight would bring to a predetermined election.[122]

---

[121] "Mubarak cornered over US push for Middle East reform," *The Telegraph*, March 7, 2004, and "The American Factor", *al-Ahram Weekly*, June 9–15, 2005.

[122] With the purpose of controlling the outcomes of the presidential elections, Mubarak's legal advisors installed a number of strict conditions that basically only the NDP candidate possessed. By controlling the roster of potential contenders, Mubarak was assured of a resounding victory. The legal opposition parties were chronically weak; none controlled the 5 percent threshold in the two houses of parliament to field a candidate. The main fear was an independent candidate affiliated with or supported by the Muslim Brotherhood. To avoid such an "unpleasant" contender, the regime imposed stiff, or more accurately prohibitive, conditions for such an independent candidate. With the aim of contriving an image of comparative elections, the regime granted opposition parties, though not independent candidates, a one-time exception. This allowed the regime to brag about the "first democratically-elected leader in Egypt's history."

With the purpose of avoiding any future constitutional review, the amendments regarding the presidential election procedures were presented to the SCC for abstract review. This prior stamp of approval is what the SCC had precisely refused to undertake during the leadership of the liberal chief justice Awad Al-Morr. However, the now tamed SCC did not hesitate to provide such a service to the regime, even though it hindered the court's authority of judicial review in the future.[123]

The controversial nature of such a constitutional amendment led many opposition parties, independent groups, and civil society organizations to call on the public to either boycott the referendum or vote against the proposed changes. The regime used all of its old tricks to rig the votes, inflate the turnout, and obtain favorable results. The Judges Club established an independent committee to report on the referendum. The committee's report contradicted the regime's repeated assertion that the voting was conducted under judicial oversight. The report lambasted the government, declaring that the referendum "was NOT conducted under judicial oversight."[124] It further exposed the substantial variation in turnout between the few polling operations under the oversight of members of the judiciary, with an average turnout of merely 3 percent and the other operations supervised by public sector employees, where the turnout reached the unthinkable rate of 100 percent.[125]

Pro-reform judges found in the report another worrisome indication of the regime's exploitation of judges to achieve narrow political goals, without providing any assurance that judges would have the power to oversee a fair and free election. Many judges concluded that the regime wanted to abuse the trust that the public endow judges with to achieve its objectives. Judges understood that the government needed their oversight to negate the growing demands for international observers. The reform camp wanted to seize the moment to force the regime into making significant concessions on two issues: strengthen their electoral mandate and boast judicial institutional independence.[126]

---

[123] In their defense, the SCC's justices were compelled to perform this function through the regime control of the legislative machinery. The SCC could not defy the law of the land. Personal interview with deputy chief justice of the SCC, March 13, 2018.

[124] *Majalat Al-Qudah*, September 2, 2005, 59.

[125] Ibid., 59–63.

[126] The British newspaper, *The Guardian*, on September 7, 2005, stated, "The judges simply refuse to continue to take the blame for rigged elections where they are only allowed partial oversight. They are also demanding an end to government interference in their affairs. These demands are in line with Egypt's legal obligations under international treaties. Britain, on behalf of the

The regime counterstrategy was predictable: it used its allies in the HJC to counter the Judges Club's demands and exploited the government-controlled media to stir up public opinion against judges. The press claimed that pro-reform judges were engaged in politics, and even alleged that some leading judges were Muslim Brotherhood sympathizers. Critical to the success of the regime strategy was the position of the HJC. To resist judges' pressure, without appearing to infringe on judicial independence, the regime enlisted the support of the HJC.[127]

The HJC rebuffed the Judges Club's threat to boycott the election unless changes were enacted to the Law of Political Participation and the Law of Judicial Authority. The HJC issued a public statement asserting its exclusive right to represent judges and claimed that election oversight was "judges' sacred duty" and subject to no conditions. This statement was published on the front pages of the semiofficial al-Ahram and other regime-controlled newspapers and widely advertised on the national TV and radio stations.[128]

The HJC went further on the attack to claim that "fewer than a handful of judges appeared on satellite channels to discuss political issues, elections, and criticize fellow judges ... This is a flagrant violation of the Law of Judicial Authority which bans judges from working with or being involved in politics." The statement also attempted to sideline the autonomous role of the Judges Club, maintaining that the HJC decided to recognize only opinions attributed to the courts' general assemblies. This served the regime well as the general assemblies of many courts, particularly the First Instance Courts, were thoroughly controlled by the regime's handpicked presidents.

The HJC allowed the regime precious time to withstand the calls to amend the Law of Judicial Authority as a precondition for judicial oversight of the election; claiming that it was gathering the opinions of judges and courts the HJC forestalled, granting the regime time to conduct the elections and at the same time disavowing any responsibility for disregarding judges' demands. This was particularly significant considering Mubarak's electoral platform.

EU, has every right to insist they are included in Egypt's action plan if the government fails to respond to the judges before the parliamentary elections planned for next month. In fact, the EU is legally mandated to do so under its association agreement with Egypt."

[127] Pro-reform judges argued that the regime lured the president and some members of the HJC through a promise of raising the mandatory retirement age that would allow those senior judges to serve for an additional two years. See, for example, the president of the Judges Club Zakaria 'Abd al-Aziz's speech before the association's general assembly, September 2, 2005. The Judges Club's assemblies' proceedings in the period of study were distributed in a multimedia form (DVD). I was able to obtain these through Judge Zakaria 'Abd al-Aziz's cooperation.

[128] *Al-Ahram*, May 17, 2005.

Mubarak's 2005 presidential program pledged to "enhance judicial independence through enacting amendments to the Law of Judicial Authority." Also, the program mandated "strengthening the independence of the judicial authority by abolishing the SCJP, the SPP, and consequently, the Court of Ethics."

After the official announcement of the results, the Judges Club, aiming to bridge the gap with the regime, sent Mubarak a congratulatory message, calling on the president to fulfill his electoral promises concerning judicial independence. In yet another sign of the regime's political calculations, all government-controlled media highlighted the Judges Club's message on their front pages. Besides, the NDP newspaper *Mayo* celebrated the Club's note on its front page, a clear indication of the regime's use of the judiciary to attain public support.[129]

The tension between judges and the regime escalated again amidst the parliamentary elections, November 9–December 7, 2005. The administrative courts were instrumental in attempting to provide for the background conditions for free and fair elections. This was exemplified in numerous rulings:[130]

- First, the courts ordered the Ministry of Interior to "clean" the electoral rolls of voters that were added to favor influential government candidates.
- Second, the courts constantly upheld the right of opposition and independent candidates to receive accurate and updated copies of the electorate rolls.
- Third, the courts upheld the candidates' representatives' right to attend and observe the ballot counting.
- Fourth, the courts granted civil society organizations the right to monitor all phases of the electoral process. Furthermore, the court ruled that civil society organizations were entitled to install closed-circuit cameras and monitors during the counting process.

Pro-reform judges wanted to oversee the electoral process in its entirety. The regime, however, sought to use judicial oversight to ensure political acceptance without sacrificing its grip on the electoral outcomes. Liberal judges rightly believed that judicial control was tied to the expanded activist political role of the courts. The leading reformist judge Hussam al-Ghiryani said, "We want a truly independent judiciary that can protect freedoms and

---

[129] *Mayo*, June 12, 2005.
[130] Iṣām al-Dīn Muḥammad Ḥasan, *Shuhūd ʿayān ʿalá al-intikhābāt al-barlamānīyah al-Miṣrīyah li-ʾām 2005* (al-Qāhirah: al-Majmūʿah al-Muttaḥidah, 2006), 85–93.

human rights. A principal right is a right not to have one's will falsified through rigged elections."[131]

The confrontation between the pro-reform judges and the executive aided by the HJC escalated during and after the parliamentary elections. The Judges Club in tandem with the civil society organizations, opposition parties and groups, and independent media exposed the electoral fraud and the security forces' interference with the electoral process. Pro-reform judges publicly condemned the corruption of some executive-friendly judges who breached the public's trust. The bar compiled a "Black List" of thirteen judges accused of electoral fraud in their oversight of the elections and published by independent newspapers and bloggers. For the first time, judges collaborating with the executive were publicly exposed. This revelation had the potential of undermining the regime's strategy of control from within. The regime persuaded the HJC to file a complaint against two leading pro-reform judges, Mahmoud Mekki and Hisham al-Bastawisi.

The government wanted the trial as a showcase to the hefty price that had to be paid for opposing the regime. Mubarak, however, miscalculated the cohesiveness of the judicial community and the public support for pro-reform judges. The Judges Club organized a sit-in at its headquarters, demonstrations, and marches before the high-court building. The club held an extraordinary session of its general assembly in support of the two judges. The power of collective judicial action proved effective.[132] Public support of the pro-reform judges was also deep and widespread. Eventually, all of Egypt's independent civil society organizations, professional syndicates, and university professors' organizations, as well as opposition parties and groups, were steadfast in their support of the two judges. Everyone understood the trial as a fight for judicial independence. An Egyptian blogger captured the essence of the conflict: "What is at stake is the future autonomy of an already embattled judiciary to assert itself as a check to executive power and will. At the core of this struggle is the state's attempt to nationalize the judiciary as its principal legitimation tool."[133]

As expected, the regime denied any responsibility for this attack on judicial independence, declaring that it is solely an internal judicial matter. Mubarak stated that this was "a dispute among judges, specifically between the Judges

---

[131] Personal interview with Hussam al-Ghiryani, May 7, 2006.

[132] Judges understand their symbolic public power vis-à-vis the regime. Shahat quotes a senior judge: "The regime considers the gathering of 100 judges much more than gathering of a 1000 simple worker in a company." Shahat, *"dor Nadi al-qudah fi ta'ziz istqlal alquda wa al'ashalh alsiasi,"* 395.

[133] https://arabist.net/blog/2006/5/17/the-judges-vs-the-state-a-primer.html?rq=judges

Club and the High Judicial Council, neither the government nor the state has anything at all to do with it." In personal interviews with the minister of justice Mahmoud Abu El-Leil and the director of the JID Intsar Nasim, both reiterated the presidential position, claiming that neither the Ministry of Justice nor the executive branch had anything to do with "purely internal conflict within the judicial authority."[134]

During the proceedings of the trial, every day was marked by violent confrontations between the security forces and the activists. Muslim Brotherhood and independent MPs who participated in the demonstrations were not spared the regime's heavy-handed repressive measures. On May 18th, the center of the capital, where the ruling in the trial of Mekki and El-Bastawisi was to be made, was under what amounted to martial law. An estimated 25,000 police officers, some uniformed, some plain clothed, some in full riot gear, all but sealed off the Freedom Tringle,[135] fearing that public protests were getting out of hand. In the end, intensive public pressure forced the regime to yield.[136]

The disciplinary board cleared Mekki and reprimanded El-Bastawisi. By any account, this outcome was a clear victory for pro-reform judges and their allies in the civil society and within the public. El-Bastawisi acknowledged the pivotal role the public opinion played: "Without the people and the street, the Board's decision would have been a slaughter for us. Devoid of the people who were beaten and imprisoned for their solidarity with us, the ruling would have been very different. We could have been fired or maybe even imprisoned."[137] Shielded by public opinion support, pro-reform judges were saved from the regime's intimidation efforts. The regime's strategy to browbeat liberal judges, through sacking two prominent vice presidents of the Court of Cassation, failed.

After the dust settled, public attention once again turned to the broader struggle on the Judicial Authority Law. As stated earlier, Mubarak made augmenting judicial independence one of his primary reelection campaign's

---

[134] Personal interviews with Minister of Justice Mahmoud Abou- El-Leil and the Director of the Judicial Inspection Department Intsar Nasim in the Ministry of Judge's Headquarter, May 9, 2006.

[135] Freedom Tringle denotes the parcel of land in downtown Cairo where the Judges Club, the Journalists Syndicate, and the bar association headquarters located.

[136] I was fortunate to conduct field research in Cairo and Alexandria during the crisis. Through professional ties to both the pro-reform camp and the ruling party, I was granted access to many closed-door events.

[137] Judge al-Bastawisi's comments before Journalists Syndicate in the occasion of the syndicate's commemoration of him and Judge Mekki, 22 June 2006.

promises. He reiterated this in his 2005 speech before the Parliament: "I spoke of deepening the rule of law and furthering the respect for the decisions of the judiciary and the provisions of swift justice."

The government, while acting to provide a perception of supporting judicial independence, did not want to forgo its influence on the judiciary. This was clear in the regime's acceptance of some of the judges' demands and disregard for others. Law 142/2006 enhanced the power of the HJC in some critical matters, including requiring the Council's approval for most judicial appointments. The amendments rescinded the minister of justice's administrative authority over public prosecutors. In addition, the judiciary was granted an independent budget, prepared by the HJC in collaboration with the minister of finance. Also, Article 83 accorded judges the right to appeal disciplinary sanctions.[138] Additionally, the regime halted its efforts to increase the mandatory retirement age, allowing the ill-famed chief justice of the SCC and the presidents of the Court of Cassation to leave the bench.[139] Nevertheless, the regime discarded other essential demands, including

1. Objective criteria for the selection of the PP, the presidents of the First Instance Courts, and seconding judges.
2. Comprehensive HJC's control over the JID.
3. Restoring the elected representatives on the HJC.
4. Legislative affirmation of the institutional independence of the Judges Club.
5. Judicial police force under the auspices of the HJC to enforce judicial rulings and assist judges in their extrajudicial functions, principally electoral oversight.

In retrospect, it appeared inevitable that the judges' bold challenge alerted the regime to the inconvenient role an independent judiciary could play in the post-Mubarak era. The regime was, for quite some time, restructuring the political landscape to favor Gamal Mubarak's bid to succeed his ailing father. Mubarak was once again torn between the quest for political survival and the struggle for control. The regime decision to disregard popular acceptance in favor of political consolidation was a fatal mistake. The 2010 parliamentary election was critical for the succession process. "Free and fair" elections, even

---

[138] Since 1972, judges demanded to have the right to appeal their disciplinary actions. At last, the amendments instituted a first-degree adjudication before Cairo's Court of Appeal and an appeal level at the Court of Cassation.

[139] In 2007, after the retirement of those judges, the regime issued Law 17/2007 that increased the mandatory retirement age to seventy.

by the very modest Egyptian standards, would have meant a strong showing for the opposition and particularly the Muslim Brotherhood. To ensure a smooth succession, the NDP decided to end judges' oversight of the electoral process. The regime amended the constitution to bring the electoral process to the pre-2000 era.

To disguise the intent to manipulate the elections, the regime created a smokescreen of other constitutional amendments. After amending a single article of the constitution in a quarter century, Mubarak in 2007 suddenly was changing thirty-four constitutional provisions.[140] Al-Khodiry criticized the proposed constitutional amendments, arguing, "I am confident that the change of Article 88 of the Constitution on the judicial oversight of the election is the primary goal behind all these amendments. In fact, all the other modifications are to disguise this change that the government wants to carry out."[141] The leading pro-reform justice El-Bastawisi put it bluntly, "the purpose of amending Article 88 is to ensure the rigging of elections."[142] This is how most Egyptians came to perceive the regime's actions.

While the amended Article 88 effectively removed the judges' watchful eyes over the electoral process, the regime, for reasons related to its political survival strategy based on the judiciary, created a High Election Commission (HEC) chaired by the president of Cairo Court of Appeal.[143] Moreover, the regime continued to insist that judges would still run the elections. The *al-Ahram* newspaper's main headline was Mubarak's statement denying that the amendment would "remove judges from supervising the elections."[144] The president stated, "All respect to judges who are not going to be away from the elections."[145] The People's Assembly Speaker Fathi Sorour, the chief

---

[140] The amendment of Article 179 granted the government massive powers that run counter to constitutional guarantees for personal freedoms and individual rights. Under the banner of combating terrorism, the president is given the right to refer any suspect to exceptional, primarily military, courts. The security services can now carry out arrests, search homes, and conduct wiretaps without a court order.

[141] *Al-Masry al-Youm*, January 8, 2007.

[142] *Al-Karama*, July 5, 2007.

[143] Law 18/2007 amended the Law of Political Participation to create this committee. In addition to the president of Cairo's court of Appeal (chair), the committee members are the president of Alexandria's Court of Appeal, a Court of Cassation's deputy-president chosen by the HJC, a Council of State's deputy-president chosen by the Special Council of Administrative Affairs, and seven other members, three of them must be from the ranks of retired judges. Nevertheless, the law mandated that the under-secretary for Judicial Inspection Affairs assumed the position of secretary general of the committee. This was another indication of the pivotal role the JID has played in service of the regime.

[144] *Al-Ahram*, January 12, 2007.

[145] *Al-Gomhuria*, January 28, 2007.

government spokesperson on legal matters, was quoted in the first page of the *al-Gomhouria* newspaper stating, "The constitutional amendments did not remove judges from electoral oversight, but just restructured it [judicial oversight]."[46] It was rather striking that the referendum on the constitutional amendments that removed full judicial oversight of the election was reported in the semiofficial *El-Akhbar* as, "36 Million Electors Will Vote under *Full Judicial Oversight.*"[47] In the *El-Akbar* 's front page, the writer cited some NDP leaders who delineated the reasons for the amendment. They claimed that the change was due to the inability of the small number of judges to cover all ballot boxes, the delay in administering justice because of judges' involvement in the electoral process, and the protection of judges from any mischiefs against them.[48] Even after the amendment of Article 88 that limited the judicial oversight of the electoral process, the regime continued to use judges to confer legitimacy on the election. During the 2008 local elections, *El-Akbar* newspaper's front page had the following headline "Judicial Oversight of the Municipal Elections."[49] Of course, this claim had no creed in the street.

Faced with a choice between maintaining its political survival strategy and losing some control at one end or forsaking the courts' RSFs and ensuring political hegemony, the regime opted for the latter. This decision proved fatal for Mubarak, his family, and his government. Removing judges from their umpire position overseeing the electoral process might have lessened their political influence in the short run, but it caused irreversible damage to the regime survival strategy. After all, "The current judicial movement is founded on the democratic reformist discourse and the patriotic discourse that the regime uses."[50]

After amending the constitution, Mubarak sought to eliminate what he perceived as the last castle of judicial activism the Judges Club. The administration hoped to weaken the Judges Club by encouraging judicial associations in the governorates to declare their institutional independence.[51] The regime encouraged its devotees to establish rival institutions to claim representation of

---

[46] *Al-Gomhuria*, February 12, 2007.

[47] *El-Akhbar*, March 21, 2007.

[48] *El-Akhbar*, March 13, 2007.

[49] *El-Akhbar*, February 28, 2008.

[50] Yūnus, *Istiqlāl al-qaḍā*, 63.

[51] Ahemd Mekki stated that after the Judges Club's strong position against Sadat's restrictive legislation in 1980, the regime tried to weaken the association. The minister of justice at that time started an idea to establish clubs in the governorates. These entities were used to attack the association in 2005 after it declared its position regarding the elections. *El-Fagr*, December 11, 2006.

crucial segments of the judicial community. For instance, the president of the Court of Cassation, Moqbel Shaker, established a new association for justices at the Court of Cassation.[152] The "new" association claimed to represent justices at the highest court, which traditionally led the charge for judicial independence.

The regime also launched a campaign against the Judges Club's leadership in Cairo and Alexandria. The strategic use of the JID and the massive interference of the state security succeeded in ousting the outspoken regime critic, al-Khodiry from the chairmanship of Alexandria Judges club.[153] The government then moved to focus on the Judges Club in Cairo. The government utilized its control over financial resources to limit the Judges Club's ability to use its resources to champion the cause of judicial independence and to provide services for its members. In addition to defending the corporate interests of the judiciary, the club historically attracted support through the services it offered. This included loans, low-cost housing, social activities, reduced cell phone plans, and subsidized transportation.

In addition, the Ministry of Justice established in each court a "benefits office" to provide the social and economic services that the Judges Clubs traditionally delivered. It was rather striking that this approach was first proposed during the late 1960s to weaken the association under Nasser. Mubarak's, who until 2005 was using Sadat's playbook, now moved to embracing Nasser's punitive strategies. In 2009, the intense pressure succeeded in bringing a change at the helm of the Judges Club. The regime's partisan, Ahmed El-Zend, was elected president and regime loyalists won most seats on the association's board of directors.

Despite being forced out of the leadership of the Judges Club, liberal judges have proved themselves true to their liberal and rule-of-law tradition and, in the process of defending such ideals, have gained significant public opinion support that is going to be an asset in judicial–executive confrontations in the years to come. A notable Egyptian law professor put it nicely:

> On the national level the "rule of law" has also transformed into perhaps the single most unifying slogan shared by the many strands of Egyptian

---

[152] This became an issue when the HJC interfered to grant the new association some of the Judges Club's quota of *Haj* visas, a highly important and symbolic issue. *El-Badeel*, July 10, 2007.

[153] A number of judges argued, during my interviews, that the JID exerted strong pressure, in the form of continuous and detailed review of their cases, on judges serving in Alexandria to abandon their support for al-Khodiry. In addition, al-Khodiry's unorthodox tactics and his interest in the broader political questions of reform, liberalism, and democracy angered many conservative judges.

opposition groups, professional associations, intellectuals and civil society activists. Though split between seculars and Islamists, liberals and Arab socialists, these diverse actors are nonetheless united today in their shared demand for the "rule of law" as a solution to national problems.[154]

Once more when the regime successfully undermined an outlet for judicial activism, another avenue became active. This was an aperture that the government could hardly control.[155] The Council of State carried the torch of judicial activism and the rule of law. While the judiciary and especially the Council have been active since the 1970s, judicial activism reached new levels in 2010. When the regime labored to limit political freedom and sideline the representative institutions, citizens view the Council as a last resort to challenge the regime's appalling policies. In many rulings, the Council sided with rights and liberties against government domination.[156] The last year of Mubarak's long reign witnessed an onslaught of rulings that undermined the basic foundations of the semi-authoritarian regime. Mubarak had two alternatives: first, follow the courts' rulings and maintain the image of legality but lose some control over the society or, second, disregard the decisions to retain power but shoulder the political damage. The regime decided again to take that second route and in doing so further undermined the judicial RSFs and opened the floodgate of a popular uprising. This was particularly true because many rulings touched on the ever-important issues of elections, corruption, state powers, civil societ, etc.

For instance, the Council was the only legal recourse to address the massive fraud that accompanied the 2010 preliminary elections. The administrative courts received more than 1,600 disputes that covered almost all districts. The rulings revealed that in many cases the polls that were held dispute prior

---

[154] Shalakany, "I Heard It All Before," 837.

[155] After the 1984 legislative amendments, the Council of State became largely a self-governing institution. The regime had only two alternatives to influence the administrative judiciary. The first was through the power of senior judges whom the regime built strong ties with. The second was through seconding judges to non-judicial posts with significant financial rewards.

[156] The Council's first vice-president, Mohamed Attia, affirmed the political role of the Council in the January 25th Revolution. In his first ever newspaper interview, Attia was asked, If the Council's rulings against the previous regime did contribute in the creation of the January 25th Revolution? His answer was straightforward: "YES, the administrative court issued a number of important rulings under my leadership since 2008. Notable among them are the rulings to stop exporting natural gas to Israel, allowing aid convoys to reach Gaze, the expulsion of university guards. These rulings were issued during the panicle of the regime's power and they offended it. These rulings made people feel that there was a judicial authority still protects them and stood guard against the infringements and illegal decisions. The rulings gave people hope and exposed the level of corruption that the Revolution irrupted to eradicate." *Shorouk*, June 21, 2011.

rulings from administrative courts.[157] The Council rescinded these results, undermining any regime's claim to legality. The court also dealt a symbolic personal rebuke to Mubarak by invalidating the results of the district in which he voted.[158] The bold headline of Shorouk during the run-off round was "The High Administrative Court: the Forthcoming Parliament is mired in illegality."[159] The public anger over the 2010 parliament was one of the immediate reasons behind the mass protest of January 2011.

The Council ordered the HEC to increase the number of judges supervising the elections to address the systematic rigging and intimidation of the security forces and ruling party thugs. The Council questioned the constitutionality of Article 24 of the Law of the Political Participation that limited the number of judges who can supervise elections.[160] Along the same lines, the administrative courts nullified an HEC decision to constrain civil society organizations' monitoring of the elections. The administrative courts ruled that these agencies are entitled to monitor the electoral process, and no government entity could forgo this right.

Other rulings undermined the regime's legitimacy in more ways than one. Corruption cases were center stage in the court docket. Exposing corruption helped to delegitimize the regime. Numerous corruption cases were adjudicated before the administrative judiciary. Arguably one of the most definitive rulings was the Council's ruling to nullify the government's decision to export natural gas to Israel below market prices. What rubbed salt in the wound was that the government fought tooth and nail against this highly publicized ruling; a course of action that shocked many ordinary Egyptians.[161] The Council's vice president Bayoumi M. Bayoumi revealed that Mubarak exerted intense pressure on the HAC's leadership during the court's deliberations on the case regarding the export of natural gas to Israel. In the end, the HAC allowed the export to continue but again condemned the unfair conditions and the incredibly low prices. The court also stated a new legal principle that any citizen is entitled to question government decisions related to natural recourses.[162]

[157] Al-Ahram, September 2, 2011.
[158] Shorouk, December 2, 2010.
[159] Shorouk, December 5, 2010.
[160] Shorouk, November 19, 2010.
[161] After the 25th of January Revolution, judicial investigations and media reports suggest that influential regime leaders including Mubarak's sons personally enriched their coffers.
[162] Shorouk, December 31, 2010.

Another highly publicized case was that of Madinaty.[163] The developer of this project is Talaat Moustafa Group (TMG), one of the largest construction companies in the Middle East. The public opinion was furious because of the conditions of the sale and the no-bidding process. The court invalidated the contract on technical grounds.[164] The government's decision to appeal the ruling added fuel to the fire. After the government and TMG appealed the ruling, the HAC upheld the lower court's ruling. The HAC decreed that New Urban Communities Authority broke the law when it sold land for the Madinaty project to a TMG. This final and binding decision did not put the matter to rest as the government continued to maneuver to circumvent the ruling.[165] The court had to intervene again to quash the illegal government decisions.[166] All this kept the scandal before the public eyes and intensified public outrage.

In the sphere of right to assembly, the administrative courts invalidated the Lawyers Syndicate's decision requiring all lawyers to acquire annual practicing licenses to be able to practice law and remain active members of the syndicate.[167] The decision was widely perceived as an attempt by the regime to deny opposition lawyers their voting rights and ensure regime control of the syndicate's governing board.[168]

Furthermore, the Council came decisively on the side of academic freedom ordering the removal of uniform police officers from all national universities. These forces dominated all aspects of academic instruction, activities, and faculty and administration appointments. The court ruled that the existence of these forces is a violation of Article 18 of the 1971 Constitution, which guaranteed the independence of universities. The court argued that this presence hampered academic freedom and integrity. The court ordered the establishment of civilian guard under the control of university administrators to replace the police and state security.[169] Again, the government

---

[163] Madinaty is a new mega-development in the outskirts of Cairo. Madinaty is a city built on 33 million-square-meter (355 million-square-foot). TMG was owned and managed by Hisham Talaat Moustafa, a leading member of the NDP ruling party, a chairman of a People's Assembly influential committee, and a close confidant of Gamal Mubarak.

[164] *Shorouk*, June 29, 2010.

[165] *Shorouk*, September 15, 2010.

[166] *Shorouk*, November 24, 2010.

[167] The syndicate is Egypt's equivalent of the bar association. Historically, the syndicate was a center of anti-regime activities to expand rights and defend liberties.

[168] *Al-Ahram* December 12, 2010.

[169] *Al-Ahram* December 12, 2010.

refused to carry out such a decision, fearing loss of control over the vibrant students' community.

The Council also guarded the freedom of speech. For the government to control news, the National Telecommunication Regulatory Authority directed all telecommunication providers to acquire its approval before disseminating any news or information via text messages. The court quashed this decision as a violation of the freedom of speech guaranteed in the constitution.[170] The government's action underscored the regime's growing apprehension of the viable alternative, "uncontrolled" media. The new press provided very different coverage from the regime-owned TV, radio, or newspapers. The Council challenged government efforts to curtail social media. This proved critical to the success of the popular uprising in January 2011.

Another critical ruling was related to torture and human rights abuses. After human rights activists exposed police brutality in police stations through cell phone photos and videos, the minister of interior issued a directive banning cell phones from police stations. Lawyers challenged the decision before the administrative courts. The courts repealed the decree and permitted citizens to use their phones in police stations. Again, this ruling put a spotlight on the security forces abuses, which was another critical cause for public anger against the brutal regime of Mubarak.

In the dominion of socioeconomic rights, the Council was as active as it was in political rights. The administrative court ruled, in March 2010, in favor of setting a minimum wage. The government tried to circumvent the ruling, and the court reasserted itself again in October 2010.[171] The decision was a sharp rebuke to the regime's neoconservative trickledown economic policies that widened the gap between the rich and the power in Egypt. The media coverage of the ruling highlighted the abject poverty of more than 40 percent of the society, who survive on less than two dollars a day. Again, the government's refusal to enforce the court's ruling kept the issue in the public spotlight. It was no surprise that "social justice" was one of the three leading slogans during the January 25th Revolution.[172]

Furthermore, the Council was the only recourse available for lower-income Egyptians to challenge the neoconservative policies of Mubarak regime.[173] The court invalidated the minster of health's decision to use substandards

[170] *Shorouk*, November 27, 2010.
[171] *Shorouk*, October 26, 2010.
[172] The three slogans were "Freedom, Dignity, and Social Justice."
[173] *Al-Ahram* January 5, 2011.

interferon treatment for Hepatitis C (HCV) patients.[174] This was highly symbolic in a country where doctors and researchers claim that the between 15 percent and 20 percent of Egyptians are HCV positive. The Ministry of Health's minuscule budget could not provide the medication for the growing number of patients. This ruling focused attention on a government that continued to increase the budget for the security forces at the expense of social services.

CONCLUSION

Judges have influenced the cycle of openness and repression that is a defining characteristic of the authoritarian regime in Egypt. Each new president, upon assuming office introduced liberalizing measures that aimed at gaining public acceptance. However, with no term limit and massive presidential powers, all of Egypt's leaders grow impatient with the limited degree of the rule of law that was instituted initially to preserve their political power.[175] Courts and judges infuriated the dominant presidency when they tried to move from the "rule by law" instituted to preserve the essence of authoritarian leadership to the "rule of law" that conceivably, in the long run, could put an end to authoritarianism.

The SCC's historical 2000 ruling and the subsequent judicial activism in 2005–2006 was a landmark change in Egypt's modern politics. "In 2006 Egypt's judges mobilized for independence of the judiciary – an unprecedented development in which dissent came from within the core structures of the state itself. The judges made a potent case against the regime, alleging corruption and malpractice within the electoral system and demanding freedom from political influence."[176]

This judicial challenge to the executive authority was instrumental for many reasons. First, it was the led by judges that the state-media could not

---

[174] This is a very serious problem in Egypt. The World Health Organization reported, "Egypt has a very high prevalence of HCV and a high morbidity and mortality from chronic liver disease, cirrhosis, and hepatocellular carcinoma. Approximately 20% of Egyptian blood donors are anti-HCV positive. Egypt has higher rates of HCV than neighboring countries as well as other countries in the world with comparable socioeconomic conditions and hygienic standards for invasive medical, dental, or paramedical procedures." www.who.int/csr/disease/hepatitis/whocdscsrlyo2003/en/index4.html.

[175] Professional jealousy of the judges' elevated stature might be another reason behind the attitudes of some regime bureaucrats. In a personal conversation with a junior minister, this person stated, "Mubarak spoiled judges."

[176] Rabab El-Mahdi, "The Democracy Movement: Cycles of Protest" in Rabab El-Mahdi and Philip Marfleet (eds.), *Egypt: The Moment of Change*, (London: Zed Books, 2009), 99.

easily discredit as part of a foreign Zionist plot against Egypt as they usually did with previous popular protests. Second, the massive popular demonstrations for political cause were a new phenomenon. While Egyptians protested in large numbers before, on many occasions, the driving forces were economic discontent or foreign policy issues. Third, the successes of the movement in forcing the government to cave emboldened the public to think that they can challenge the oppressive state apparatus. The spark of massive protests was ignited in 2006 and continued to simmer for the next five years until it came to full bloom in January of 2011.

The courts and especially the administrative judiciary shed light on all ill policies and practices of the regime. From systematic, widespread corruption to the widespread rigging of elections the government seemed to be beyond repair. The Council rather than "elected" officials was the warden of citizens' rights and liberties. It was no surprise that the influential daily newspaper *Shorouk* pronounced, "The Council of State: The Hero that Ruled Egypt in 2010."[177] The vocal voice of the Council coupled with the government refusal to implement rulings helped to weaken Mubarak's claim to legality and the rule of law and hence his courts' based survival strategy. As one leading lawyer put it, "People are convinced that the rulings of the administrative judiciary regarding elections are worthless because they were not enforced."[178] Many ordinary Egyptians became convinced that the regime could not be reformed.

Mubarak's regime's refusal to enforce the Council's rulings helped to undermine the regime's credibility and convince many on-the-fence Egyptians that this government had to be overthrown. An administration that had at least partially based its political survival on the rule of law became naked in the eyes of its citizens when it refused to follow adverse rulings for narrow political interests. The regime that preached legality for thirty long years undermined its authority when it defied its own stated principles.

---

[177] *Shorouk*, December 31, 2010.
[178] *Shorouk*, December 18, 2010.

6

The SCAF, the Courts, and Islamists

Judges and Political Transition (2011–2012)

I wish to make the judicial authority prevail over the other two authorities, after establishing enough guarantees for the judiciary and its integrity.[1]

The esteemed jurist and president of the Council of State
Abd al-Razzāq Al-Sanhuri

The regime assault on the courts had devastating consequences. Absent the critical regime survival functions supplied by the legal system, repression, and corruption became the defining features of Mubarak's regime. Mass antagonism reached new levels. Mubarak's long tenure, the widening income gap, and the grooming of Gamal Mubarak convinced many that no natural way out of the miserable state of affairs. This deadlock coupled with the work of a plethora of brave activists, bloggers, and journalists widening the cracks in the oppressive regime's armor.

Calls for mass demonstrations on Police Day (January 25, 2011) gathered an unprecedented momentum.[2] The masses that flocked to the streets of Cairo, Alexandria, Suez, and many other cities and towns surprised the ruling party, the security forces, and the media apparatus. The symbolic act of reaching

---

[1] Al-Sanhuri's daughter Nadiyah Al-Sanhuri and his student Tawfīq al-Shawi pointed rightly that the idea of judicial supremacy over both the legislative and executive branches was, in the 1920s, not present in the French judiciary or jurisprudence and it has no place in the Anglo-Saxon law. They argued that Al-Sanhuri derived this idea from the Islamic principles, which make Shari'a supreme over legislation and hence empower the judiciary to ensure that all legislation adhere to Shari'a principles. Nadiyah Al-Sanhuri and Tawfīq al-Shawi eds., *'Abd al-Razzāq Al-Sanhuri min khilāl awrāqihi al-shakhiīyah* (al-Qahirah: al-Zahrā' lil-I'lām al-'Arabī, 1988), 82–83, 265.

[2] January 25th marks the National Police Day. This day became an official holiday in 2009. It commemorates and is a remembrance for fifty police officers killed and more wounded resisting the British demands to hand over weapons and evacuate the Ismailia police station on January 25, 1952.

Tahrir Square was uplifting for the young revolutionaries of the left and the right, seculars and Islamists. The masses proved they could take on the Leviathan and prevail, even for a short while. The security forces repressive crackdown inspired many to call for another challenge on Friday, January 28th. Mubarak's actions proved lacking and void of clear strategy or appreciation of the scale of public anger. The Day of Rage, as Friday, January 28, 2011, was dubbed by the young revolutionaries, proved faithful to its calling, and the masses overwhelmed the oppressive regime forces. The slogans in the streets were indicative of the goals of the protestors: bread, liberty, and social justice. These demands reflect the degree to which the regime's social contract became defective. The old formula created by Naser and his fellow Free Officers sixty years ago lost all meaning or value. The regime long ago stopped providing its share of the bargain (social and economic welfare) but in the same time maintained all the privileges of political power. If we would like to borrow from Marting Luther King Jr., it is apparent today that the 1952 state has defaulted on this promissory note. The regime has given most Egyptians a bad check, a check which has come back marked "insufficient funds."

Mubarak's actions in the aftermath exemplified his poor judgment and slow decision-making mechanisms. In the end, the army leadership concluded that Mubarak's departure was a price to be paid to avoid the escalation of the revolutionary demands.[3] Otherwise, the revolutionary wave could undermine the foundations of military hegemony enshrined after the 1952 army takeover and maintained with varying degrees of intensity through the reigns of Nasser, Sadat, and Mubarak. Mubarak, it seemed, did not resist the generals. He agreed to resign after his family departed to their preferred residence in the Red Sea resort town of Sharm El-Sheikh. In his resignation speech, dated February 11th, Mubarak handed power over to his lieutenants in the armed forces. A new era in Egypt's political history seemed to be taking a foothold.

This chapter sheds light on the judicialization of politics after the end of the Mubarak's era in 2011.[4] It investigates the political role the courts played in the transition process. It explains how judicial rulings and actions during the transition period influenced politics in the post-transition Egypt. It analyzes the constitutional changes related to the institutional independence and the political role of the courts. Understanding the active role, the courts played in

---

[3] The army high command was not quite pleased with the grooming of Gamal Mubarak. Generals were not ready to surrender power to a civilian.

[4] This discussion is partially based on Mahmoud Hamad, *Egypt's Litigious Transition: Judicial Intervention and the Muddied Road to Democracy*, The Rafik Hariri Center for the Middle East, Atlantic Council, May 2013.

2011–2012 as well as judges' intense interactions with generals and Islamists is key to predicting the future of judicialization in Egypt. The chapter is divided into three sections. In the first, I examine the judicial role in the destruction of the pillars of the Mubarak's regime. The second section underscores how judges help build and dismantle the political institutions of the new political order. The last and third section zeros in on how the courts' molded the constitutionalization process under the Supreme Council of the Armed Forces (SCAF) leadership.

THE SCAF, THE COURTS, AND THE ISLAMISTS

Mubarak's departure ushered the era of the SCAF.[5] The generals, who remained in the shadows during Mubarak's long tenure, assumed full control of the boiling Egyptian streets. Amidst the euphoria that followed Mubarak's removal, two main views dominated the Egyptian political scene: revolutionary and conservative. The young activists who led the uprising coveted a complete restructuring of the state's institutions, redefining the government's social responsibility, and repositioning Egypt's foreign policy. On the other end of the spectrum, leaders of the state institutions (military, security, and judiciary) sought to limit change to amputating the head of the regime. This second group wanted to maintain the power structure of the First Republic. The junta only implemented the least possible changes necessary to calm down the masses. The strategy of the most significant opposition group, the Muslim Brotherhood and its political arm the Freedom and Justice Party (FJP) fluctuated from supporting substantial reforms to maintaining the status quo.

---

[5] The previously little known Supreme Council of the Armed Forces (SCAF) became Egypt's de facto junta after Mubarak's transferred power to them on February 12, 2011. The Council, which was traditionally chaired by the president of the Republic, was headed by Field Marshal Mohammed Hussein Tantawy. Lieutenant General Sami Anan, armed forces Chief of Staff, was its deputy chairman. The SCAF, as the Council became widely known included the service heads and other senior commanders of the Egyptian Armed Forces, namely Air Marshal Reda Mahmoud Hafez, air force commander; Lieutenant General Abd El Aziz Seif Eldeen, commander of air defense; and Vice Admiral Mohab Mamish, navy commander in chief. The commanders of Egypt's two field armies and the commanders of the four military zones are also included, in addition to the chief of operations of the armed forces, chief of the engineering authority of the armed forces, commander of the border guards force. The Council's members also included other assistants to the minister of defense. The SCAF ruled Egypt until the swearing in of Mohamed Mursi is president of the Republic, on June 30, 2013. The Council, nonetheless, remained the power behind the throne until the dismissal of its leadership in August 2013.

Generals and judges rediscovered their institutional affinity. The military–judicial collaboration proved critical during the transition and beyond. The SCAF's close relationship with the judiciary and notably the Supreme Constitutional Court (SCC) manifested itself early on. The SCAF team of legal advisors were all recruited from the high court. Two days after Mubarak departure, the depth of the SCC–SCAF collaboration became apparent. The committee tasked by the SCAF to amend the 1971 Constitution counted in strong SCC representation with three members (including the influential position of rapporteur) drown from the SCC.[6] According to concurring news reports and personal interviews with individuals of knowledge of the process, the three SCC members had an outsized imprint over the committee deliberations and decisions. The committee retained the constitutional structure of the 1971 Constitution, endowed the SCAF with sweeping power, designed the transition process to SCAF liking, and sustained the competencies of the SCC. All these outcomes would pay dividends to the SCAF and the SCC during the transition and beyond.

It was also noticeable that the first key legislation the SCAF decreed pertained to the SCC. On June 18, 2011, SCAF chairman, Field Marshal Mohamed Hussein Tantawi, issued Law-decree 48/2011. The law was rather short as it only included two articles, but its impact was drastically significant. The first article related to the appointment of the chief justice. Under Sadat and Mubarak, the president of the Republic had free reign in appointing the chief justice. A prerogative that Mubarak used to a great effect to transform the SCC's jurisprudence after its landmark decision in 2001. Law No. 48 removed this presidential power altogether. The chief justice is to be appointed from amongst the three most senior justices on the court and only after the approval of the court's general assembly. Furthermore, the general assembly became the only authority to appoint justices on the court. The law also mandated giving priority in the appointment process to members of the commissioner's body (junior and midlevel judges assisting justices in preparing cases and other functions performed by law clerks in the US Supreme Court).

---

[6]   Chairman of the SCAF Decision No. 1 issued on February 14, 2011.

   The Committee was chaired by the former first vice-president of the Council of State. It included in its membership three constitutional law professors, the Muslim Brotherhood lawyer Sobhy Saleh and two SCC justices Maher Sami and Hussein al-Badrway and Hatem Bagato, then chairman of the commissioners body of the SCC. The SCAF narrowly defined the mandate of the committee to include only Articles 179, 88, 77, 67, 189, 39. In addition to any articles related to guaranteeing democracy, transparent elections for the president of the Republic, the Peoples' Assembly, and the Shura Council.

In a nutshell, the SCC, now staffed by pro-regime conservative justices, became a self-perpetuating body, wholly insulated from the political system and even the judiciary itself. This basically transformed Egypt's highest court from the least autonomous among the nation's judicial institutions to arguably the most independent high court in the world. The law not only reflected the close relationship between the SCAF and the SCC but also indicated a desire to utilize the high court as an insurance policy during and after the transition period. Uncertain about the political affiliations or persuasions of future office holders, the SCAF sought to encapsulate its ideological allies in the court. Enhancing judicial independence before or during a period of political transition was not a novel idea but a customary practice of their counterparts in Latin America.[7] The junta created a judicial insurance policy to be cashed if needed.

The SCAF's alliance with judges not only manifested itself in enhancing the SCC's institutional independence but also extended to the courts and the Public Prosecution Department (PPD). The SCAF resisted revolutionary demands to undertake any major reform in the judiciary or purge old regime supporters on the bench and the PPD. The SCAF withstood calls to establish revolutionary courts to try Mubarak's regime with corruption and human rights atrocities. These decisions would pay dividends for the generals on more than one occasion.

On the other hand, judges, benefiting from their role in undermining the Mubarak's regime, emerged as the most respected state institution (alongside the military). Removing Mubarak also freed judges from the institutional shackles of the old regime. Judicialization during the transition process is arguably the most visible judicial role in any political transition in recent memory.

The transition from authoritarian role is a protracted, complicated, and chaotic process. It encompasses breaking with the nation's tyrannical past, dismantling authoritarian institutions and building the foundations of a democratic polity. While remnants of the old regime were expected to sabotage the process, transition became further complicated when "forces of change" disagreed about the nature of the new political order. These forces, which collaborated to bring down the vestiges of authoritarianism, promoted conflicting proposals about the structure and objectives of the new polity. Absent a complete triumph of one side over the others, an arbitrator to adjudicate transition disputes would be critical. The judiciary was a prime candidate

---

[7] For more information on this, please see Jodi S. Finkel, *Judicial Reform as Political Insurance Argentina, Peru, and Mexico in the 1990.*

for this task. It had developed a reputation for impartiality and willingness to tackle politically sensitive disputes. Egypt's transition was one of the most fragmented in recent memory. With increased fragmentation came increased adjudication, particularly when judges demonstrated their inclination to engage in solving political problems.

In these circumstances, it came as no surprise that the judiciary played an indispensable role in every aspect of the transition. In many occasions, judicial overreach confounded the transition process. In this section, I explain how courts shaped the three processes of transition: undermining the old order, building democratic institutions, and negotiating the new constitutional order.

1. *Courts and Devaluation of Old Order*

The SCAF sought to limit the scope and pace of change. After dissolving the 2010 parliament, the junta refused to implement any decisive restructuring of the political system. Activists, emboldened by the Council of State rulings before Mubarak's abdication, hounded two vestiges of the old regime: The National Democratic Party (NDP) and the local (municipal) councils.

The NDP was Egypt's ruling and de facto single party since its establishment in 1978. Under the auspices of prince-regent Gamal Mubarak, the NDP became a cartel of notable family chieftains, government bureaucrats, and business tycoons. The party was instrumental in manufacturing the regime's majorities in all elections. Even after the NDP's national headquarter was torched during the revolution, the party remained lawful. The NDP's electoral infrastructure could be used to elect old regime loyalists to the new parliament. Revolutionary appeals to dissolve the NDP and ban its leading members from political participation fell on deaf ears. Fearing that many NDP leaders weathered the storm, blotting a comeback, activists petitioned the Council of State to dissolve the party. On April 16, 2011, only sixty-five days after Mubarak's ousting, an administrative court ordered the dissolution of the NDP and seized its funds and property.

The enormously popular ruling was plainly the work of activist judges. The verdict's justification was more political than legal. The ruling stated,

> The NDP since 1978 played a principal role in selecting corrupt governments, passing unconstitutional legislation, implementing policies contrary to the national interests, and preventing the enforcement of judicial rulings. The party also damaged political life and hindered national unity. Hence the said party lost its license to operate as a party.

Many of those who welcomed the ruling did not foresee it as the beginning of judicial intrusion into the political arena. This verdict ushered a slippery slope of extreme judicialization with both legal and political ramifications. Rival political factions concluded that political victories could be scored in courtrooms rather than in ballot boxes. Therefore, in a transition period, where the rules of the game were still being negotiated, all political disputes had the potential of ending up on a docket of one court or another.

Predictably, this ruling fostered a trend of seeking judicial remedies for political questions. One such problem was the SCAF's unwillingness to eradicate the NDP's last institutional stranglehold on municipal councils. The NDP controlled 98 percent of the 1,750 councils, which touched every aspect of citizens' lives. These councils could provide an electoral platform for NDP members. Legal advocates filed a case before the Council of State requesting the dissolution of these councils. In June 2011, the court delivered a verdict ordering the government to dissolve all local councils across the country. Yet again, the court based its ruling on political rather than legal reasoning.

The ruling's reasoning for a second time was rather political. The court based its decision on the premise that these councils were the tools of the previous regime and hence has no value after its demise. The court went further to maintain that the dissolution is mandatory because of these councils' rampant corruption and their failure to provide accountability, causing the inferior conditions of healthcare, education, and other services. The verdict went further to argue that "these councils lost its legitimacy as a direct outcome of the success of the people's revolution and as an inevitable consequence to suspending the former constitution, which situated them as part and parcel of the executive branch that destroyed all appealing things in this state." The court had to find a workaround Article 144 of the Local Governance System Law (43 of 1979), which strictly forbids the dissolution of the entire system of local governance. The verdict reasoned that this provision only applies to the usual situation, not the exceptional circumstances of Egypt after January 2011.

After the administrative courts seized the initiative in undermining the institutional foundations of authoritarianism, the criminal courts became the arena where old regime leaders faced justice, or so it seemed at that moment. In 2011–2012, Egypt's criminal courts were visited by who's who of the old regime. The extensive list included Mubarak, his two sons, the speakers of the two houses of parliament, two former prime ministers, many cabinet members, chieftains of the interior ministry including the head of the dreaded secret police, and scores of leading businessmen. The role of the criminal courts was significantly amplified when the SCAF, for reasons that will become apparent later, refused demands to establish revolutionary courts to hold former regime leaders accountable.

Mubarak's trial, dubbed the trial of the century, was undoubtedly the most significant criminal case in the nation's judicial history. The SCAF, possibly out of loyalty or deference for a fellow senior officer, refused to take any legal action against the former president or his family. The former air force commander remained in his villa in Sharm El-Sheikh. The SCAF did not relent until popular demands and weekly mass protests threatened to overwhelm the generals. On April 13th, two full months after his abdication, the military authorities detained Mubarak and his two sons in an investigation into corruption, abuse of power, and the murdering protesters. Mubarak, however, did not stand trial until August 3, 2011.

For the first time, a pharaoh stood before a court to answer accusations of complicity in the murder and attempted murder of hundreds of peaceful demonstrators in addition to receiving bribery and facilitating corruption. The trial was marked with drama inside the courtroom and violent clashes outside. The highly anticipated verdict came on June 2, 2012, a few days before the crucial second round of the presidential elections.

The presiding judge announced the life sentence for Mubarak and his minister of interior, Habib El Adly, and the acquittal of Mubarak's sons and several senior security officials. The ruling reasoning was quite feeble. The court dismissed the corruption charges against the former president and his sons by claiming a statute of limitations had expired, a legal technicality that exasperated the masses. Judge Ahmed Rafaat maintained that prosecutors failed to provide evidence that either Mubarak or his police generals had directly ordered the killing of protesters. Instead, he found that Mubarak and his minister of interior were an "accessory to murder" because they failed to stop the killing. *The New York Times'* Cairo veteran bureau chief summed the reaction to the conviction nicely:

> But a conviction that once promised to deliver a triumph for the rule of law in Egypt and the Arab world – the first Arab strongman jailed by his own citizens – instead brought tens of thousands of Egyptians back into the streets. They denounced the verdict as a sham because the court also acquitted many officials more directly responsible for the police who killed the demonstrators, and a broad range of lawyers and political leaders said Mr. Mubarak's conviction was doomed to reversal on appeal.[8]

8 "New Turmoil in Egypt Greets Mixed Verdict for Mubarak," *The New York Times*, June 2, 2012.

TABLE 6.1 *Votes in the first round of the presidential elections*

Candidate	Political Orientation	Votes / Percentage%
Mohamed Mursi	Muslim Brotherhood	5,764,952 (24.78)
Ahmed Shafiq	Old Regime	5,505,327 (23.66)
Hamdeen Sabbahi	Leftist / Nasserite	4,820,273 (20.72)
Abdel Moneim Abol Fetouh	Moderate Islamist	4,065,239 (17.47)
Amro Mousa	Liberal	2,588,850 (11.13)

The verdict put its mark on Egypt's presidential elections. The disappointing decision worsen the chances of Ahmed Shafiq, Mubarak's last prime minister, and helped the Muslim Brotherhood's candidate, Mohamed Mursi to win the support of the many liberals who spearheaded the revolution. The support of these groups was critical in the very tight presidential race.[9]

The 2012 presidential election was a landmark event in Egypt's history. It was the first time the people would directly elect the head of state in a competitive election that included candidates from all the four corners of the political spectrum. The rules set by the SCAF mandated an absolute majority of the votes for any candidates to win outright. The first-round was held on May 23–24. With 23,672,236 (46.42%) votes casted, the results were shocking for Egyptians and observers alike.[10]

As no candidate won the needed 50 percent + 1 majority, a runoff election was scheduled for June 16–17. Only the top two vote-getters advanced to the second round. Mohamed Mursi and Ahmed Shafiq battled for every vote. The heated contest boosted voting turnout. Total number of votes cast were 26,420,763 or 51.85 percent. The old regime electoral machine went into high gear to elect Mubarak's last prime minister to the presidency. Mursi, however, triumphed by attracting support from young revolutionaries and non-Muslim Brotherhood Islamists.

The verdicts in many other criminal trials did not sooth public wrath either. To the dismay of many revolutionaries, most of the court cases against police

---

[9] As Mubarak's last prime minister, Shafiq was perceived as guilty by association as he presided over the cabinet when the police failed to protect unarmed protesters in Tahrir Square from a deadly assault by a mob of Mubarak supporters known as the "battle of the camels." On the other hand, Mursi pledged that if elected, he would assemble a team of top prosecutors to determine the responsibility for the killings and press new charges against Mubarak and his aides.

[10] Sources for these statistics are the two PEC press conference held on May 28, 2012, and June 24, 2012, aired on state TV.

TABLE 6.2 *Votes in the second round of the presidential elections*

Candidate	Votes / Percentage%
Mohamed Mursi	13,230,131 (51.73)
Ahmed Shafiq	12,347,380 (48.27)

officers and personnel accused of murdering protesters during the troubling days of January–February 2011 ended with non-guilty verdicts. Lawyers and relatives of the victims put all the blame on the PPD and the Mubarak's appointed Public Prosecutor (PP) for failing to present enough evidence in the cases. Many legal experts concluded that the PPD did not carefully prepare the cases. Calls to remove PP Abdel Meguid Mahmoud were echoed in courtrooms and TV talk shows. Angry mobs attacked courtrooms in unprecedented episodes in Egypt's history. Faith and confidence in the legal system dwindled.[11] Judges, on the other hand, became very defensive on accusations of ties to the old regime.

It did not help one bit that SCAF used the courts to score some political points domestically and internationally. With many national and foreign nongovernmental organizations (NGOs) exposing the SCAF's human rights abuses, the generals sought to silence these independent voices. The authorities raided seventeen NGOs working on democracy and rights issues. Publicly, Planning and International Cooperation Minister Fayza Abou El-Naga and other Egyptian officials accused the NGOs, including the American organizations International Republican Institute (IRI), National Democartic Institute (NDI), and Freedom House, of working to sow unrest in Egypt. The security forces and the PPD claimed that these groups worked to implement an American–Israeli plot against Egypt and accused the NGO workers of having links to the CIA.

The PPD filed indictments against forty foreign and Egyptian activists. The foreign defendants included eight Americans, three Serbs, two Germans, one Norwegian, and one Palestinian. The Americans included Sam LaHood, director of the IRI and son of then transportation secretary Ray LaHood. The raids caused fury in Washington, where lawmakers threatened to cut off the roughly $1.5 billion Egypt gets in US aid. The pressures, apparently, yielded results. The SCAF was forced to seek a way out of the crisis. To allow foreign nationals to leave Egypt, the president of Cairo Appeals Court Abdel

---

[11] In fairness, while some judges and prosecutors condoled with the police officers, the verdicts were not only due to judicial prejudice. The PPD depended on the police to investigate the cases, and many police officers were in lockstep with their brothers in arms.

Motaz Ibrahim changed the composition of the circuit presiding over the case. Defendants, who were freed on bail, hastily left Egypt. This created uproar within the judiciary and further undermined the trust in the legal system. Aggrieved judges called for the removal of Judge Ibrahim, but the SCAF would have none of it.

2. *Judges' Role in Building (and Dismantling) Political Institutions*

Over and above their judicial duties, Egyptian judges were once more tasked with overseeing the presidential and parliamentary elections. Managing elections was no easy task in a country that lacked electoral infrastructure and where election rigging was commonplace. The parliamentary elections were entrusted to the High Elections Commission (HEC). The HEC was chaired by the president of Cairo's Court of Appeal and included in its membership two senior judges from the Courts of Appeal and two senior vice-presidents of the Court of Cassation and two senior vice-presidents of the Council of State. The Commission's administration of the election was adequate. International and local observers testified to the fairness of the process. Nevertheless, some judicial rulings complicated the process.

Administrative courts delivered several rulings that influenced the process. The first verdict obliged the HEC to grant Egyptians abroad the right to vote. Prior to this decision, millions of Egyptian expatriates never participated in elections. The HEC complied, and SCAF issued a decree amending electoral laws. The HEC carried out the tasks of registering voters overseas, distributing ballots, and counting in each embassy and consulate successfully and few complaints were registered.

The eligibility of NDP members to run for parliamentary seats was a very different matter. Revolutionary forces, Islamists and seculars alike, petitioned the SCAF to exclude ex-NDP candidates. The junta refused to pass any "disenfranchisement laws" calculating that this conservative old-regime block could balance liberal and Islamist MP's in the elected assemblies. Once more, lacking a political solution, activists appealed to the administrative courts. Different administrative courts issued conflicting verdicts with some courts allowing NDP candidacies and some others banning them. The High Administrative Court (HAC) was called on for a binding decision. To the chagrin of revolutionary forces, the HAC permitted all ex-NDP candidates to run.

In the end, the revolutionary wave was quite strong. Former NDP candidates only won a handful of seats. The results represented an overwhelming victory for Islamists. Two new parties won more than two-thirds of the seats. The Muslim Brotherhood's FJP came first gaining 47 percent of seats in the

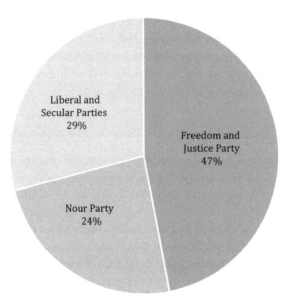

FIGURE 6.1 The percentage of seats by party in the 2011–2012 People's Assembly elections

People's Assembly and the Salafi Nour Party was second winning 24 percent. Liberal and secular parties all together took slightly less than 30 percent of People's Assembly seats. Islamist parties also gained nearly 90 percent of contested seats in the Shura Council (upper house), resulting in an Islamist majority in both houses.

While legislative elections ended with relatively little judicial drama, the presidential election was a very different story. The five-member Supreme Presidential Elections Commission (SPEC) was chaired by the chief justice of the SCC and included the first deputy chief justice of the SCC, the first vice-president of the Court Cassation, the first vice-president of the Council of State, and the president of Cairo Court of Appeal. The SPEC had exclusive jurisdiction in running the elections, and its decisions were final and not subject to appeal before any entity – judiciary or otherwise. A three-person majority needed to take any decision. The commission's decisions were not subject to any form of judicial review. The animation in the presidential election began with the nomination process. The SPEC, in a surprising twist, disqualified three top candidates: Mubarak's spy chief and former vice-president Omar Suleiman, the Muslim Brotherhood leader Khairat El-Shater, and the firebrand Salafi preacher Hazem Salah Abu Ismail. The justifications for the disqualifications was rather conspicuous. Suleiman was disqualified for not having the required number of voter endorsements, El-Shater for his past criminal convictions and Abu Ismail for his deceased mother dual nationality

Many speculated that the disqualifications were not purely legalistic and that the SPEC was doing the SCAF's bidding.[12] The elimination of these three candidates dramatically transformed the electoral landscape. Former air force commander Gen. Ahmed Shafiq, Mubarak's last prime minister, emerged as a serious contender representing the interests of the old regime. The Islamist-dominated People's Assembly sprang into action and quickly produced a "political exclusion" (*disenfranchisement*) law to disqualify Shafiq from contesting the elections.

The SPEC had no alternative but to disqualify Shafiq. A few days later, in a startling move, the commission accepted the General's appeal and reinstated his candidacy. The SPEC then transferred the matter to the SCC asking the high court to rule on the constitutionality of the law. The legal grounds for such a decision was highly questionable. Because Shafiq was the SCAF's favored candidate, many doubted the commission's motives and questioned the legality of its decision. Apprehension escalated when the results of the first round pitted Shafiq against the Muslim Brotherhood's candidate Mohamed Mursi.

Two days before the crucial second round, all eyes were on the SCC, which was expected to rule on two important cases: Shafiq's eligibility and the People's Assembly election. Most seasoned observers speculated that the court would show some political cunning in rendering the historical verdicts, either by allowing both Shafiq and the People's Assembly to stand or ruling both illegal. Put another way, the court was not expected to tilt the balance entirely in favor of the Islamists (allowing the parliament to stand and excluding Shafiq) or to favor the old regime (dissolving parliament and allowing Shafiq to run). In the end, the verdict raised eyebrows around the world and flabbergasted Islamists and many revolutionaries. The SCC dissolved the Islamist-dominated parliament and ruled that the old-regime candidate could stay in the race.

In addition to the legal and political questions about the two rulings, the timing of the decision on the People's Assembly was highly questionable. The case was transferred to the SCC on February 20, 2012, and the court delivered its verdict on June 14, 2012. The SCC historically has taken a much longer

---

[12] When asked if this was a political or a judicial decision, MP and political commentator Wahid Abdel Magid answered, "Political decision, all political decisions. Unfortunately, the judiciary was severely abused in this political battle." *El-Watan*, September 18, 2012.

time to reach such earth-shattering rulings.[13] On average the SCC took three years to rule on similar cases. *The New York Times'* correspondent in Cairo summed the impressions after the ruling:

> A panel of judges appointed by Egypt's ousted president, Hosni Mubarak, threw the nation's troubled transition to democracy into grave doubt Thursday with rulings that dissolved the popularly elected Parliament and allowed the toppled government's last prime minister to run for president, escalating a struggle by remnants of the old elite to block Islamists from coming to power.[14]

It did not help the court's public image one bit that SCC issued its decision only two days before the second round of the presidential election, just after one session of oral arguments, and in an unprecedented second session during the same month for the first time in recent memory. The SCC typically would hold a single session each month on Sunday. The June 14th session was held on a Thursday, the last working day in Egypt (Friday is a holiday). The court would repeat this practice only once more in 2012 also in a matter pertaining to the Peoples' Assembly, (details in Chapter 7).

Many understood the decision, if not as a clear handout to SCAF, then as a *preemptive strike* against the parliament. The ruling came after a few MP's proposed an amendment to the SCC law that could have curtailed the court's jurisdiction and limited its institutional independence. Former political adviser to the Prime Minister Motaz Abdel-Fattah put it nicely, "the Parliament and the SCC both have guns and the party who can draw his gun first would win. The SCC drew its gun and fired first."[15] It is evident that the SCC considered the legislature a threat and the ruling could be considered an act of self-preservation.[16]

The verdicts forced the public to recall that Prime Minister Kamal Ganzouri had threatened, during an institutional crisis with the People's Assembly that "The verdict regarding the dissolution of the parliament is in the drawer of the SCC and can come out in any time."[17] One veteran expert had no alternative but to conclude, "The final yet no less troubling aspect of the

---

[13] The legal challenges to the constitutionality of the 1984 elections lasted until 1987 when the SCC ordered the dissolution of the People's Assembly and the same for the People's Assembly elected in 1987 and dissolved by the SCC in 1990.

[14] *The New York Times*, June 14, 2012.

[15] *El-Watan*, September 12, 2012.

[16] Personal interview with a deputy chief justice of the Supreme Constitutional Court, March 13, 2018.

[17] Wahid Abdel Magid, who was close to these developments, agreed with this analysis, stating "The dissolution of the Majlis (People's Assembly) was a reaction to the attack on the government." *El-Watan*, September 12, 2012.

TABLE 6.3 *SCC sessions in 2012 (judicial year 34), source: the SCC's official website*[18]

SCC Session	Comments
Sunday 1/15/2012	Regular Session
Sunday 2/05/2012	Regular Session
Sunday 3/04/2012	Regular Session
Sunday 4/01/2012	Regular Session
Sunday 5/06/2012	Regular Session
Sunday 6/03/2012	Regular Session
Thursday 6/14/2012	Extraordinary Session: Peoples' Assembly & disenfranchisement Law
Sunday 7/01/2012	Regular Session
Tuesday 7/10/2012	Extraordinary Session: Mursi's decision to recall the Peoples' Assembly
Sunday 8/05/2012	Regular Session
Sunday 9/30/2012	Regular Session
Sunday 10/14/2012	Regular Session
Sunday 11/04/2012	Regular Session
Sunday 12/02/2012	Regular Session

decisions is that the SCC looks as if it has done the full political bidding of the Ancien Régime."[19]

In retrospect, it is entirely plausible that the SCAF wrote the law in such a way to allow for the dissolution of the legislature if need be. Ibrahim, the president of Cairo Court of Appeal who chaired the election commission that supervised 2012 legislative elections revealed that he informed the SCAF about the shortcomings in the law and that the SCC will dissolve the House. Judge Ibrahim stated that before the elections, "I advised Major General Mamdouh Shahin (the SCAF legal and constitutional adviser) that law violates the equality of opportunity and that the SCC has dissolved the Peoples' Assembly for the same reason before. Major General Shahin told me 'I know, and the Field Marshal knows. There is a directive to go in this direction, and we will carry out this legislation.'"[20] It is important to note that the SCAF

---

[18] Information compiled from the SCC official website: http://sccourt.gov.eg.

[19] Chibli Mallat "Saving Egypt's Supreme Constitutional Court from Itself" http://english.ahram .org.eg/News/45009.aspx.

[20] *El-Waten*, December 11, 2013.

principle legal advisers came from the SCC, and such deficiencies were not new to them.

In addition to the SCC anti-Islamist rulings, some of the SCC's justices did not shy from openly collaborating with the SCAF and endorsing its policies. Former deputy prime minister Ali El-Selmi, a harsh opponent of the Islamist, revealed that justice Tahani al-Gebali was a member of a troika entrusted to draft supra-constitutional principles that created quite a stir in late 2011.[21] Hatem Bagato, the former head of the SCC commissioners' body, was also an unofficial legal adviser to SCAF and attended many of the meetings with political parties.[22]

Furthermore, several leading judges tacitly and sometimes openly supported Shafiq's presidential bid. Then president of the Judges Club Ahmed El-Zend is a quintessential example of judicial meddling in political contestation. A few days before the second round of the presidential election and the SCC ruling, El-Zend, in a televised speech, spared no effort in harshly censuring the People's Assembly with its Islamist majority. The Judges Club's president had all but threatened MPs with a firing squad and publically asserted that judges would not enforce any legislation enacted by the parliament. The Judges Club and the SCC emerged as the enemy of political Islam and as the spearhead of the SCAF. The two institutions put their bets on the wrong horse in the presidential election, and it became clear that their relationship with the Mursi presidency would be troubling.

3. The Courts Mold the Constitutional Order

On the heels of Mubarak's abdication, two routes were put forward. Secular forces preferred drafting a constitution before holding elections; this option came to be known as "Constitution First." The SCAF, however, advocated a different roadmap called "Election First," which entailed holding legislative elections, then the two houses of Parliament would elect a constitute assembly to draft the new constitution.

Naturally, the generals did not desire to write a constitution in the aftermath of the mega revolutionary wave that forced Mubarak's departure. The junta was playing for time, confident in its ability to drive a wedge amongst the different factions of the January 25th uprising. Besides, an indirectly elected assembly would be easier to cajole and pressure than an elected commission with a mandate from the masses.

---

[21] *El-Waten*, September 11, 2012.
[22] *El-Waten*, September 15, 2012.

The referendum on constitutional amendments of March 19th endorsed the second route after the SCAF was able to enlist the support of the Muslim Brotherhood and other Islamist parties.[23] This referendum was the beginning of a major rift between the two components of the revolutionary camp: secular and religious – a rift the SCAF cleverly nurtured to ensure political dominance.

The SCAF projected a divided parliament in which the generals could be the balance holders. Abdel-Fattah argued that the SCAF believed the new parliament would be divided into three relatively equal groups: the Muslim Brotherhood and other Islamists, the revolutionary forces, and the traditional forces.[24] Election results, however, brought an overwhelming majority of Islamists. As expected, the Muslim Brotherhood's FJP emerged with the largest number of seats. The big surprise, however, was the number of seats won by the newly politicized Salafis at the expense of the NDP.

The two houses held their joint meeting to elect the Constituent Assembly (CA). The CA composition reflected an overwhelming majority of members from the FJP and Noor party. Half the members were members of parliament, and the other half from public figures. Non-Islamist members walked out in protest, and a stalemate was reached between the two sides. Secular forces sought to find judicial remedies for their dilemma and petitioned the Council of State to invalidate the selection on the politically justified but legally dubious proposition that the selection did not reflect the diversity of the Egyptian society.

In another episode of extreme judicial activism, an administrative court panel issued a ruling on April 10, 2012, suspending the CA. The ruling's rationale included a wealth of legal creativity. The court reasoned that Article 60 of the Constitutional Declaration delegated the selection of the 100-member committee is a separate process from the election of the houses of parliament. Hence, the membership of the Peoples' Assembly and Shura Council's members is illegitimate.[25]

---

[23] Article 60 of the March 30th constitutional declaration delineated the process: "The members of the first People's Assembly and Shura Council (except the appointed members) will meet in a joint session following an invitation from the Supreme Council of the Armed Forces within 6 months of their election to elect a provisional assembly composed of 100 members which will prepare a new draft constitution for the country to be completed within 6 months of the formation of this assembly. The draft constitution will be presented within 15 days of its preparation to the people who will vote in a referendum on the matter. The constitution will take effect from the date on which the people approve the referendum."

[24] *El-Waten*, September 12, 2012.

[25] Justice Maher Sami, a staunch critic of Islamists and a member of the committee that drafted the constitutional amendments in 2011, maintained that during the discussion of the

The Parliament decided not to appeal the verdict, opting for forming another CA. Negotiations among the different political factions resulted in the selection of a more balanced selection for the CA on June 12, 2012. The new panel included a range of politicians, members of the armed forces, police, judiciary and trade unions, as well as Muslim and Christian leaders. It was noticeably less Islamist than the first one.

Once more, legal challenges were filed before the ever-welcoming administrative courts. Furthermore, many CA members representing the different Christen churches, liberals, government officials, and public figures close to the military announced their withdrawal. Two days later the SCC dissolved the People's Assembly, and the SCAF seized the moment to issue a constitutional declaration. The constitutional declaration, announced by state media minutes before polls closed at the end of two days of voting in the presidential elections, gave SCAF the power to form a new constituent assembly if the current CA could not fulfill its mission.

Another amendment gave the SCC the equivalence of veto power over the drafting process. Article 60-B1 of the constitutional declaration stipulated that

> If the President, the head of SCAF, the Prime Minister, the SCJP or a fifth of the CA find that the new constitution contains an article or more which conflict with the revolution's goals and its main principles or which conflict with any principle agreed upon in all of Egypt's former constitutions, any of the aforementioned bodies may demand that the constituent assembly revises this specific article within 15 days. Should the CA object to revising the contentious article, the article will be referred to the SCC, which will then be obliged to give its verdict within seven days. The SCC's decision is final and will be published in the official gazette within three days from the date of issuance.

This was how matters stood when Mohamed Mursi was sworn on June 30, 2012, as Egypt's first civilian head of state in sixty years. The tense relations between the Islamists and the courts were expected to overshadow the executive–judicial relationship after the end of the transition.

Constituent Assembly (CA) article, the committee decided to allow the Parliament unrestricted freedom to select the Constituent Assembly members. He stated, "the Committee debated the pool from which to choose the Constituent Assembly members. The selection could be from outside the electoral college or from inside it. The Committee consented to leave the provision without restricting the electoral college or confiscating its prerogative to select from outside it or within it or to mix between these and those. The committee granted the electoral college unlimited authority to elect the Constituent Assembly." Maher Sami, *Al-Dustūrīyah*, al-Qāhirah: al-Maḥkamah al-Dustūrīyah al-'Ulyā, al-Sanah 11., al-'adad 24: (2013).

7

Mursi and the Judiciary

The Self-Fulfilling Prophecy (2012–2013)

The judiciary continued to play a dominant political role during the short tenure of President Mursi in office (June 30, 2012–July 3, 2013).[1] This period is indicative of the role the judiciary in collaboration with the military could play in undermining a democratically elected regime. If judicial rulings and actions were contributing factors to the demise of Mubarak's authoritarian regime, judges were instrumental in bringing down Mursi's government.

Upon assuming office, it was clear that Mursi inherited a complicated political scene. Almost half the electorate did not vote for him. The main institutional pillars of the state (military, security, and judiciary) perceived him as an outsider with questionable intentions. The Peoples' Assembly was dissolved. The upper house lacked legislative authority and was also threatened with the Supreme Constitutional Court's (SCC) guillotine. The Constituent Assembly (CA) was at the mercy of less-than-sympathetic courts.

Furthermore, the Supreme Council of the Armed Forces (SCAF), taking full advantage of the SCC's ruling to dissolve the People's Assembly, issued a declaration to strip the newly elected president of power. In addition to mandating that the president-elect takes the oath of office before the SCC,

---

[1] Mohamed Mursi (Morsi) is Egypt's first democratically elected president. He is also the first and, until the present day, the only civilian to assume the post of chief executive since the army takeover in July 1952. Mursi was born August 8, 1951. He studied engineering at Cairo University, where he received his BA and MS degrees. He then moved to the United States to continue his doctoral studies. He received a PhD in materials science from the University of Southern California in 1982. Mursi returned to Egypt in 1985 and joined the engineering faculty at Zagazig University. He was elected to parliament in 2000 and served until 2005. Mursi was a leading figure in the then-outlawed Muslim Brotherhood. After the January 25th uprising, Mursi became the president of the Freedom and Justice Party (FJP) in 2011; a position he maintained until his election to the presidency in June 2012. He took the oath of office on June 30, 2012, becoming Egypt's fifth president. He was deposed on July 3, 2013, after an army takeover.

the SCAF acquired the power to appoint another CA if the current one was to fail or get disbanded by the courts as its predecessor. Furthermore, the June Declaration, issued in the waning hours before the end of voting in the second round of the presidential elections, included a plethora of constraints on the presidency:

1. Removing the armed forces from any degree of supervision by elected officials. The amended Article 53 stipulated: "The Supreme Council of the Armed Forces, as it was composed on the day on which this Constitutional Declaration entered into force, is responsible for deciding on all issues related to the armed forces, for appointing its leaders, for extending their terms of office. The head of the SCAF will exercise all the powers that are granted by the laws and regulations to the commander-in-chief of the armed forces and the minister of defense until a new constitution enters into force."

2. The president can only declare war or dispatch the armed forces to perform duties at home with the approval of the SCAF. Article 53(1): "The President declares war pursuant to the approval of the Supreme Council of the Armed Forces." Article 53(2): "In the event of unrest within the country that requires the intervention of the armed forces, the president may, with the Supreme Council of the Armed Forces' approval, issue a decision to join the armed forces in the mission to maintain security and defend vital state institutions. Egyptian law sets out the armed forces' powers, its mission, the situations in which force may be used and in which detentions and arrests may be made, its judicial mandate, and the situations in which it enjoys immunity."

3. The SCAF, not the president or the upper house of parliament, will command the legislative powers vacated with the dissolution of the Peoples' Assembly. Article 56: "The Supreme Council of the Armed Forces will assume the authorities set out in Article 56(1) of the Constitutional Declaration dated 30 March 2011 until a new parliament is elected and assumes its authorities."

Mursi failed to develop an effective strategy to deal with the judiciary (and the military and security complex). Regime leaders believed that "the courts were out to get them" and acted in that manner, rendering executive–judicial clashes a self-fulfilling prophecy. The president and his associates mishandled the courts and allowed remnants of the *ancien régime* to stir anti-Brotherhood sentiments, undermine the regime's popular support, and facilitate military intervention. Executive–judicial interactions abetted the creation of a unified structure of contestation that allowed all anti-Brotherhood factions to collaborate in bringing down the regime. This role is similar to the role the courts played during Mubarak's final years in office and the complete opposite of how the courts functioned under Sadat and most of Mubarak's reign.

The executive–judicial confrontations are the nucleus of this chapter, which is divided into two sections. In section one, I analyze the regime's discourse and policies toward the courts, with a particular focus on two case studies: the conflict over the Public Prosecutor (PP) and the constitutional drafting process. I conclude with an analysis of the changes related to the judiciary in the 2012 Constitution. In section two, I move to study judicial counteroffensives on the regime. I concentrate on scrutinizing judicial behavior on and off the bench and demonstrate how these actions dealt a massive blow to the regime's public standing and facilitated its demise.

THE REGIME'S FRAY WITH JUDGES

The problems between the Brotherhood and the judiciary were bubbling beneath the surface even before Mursi's ascendency to power. The Islamists did not forget that the SCC dismantled their legislative fortress, the Council of State undermined the constitutional drafting process, and the leadership of the Judges Club supported Shafiq. Mursi's swearing-in ceremony was an early indication of the strained relations to follow. As per the SCAF's Constitutional Declaration, the president-elect ought to perform the oath of office before the SCC.[2] The junta perceived this as an affirmation of the Mursi's submission to their June Constitutional Declaration, which drastically enhanced the power of the military vis-à-vis the presidency.

Mursi tried to maneuver away from this legal hurdle. His advisors floated several ideas, including taking the oath before the Shura Council, in Tahrir Square (the birthplace of the revolution), or at the Cairo International Conference Center. After all, no previous Egyptian constitution ever required the president of the Republic to take the oath of office before a court. In addition, the natural alternative to the dissolved Peoples' Assembly was not the SCC but the Shura Council.

The SCC, arguably with the SCAF backing, utterly refused any compromise in this regard. The SCC insisted that Mursi had to take the oath in the SCC headquarter. In the end, it became clear that military–judicial alliance would not permit Mursi to assume office unless he carried out the oath before

---

[2]   Article 30(3): "Where parliament is dissolved, the president will take the oath of office before the Supreme Constitutional Court's General Assembly."

the SCC. The president-elect reluctantly acquiesced.[3] Mursi then sought a low-key ceremony before the SCC and ordered that the inauguration not to be carried live on national TV. Many justices rebuffed this demand and threatened to boycott the ceremony, which could potentially invalidate it. Yet again, Mursi had to yield. It was clear, however, that he considered this to be a deliberate affront to him and his office.[4]

PRESIDENTIAL DISCOURSE

Mursi did not deliver an annual speech to parliament that could be compared to his predecessors, simply because there was no People's Assembly during his short tenure in office. Mursi's most significant speech, however, could well be the one he delivered before assuming office in Tahrir Square on June 29, 2012. In this speech, the president-elect did not mention the judiciary plainly but stated what some judges believed to be a challenge to their authority. First, Mursi performed the presidential oath in Tahrir before he took the official oath before the SCC. Second, the president-elect maintained, "I confirm my utter rejection to confiscating the authority of the people and its deputies." He repeated this assertion twice before stating his respect for the constitution, the institutions, and the judiciary. Many considered these two gestures as an early indication of Mursi's plan to take on the courts. Mursi, in the end, tried to make amends stating that he "respects the rulings of Egypt's exulted judiciary." This modest tribute was a far cry from Mubarak's lavish praise on the courts. Judges took notice of the change in tone.

In the following months, the struggle between judges and the president escalated. Mursi hinted at judicial conspiracies to undermine his administration, a claim that the SCC publicly denied. The president's assistant on foreign relations issued a statement to the foreign press criticizing the SCC.[5]

---

[3] Mursi, nonetheless, added another oath ceremony in Cairo University (where members of the dissolved People's Assembly gathered) and a third at Tahrir Square.

[4] Personal Interview with a Deputy Chief Justice of the SCC, March 13, 2018.

[5] The long communique published on December 13, 2012, included the following statements: "Restore the *dubiously* dissolved Parliament (8 July 2012). The decision by the President to restore parliament was immediately overturned by a second decision of the Supreme Constitutional Court (SCC)." The SCC took exception to the reference of the ruling to dissolve the Peoples' Assembly as dubious. It also did not appreciate another reference "Signals from a number of quarters that the SCC will dissolve the CA."

"The Constitutional Declaration of 22 November 2012 was aimed primarily at doing this by extending the life of the CA in order to facilitate consensus and by immunizing these decisions from intervention by the SCC." The SCC responded stating that the presidency seeks to "undermine the reputation of this court internationally . . . without giving one piece of truthful

The SCC's General Assembly responded by releasing a fiery statement defending itself and criticizing its detractors. Some justices flocked to the nightly talk shows defending themselves and their court.

The Shura Council further infuriated the SCC when it revealed the details of its budget, claiming that each justice receives a *monthly* salary of EGP 120,000 (about $17,100 at that time) in a country where the average *annual* household income during 2010–2011 was EGP 25,353.[6] The Shura Council's Constitutional and Legislative Affairs Committee refused to grant the SCC its proposed raise and mandated the appearance of one of its members before approving the proposed budget.

The Freedom and Justice Party did not do Mursi any favor when it organized mass demonstrations on April 19, 2013, under the slogan of "cleansing the judiciary." These demonstrations were marked by vicious verbal attacks on judges and the courts. Furthermore, Mursi judicial allies tried to revoke the judicial immunity of Ahmed El-Zend, the president of the Judges Club. The High Judicial Court (HJC), however, did not cooperate. Mursi could not enlist the support of high-ranking judges as Mubarak before and Sisi after would do.

In his last televised speech on June 26, 2013, Mursi launched scathing attacks on the judiciary. The president claimed that Judge Ali M. al-Nemr rigged the 2005 election and this judge is among "a group of 22 judges that should be under investigation and dismissed because of their election rigging." Indeed, most judges felt that the public attacks on one of their own was an attack on the institution itself. Mursi also mocked the non-guilty verdicts against the leading members of the Mubarak regime as well as the thugs who were released by the Public Prosecution Department (PPD) or the courts.[7]

---

evidence to support his [The President's Assistant on Foreign Relations] allegations and claims."

[6] The figures are according to the Central Agency for Public Mobilization and Statistics. The SCC's salaries are a remarkably sensitive matter for the justices. SCC justices receive much higher pay and many generous benefits than the counterparts in the courts or the Council of State. When the Court of Cassation and the Courts of Appeal issued rulings requiring the SCC to reveal the salaries, the SCC responded by issuing a counter ruling declaring the salaries "internal matters of the SCC and revealing them an attack on SCC' autonomy." When a senior judge at the Cairo Court of Appeal accompanied a court clerk to enforce the ruling, he was politely kicked out of the SCC's headquarters and advised not to return. SCC justices would argue that other judges at the courts and the Council of State receive much higher overall income through their secondment income and the SCC justices cannot be seconded. Personal Interview with a Deputy Chief Justice at the SCC, March 13, 2018.

[7] In one occasion, the Public Prosecution Department released three activists who were accused of attacking the Brotherhood office in Alexandria. *Shrouk*, April 22, 2013.

REGIME POLICIES TOWARD THE JUDICIARY

Mursi advisors believed that the power of the generals and judges bolstered each other and undercut presidential authority.[8] Mursi first resolved to restore the People's Assembly to counterbalance the military–judicial partnership. The presidential order recalled the parliament and mandated legislative elections in sixty days. The Peoples' Assembly convened and asked the Court of Cassation for its opinion on the implementation of the SCC ruling. This decision was a crude attempt to pit one high court against another. The Court of Cassation, however, refused to be drawn into a battle with a fellow high court and declared it had no jurisdiction to review such ruling.

The presidential decree to recall the "dissolved" lower house was met with an uproar from the SCC and many judges. Prominent judges launched fiery public criticism against the decision in a televised news conference organized by the Judges Club. The SCC sought to nullify Mursi's decree by convening an emergency session, an innovative practice in the court's institutional history. In less than forty-eight hours after Mursi announced his presidential order, the SCC held a hearing to review implementation disputes filed against the decree.[9] After one brief session, the SCC ordered the suspension of the presidential order immediately.[10]

The extreme speed with which the SCC responded to his decree confirmed Mursi's doubts about the adversarial nature of the high court. The president, however, concluded that he could not take on the SCC before affirming his authority over the military. Mursi seized on the public's discontent after the murder of army soldiers in Sinai and issued his first constitutional declaration on August 11, 2012.[11]

---

[8]   Personal Interview with a close aide to Mursi's advisor, August 10, 2013.

[9]   Implementation dispute is a legal technique in which an affected party petitions the court to issue a stay to suspend the implementation of a law, an executive decision, or even a court ruling on the premise that ramifications would be detrimental if the party had to wait for the final ruling on the merit of the case.

[10]   In this short interval, the People's Assembly convened and sent a bill on the selection process for the Constituent Assembly (CA) to Mursi, who quickly signed it into law, rendering the case outside the jurisdiction of the administrative courts, and protecting the CA from another suspension by an administrative court.

[11]   The declaration stated, "1- The 17 June 2012 constitutional addendum is to be abrogated. 2- Article 25, clause 2 of the 30 March 2011 Constitutional Declaration is to be replaced with the following text: "And he [the president] will undertake all his duties as stipulated by Article 56 of this declaration." [Article 56 outlines the authorities of the Supreme Council of the Armed Forces (SCAF) and grants the latter full executive and legislative powers]. 3- If the Constituent Assembly is prevented from doing its duties, the president can draw up a new assembly representing the full spectrum of Egyptian society mandated with drafting a new constitution

The August Declaration effectively removed the SCAF from its formal role in politics. The declaration sacked most SCAF members, including its chief field marshal Tantawi. Mursi promoted the director of military intelligence Major General Abdel Fatah El-Sisi, the youngest SCAF member, to the rank of general and appointed him minister of defense and commander-in-chief of the armed forces, a decision that Mursi would come to regret.[12] In addition, Mursi announced the appointment of senior judge Mahmoud Mekki as vice-president. The first ever judge and civilian to assume the high office. This olive branch, nonetheless, was not enough to bring judges on board.

After what seemed at that time to be a solution to the civil–military problem, Mursi's immediate goals were to conclude the constitutional drafting process, protect the upper house of parliament, and ensure control over or at least to secure the neutrality of the PPD. Courts' interventions promised to threaten these goals. Hence; the president issued another constitutional declaration on Thanksgiving Day, November 22, 2012. This was the most consequential of Mursi's order during his short tenure. The declaration first attempted to anchor the measures on the goals of the January 25th Revolution and the president of the Republic as the officer in charge of fulfilling these objectives. With the purpose of building "new legitimacy based on a constitution" to promote "principles of freedom, justice, and democracy," decree the following:

- Article I: "Reopening the investigations and prosecutions in the cases of murder, attempted murder, and wounding of protesters as well as the crimes of terror committed against the revolutionaries by anyone who held a political or executive position under the former regime, according to the Law of the Protection of the Revolution and other laws."
- Article II: "Previous constitutional declarations, laws, and decrees issued by the president since he took office on 30 June 2012, until the constitution is approved and a new People's Assembly [lower house of parliament] is elected, are final and binding and cannot be appealed by any way or to any entity. Nor shall they be suspended or canceled, and all lawsuits related to them and brought before any judicial body against these decisions are annulled."

within three months of the assembly's formation. The new draft constitution is to be put before a nationwide referendum within 30 days after it is written. Parliamentary elections are to be held within two months of the public's approval of the draft constitution."

[12] Gen. Sisi's aspirations to play a political role outside his military preview were transparent from the very beginning. Mursi, however, had complete trust in the former intelligence chief, who appeared to be profoundly religious.

- Article III: "The public prosecutor is to be appointed from among the members of the judiciary by the President of the Republic for a period of four years commencing from the date of office and is subject to the general conditions of being appointed as a judge and should not be under the age of 40. This provision applies to the one currently holding the position with immediate effect."
- Article IV: "The text of the article on the formation of the Constituent Assembly in the 30 March 2011 Constitutional Declaration that reads, "it shall prepare a draft of a new constitution in a period of six months from the date it was formed" is to be amended to "it shall prepare the draft of a new constitution for the country no later than eight months from the date of its formation.""
- Article V: "No judicial body can dissolve the Shura Council [upper house of parliament] or the Constituent Assembly."
- Article VI: "The President may take the necessary actions and measures to protect the country and the goals of the revolution."

The declaration was an apparent attempt to get the courts out of the transition process. It prevented all courts from reviewing (suspending or canceling) all constitutional declarations, laws, and decrees promulgated by the president since he took office on June 30, 2012. No judicial body, read the SCC, could dissolve the Shura Council or the CA. The CA was given two extra months to conclude its proceedings. The Mubarak-era PP was sacked, and Mursi appointed a replacement.

Mursi's actions, dubbed a power grab by his critics, angered the opposition and unified all anti-Brotherhood forces against the president. Rallies were held in Tahrir Square and some major cities. Judges spearheaded the opposition to what they saw as a blatant attack on the independence of the judiciary. Most courts, including the Court of Cassation, suspended their proceedings. Violent clashes near the presidential palace added fuel to the fire. These actions created two gargantuan crises with the judiciary and the opposition involving the PP and the CA.

THE PUBLIC PROSECUTOR CRISIS

The PP is arguably the most critical judicial assignment. Since 1952, the government made it a norm to appoint political allies to this post. Mubarak went to great pains to select highly trusted protégés. Mahmoud was named public prosecutor in 2006. The appointment of a relatively young judge reflected Mubarak's complete confidence in Mahmoud's political inclinations. Traditionally, the PP was appointed for no more than three years. Mahmoud served the regime's interests well and delivered valuable RSFs to Mubarak. Some revolutionaries would even argue that he served his old masters after they left office by not fully prosecuting their crimes after the 2011 uprising. No wonder revolutionary demands to remove Mahmoud were echoed since Mubarak's departure. The SCAF, however, turned a blind eye.

Mursi was expected to attempt to remove the PP; after all, it was Mahmoud who imprisoned thousands of the Brotherhood's activists, including Mursi himself. Initially, the president tried to remove Mahmoud by offering him the ambassadorship to the Holy See. After initially consenting, the PP, buttressed by the Judges Club, secular parties, the military, and security apparatus, backtracked. The presidency capitulated, and Mahmoud kept his post. These ill-advised actions further widened the wedge between the administration and the courts and enormously weakened presidential prestige.

The November Constitutional Declaration crudely removed Mahmoud and appointed a replacement without consultation with the HJC. These actions were met by an uproar among the judicial corps. Most judges perceived such decisions as clear infringements on judicial independence; something that even Mubarak did not dare to do. Even those who suspected Mahmoud's relations with the old regime and earlier demanded his departure objected to the way he was removed. It appeared that Mursi replaced Mubarak's protégé with his own.

Many judges and prosecutors bitterly protested Mahmoud's removal. The Judges Club spearheaded the effort to restore Mahmoud to his post and many prosecutors organized a sit-in in the PPD headquarter in downtown Cairo. The anti-Mursi camp benefited from Mahmoud's popularity with the rank and file. After serving for years, the ousted PP commanded loyalty within the judicial corps, particularly among young prosecutors for the services he provided and his fatherly treatment of younger subordinates.[13] The Judges

---

[13] One mid-level judge narrated an indicative incident of how Mahmoud built support within the judicial corps. "Two young prosecutors wanted to purchase apartments sold by the Ministry of Housing. The two young men stormed the office of the official responsible for making such decisions, demanding the approval needed to purchase the prized apartments (Egypt has a chronic shortage of housing). The prosecutors argued with the official, who refused to grant them the preferential treatment and reported the incident to their superiors. The district attorney warned the young prosecutors from repeating such offenses and as guidelines dictate related the incident to the office of the PP. A week or so later, the two prosecutors were summoned before the PP. The young prosecutors were naturally apprehensive of the expected disciplinary actions. When they met Mahmoud, the Public Prosecutor (PP) asked them to

Club and anti-Brotherhood media launched a barrage of attacks against the newly appointed PP.

Abdullah, who did not comprehend the inner workings of the PPD, was hardly the right choice to replace Mahmoud. A judicial mutiny erupted and undermined his authority and standing. The insurrection against the PP reached a new height when junior members of the PPD challenged a directive from the newly appointed PP before the HJC.[14] Abdullah did not do himself any favors when he appeared to be intervening in investigations of the violent clashes near the presidential palace (*Ittihadiya*), where the opposition alleged that the Brotherhood's henchmen attacked protestors.[15]

Mahmoud filed a lawsuit before the Judicial Personal Circuit (JPC) of Cairo's Appeals Court. This was a smart tactic as most judges naturally sided with the PP against what they perceived as a breach of judicial independence. As expected, the highly anticipated ruling came in favor of Mahmoud. On March 27, 2013, the JPC invalidated the removal of Mahmoud and the appointment of Abdullah. The verdict was patently the work of activist judges who wanted to further judicial independence (or weaken the presidency). In concluding that the president lacked authority to remove judges, the JPC characterized judicial independence as a "basic and salient feature" of Egypt's constitutional structure. The court considered judicial independence a "supra-constitutional" principle superior to presidential decrees and legislation. Evidently, the ruling was a significant boost to anti-Mursi factions. Mahmoud and his allies demanded his immediate return to the post. Abdullah naturally appealed the decision to the Court of Cassation.

The Court of Cassation lent its support to the anti-Mursi camp on July 2, 2013. Amidst the political crisis that was the pretext for the military takeover, the Court of Cassation annulled the presidential constitutional declaration

---

describe the details of the incident. After they finished, the PP picked up his phone, called the minister of housing and got the two prosecutors the apartments they wanted!" These types of tales of generosity traveled fast in a close-knit community like the Egyptian judiciary. An interview with a judge seconded to the Ministry of Justice, Cairo, July 18, 2013. Mahmoud also turned a blind eye to the large numbers of loyalist judges and prosecutors who received land grants at reduced prices from the government. The president of the Central Auditing Organization reported that member of the State Security Prosecution Office has illegally acquired land in a prime location the suburbs of Giza. *Almasry Alyoum*, February 17, 2014.

[14] *Youm 7*, January 30, 2013.

[15] The clashes started on December 5th when hundreds of Muslim Brotherhood supporters marched to the presidential palace in response to several days of protests and sit-in by Mursi's opponents. Brotherhood and FJP supporters then broke up a sit-in of several dozen anti-Mursi protesters. Over the next twelve hours, violent clashes between the two sides escalated. Egypt's riot police and other security forces stationed nearby made no serious effort to halt the violence.

and mandated the return of Mahmoud. This was a symbolic and practical setback for the presidency. From a symbolic standpoint, the ruling reinforced the claim that Mursi did not have the legal authority to issue a constitutional declaration. From a practical perspective, the vast legal powers of the PP were transferred to Mursi's rivals. Mahmoud and his allies in the PPD instantaneously sprang into action, issuing several arrest warrants to many of Mursi's close associates and confidants.[16] The political significance of the office of the PP would manifest itself clearly after Mursi's removal.

THE CONSTITUTIONAL DRAFTING PROCESS

The supposedly straightforward constitutional drafting process was thwarted by political disagreements, judicial intervention, and the SCAF's manipulation. Mursi inherited the problem, and his actions did not help cultivate a consensus-building process. After the failed attempt to restore the Peoples' Assembly, the Administrative Court decided to expedite its review of the legal challenges against the Second Constitutional Assembly. While, initially, the court had scheduled a session on September 4th to review the petition, it decided on July 12, 2012, to hear the oral arguments on July 17th. Again, this was perceived by Mursi's supporter as another judicial assail against the Islamists.[17]

One of the key provisions of the August Constitutional Declaration was to empower Mursi rather than SCAF to select a different assembly if the CA did not conclude its assignment. The president, however, wanted no part in this lose-lose game and very much preferred that the CA would accomplish its missions. Any assembly selected by Mursi would either undermine the Islamist alliance or infuriate liberals. For this purpose, lawyers defending the CA exhausted all legal maneuvers to delay the bending ruling, which most expected to be detrimental to the assembly. In the end, the Administrative Court referred the dissolution case against the assembly to the SCC questioning the constitutionality of Law 79 of 2012 on the composition of the CA.[18]

If ruled unconstitutional, the assembly would have been dissolved for the second time. Nevertheless, because of the minimum time needed for the SCC to issue a ruling, it looked as if the CA would survive long enough to finalize the draft constitution. However, in a complicated legal maneuver to

---

[16] *Ahram*, July 2, 2013.
[17] The court argued that its decision came as a response to the plaintiff in the case and it is within the legal norms. *Almasry Alyoum*, July 12, 2012.
[18] *Ahram*, October 23, 2012.

negate the adjudication deadlines, two "implantation disputes" were filed demanding to suspend the aforementioned law and hence the work of the CA.[19] The SCC raised apprehension when it put these two motions on its docket for its monthly session on December 2, 2012.[20] If the SCC ruled for the plaintiff, the assembly could be prevented from completing its work. Mursi seemed to have taken this peril seriously.[21] This fear was the cardinal reason behind Mursi's November Declaration.

The CA held an overnight meeting to railroad the final approval of the draft constitution on November 30th, preempting adversarial judicial actions. Mursi promptly scheduled the referendum to take place two weeks later (December 15, 2012). However, one potential source of danger remained. The SCC had two implantation disputes on its docket for the December 2, 2012, session. The Islamists were sufficiently worried that the SCC might still rule on the pending cases against the Shura Council and the Constitute Assembly.[22] In a show of force, Mursi's supporters besieged the SCC's head-quarter and publically declared they would not leave until the referendum was held.

The SCC issued a strongly worded statement to condemn the protestors and their leaders and suspended its sessions until further notice.[23] Justice Mohamed El-Shenway stated, "the Brotherhood sympathizers' siege of the SCC was the hardest moment in the court's history and the most painful for its justices."[24] This episode further widened the gap between judges and the presidency. The regime and its supporters repulsed many judges. The antagonistic media and secular opposition seized these developments to also cast the government as illegitimate.

In a last-ditch attempt to block the referendum, judicial associations announced they would boycott the referendum. The president of the Judges

---

[19] This legal tactic was the same one that the SCC used to suspend Mursi's decree calling the parliament a few months ago. Implantation Dispute No. 6 of the 34 Judicial Year.

[20] Implantation Dispute No. 8 and Implantation Dispute No. 10 of the 34 Judicial Year.

[21] After all, the SCC had all the motives in the world against the proposed draft constitution. The SCC, also, was widely expected to dissolve the Shura Council on the same grounds it used to dissolve the People's Assembly.

[22] In retrospect, it seems that the regime supporters were accurate in their anticipation of the court's actions. On June 2, 2013, the SCC ruled unconstitutional both the CA selection law and the Shura Council electoral law.

[23] The SCC official spokesman Justice Maher Sami wrote in the SCC journal criticizing those who attacked the court and prevented the justices from performing their functions. Sami seemed pessimistic about the future of the SCC in the light of the proposed changes to its mandate. *Al-Dostoriah*, Issue 23 http://sccourt.gov.eg/SCC/faces/Portal_Pages/PortalHome .jspx?_afrLoop=159341179731153&_afrWindowMode=0&_adf.ctrl-state=kdeqgnw54_4.

[24] *Ahram*, July 10, 2014.

Club petitioned the administrative courts to nullify the presidential decree to call for a referendum on the new constitution.[25] Mursi withdrew his initial constitutional declaration to coax enough judges into supervising the vote. He issued a third declaration that removed several restrictions on the judiciary. The December 9th Declaration voided the November 22nd Declaration but mandated that "all its consequences remain in effect." Mursi's fear of judicial meddling is quite apparent in his insistence on maintaining in the new declaration the provision that "All constitutional declarations, including the current one, are immune from any challenge in any court and all related lawsuits are considered void."

Furthermore, taking into consideration the possibility of a "no-vote" on the draft, the president agreed to remove himself from the process of selecting a replacement CA and provided guarantees of the voting process. Article 3 of the Declaration mandates,

> If the people vote against the draft constitution in the referendum on Saturday, 15 December 2012, the President is to call for the direct election of a new Constituent Assembly of 100 members within three months. The new Assembly is to finish its task within six months from its election date. The President is to then call for a referendum on the new draft presented by the Assembly within thirty days of receiving it. In all cases, vote counting and the announcement of results of the constitutional referendum is to take place publicly in election subcommittees as soon as the voting process is finished. The results are to be validated by the head of the subcommittee.

Despite this concession, judges and the other regime's foes did not lessen their opposition to the draft constitution. Due to the insufficient number of judges willing to oversee the referendum, the Elections Commission was forced to hold the referendum in two rounds. The constitution was ultimately approved with nearly a two-thirds majority on December 25, 2012, but neither Mursi nor judges could forget the bitter conflict.

THE JUDICIARY IN THE 2012 CONSTITUTION

This visible and highly controversial meddling in the transition process was reflected in the constitution. The constitution broadened the powers of all judicial institutions except the SCC. The constitution added many provisions that furthered the institutional autonomy of the courts. The constitution mandated financial independence for the courts and the Council of State

---

[25] *Ahram*, December 11, 2012.

and provided a constitutional mandate for the first time for the Administrative Prosecution Authority (APA) and the State Cases Authority (SCA). The Council of State gained explicit affirmation of its prerogatives in the constitutional text, safeguarding it from any legislative diminution. The constitution authorized the HJC to appoint the public prosecutor in a way that guarantees his independence from the presidency. The constitution prohibited the despised practice of part-time seconding, which was used under Mubarak as a carrot to elicit support from specific judges. Under the new provisions, "Judges can only be seconded for full time and only to entities and perform duties subscribed by legislation."

The constitution removed several of the 1971 constitutional clauses that judges regarded as infringements on judicial independence. For instance, Article 170 allowed the inclusion of laypersons in the composition of judicial circuits. Article 171 organized the much-despised State Security Courts, and Article 173 created the Supreme Council of Judicial Bodies to ensure executive control over judicial affairs.

On the other hand, the SCC was evidently the biggest loser in the 2012 Constitution. The constitution curtailed the SCC's power and limited its independence. Articles 175–178 and 233 of the constitution delineated many structural changes pertaining to the SCC's powers and composition. The SCC membership was reduced from eighteen to eleven justices. The day the constitution went into effect, seven justices received their pink slips. Proponents of such a provision argued that reducing the number of judges would limit the power of the presidency to increase the number of judges at will, cut costs, and eliminate the power of the chief justice to assign justices into different panels for political reasons. Presumably, this ceiling was enacted to get rid of the most divisive justices, especially the highly controversial Tahani Al-Gebali, who was number twelve in the rank of seniority.[26] Furthermore, eliminating junior justices had the added benefit of limiting tenure on the bench. Most junior justices were relatively young and were expected to serve for at least a decade.[27]

---

[26] Justice al-Gebali's vociferous criticism of the forces of political Islam and her open cooperation with the SCAF gave the impression of a political partisan rather than an impartial judge. It did not help her image a bit that *The New York Times* titled its report after the dissolution of the People's Assembly "Judge Helped Egypt's Military to Cement Power." *The New York Times*, March 7, 2012.

[27] With a retirement age set at seventy years for all justices, the oldest justice of those who were removed was expected to retire in 2021, and the rest were expected to leave the court in or after 2027.

In addition to reducing its manpower, the constitution curtailed the SCC's institutional independence in selecting its members.[28] Since the SCAF's legislative amendments in 2011, the SCC General Assembly had exclusive competence to appoint all justices, including the chief justice. Article 176 of the constitution changed this. It stipulated, "The Supreme Constitutional Court is made up of a president and ten members. The law determines the judicial or other bodies and associations that nominate them, the manner in which they are to be appointed, and the requirements to be satisfied by them. Appointments take place by a decree from the President of the Republic." This was a grave danger from the perspective of the SCC and its allies in the state institutions. The constitution empowered other entities with the authority to nominate justices to be appointed by the president of the Republic.[29] With the Islamist in control of the presidency and likely to regain control of the legislature once the elections were held, nominations were expected to reflect their ideological commitments, which stands in sharp contrast to those justices serving on the SCC. Furthermore, the SCC also lost its authority to call its members into account as per Article 177 of the 1971 Constitution. The constitution was deliberately silent about this, and some expected that amendments to the SCC law would empower other institutions with authority to discipline the justices.

The desire to limit the SCC political power is also evident in other provisions in the 2012 Constitution. The SCC was stripped of the ability to dissolve elected assemblies at the national or local levels. The court's judicial review of legislation related to local, parliamentary, and presidential elections was restricted to abstract review of the legislation before enactment. Article 177 of the 2012 Constitution stipulated,

> The President or the House of Representatives shall present the proposed laws regulating presidential, legislative, and local elections to the Supreme Constitutional Court prior to their issuance to opine on the extent of their conformity with the constitution. The Court issues its decision in this matter within forty-five days from the date the matter is presented thereto, otherwise the Courts' non-issuance of the decision would be considered an approval of the proposed texts. In the event the Court decided the unconstitutionality of

---

[28] A deputy chief justice of the SCC stated that the SCC's justices believed that Mursi intended to abolish the court altogether if he was able to consolidate power. Personal interview with a Deputy Chief Justice of the SCC, March 13, 2018.

[29] These changes were enacted despite repeated calls from the SCC chief justice expressing the court's desire to maintain its control over selecting its members as mandated by Law 48 of 2011. The SCC maintained that this was one of the achievements of the January 25th Revolution. *Ahram*, October 22, 2012.

a provision or more, its decision shall be applied prior to the issuance of the law. These laws are not subject to succeeding oversight stipulated under Article (175) of the Constitution.

The constitution also specified the main structure of the electoral process to deny the SCC the power to shape legislative elections or outcomes. Article 231 stipulated, "In the legislative elections that follow the entry into effect of the Constitution, two-thirds of the seats are to be filled through the list system. One third is to be filled through the single winner system. Parties and independent candidates may run under either of the two systems."

Naturally, the SCC was not particularly thrilled with these dramatic restrictions of its power.[30] Furthermore, the SCC also lost its prerogative to provide binding interpretation of legislative texts as per Article 175 of the 1971 Constitution. The distrust in the SCC is also evident in provisions related to the National Elections Authority (NEA). The NEA entrusted with supervising all elections was to have no members from the SCC.[31] The NEA was to be chaired by a Court of Cassation judge and included in its membership nine additional members drawn from the Court of Cassation, the Courts of Appeals, the Council of State, the APA, and the SCA. Legal disputes pertaining to the elections were also to be decided before the Court of Cassation and the Council of State.

Furthermore, the constitution removed the SCC judicial review over presidential decrees endorsed in a referendum. While the power to bypass

---

[30] Abdel Aziz Salman, then the head of the SCC commissioners body wrote in the SCC periodical, a scathing analysis of the abstract review in the 2012 Constitution, maintaining, "Anyone who appraises this constitutional text, finds it completely narrow the domain of legitimacy and even the principle of legality and the notion of legal state in their understanding in true democratic countries or those that want to efficiently move in this direction. That is because the Constitution has closed the road for concrete judicial review, practiced by the SCC as a standard method to review the constitutionality of legislation without the existence of a mechanism to ensure that the legislature has entirely and faithfully implemented the SCC decision on abstract review." Abdel Aziz Salman, *Al-Dostoriah*, Issue 23.

[31] The SCC also lost its dominant position in managing the presidential elections. Previous provisions enacted in 2005 and continued until the passing of the Constitution created the Supreme Presidential Elections Commission (SPEC) with draconian powers not subject to any form of judicial review or legislative oversight. Article 28 of the 2011 Constitutional Declaration stated, "A supreme judicial commission named the "Presidential Elections Commission" will supervise the election of the president of the republic beginning with the announcement of the opening of candidate nomination and ending with the announcement of the election result." The five-member SPEC was headed by the SCC's chief justice and included the most senior justices of the SCC. The SPEC's secretary-general, who controlled the day-to-day management of the elections was also the head of the SCC's commissioner's body.

parliament and appeal directly to the public was not novel, as it did exist in the 1971 Constitution (Article 152), the new provision explicitly shielded these actions by stating that "the results of the referendum are binding on all state authorities and everyone." (Article 150) Moreover, the president of the Court of Cassation, not the chief justice of the SCC, was to preside over the trial if the House of Representatives impeached the president of the Republic.

In addition to the constitutional changes in relation to the judiciary, intense debate over amending the Law of Judicial Authority continued under Mursi. The lack of trust between the two sides was apparent in the discussions regarding the amendments to the Judicial Authority Law. Demands to implement changes converged during July 2012 – June 2013. These demands echoed the debate that emerged since the 1980s and intensified in the last years of Mubarak's reign. This included the appointment of the PP, Judicial Inspection Department (JID), seconding judges, powers of presidents of the courts, judicial salaries, and the retirement age.

The proposed law presented by Al-Wast Party (a moderate Islamic party, considered close to the ideological line of the Muslim Brotherhood) angered many senior judges because it included a provision lowering the retirement age for all judicial personals to sixty years. Junior judges supported decreasing the retirement age. This reduction would have allowed faster promotions to the painfully scarce top judicial post. Many judges, however, perceived the proposed change as a stepping-stone to packing the courts with pro-Brotherhood judges. The Judges Club was steadfast that the Shura Council lacked the authority to draft such significant legislation.

When a compromise was reached to organize the Second Justice Conference to bridge the gap with judges and reach a consensus bill to be adopted by parliament, the Shura Council continued the deliberations. Judicial associations responded angrily and forced the HJC to suspend the work of the organization committee. Regardless, Mursi could have introduced some changes to the Law of Judicial Authority to ensure the political neutrality of the judicial system. These changes could have included the following:

- Separating the investigative power from the prosecution authority (as it was before 1952);
- Removing the JID from the auspices of the Ministry of Justice and grant it to the HJC;
- Transferring the appointment of presidents of first instance courts from the Ministry of Justice to the HJC;
- Empowering the courts' general assemblies and prohibiting the delegation of authority from the general assemblies to the presidents.

The Brotherhood must surely regret squandering this opportunity. Enacting all or some of these proposed changes could have lessened the politicization of the courts and ensure more guarantees of due process and fair trials.

JUDGES ON THE OFFENSIVE

Like other corporate judges, Egyptian judges put a premium on their institutional independence and public image. Many of the regime actions were perceived as an attack on judicial independence and the stature of judges. The anti-Mursi camp within the judicial corps capitalized on these blunders to beget a majority of judges to view the regime as an enemy of the judiciary. The anti-Mursi camp was able to cast the debate over judicial reform as an attack on judicial independence and in doing so was able to attract support from judges who predictably worry about this crucial corporate goal. In addition, Mursi paid dearly for the undisciplined discourse of several of his allies. Public statements accusing the judiciary of corruption and demanding a large-scale purge did not sit well with the rank and file. Radical Islamists' raging calls to besiege judge's houses were met with an uproar. A Judges Club statement left no doubts about how many in the judiciary felt:

> Since the election of Muslim Brotherhood members to the Parliament, and the election of President Mursi, numerous and unprecedented hostile attacks against the judiciary and courts have taken place, these actions were under the patronage of the ruling party; the Justice and Freedom Party, which is the political arm of the Muslim Brotherhood.[32]

---

[32] The statement went further to maintain "Undermining the Rule of Law and the right to a fair trial took many forms, to name a few: issuing a Presidential Decree stating that Presidential decrees and laws – past and present – shall be immune from the judicial review process; the dismissal of the Egyptian Public Prosecutor despite his constitutional immunity; refusing to uphold a court decision reinstating the Public Prosecutor; the transfer of judges from their courts as a punishment for rendering a ruling, concerning the legality of the process upon which the President appointed a new Public Prosecutor; the constant and systematic ridicule of court decisions and verdicts in an attempt to polarize the public against the judiciary; and finally the current attempt to dismiss 3500 judges. The Egyptian Judiciary has stood firm during the reign of all previous regimes, to protect civil liberties and the right to a fair trial, and have fought to secure Egyptians' rights to cast their votes freely despite the previous regime's attacks on them. Today, they continue their long struggle for democracy, human rights, civil liberties and judicial independence. The Judge' profoundly appreciates the support it received from professional associations, civil society, Media and members of the public, for their struggle to secure a free, modern and democratic Egypt. The Egyptian judiciary is here to defend the rule of law and protect civil liberty, that was our oath, and we will uphold it."

Many judges interviewed during the process of researching this book, believe that Mursi committed the following offenses against the courts:

1. Recalling the People's Assembly that was dissolved by the SCC.
2. Removing the public prosecutor and unilaterally appointing a replacement.
3. Preventing the courts from examining presidential orders (above the law).
4. Besieging the SCC.

The judiciary proved it could make the president's life very difficult. Judicial actions were instrumental in unseating Mursi and facilitating the generals return to power. These positions were clear in judicial rulings that delegitimized the regime's central institutions on one hand and prevented the completion of the transition process on the other.

FIRST, DELEGITIMATION OF THE REGIME

Chief executives in authoritarian or democratic countries have been accused of an assortment of moral and legal offenses. However, a claim that a sitting president was a mole and a conspirator with a foreign power is arguably unique to Egypt. In a somewhat bizarre judicial drama, a trivial misdemeanor related to the instance of the Wadi El-Natrun prison break during the January 2011 uprising, was transformed into a major criminal case. This lawsuit included Mursi himself and many of the top leaders of his Muslim Brotherhood.[33] The case and the intensive media coverage it received provided ammunition for the opposition's unremitting campaigns against the presidency and the Brotherhood.

One week before the June 30th protests, The Ismailia Misdemeanor Court decided to refer the Wadi El-Natrun case to the PPD for further investigation. The presiding judge asserted that Muslim Brotherhood members conspired with Hamas, Hezbollah, and local militants to storm the prison in 2011 to free Mohamed Mursi and thirty-three other Islamist leaders.[34] The verdict

[33] In the early days after Mubarak's removal, Mursi was seen as one of those that suffered injustice and illegal detention by the former authorities and was accidentally freed during the chaos prevailing in the country.

[34] There were a lot of dark clouds surrounding the presiding judge, Khaled Mahgoub, who is the son of Mohamed Ali Mahgoub, a leading member of the Mubarak's ruling party. Mahgoub is on record in a number of TV interviews after Mursi's removal praising the army. Mahgoub was rewarded with an assignment to the PP's technical office after Mursi's removal. *Ahram*, October 2, 2013.

mentioned all the names of the Brotherhood, including the president, the former speaker of the People's Assembly, and scores of other top leaders.

The consequences of this case undoubtedly added another strong reason for many Egyptians to question the loyalty of the president and the Muslim Brotherhood. In Egypt's polarized political climate, Mursi's opponents used his escape from Wadi El-Natrun against him, declaring the Brotherhood's collaborators violated the country's security and fed its instability. The eagerness of some in the intelligence and security agencies to blame Hamas could in part reflect resentment of the Brotherhood's ties with the Palestinian group, which they have long seen as a threat. The political opposition used the case to deprecate the presidency further, claiming that Mursi committed treason and conspiracy against the state.[35]

In another judicial effort to cast doubts on Mursi's presidency, the Supreme Presidential Election Committee (SPEC) announced on June 20, 2013, ten days before the expected mega protest, it would convene to review Shafiq's appeal to invalidate Mursi's election. The SPEC did not convene since delivering the results of the 2012 presidential elections and miraculously rose from the ashes, casting more doubts on the embattled president at a critical juncture of his tenure.[36] The anti-Mursi media seized this news to recall accusations of foul play during the elections. The SPEC's decision came as a surprise to most legal experts for three reasons: first, the SPEC already addressed these allegations and concluded that it did not influence the results. Second, SPEC's membership had changed extensively with the retirement of most of its members and the appointment of its secretary general to a ministerial post. Third, and arguably most importantly, the March 2011 Constitutional Declaration, which governed the transitions period, is abundantly clear in shielding all SPEC's decisions from any and all legal appeals.[37] Once more, this was used by the regime's antagonists to cast doubts on the president's legitimacy.

The judicial actions did not only target the president but extended to other pillars of his regime. For example, Prime Minister Hisham Qnadil was not spared from the barrage of judicial attacks. A lower court sentenced him to a year in jail and ordered his removal from office on the count of refusing to

---

[35] This ruling was a legal excuse used by the regime to detain Mursi after his removal from office.

[36] *Shrouk*, June 20, 2013.

[37] Article 28 states, "The Commission's decisions will be final and carry the force of law, and will not subject to objections from any party, in the same manner as it is forbidden for the decisions to be stopped or canceled."

implement an administrative court order.[38] In a surgically timed ruling delivered a few minutes before Mursi's highly anticipated speech before the June 30th demonstration, the administrative court issued a decision ordering the minister of information, a close ally of the president, to pay back EGP 269,000 that he received as financial incentives. The court scolded senior government officials for receiving monetary benefits beyond what the law granted to them. The ruling went further to argue that the revolutionary regime followed archaic practices of the corrupt old regime.[39]

The courts also ventured to emasculate public trust in the legislative authority. After the dissolution of the People's Assembly, only the Shura Council remained as a representative institution. Mursi did everything in his power to keep the upper house despite legal challenges. The SCC issued a ruling on June 2, 2013. The SCC ruled that the Shura Council was elected on the basis of unconstitutional electoral law, severely damaging its legitimacy.[40] According to the SCC's judgment, "although the articles ruled unconstitutional entails that Shura Council is invalid completely, Article 230 of the constitution passed in December 2012 made the (Shura) Council immune to dissolution and granted it legislative powers until a House of Representatives is elected." On the same day, the SCC also deemed unconstitutional Law 79 of 2012 that established the criteria for selecting the members of the CA. The SCC ruled that the CA that was established in June 2012 was unconstitutional. The judgment came as another legal blow to the embattled Mursi regime. The SCC casted doubts on the legitimacy of the 2012 Constitution.[41]

The administrative courts even ventured into national security and foreign policy ordering the government to demolish the tunnels between Sinai and

---

[38] *Ahram*, June 5, 2013.

[39] *Ahram*, June 26, 2013.

[40] The SCC ruled that the first paragraph of Article 8 of the 1980's Shura Council election law (amended by military decrees No. 109 and 120 of 2011) was unconstitutional. As it did with its previous ruling in May, the SCC reasoned that this article discriminated against independent candidates because it allowed political parties to compete for the one-third of seats reserved for independents, while it stripped independents of the right to compete for the two-thirds of seats reserved for party-based candidates. This article was deemed unconstitutional because it "violated articles 37 and 39 of the constitutional declaration passed by the SCAF) on 30 March 2011."

[41] The HCC also indicated that law No. 79 of 2012 regulating the selection of members of the CA that drafted the constitution violated Article 48 of the constitutional declaration passed by the SCAF on March 30, 2011. "While this declaration granted the State Council the right of reviewing administrative orders, the 2012 law elevated the decisions of the CA above any kind of administrative scrutiny." This happened even though the lawyer who petitioned the court in the first place had withdrawn his appeal during the SCC's deliberations. *Ahram*, May 12, 2013.

Gaza.[42] This initiative was an indirect rebuke to Mursi's government that maintained close ties with Hamas, which controls the Gaza Strip. The administrative court likewise provided protection for anti-Mursi officials. On one occasion. the court reversed a decision to suspend a government official who harshly criticized the president.[43]

The judiciary furthermore was used to drive a wedge between the presidency and the young revolutionaries who spearheaded the January 25th protests. In one famous case involving Hassan Mustafa, a well-known activist from Alexandria, a young district attorney claimed that Mustafa insulted him. In a highly publicized case, the activist received a one-year sentence. Miraculously, a few days after the removal of Mursi, the young district attorney submitted a memo to withdraw his accusations. All this happened after Sisi promised young activists that Mustafa would be released shortly.

SECOND, DELAYING LEGISLATIVE ELECTIONS

The SCC and the Administrative Courts were instrumental in shelving the House of Representative elections. Legislative elections could have brought a representative parliament and an accountable cabinet. Parliamentary elections could have defused the blame from the presidency for all the shortages (real and artificial) in electricity, gas, and other basic needs. Under the 2012 Constitution, the SCC was to perform an abstract review of legislation related to presidential, legislative, and local elections. The abstract review was designed to prevent the court from flexing its muscles later and dissolve elected institutions. This reflected the genuine fear that the Islamists had for the SCC.

The abstract review was first introduced in 2005 to shield the flawed presidential election procedures enacted by Mubarak from further judicial scrutiny. The SCAF used the same method on four different occasions. The SCC typically needed a very short period to issue a decision. For example, the SCC was swift in reviewing the Law of Presidential Elections. The proposed legislation was presented to the SCC on June 18, 2005, and the SCC issued its opinion promptly on June 26, 2005. The SCC did not demand that the People's Assembly return the law to the court to ensure the faithful application of its opinions. The People's Assembly issued the Law on July 2, 2005, and it was published in the official *Gazette* on the same day. During Mubarak and the SCAF's tenure in office, five instances of abstract review occurred.

---

[42] *Ahram*, February 26, 2013.
[43] *Ahram*, April 29, 2013.

The fastest decision came after only four days, and the longest was after twelve days, with an average of 8.2 days. The SCC amendments were somewhat symbolic with no substantial modification to the essence of the proposed legislation.

Under Mursi, however, the SCC abstract review was much lengthier and meticulous. The amendments to the Law of Political Participation and the House of Representatives Law were presented to the SCC on January 20, 2013, and the court issued its opinion on February 17, 2013. The SCC rejected the electoral law's first draft on several grounds, including that some electoral districts were proportionally allocated more seats than other districts for no apparent reason. The Shura Council quickly produced a second draft of the law, which was referred to Mursi for signature, arguing that the SCC should not be given a second opportunity to review the draft law.

Mursi signed the bill into law and issued a presidential decree to call for elections on March 6, 2013. The election procedures were to start on March 9, 2013. However, the Administrative Court, presided over by Judge Al-Dakroury,[44] suspended the presidential call for elections on technical grounds and accepted the unconstitutionality claim based on not returning the law to the SCC to ensure the conformity to its opinions. Amro Mousa, a former presidential candidate and the president of the Congress Party, remarked that the ruling to suspend elections was a "gift from heaven."[45]

The High Administrative Court (HAC) affirmed the lower court decision to suspend the President's call for elections. The HAC reversed the Council's established jurisprudence that classified this type of presidential decree as "matters of sovereignty" and hence excluded from judicial review. Matters of sovereignty, the HAC stated, "change with the changes in the constitutional foundations of the state. These types of matters expand under dictatorship and contracts with the advance of democracy. Only the courts have the right to decide what lies within the issues of sovereignty and what does not. The new constitution removed the call to elections from matters of sovereignty when it included the cabinet in the process."[46] Mursi, embattled from his previous battle with the courts, had to capitulate, and the law was sent back to the Shura Council. The Council returned the proposed legislation to the SCC on

---

[44] Al-Dakroury believes that the scope of "sovereign matters" decreases with the advancement of democratization. Personal interview with Council of State first vice-president Yahia Al-Dakroury, December 2, 2017.

[45] *Ahram*, March 6, 2013.

[46] *Almasry Alyoum*, April 22, 2013.

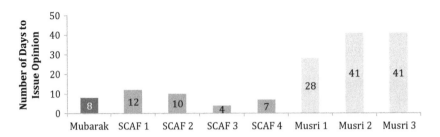

FIGURE 7.1 The number of days the SCC needed to conduct abstract review

April 11, 2013. In the second review, the SCC found four provisions to be unconstitutional:

1. The allocation of seats to different governorates.
2. The usage of religious slogans in campaigns.
3. The president of the republic authority to determine election dates and shortens its duration.
4. The ability of army and police officers to vote.

The Shura Council presented the third draft to the SCC. On May 25th, the SCC again rejected the draft electoral law that the Shura Council had referred to it forty-one days before. The SCC found that the draft law did not conform to the constitution on ten different grounds, some relatively minor and others far more consequential. It was quite eye-opening that the SCC found more shortcomings with the draft laws as time went by. Some of Mursi's supporters found this yet another indication of the SCC's intentions to throw curve balls at the regime. The net result was the inability of the government to organize the legislative elections that could have focused the attention of many Egyptians on campaigning rather than street protests.

This delay was vital to the anti-Brotherhood strategy of creating a unified structure of contestation, which allowed for the formation of a cohesive opposition front from all shades of political opposition to challenge the regime. The broad coalition that included leftist and liberals, old regime reactionaries and young revolutionaries, and seculars and Salafis could have easily fractured if elections were permitted to take place. These groups would have competed against each other to win seats in the legislature.

CONCLUSION

Mursi's tense relation with the courts started early in his presidency. The regime failed to build a cooperative relation with judges. This was a fatal error.

In the critical days prior to the army takeover, judges came decisively on the side of the anti-Mursi camp. The Judges Club organized a march and a sit-in on June 30th to voice their opposition to Mursi and his accusations against a number of judges. These actions coincided with the June 30th public protest organized by the opposition. On July 2nd, the Judges Club president lent full weight of his organization publicly to the military in the crucial days that preceded Mursi's removal stating, "judges affirm their unconditional support to the armed forces."

In doing so, judges were answering the call by the secular intelligentsia, who had been openly calling upon the old guardians of the state – namely, the military and judiciary – to intervene to save the state. The mass protests, widely covered in state-media and cheered on by the state institutions provided the background for the military to regain the political power. Judges' decision to throw their lot with the military is a decision that most likely would come back to haunt them. After all, judges have previously supported another army takeover before, only to regret the outcomes later. If Sisi is the new Naser, as his supporters averred, judges most certainly will cry over spilled milk.

8

Patricians and Plebeians

The Chief Justice Paves the Road to the General (2013–2014)

It has become difficult for me to continue bearing responsibility for decisions that I do not agree with and whose consequences I fear. I cannot bear the responsibility for one drop of blood.

Interim Vice-President, Nobel laureate Mohamed ElBaradei's resignation letter.[1]

July 3, 2013, ushered a new (old) chapter in Egypt's politics. The revolutionary wave that reached its zenith with the ousting of Mubarak and the election of the first civilian president in Egypt's only free, fair, and competitive elections came to an abrupt halt. The counterrevolutionary surge, fostered by the army high command, triumphed. Mursi and the Muslim Brotherhood were removed. The forces of the *ancien régime* came back to dominate Egypt's political scene as they did since the military takeover of 1952. The Islamists proved lacking in taming the powers of the deep-state.

The security–bureaucratic alliance undermined Mursi's administration. It devised and implemented a calculated strategy to alienate the people. This strategy included an intense media campaign; manufactured shortages in goods and services, including electricity, gasoline, and natural gas; and systematic absence of law and order.[2] A restoration of the military heavy hand

---

[1] ElBaradei submitted this letter of resignation in protest after the security forces violently broke up protest camps set up by supporters of the deposed President Mursi in *Rabaa* and al-*Nahda* Squares (August 14, 2013).

[2] In carrying this extensive plan, the deep state received broad support from regional forces worried from the rise of political Islam. The United Arab Emirates and the Kingdom of Saudi Arabia provided staging ground, financial resources, and media to the anti-Mursi campaign. The Sheikhs of Abu Dhabi and Riyadh perceived the triumph of revolutionary forces particularly the Islamists as an imminent danger to the stability of their regimes and their dominant position in the Arab World. Furthermore, Israel also was not especially happy with the alliance between the Brotherhood and Hamas and Mursi's expressed support to the group that ruled Gaza since 2007.

over the polity and society became apparent on the horizon. The army takeover was the climax of this year-long plan. It represented the triumph of the counterrevolutionary wave. Now, all revolutionary forces, not only those of political Islam, are branded enemies of the state and were to suffer harsh consequences. The list would even include political parties, groups, and intellectuals that opposed Mursi and supported the army takeover.

The synergy between generals and judges is quite evident during the second transition period (July 2013–June 2014). The generals harbored great pains to give their policies a patina of legal formality. Generals needed judges to perform crucial regime survival functions (RSFs). The courts were called on to bolster the new political order and to provide legal cover for regime actions. In the absence of judicial cooperation, military dominance would be transparent, rendering resistance easier and more widespread. The judiciary performed three critical RSFs in service of the new regime: undercutting the remaining foundations of the ousted government, curtailing the opposition to the new regime, and legitimizing the new political order. Legality, or even the appearance of legitimacy, is also valuable to market the regime's positive image amongst the regional and international allies, whom the government desperately needed to shore up its dry coffers. This cooperation was crucial because, in the modern world (all else equal), there are advantages to keeping some pretenses to legality and to legitimize authoritarian rule with some appeal to the law. Pereria put it nicely:

> Legal manipulations and political trials are useful for an authoritarian regime because they can demobilize popular oppositional movements efficiently, reducing the need to exercise force; garner legitimacy for the regime by showing that it 'plays fair' in dealing with opponents; create positive political images for the regime, and negative ones for the opposition.[3]

This chapter covers the period commencing with the military takeover in July 2013 through the election and inauguration of President Sisi in June 2014. This chapter is divided into three sections. The first covers the role of the interim president, Adly Mansour, in restoring the old order. The second investigates the judicial policies during the second transition. The third section highlights the changes pertaining to the judiciary and the military in the 2014 Constitution.

---

[3] Pereria, "Of Judges and Generals," 55.

FIRST, THE POLITICS OF THE INTERIM ADMINISTRATION

The generals needed a political cover to mask the aggressive military takeover. This explains the junta's decision to place the President of the Court of Cassation and the High Judicial Court (HJC) (Egypt's most senior judge) in a prime position during the proclamation of Mursi's removal. The carefully choreographed photo positioned Egypt's most senior judge alongside the spiritual leaders of Egypt's Muslims and Christians: the Sheikh of Al-Azhar and the Patriarch of Alexandria. The guardians of the rule of law and the guardians of the faith support the measures taken by the army against a democratically elected president. In addition, during the same speech, Sisi announced the appointment of the chief justice of the Supreme Constitutional Court (SCC) as interim president.[4]

Installing the chief justice of the SCC, as an interim president is an affirmation of the symbolic value that the judiciary commands and how the junta wanted to use it to its advantage. There was nothing in the 2012 Constitution, or for that matter previous Egyptian constitutions, that would permit such an appointment.[5] The generals' choice of the chief justice to assume the presidency conveyed two messages. At one end, the military believed that the stature of the SCC would make such an appointment acceptable to important segments of the society. Secondly, the army trusted the chief justice to assume the enormous powers of the presidency and do "the right things" to facilitate the creation of a "new" political order, molded in the image of the military high command. Actions by the interim president Adly Mansour would prove the generals vindicated. Mansour did everything to undermine the opposition of the army takeover, facilitate the transition process, and advance the ascendance of the army chief to the presidency.[6]

The interim president's first decision was to replace the director of the influential General Intelligence Directorate (GID) with a Sisi loyalist. The

---

[4] It is logical to conclude that such announcement did not come as a surprise to the chief justice. An understanding must have been reached between the generals and Mansour. The precarious situation after Mursi's removal and the calculated nature of Egypt's former military spy chief negate any idea that such decision was not cleared in advance.

[5] Article 153 of the 2012 Constitution mandated that the prime minister assumes presidential responsibilities, "should the president be temporarily unable to exercise his powers. If the presidency became vacant, be it due to resignation, death, long-term disability, or any other cause, the speaker of the House of Representatives or the speaker of the Consultative Assembly, if the House was dissolved temporarily assumes the powers belonging to the president."

[6] In addition to changing the roadmap for political transition to suit the interests of the army chief, the interim president transferred important economic assets to the military including the Port of Arish and the vital Cairo–Alexandria highway.

new appointee was no other than Gen. Mohamed Farid El-Tohamy, a mentor of Sisi and former head of military intelligence, whose animosity toward Mursi is common knowledge.[7] The "new" spy chief has emerged as the most hardline of the new regime leaders.[8] His appointment reflected Sisi's cunning in surrounding himself with people who reflect the Benjamin Franklin aphorism, "We must hang together, gentlemen ... else, we shall most assuredly hang separately."

In another attempt to garner broad political support for the regime, Mansour's first administration included many prominent liberals and leftists that opposed Mursi's government. The list included the former chief of the International Atomic Energy Agency, Mohamed ElBaradei, who assumed the position of vice-president. The cabinet included the liberal economist, Ziad Ahmed Bahaa-Eldin (deputy prime minister and minister of international cooperation), the leading leftist academic Hossam Eisa (minister of higher education), the longtime labor activist Kamal Abu-Eita (minister of manpower), the leftist lawyer Ahmed Borai (minister of social solidarity), and the Wafd Party leading businessman Mounir Fakhry Abdel Nour (minister of industry, trade and investment).

Equally significant was Mansour's legal agenda. Mansour dissolved the Shura Council, which was the last Brotherhood stronghold, assuming its legislative power. This decision was critical to implement the coordinated program to reconstruct the heavy hand of the state over the public sphere; the interim president issued scores of laws to undermine popular resistance to the new regime. Less than three months after assuming office, Mansour issued Decree-Law No. 83 of 2013 that removed time limits on protective (or pretrial) detention.[9]

Previously, codes had imposed limits on the authority of the Public Prosecution Department (PPD) and the courts on issuing such orders. Article 143 of the Criminal Procedure Code had a limit of two years for accusations that could carry the conviction of death or a life sentence, eighteen months for lesser felonies, and six months for a misdemeanor. The interim president changed this to allow the courts to place any individual accused of crimes that could carry death or life sentence for forty-five days renewable without

---

[7] Sisi succeeded El-Tohamy to the post of army intelligence chief after the later was transferred to preside over the Administrative Control Authority (ACA). Allegations surfaced after January 2011 that the ACA under El-Tohamy had covered the wide-speared corruption under Mubarak and failed to help to find the stolen assets abroad. Mursi fired El-Tohamy after assuming office.

[8] *The New York Times*, October 30, 2013, "Ousted General in Egypt Is Back, as Islamists' Foe."

[9] Protective custody or detention pending investigation is the practice of imprisoning individuals under investigation until the beginning of the trial.

limits. This permitted the security apparatus to keep any individual locked up perpetually if they secure the cooperation of the judicial circuit in charge. In fact, pretrial detention became a punishment. This decision was a critical move in the regime's strategy to detain thousands on questionable legal grounds. This essentially created conditions very similar to what Egypt witnessed during the state of emergency (administrative detention without court orders).

Furthermore, the interim president issued Decree-Law No. 107/2013 that severely restricted public gatherings, protests, and demonstrations. The law imposed harsh penalties on individuals accused of organizing or participating in unauthorized activities. Many "law and order" judges enthusiastically implemented the new decree. A great number of liberal and Islamist activists received lengthy jail sentences and hefty fines. From the very beginning, the law appeared to fly in the face of the guarantees of peaceful assembly prescribed in the army-backed constitution. It is no wonder that the Administrative Court transferred the Protest Law, as is commonly known in Egypt, to the SCC on suspicion of unconstitutionality. However, even if the SCC invalidates the law (or parts of it), the regime would have achieved its objective of constraining mass-mobilization in the critical juncture after July 2013.

Mansour also altered the sequence of the transition process to secure the election of Gen. Sisi and to ensure a malleable legislature. The transition roadmap announced by Sisi on July 3rd stipulated that presidential elections would follow the legislative elections. However, it seemed that the security apparatus concluded that parliamentary elections would undermine the fragile anti-Brotherhood coalition, hindering the general's chances of a big electoral victory that could be portrayed as a political mandate. Hence, Mansour reversed the order and mandated holding the presidential elections first. The result was a 97 percent majority for Sisi. This decision also permitted Sisi to rule as a virtual dictator until the House of Representatives was elected, using presidential decrees to change many critical aspects without any public input. This change was crucial in the engineering of a submissive legislative majority.

Additionally, Mansour amended the Law of Political Participation to ensure that Islamist candidates would not achieve the same degree of success as they did in the previous legislative election. This law assigned the greatest majority of seats to independent candidates sidelining political parties. Most experts presumed that independent MP's would dominate the House. These members have been traditionally easier to cajole and pressure to toe the regime's line. Furthermore, before leaving office, as interim president, Mansour issued Decree Law No. 45 of 2014, which excluded active military and police personnel from political participation. This was rather striking as the SCC, where Mansour was the deputy chief justice, had previously granted this right to members of the armed forces and the police.

After promoting Sisi to deputy prime minister, Mansour also bestowed on him the rank of field marshal. This was another shot in the arm to the aspiring army officer. The new rank, the highest in any military hierarchy granted Sisi more symbolic power over the army.

SECOND, THE COURTS AND THE REGIME

In an attempt to capture the high legal ground, Sisi repeatedly declared that the "Brotherhood Regime" had undermined the rule of law. An administrative court supported this position in a ruling issued a couple of days after Mursi's removal. The verdict did not hesitate to scold the ousted president, maintaining, "There is no harsher transgression on the authority of the judiciary except which comes from the president of the republic." The ruling went further to state that the president's humiliation of a judge is, "an incredibly dangerous matter that undermines the billers of justice and hinders the dignity and prestige of judges."[10]

The regime used the court's attacks on the previous administration and judges' backing of the army takeover to its full advantage. This tactic is similar to other military regimes that enjoyed the collaboration of the courts. Chile is an excellent example in this regard. "In its first official statement justifying the coup, Edict No. 5 (Bando No. 5), the governing Junta declared that the Allende government had, 'placed itself outside the law on multiple occasions, restoring to arbitrary, dubious, ill-intentioned, and even flagrantly erroneous [legal] interpretations,' and had, 'repeatedly failed to observe the mutual respect which one power of the state owes to another.'"[11] This is the same discourse that the junta in Egypt and their civilian protégées used to delegitimize the Mursi regime and justify the military takeover.

---

[10] The court even ventured into foreign affairs when it called on "the United States and regional and international organizations to respect the will of the Egyptian people and not intervene in the will of the people aspiring to freedom according to the principles of international law and international Declaration of Human Rights which granted people the right to select their leaders as the preamble of the Declaration." The court added, "for all its long history, the Egyptian military is conscious of the nation, and it's the trusted guardian of the people's hopes for stability. The Egyptian people guarded by its resilient army are the final arbiter in selecting a just political system." Ahram, July 5, 2013.

[11] Lisa Hilbink, "Agents of Anti-Politics: Courts in Pinochet's Chile" in Tom Ginsburg and Tamir Moustafa eds., *Rule by Law*, 104.

The collaboration of the judiciary went much further. The role judges and prosecutors played since the removal of President Mursi has been undeniably extensive as well. The visible role played by the Judges Club in opposition to the Muslim Brotherhood paid dividends. Early on, the Judges Club seemed to have acquired a veto over the selection of the minister of justice during the 2013–2014 period. After Prime Minister Hazem El-Beblawi announced the candidacy of the highly respected jurist Mohamed Amin El-Mahdi, a former judge at the International Criminal Tribunal for the former Yugoslavia and a former president of the Council of State, the Judges Club declared its opposition to his candidacy. The club demanded that the justice portfolio carried by a senior judge from the Courts of Appeal or the Court of Cassation; on the premise that most judges belong to these institutions. The prime minister obliged and created a new portfolio for El-Mahdi, leaving the justice portfolio vacant for the time being.[12] Also, the regime rewarded one of the staunch anti-Brotherhood, retired judges Ezzat Agowa with a governorship post. Others were rewarded with leading positions inside and outside the Ministry of Justice.

Furthermore, many judges seemed to be in lockstep with the generals since July 3rd. The HJC voided the appointment of new members of the judiciary who were accused of ties to the Brotherhood, including the son of the last minister of justice under Mursi.[13] The HJC and the Ministry of Justice put under investigation all the judges and prosecutors who supported Mursi during his tenure or opposed his ouster. The HJC decided to withhold promotion for judges accused of supporting the former president until the end of the investigation.[14]

The regime benefited from the Court of Cassation's ruling invalidating Mursi's removal of Public Prosecutor (PP) Mahmoud. The enormous powers of the PP would prove valuable against Mursi, his supporters, and all who opposed the army takeover. The first decision of "returning" PP Mahmoud was to deny thirty-five prominent Brotherhood members and other Islamist leaders, including President Mursi, former Speaker of the House, and the Muslim Brotherhood Supreme Guide the right to travel abroad. Shortly after, Mahmoud announced his resignation and Mansour replaced him with another regime stalwart Hisham Barakat.

---

[12] Naturally, Council of State judges were exasperated by these actions. Many quietly complained that no administrative judge every assumed the justice portfolio or occupy the senior undersecretary or assistant secretary positions. Personal Interview with a member of the Board of Directors of the Council of State Club, Cairo, November 28, 2017.

[13] *Shrouk*, December 1, 2013.

[14] *Shrouk*, December 10, 2013.

Under Barakat, the PPD issued thousands of warrants to arrest all types of regime opponents.[15] This policy allowed the regime to claim that they had no political detainees while imprisoning thousands of its opponents.[16] Some in the Egypt's judicial community exhibited pro-prosecutorial bias. As in other cases, this "bias allows investigators, prosecutors, and judges to become sloppy about evidence and procedures, violating rights and giving the executive branch the consistent upper hand."[17] Those with the strongest allegiance to the military staffed the critical State Security Prosecution Department, which gained a more substantial role after Mursi's ouster.

The PPD also placed a large number of regime detractors under pretrial detention for extended periods of time. Mursi himself was formally placed in detention on July 26, 2013, over his alleged ties with Hamas. In addition, Prime Minister Hisham Qnadil, the supreme guide of the Muslim Brotherhood, leading government ministers, thousands of Brotherhood members and activists, as well as other regime critics, were all detained on questionable charges. The PPD provided legal cover for arresting many prominent figures that either collaborated with Mursi or declared their opposition to the new regime. One flagrant example of a detainee is former president of Alexandria Judges Club Mahmoud El-Khodiry, a staunch defender of judicial independence, and the former chairman of the People's Assembly Committee on Legislative Affairs. The security forces maintained that they were acting on orders from the PPD in relation to accusations that El-Khodiry, an ailing seventy-three year old (born January 1940), was implicated in torturing a Mubarak supporter during the January 2011 Revolution.

The PP also took actions to defuse the increasingly rampant accusations of torture in detention centers. Media reports revealed that teams of district attorneys acting on orders from the PP inspected four prisons. The stories, understandably so, affirmed the suitable conditions and reported that in three of the four facilities detainees had no complaints.[18] The PPD also turned a blind eye to many violations of the Penal Code. Chief among these abuses were the integration of persons accused of committing crimes without the presence of their lawyers.

[15] Many judges refused to serve as prosecutors because of the Public Prosecutor's directives to place protestors and Muslim Brotherhood sympathizers in protective custody based solely on reports by the police. Personal interviews with a first public attorney on January 9, 2014, and a chief prosecutor January 11, 2014.

[16] Human Rights Watch put the number at 22,000, Human Rights Watch Report: "All According To Plan: The Rab'a Massacre, August 2014, 27. Mass Killings of Protesters in Egypt

[17] Pereria, "Of Judges and Generals," 52.

[18] *Shrouk*, February 19, 2014.

Besides, the regime used the judiciary as a tool of legal oppression. "Courts carry heavy symbolic weight that can lend an air of gravity and judiciousness to even the most trumped-up charges and the most blatantly unfair proceedings. This can provide legitimacy both domestically and internationally."[19] Criminal courts have issued harsh sentences on hundreds of members of the Brotherhood and other opponents of the army takeover. Without judicial cooperation, the regime would have been obliged to extensively use the Argentinian juntas approach to political dissidents (i.e., involuntary disappearance, extrajudicial killings, etc.). This approach would have been costly domestically and internationally. With this judicial cooperation, the regime minimized the use of these apparent ultra-oppressive measures.

Furthermore, the new regime exploited its judicial allies to issue rulings on many sensitive matters. One of the clearest examples is the Urgent Matters Circuit (UMC). A single judge selected by the president of the First Instance Court staffs this circuit.[20] The minister of justice appoints all presidents of the first instance courts. This circuit, hence, is typically staffed with highly trusted judges who have close ties to the regime and usually follow the political wind in their rulings. A judge has off-the-record confirmed the litmus test for UMC appointments, stating the president of the Southern Cairo First Instance Court offered him this assignment and indicated that it could be a beginning of a career of lucrative appointments in the Ministry of Justice or the Economic Courts.[21] The UMC's rulings were directed at the regime's strategic opponents of political Islam, the youth movements, and the professional syndicates. Non-exhaustive examples of such are explained below.

The first critical ruling declared the Muslim Brotherhood a terrorist organization and ordered the confiscation of all its financial assets and headquarters. This decision buttressed the regime's claims against the movement and was

---

[19] Pereira, "Political (In)Justice," 33.
[20] Technically, the court's general assembly should make this assignment and all other judicial assignment during each judicial year. The norm, however, has been for the general assembly to authorize the court president to make such assignments.
[21] Judges selected for such assignment are tested before receiving it and usually receive plum assignments in the JID or the economy courts after finishing their term. During an interview with a judge at Southern Cairo First Instance Court, he narrated the following: "the president [of the Court] summoned me to his office and praised my work ethics and spoke of his personal trust in me. He asked if I will be interested in serving on the Urgent Matters Circuit adding that this 'sensitive' position is the fast track to other lucrative assignments in the judiciary and beyond. He added that because of the sensitivity of some 'political' matters, I should 'consult' with him before issuing my rulings. Knowing that this would mean that I just put my name on his decisions, I politely declined." An interview with a judge at Southern Cairo First Instance Court on June 27, 2013.

repeatedly publicized on the regime-friendly talk-show programs.[22] The over-reaching ruling extended to any organization that received any funding or had any ties to any organization related to the Muslim Brotherhood. The regime used this judgment to seize the assets of more than 1,000 NGOs in the fields of healthcare, education, and social services.[23] These organizations are the backbone of the Brotherhood and other Islamic organizations' social capital particularly among the millions of poor and working-class Egyptians. The court also issued a ruling disbanding the Freedom and Justice Party, the political wing of the Muslim Brotherhood, denying the group legal and political representation.

Another ruling proclaimed Hamas, which the regime considers an arm of the international Muslim Brotherhood movement, a terrorist organization. The decision prohibited the activities of the group in Egypt and ordered the closure of its offices and mandated cutting all official ties with the movement that control Gaza.[24] This ruling was critical to the regime's media campaign against the Muslim Brotherhood. It helped to cement the image the regime strived to create about the Brotherhood as an outlaw, violent, and extremist group.

The court also issued a ruling amidst the waves of protests that swept campuses across Egypt, prohibiting demonstrations inside college campuses without the prior approval from the university administration. The widespread protests organized by university students forced the regime to shut down universities. The same circuit issued a ruling mandating the return of police presence in public universities.[25] Despite a previous ruling from the Council of State prohibiting such a presence, the verdict was met with a legal uproar even from some law professors close to the regime.[26] The High Administrative Court had to weigh in again, reaffirming the prior ruling.

Another UMC's verdict panned the activities of April 6th Youth Movement and ordered the confiscation of its assets.[27] The court's reasoning was overtly political. The verdict maintained that "April 6th members benefited financially without loyalty to the nation or remorse for the consequences of their actions which spilled blood. They assaulted a security post (state security headquarters)." The ruling identified many April 6th leading members as

[22] *Ahram*, February 24, 2014.
[23] *Shrouk*, December 31, 2013.
[24] *Shrouk*, March 4, 2014.
[25] *Ahram*, February 24, 2014.
[26] The president of Cairo University Gaber Nassar, a constitutional law professor, described the ruling as "illegal, from a court without jurisdiction." *Shrouk*, March 4, 2014.
[27] *Shrouk*, April 28, 2014.

instigators of anarchy and lawlessness. This was the same group that played a vital role in the original wave of protests, which led to the removal of Mubarak in January–February of 2011, and the demonstrations that facilitated army intervention in July 2013. The regime was understandably worried about the movement's ability to mobilize young people and sought to use the courts as a cover for legal repression.

The same is true concerning the professional and labor associations. These organizations caused a headache for both Mubarak and the Supreme Council of Armed Forces. The court issued rulings to weaken the syndicates with board members close to the Brotherhood. For example, the court ordered the dissolution of the board of directors of the Pharmacists Syndicate (controlled by Brotherhood members).[28]

These rulings were not well received by the legal community. Activists and legal scholars criticized these politicized rulings. A senior administrative judge criticized the UMC as engaging in politics and ruling on matters exclusively within the domain of the administrative courts.[29]

In addition to the UMC, many criminal courts issued extremely harsh verdicts (executions and lengthy jail sentences) against regime opponents. The Terrorism Circuits were established in the waning days of 2013. These circuits have adjudicated cases related to the anti-regime activists. These circuits were stuffed with staunch anti-Brotherhood judges who are known for their hardline rule of law outlook.

The idea to establish specialized terrorism circuits emerged from a Council of Ministers' suggestion.[30] While the Council has no authority over the courts, the president of Cairo Court of Appeal acted on the recommendation and established six terrorism circuits. The composition of these legal panels ensured that the regime opponents would receive the harshest treatment. Hardline anti-Brotherhood judges with a reputation for issuing tough sentences were handpicked to staff these circuits. One senior judge described how these circuits were staffed: "the president convened the general assembly of the court to receive the formal approval to establish the new circuits. After the assembly agreed to the demand, the president asked, 'who would like to rule on the Brotherhood members?' Only those who are dogmatically hostile to political Islam raised their hands and hence were selected. Most judges understood that the president wanted hardline judges on these circuits and many realized that these trials are not going to adhere to due

---

[28] *Shrouk*, January 20, 2014.
[29] *Shrouk*, March 7, 2014.
[30] *El-Waten*, November 25, 2013.

process."[31] A number of judges who sat on the criminal bench before asked to be transferred to the civil circuits because they could not survive the feverish atmosphere that surrounded many cases. Many judges were between a rock and a hard place. Applying due process and fair trials would lead to the acquittal of many defendants but would make them juxtaposed as anti-regime and could seriously hinder their judicial careers.[32]

In addition to the six circuits, the minister of justice added two more judicial circuits to accommodate the growing number of cases: one under the chairmanship of Mohamed Sherien Fahmi and the other chaired by Ahmed Sabri. Judge Sabri's circuit was the one selected to try ousted president Mursi and sentenced. The courts sentenced the former president to twenty years of hard labor. The jurisdiction of these circuits was deliberately set in very broad terms. This jurisdiction included:

- felonies that harm public interest and national security domestically or abroad;
- explosives, spying, and collaboration with foreign entities or states to damage national interests;
- revealing state secrets pertaining to national security;
- establishment and administration of groups, entities, or gangs not in accordance to the law with the goal to stop constitutional rules or legislations;
- preventing state institutions or public authorities from performing its functions;
- threatening citizens' personal freedoms or other public rights and liberties mandated by the constitution or law;
- harming national unity or social peace.

The number of capital punishment verdicts in 2014 reached the staggering number of 1,473, arguably the highest in Egypt's legal history. The aggressive onslaught of rulings against the Muslim Brotherhood stunned observers. Hundreds were sentenced to death after very short trials on account of their participation in attacks on police stations, government facilities, or assaulting security personnel.

Furthermore, many distinguished judges lent their support to then-presidential candidate Sisi. The Judges Club president, Ahmed El-Zend, was vocal of his support for Sisi's candidacy. Some former senior judges including Abd El-Rahman Bahloul, a member of the HJC, did not shy to declare his

---

[31] Personal interview with a senior judge at Cairo Court of Appeal, Cairo on June 11, 2014.
[32] Multiple interviews with a judge at Mansoura Court of Appeal, May–December 2017.

support for General Sisi's candidacy. Bahloul stated, "El-Sisi is the only suitable person for Egypt's presidency." He added that he signed a petition to ask Sisi to run for the presidency.[33]

This enthusiastic collaboration with the military has stunned observers of Egyptian judicial politics. Judges, who historically have been the most liberal amongst the state institution, now readily embrace the role of the legal oppressor. Why? This judicial behavior can be understood if we take into consideration the following factors. First, the corporate identity of judges expounds their preference for cooperation. Judges value the judiciary as an institution and understand that both a failed state or a weak government will harm them. Judges, who picked up the mantle of reform within a stagnate conservative regime of Mubarak expressed a strong commitment to limited change within the revolutionary environment of post-January 2011. This is not schizophrenic behavior. Most judges are traditional or cautious reformers, not revolutionaries. They will always prefer the status quo if they believe that the state, which they serve and receive their institutional rule from, is threatened.

Secondly, judges are the guardians of law and order. Many judges came to despise the chaos that marked the post-Mubarak era. Simply put, judges who witnessed their courthouses attached by the *plebs* decided to support a fellow *patrician*. For many judges as well as many Egyptians, another military strongman seemed to be the cure for the law and order problems that plagued Egypt since 2011. That was the experience of many courts in Latin America under the military dictators in the 1970s and 1980s.[34] Sisi's law and order message resonated with judges who became fed up with the vicious attacks on courthouses and the verbal attacks on TV and print media. The general's law and order message has strengthened the affinity between the gavel and the tank, something that is not unique to Egypt. As Shapiro put it, "a certain

---

[33] *Al-Masry Al-Youm*, January 31, 2014.

[34] Hilbink, in her study of the Chilean case, maintained, "To the dismay of justice seekers, Chilean judges cooperated fully with authoritarian regime in the months and years that followed. Not only did the courts grant the military government nearly complete autonomy to pursue its 'war' against Marxism, but also offered repeated legal justification of the regime's expansive police powers. Judges unquestioningly accepted the explanations offered by the government regarding the fate of the disappeared and readily implemented arbitrary decrees, secret laws, and policies that violated the country's legal codes ... Moreover, the Supreme Court unilaterally abdicated both its review power over decisions of military tribunals and its constitutional review power. *Throughout, the justices insisted that the military government was restoring the rule of law, even as general made a mockery of the Constitution.*" Lisa Hilbink, *Judges beyond Politics in Democracy and Dictatorship: Lessons from Chile* (Cambridge: Cambridge University Press, 2007), 1, emphasis added.

affinity or even alliance may sometimes arise between two professional corps, each respecting the other's professional integrity. That alliance may move judges to greater tolerance of security rationales for government actions, or greater tolerance of judicial interventions, or both simultaneously."[35] Not surprisingly, many judges have believed that their long-term interests are best served by remaining within "statist coalition." This affinity was reinforced by the post-January 2011 circumstances. The collapse of the police force made the armed forces the protector of courtrooms. Army troops provided physical security for judges and prosecutors. Many judges came to perceive the generals as the guarantor of their protection.

Third, the terrorism circuits played a critical role. A handful of judges were selected to handle all sensitive cases. Furthermore, some opportunistic judges sought to be in the regime's good graces by being extra tough on the Brotherhood and other opposition members. Because of the intense media coverage of these cases, a not-so-well-known judge in the provinces could get his name recognized in the regime circles through his extreme rulings.

Fourth, most secular and Christian judges were at the outset hostile to the Brotherhood for obvious ideological reasons. Those judges, alongside significant elements of the upper and upper middle class, bought into the anti-Muslim Brotherhood propaganda. They became convinced that the Brotherhood aimed to change the nature of the society and the lifestyle of the citizens. They also were persuaded that Mursi's administration thought to impose a conservative, rigid, and strict interpretation of Islam. Many less-ideologically committed judges became fierce critics of the Brotherhood because of the Muslim Brotherhood's attacks on the judicial corps during the Mursi tenure.

Fifth, Mursi did not implement any reforms concerning the judiciary. Many judges developed an impression that the Brotherhood wanted to install Mursi's loyalists to replace old regime loyalists, without furthering judicial independence. Also, many judges were disappointed for financial reasons.[36]

---

[35] Martin Shapiro, "Courts in Authoritarian Regimes," in Ginsburg and Moustafa (eds.), *Rule by Law*, 332.

[36] Judicial salaries, while amongst the pay scale in the bureaucracy, are still inadequate. A spokesman for the HJC stated that the president of the Court of Cassation receives a monthly salary of 35,000 LE. *Shrouk*, July 15, 2014. Judicial salaries are variable. The Ministry of Justice sets wages, and it includes a whole set of bizarre cash allowances specifically, a medical insurance allowance (even though all judges and their family are fully covered), Ramadan allowance (before the sacred month), and summer holiday allowance (July through September). Members of the PPD receive higher overall salaries than their counterparts in the same rank who sit on the bench. For example, prosecutors receive a variable amount every month based on the traffic fines that are imposed on the public. Within the prosecutors

The 2011–2012 president of the HJC Hussam Al-Ghiryani, who is considered close to the Brotherhood, refused to implement rulings that would have increased salaries of judges in the courts to match counterparts in the Council of State and the State Cases Authority (SCA).[37] These decisions were implemented after Mursi's departure as a goodwill gesture to judges.

Sixth, the generals used their allies at the pinnacle of the judicial hierarchy to launch an intimidation campaign against judges with close ties to the ousted regime. The minister of justice and the HJC put judges under investigation. The disciplinary board convicted many judges on accusations of engaging in politics, and excessive appearances on media.[38] Quite a few judges were removed from the bench. These efforts succeeded as a scare tactic against many judges. However, these harsh actions were not as prevalent in the Council of State or the SCC. The SCC admitted back to its ranks a former justice Hatem Bagato who held a ministerial portfolio under Mursi. The Council was much more even-handed in its dealings with political cases after the army takeover. The Council was far more accommodating in its dealing with administrative judges accused of cooperating with the Brotherhood regime. No administrative judge was removed from office, only five judges were put under investigation, and the Council admitted back into its ranks one of its vice-presidents who left the Council to assume the governorship of Alexandria.[39]

The Council of State remained true to the rule of law. The administrative court suspended an executive order, freezing the assets of a religious organization that the government claimed to be linked to the Muslim Brotherhood.[40] Another administrative court ordered the government to suspend the state of emergency and curfew imposed since August 14, 2013. The administrative courts reversed the expulsion orders placed on scores of al-Azhar students for holding a protest inside the university campus.[41] An administrative court also ruled that security reports could not stand by themselves as a reason to dismiss civil servants. The court mandated the reinstatement of a teacher that was fired and ordered 5,000 *LE* in restitution.[42]

department, those who work within the State Security Prosecution receive further financial and nonfinancial benefits.

[37] Personal interviews with mid-level judges, June–July 2013.
[38] Ruling in Disciplinary Case No. 17/2013 issued January 27, 2014.
[39] *Shrouk*, June 24, 2014.
[40] *Ahram*, July 7, 2014.
[41] *Shrouk*, August 17, 2014.
[42] *Al-Gomhuria*, April 6, 2014.

What is more, the same equitable approach was evident in many criminal courts outside the domain of the handpicked circuits. Some criminal courts ordered the release of activists whom the PPD put under protective custody. Most of these rulings, however, did not receive the same intensive medical coverage. For example, a Criminal Circuit of Cairo Court of Appeal dismissed the case against opposition lawyer Issam Sultan who was accused of insulting the judiciary.[43] The Court of Cassation accepted Mursi's Prime Minister Qnadil appeal and reversed the judgment against him. The regime was naturally not pleased with these pockets of resistance and was expected to exert more control over the different judicial institutions upon Sisi's formal assumption of power.

THIRD, THE 2014 CONSTITUTION: THE TRIUMPH OF JUDGES AND GENERALS

The depth of the alliance between the judiciary and the military manifested itself in the process that led to the drafting of the 2014 Constitution.[44] The Constitutional Amendment Committee, generally known as the committee of ten, set by the military and formally appointed by the interim president to examine the constitutional future of Egypt had a clear judicial majority. Six judges staffed the ten-member committee. Two were drawn from the SCC, two from the administrative courts and two from the courts of general jurisprudence (cassation and appeals). The committee proposals favored the institutional interests of the men in uniform: robed and camouflaged. These propositions included an unprecedented degree of institutional and financial autonomy for the armed forces and the judiciary.

The 2014 Constitution sustained the extensive judicial powers under the 2012 Constitution and expanded the mandate of the courts and acquiesced to many of the demands of the judges. These changes admittedly looked like a "pay-back" for judicial support of the generals. The 2014 Constitution mandated several important changes to Egypt's constitutional structure.

First, all judicial institutions secured constitutionally mandated financial autonomy. Article 185 states "Each has an independent budget whose items are all discussed by the House of Representatives. After approving each budget, it is incorporated in the state budget as a single figure." The same

---

[43] *Ahram*, July 5, 2014.
[44] Technically, the 2014 Constitution is an amended version of the 2012 Constitution. The junta decided to suspend, not cancel, the 2012 Constitution to avoid the calls to elect another constituent assembly to draft a new constitution.

privilege is granted to the SCC. According to Article 191, the SCC "has an independent budget whose items are all discussed by the House of Representatives. After it is approved, it is incorporated in the state budget as a single figure." The inclusion of these budgets as a single number means that the details of the budgets are not available to the public and hence are not subject to the scrutiny of public opinion. This privilege was originally granted to the armed forces on the pretext that discussing the details of the budget would harm national security. Also, the 2014 Constitution mandates the HJC, stating in Article 188 "Its [The Judiciary and Public Prosecution] affairs are managed by a higher council whose structure and mandate are organized by law." Furthermore, the constitution obliges the House of Representatives to consult with each judicial organization before enacting laws related to its affairs, (Article 185 and Article 191).

Second, the Council of State secured two essential objectives. One, the Council commands exclusive jurisdiction to provide advice on legal matters to the executive branch. Two, the Council successfully defeated attempts by the Administrative Prosecution Authority to exclusively control disciplinary actions against public servants (Article 190). The Council also regained the prerogative granted to the SCA in the 2012 Constitution pertaining to "settling of disputes in which the State is a party" (article 179). Members of the Council hinted at their ability to issue rulings deeming the fifty-member drafting committee unconstitutional as the Council previously did with the 100-member assembly selected by the previous parliament to draft the 2012 Constitution.[45] Furthermore, the 2014 Constitution expands the scope of draft contracts under the mandatory review of the Council to include in addition to draft contracts to which the state is a party, draft contracts that any public entity is a party (Article 190). Because of the nature of the Egyptian economy, where the state participates in a great many joint ventures, this added provision extends the Council's domain exponentially.

Furthermore, the prohibition on seconding judges part-time to non-judicial duties that were enacted per Article 170 of the 2012 Constitution was removed. Many judges, particularly in the Council of State, were steadfast in their opposition to this prohibition for financial reasons. Article 239 instead invites the House of Representatives to issue a law "organizing the rules for assigning judges and members of judicial bodies and organizations, ensuring the

---

[45] The representatives of the Council of State inside the drafting committee were quite explicit in their threats to retaliate in case of any minimization of their jurisprudence. A personal interview with a member of the Administrative Prosecution Authority who participated in the constitutional drafting deliberations, Luxor, May 17, 2014.

cancellation of full and partial assignment to non-judicial bodies or committees with judicial jurisdiction, or for managing justice affairs or overseeing elections, within a period not exceeding five years from the date on which this Constitution comes into effect."[46] This was the compromise between those who wanted to keep the prohibition stipulated in the 2012 Constitution, knowing the problems that seconding creates at one end and those judges, who for financial gains, desired to rescind the provision altogether.

The SCC's role as guardian of an image of the state and as an insurance policy against future elite transformations received further constitutional augmentation. Relevant articles leave no doubt that the SCC emerged as the most significant beneficiary of the new constitution. The 2014 Constitution expanded the institutional independence, financial autonomy and legal mandate of the court. Article 191 stipulates: "The Supreme Constitutional Court is an autonomous and independent judicial body . . . It shall have an independent budget . . . The General Assembly of the court shall manage its affairs, and it shall be consulted regarding bills relevant to its affairs." The 2014 Constitution removed the eleven-member limit on membership in the court. Article 176 of the 2012 Constitution stated, "The Supreme Constitutional Court is made up of a president and ten members." The 2014 Constitution does not set a limit. Article 193 stipulates, "The Court is made up of a chief justice and a sufficient number of deputies to the chief justice." This omission was considered a symbolic victory for the SCC and removal of the last traces of the perceived interference in its affairs.

The same article permits the SCC to convene outside the capital. "If necessary, it may convene anywhere else in the country with the approval of the Court's General Assembly." Arguably, this provision was added as a result of the "siege" of the SCC in 2012 and to allow the court some flexibility in future similar circumstances.

For the first time in Egypt's constitutional history, the SCC's ability to control its membership is fully guaranteed in the constitution. As per Article 193, the court's general assembly elects the chief justice from among the three most senior deputy chief justice serving on the court. Additionally, the general assembly has the sole authority to select all justices and commissioners. The president of the Republic only issues decrees to implement the general assembly decisions. This complete autonomy, unprecedented in modern judicial history, put the court beyond any form of accountability from any state institution or public opinion. Furthermore, the court according to

---

[46] The prime minister issued a decree preventing state institutions from seconding judges to more than one extrajudicial post.

Article 192 is solely competent to adjudicate on disputes about the affairs of its members. No other court or institution can meddle in the SCC affairs.

Additionally, the mandate of the SCC has expanded. The 2014 Constitution removed the provisions related to the role of Al-Azhar in the interpretation of the principles of Islamic Shari'a.[47] The preamble of the constitution assigned the SCC to be the sole arbiter in matters related to the interpretation of the said principles, stating "the reference for the interpretation of such principles lies in the body of the relevant Supreme Constitutional Court Rulings." The SCC's jurisprudence henceforth is the only demarcation of what is included in the "principles of Shari'a" and what is not. Because the SCC's rulings have narrowly defined such principles, any House of Representative with an Islamist majority would have a hard time changing Egypt's legal code. This provision endows the SCC with immense power and could be considered as another insurance policy to preserve a specific ideological outlook of the state, as was the case with Turkish Constitutional Court for decades.

Furthermore, if the president of the Republic's office becomes vacant due to his resignation, death, or permanent inability to work, and the House of Representatives has not been elected, the chief justice of the SCC shall temporarily assume the powers of the president of Republic (Article 160). This was basically codification of the practice enshrined after the army takeover in 2013. It, nonetheless, remains novel in Egypt's constitutional tradition.

In addition to the judicial review of laws and regulations, the SCC has secured for the first time constitutional guarantees of its exclusive jurisdiction to

- Interpret legislations,
- Adjudicate jurisdictional disputes amongst judicial bodies and entities that have judicial jurisdiction,

---

[47] Article 4 of the 2012 Constitution maintains, "Al-Azhar is an encompassing independent Islamic institution, with exclusive autonomy over its own affairs, responsible for preaching Islam, theology and the Arabic language in Egypt and the world. *Al-Azhar Senior Scholars are to be consulted in matters pertaining to Islamic law.*" Emphasis added. Article 7 of the 2014 Constitution states, "Al-Azhar is an independent scientific Islamic institution, with exclusive competence over its own affairs. It is the main authority for religious sciences, and Islamic affairs. It is responsible for preaching Islam and disseminating the religious sciences and the Arabic language in Egypt and the world. The state shall provide enough financial allocations to achieve its purposes. Al-Azhar's Grand Sheikh is independent and cannot be dismissed. The method of appointing the Grand Sheikh from among the members of the Council of Senior Scholars is to be determined by law."

- Adjudicate disputes pertaining to the implementation of two final contradictory judgments, one of which is rendered by a judicial body or an authority with judicial jurisdiction and the other is rendered by another,
- Adjudicate disputes pertaining to the implantation of its judgments and decisions.[48]

The constitution also restored the SCC authority in relation to electoral laws related to local, legislative, and presidential elections. While the 2012 Constitution mandated only abstract review and denied the court the power of concrete judicial review, the 2014 Constitution empowers the SCC to declare any electoral law unconstitutional and hence dissolve elected assemblies. Even more, the interim president also issued a Decree-Law to amend the SCC Law (Law No. 48 of 1979) to expedite the adjudication of judicial review in matters related to the presidential and legislative elections. All adjudication related to these elections can now be fast-tracked without observing the mandatory times for hearing all other cases. It is entirely conceivable that this amendment allows the SCC to swiftly terminate a hostile parliament or unfriendly chief executive without delay.[49]

The judges-dominated ten-members experts committee made sure that the military also secured extensive benefits. First, the armed forces' budget is incorporated as a single figure in the state budget without details or description and the opinion of the National Defense Council with a clear military majority must be sought in relation to draft laws on the armed forces (Article 203).[50] The jurisdiction and powers of the Military Judiciary were expanded enormously. After repeated demands by various forces in society – particularly after the January 2011 Revolution and expiration of the state of emergency in 2012 – a significant amendment was made to the constitution. It stipulated that "Civilians may not stand trial before military courts, except for crimes that harm the armed forces, and the law shall define these crimes." The 2014 Constitution lists the cases that are considered as attacks on the armed forces and related entities. The 2014 Constitution was criticized for significantly broadening the jurisdiction of military courts over civilians. According to the broad interpretations in Article 204 of the constitution, any attack on armed forces personnel or facilities, the perpetrators, even of civilians, will be referred to military prosecution.

[48] Article 192 of the 2014 Constitution.
[49] Decree-Law No. 26 of 2014, issued April 1, 2014.
[50] This article was perceived as a constitutional guarantee to Sisi to prevent his removal from office. After the army takeover, Sisi promised not to seek political office.

Military courts secured competence concerning crimes committed by the GID personnel during and because of the service. More to the point, civilians became under the mercy of the military judiciary for a plethora of offenses.[51] To avoid any constitutionality challenges to the military judiciary, Article 204 adds, "Members of the Military Judiciary are autonomous and cannot be dismissed. They share the securities, rights, and duties stipulated for members of other judiciaries." Article 234 granted the minister of defense tenure protection for two presidential terms after the ratification of the constitution.

All these changes reflected the organic and close ties between two state institutions that found value in furthering close institutional ties. The changes also revealed the growing interdependence between the generals and judges and their collaboration to secure institutional objectives.

Judges enthusiastically oversaw the referendum on the new constitution and supervised the election of Sisi to the presidency. The judicial commission monitoring the presidential election, chaired by the first vice-president of the SCC, spared no effort to inflate voter turnout. The committee added an unscheduled day of voting for expats elections and voting inside Egypt. This was critical in the regime quest to bestow a mandate on Sisi after a low voting turnout in the previously scheduled two-day voting. The SCC also warmly welcomed Sisi during his swearing-in ceremony, a sharp contrast to Mursi's swearing-in ceremony two years earlier.

CONCLUSION

Judges' collaboration with the generals is evident, deep, and widespread in the 2013–2014 period. The leaders of the two state institutions found common ground in their efforts to remove an "interloper" from the presidency. The two institutions worked together after the army takeover to restore the old political order.

Despite this seemingly strong military–judicial alliance, clouds were gathering in the horizon. The junta's resolve to assert complete control is evident in the expanded preview of the military courts. This was an early

---

[51] Article 204 states, "Civilians cannot stand trial before military courts except for crimes that represent a direct assault against military facilities, military barracks, or whatever falls under their authority; stipulated military or border zones; its equipment, vehicles, weapons, ammunition, documents, military secrets, public funds or military factories; crimes related to conscription; or crimes that represent a direct assault against its officers or personnel because of the performance of their duties. The law defines such crimes and determines the other competencies of the Military Judiciary."

indication that the men in uniform would desire to limit judicialization and limit the expanded judicial political role. The generals and judges' alliance, however, is going to be severely tested after the generals succeed in their consolidation of power. If history provides any indication, the rosy picture of judicial–military collaboration will not remain for long.

9

Old Wine in a New Bottle

Sisi, Judges, and the Restoration of the Ancien Régime (2014–2018)

لا وجود لمعتقلين سياسيين في مصر... ولا يوجد لدينا سجناء سياسيون" مؤكدا أنه في مصر "هنالك إجراءات قضائية حقيقية يتم من خلالها مراعاة كافة الإجراءات القانونية طبقا للقانون المصري."

We have no political detainees in Egypt ... We do not have political prisoners ... We have genuine judicial measures that adhere to all legal procedures according to the Egyptian law.

President Sisi comments on a TV interview.[1]

Abdel Fattah el-Sisi was sworn in as Egypt's sixth president on June 8, 2014.[2] Sisi, however, has been the de facto leader since the army takeover on July 3, 2013. He played a domineering role over the polity even before his formal assumption of the presidential power. Sisi's high media profile, control of the army, and popular support left no illusion that the general was the power behind the throne soon to clinch the presidency after the finalization of mere formalities. After all, it was Sisi who appointed Mansour president. Egypt under Sisi and judicial politics during general's first term in office (2014–2018) is the subject of this chapter, which is divided into two sections. The first investigates President Sisi's program to establish full presidential

---

[1] President Sisi interview with *France 24* on October 24, 2017.
[2] Incidentally, Sisi was born in 1954, the same year when Nasser consolidated power. He ascended to the presidency sixty years after Nasser's predominance of the Egyptian polity. President Sisi graduated from the Egyptian Military Academy in 1977. Like other Egyptian officers of his generation, he never saw combat. Sisi advanced through the ranks after serving as a military attaché in Riyadh and attending the United States Army War College in 2006. He became commander of the Northern Military Region in 2008. In 2010, he was appointed director of military intelligence and reconnaissance. Sisi was the youngest member of the Supreme Council of the Armed Forces (SCAF). In December 2012, he was appointed commander-in-chief and minister of defense, making him the first Egyptian army chief trained in the United States.

hegemony over the state and society. This section details the regime policies to consolidate power in the security and civilian sectors of government. It then moves to underscore the strategies to restore state's control over the polity and the society. Section two analyzes the state–courts interaction. This section details the regime survival functions (RSFs) provided by the judiciary in service of the regime, investigates judicial rulings and actions that defied regime's policies, and concludes by examining President Sisi's legal changes to the laws governing judicial institutions to increase executive control over the courts.

THE QUEST FOR CONTROL

President Sisi's admiration of the image and practices of fellow strongman is evident in his actions and public statements. The general-turned-president did not hide his veneration of like-minded autocrats such as Vladimir Putin.[3] Sisi ascended to power without much political experience. He often gloated about being apolitical. The president has kept his inner circle of military advisers who accompanied him from his time at the Military Intelligence and Reconnaissance Administration (MIRA) to the defense ministry to the presidency. President Sisi and his supporters seem to believe that a dominant imperial presidency is the only cure for Egypt's illness.

To this end, the newly inaugurated president has acted from day one to consolidate power. Borrowing several pages from Nasser's playbook, President Sisi implemented a comprehensive plan to establish firm control over the state and society. Maintaining his grip on the armed forces has been the top priority. Noting that the position of the defense minister and commander-in-chief is constitutionally protected for two presidential terms;[4] President Sisi made sure to leave his trusted lieutenants in influential positions in the military establishment. Following in the footsteps of Nasser, who appointed his close friend Abdel Hakim Amer as commander-in-chief of the armed

---

[3] It was also noticeable how Sisi's inauguration on June 8, 2014, was modeled after his fellow former spy master, Putin, in 2012. Many of Sisi's administration policies toward the opposition and the press reveal a remarkable resemblance to Putin's. Both have used less-than-savory tactics to domesticate political adversaries and control the media.

[4] According to Article 234 of the 2014 Constitution, "The Minister of Defense is appointed upon the approval of the Supreme Council of the Armed Forces. The provisions of this article shall remain in force for two full presidential terms starting from the date on which this Constitution comes into effect." Hence, barring a constitutional amendment, General Sedky Sobhy is expected to remain in office until 2022. This guarantee was explicitly designed to protect Sisi as defense minister.

forces, Sisi named his confidant Lieutenant General Mahmoud Hegazy to the all-influential position of chief-of-staff of the armed forces.[5] Sisi also made sure to curry favor with the rank and file of the military through expanding their political and economic role, increasing their salaries, and the constant emphasis on both the elevated position of the army and his personal connection to the institution.[6]

Likewise, President Sisi found in the security apparatus a willing partner. Their support was critical during and after the crackdown on the Brotherhood and other rivals. Sisi returned the favor by granting them a blank check to use force with immunity. In the words of one mid-level police officer, "the good old days of Mubarak is back. We are back on top."[7] After securing his power, President Sisi made sure that Gen. Mohamed Ibrahim, the minister of interior during the army takeover and the person who oversaw the violent crackdown in the aftermath, faded into obscurity after he was removed from his post.

Sisi also has tried to assert control over the powerful General Intelligence Directorate (GID). The *Mukhabarat*, as the GID is often referred to, played a magnified political role under Mubarak but lost a good deal of influence to the MIRA since 2011.[8] After significant reshuffles at the pinnacle of the institution and the forced retirement of scores of officers, Sisi named his alter ego and right-hand man General Abbas Kamel acting director of the GID in early 2018. Kamal is expected to continue the purge of the intelligence apparatus. With all these measures, the president seems confident that the military–security coalition has produced the devoted coterie needed to shore up his regime amidst the increasing public anger over the many domestic and foreign policies fiascoes.

---

[5] Hegazy is related to Sisi through the marriage of their respective children. Sisi's youngest son, Hassan is married to Hegazy's daughter, Dalia.

[6] Sisi has visited military posts with an astonishing frequency. He paid a visit to the military academy at least three times a year since assuming office.

[7] Personal interview with a major in the police's special forces division, Cairo, July 24, 2016.

[8] Arguably, one of the cardinal outcomes of the 2011 uprising is the rearrangement of the balance of power within Egypt's complex web of security services. Under Mubarak, the General Intelligence Directorate played an oversized role because of the close ties between Mubarak and spy chief Omar Suleiman. The State Security Investigations Service (SSIS) also played a prominent role, particularly since the ascendency of Gamal Mubarak. The Military Intelligence and Reconnaissance Administration (MIRA), on the other hand, was considered a specialized and small institution that generally had no apparent role in domestic politics and foreign relations. All this will change. Sisi benefited from his exceptionally close ties to the SCAF's chairman Field Marshal Hussein Tantawi. The MIRA also seized on the vacuum after the apparent collapse of the SSIS and the demise of Omar Suleiman to expand its mandate and power. Since 2013, the MIRA is considered the most influential security institution in Egypt. Its mandate extended well beyond the barracks, to include many aspects of civilian life.

After securing a firm grip over the security sector, President Sisi moved to implement a thorough and systematic plan to establish control over the state and the society. This program involved ensuring presidential dominance over the legislature, independent agencies, civil society, political parties, and the press. Control over the judiciary would shortly follow.

Dominating the legislature was the bedrock of the regime's power consolidation strategy. Under the 2014 Constitution, the parliament commands extensive powers. According to Article 101, "The House of Representatives is entrusted with legislative authority, and with approving the general policy of the state, the general plan of economic and social development and the state budget. It exercises oversight over the actions of the executive authority." In addition to the regular powers over the purse, appointment, and oversight, Article 146 grants parliament authority over the selection of prime minister and government.[9] Furthermore, the House of Representatives has the power to affirm or rescind presidential orders declaring the state of emergency; a prerogative much needed to implement the regime's iron-hand policies.[10] The House also plays a significant role in the presidential nomination process. Twenty MPs' endorsements are needed to stand for presidential elections.

---

[9] Article 146: Government Formation stipulates, "The President of the Republic assigns a Prime Minister to form the government and present his program to the House of Representatives. If his government does not obtain the confidence of the majority of the members of the House of Representatives within no more 30 days, the President appoints a Prime Minister based on the nomination of the party or the coalition that holds a plurality of seats in the House of Representatives. If his government fails to win the confidence of the majority of the members of the House of Representatives within 30 days, the House is deemed dissolved, and the President of the Republic calls for the elections of a new House of Representatives within 60 days from the date the dissolution is announced.

In all cases, the sum of the periods set forth in this Article shall not exceed 60 days.

In the event that the House of Representatives is dissolved, the Prime Minister presents the government and its program to the new House of Representatives at its first session.

In the event that the government is chosen from the party or the coalition that holds a plurality of seats at the House of Representatives, the President of the Republic may, in consultation with the Prime Minister, choose the Ministers of Justice, Interior, and Defense."

[10] Article 154: State of Emergency, "The President of the Republic declares, after consultation with the Cabinet, a state of emergency in the manner regulated by law. Such proclamation must be submitted to the House of Representatives within the following seven days to consider it. If the declaration takes place when the House of Representatives is not in regular session, a session is called immediately in order to consider the declaration. In all cases, the declaration of a state of emergency must be approved by a majority of members of the House of Representatives. The declaration is for a specified period not exceeding three months, which can only be extended by another similar period upon the approval of two-thirds of House members. In the event the House of Representatives is dissolved, the matter is submitted to the new House in its first session."

This is key to keep "undesirable" prospective candidates from contesting the high office.

Furthermore, Article 156 obligated the House to review the decree-laws issued by both Mansour and Sisi within fifteen days from the date the new House convenes. Any decree not approved is revoked retroactively. Theoretically, the legislative engineering of the autocratic state since the army takeover could have been reversed.[11] As of July 2013, a staggering 342 law-decrees were enacted. Between July 3, 2013, and June 7, 2014, Mansour issued 147 law-decrees while Sisi claimed 195 law-decrees after assuming power on June 8, 2014, until the House of Representatives convened.

Because of these extensive powers, an abiding legislative majority is key to all presidential aspirations for control. This explains the rescheduling of the legislative elections until after President Sisi's inauguration. This delay allowed the new czar to labor to create an acquiescent legislature. Sisi delegated the critical task of forming a loyal majority to a handful of trusted advisers in the intelligence apparatus. The group assembled a political coalition conveniently labeled "For the Love of Egypt." This statist coalition won the desired two-thirds majority. As one commentator put it, "It is, unfortunately, a legislature of, by, and for President Abdel Fattah al-Sisi."[12]

Members of the House of Representatives proved loyal to their masters in the deep state. The House affirmed 341 law-decrees, rejecting only one, mostly to save some face (the act was shortly approved after a few changes). The majority also extended the state of emergency repeatedly without regard to the constitutional provisions. Of the 596 House members, 549 endorsed President Sisi for a second presidential term, while twenty other MPs were tabbed to nominate his hand-picked "opponent" Mousa Mostafa Mousa. The legislature would undoubtedly pose no threat to the general.

---

[11] Article 156: Decrees that have the force of law, "In the event that the House of Representatives is not in session, and where there is a requirement for urgent measures that cannot be delayed, the President of the Republic convenes the House for an emergency session to present the matter to it. In absence of the House of Representatives, the President of the Republic may issue decrees that have the force of law, provided that these decrees are then presented to the House of Representatives, discussed and approved within 15 days from the date the new House convenes. If such decrees are not presented to the House and discussed, or if they are presented but not approved, their legality is revoked retroactively, without the need to issue a decision to that effect, unless the House affirms their validity for the previous period or chooses to settle the consequent effects."

[12] Charles Tiefer, "Egypt's Parliamentary Election Ends on an Undemocratic Note," www.forbes.com/sites/charlestiefer/2015/12/21/egypts-parliamentary-election-ends-on-an-undemocratic-note/#f29872755a56.

To consolidate control on the long term, the regime heavily utilized its legislative powers. The most vital assault on rights and liberties, however, came through the Terrorism Law of 2015. The law significantly expanded the definition of actions on the basis of which individuals or groups may be designated terrorists. Under this definition, human rights defenders, political parties, or developmental associations may be easily labeled terrorist entities and their members terrorists. Article 1 maintains that terrorism includes "infringing public order, endangering the safety, interests, or security of society, obstructing provisions of the constitution and law, or harming national unity, social peace, or national security." Most troubling is that the definition of terrorist entities and terrorists in the law is broader even than the definition of terrorism in Article 86 of the Penal Code, which was also condemned by rights groups for its overly broad language. Even more seriously, as was the case under the emergency law and despite the Supreme Constitutional Court (SCC) rulings on the unconstitutionality of arbitrary arrest, Article 40 of the new law allows the arrest of persons not caught in a criminal act and without a judicial warrant by calling the arrest "holding."

The same could be said about changes to the Penal Code. The amendments dramatically increased the minimum penalties and fines in many cases. The changes also loosened the definition of criminal offenses to criminalize a plethora of acts.

Furthermore, President Sisi issued a law empowering the executive to take any measure, including the imposition of a curfew, to "preserve public security and order" in the event of a terrorist danger. Such procedures establish an undeclared state of emergency that is not subject to constitutional protections. The president may declare this disguised state of emergency to counter the dangers of terrorist crimes or environmental disasters for a period of six months, renewable indefinitely with the approval of a parliamentary majority.

The regime as well inserted several critical changes to the legal frameworks in criminal cases. Law 11 of 2017 amended the Penal Code and the Code of Criminal Procedures by allowing the court to refuse to hear any testimony requested by the defense.[13] Lawyers and human rights activists have vehemently protested this law as a clear violation of defendants' rights, particularly in political cases. They argue that such a law undermines any claim to due process and fair trial.

---

[13] *Shrouk*, October 11, 2017.

The regime as well moved expeditiously to assert control over the constitutionally mandated independent agencies. The regime enacted Decree-Law No. 89 of 2015 on circumstances to remove presidents and members of independent commissions and supervisory authorities from their posts. This decree-law, despite numerous constitutional provisions to the contrary, empowered the chief executive to dismiss those officials on the following grounds:

1. If credible indications emerged that he distressed state security and safety;
2. If he lost trust and respect;
3. If he miscarries the duties of the position that could hinder the high national interest or individual public dignitary;
4. If he lost any of the qualifications to assume the position other than health qualifications.

The law was popularly dubbed the "Genina Law" because it was clear that its target was the chairman of the General Accounting Authority (GAA) Hisham Genina. Genina, a former liberal senior judge, did not endure himself to the regime by his outspoken, critical, and anticorruption rhetoric. The GAA published a report declaring that the cost of corruption was *EGP* 600 Billion.[14] The GAA exposed massive corruption in critical state institutions such as the PPD, the courts, the police and the intelligence. In a press conference, Genina revealed that members of the State Security Prosecution Department (SSPD) in Cairo and Giza as well the officers in the powerful Administrative Control Authority (ACA) have illegally seized 35,000 acres of land in the suburban neighborhood of Giza.[15] The removal of the popular Genina killed two birds with one stone. The regime got rid of an official who could not be controlled and in the same time delivered a shockwave through

---

[14] Genina did not do himself any favor by publicly supporting his colleagues Ahmed Mekki, minister of justice under Mursi; Mahmoud Mekki, former vice-president of the republic; and Hussam El-Ghiryani, the chairman of the 2012 Constitutive Assembly. He also defied the regime's frenzied attack on the Muslim Brotherhood stating that "the Muslim Brotherhood is part of the fabric of the society ... and only a small fraction of the group commits actions that could hinder the state." After an ostentatious investigation where Janina's enemies were in control, President Sisi ordered the dismissal of Janina from his post. Genina was later investigated and sent to court. The attacks on Genina did not stop with removing him from office. His daughter who worked in the Administrative Prosecution Authority was fired from her work on allegations of posting on Facebook against then minister of justice Ahmed El-Zend. *Shrouk*, June 13, 2016.

[15] *Almasry Alyoum*, February 17, 2014.

the bureaucracy: no one is immune from the long reach of the regime. The message was loud and clear "get in line or get out."

Along the same lines, the government changed the rules governing the appointment of presidents of universities and deans of colleges. University administrators are to be appointed rather than elected as was the case since the law was changed after the Mubarak's ouster. In all likelihood, this meant that appointments are principally based on favorable reports from the security apparatus. Another legislative change eased the process of sacking tenured professors and expelling students. These changes were critical to put on a leash the vibrant political life on Egyptian college campuses.

The regime as well strived to cleanse the political scene from any meaningful political institution. To prevent any chance of legal opposition from within the political system, the Political Parties' Affairs Committee worked to weed out "unwanted" political forces. In addition to outlawing Islamist political parties and severely weakening the Salafi parties that supported the military takeover, the regime worked to undermine any political party not under the firm control of the security apparatus.

The liberal-secular Free Egyptians Party, a party founded by the Christian business tycoon Naguib Sawiris, is a telling example. The party, which did well in the 2015 parliamentary elections, became a target of the security interventions to remove the party's founder and the board of trustees, some of which did not follow the regime's line fully. The interventions led to the split of the party into two factions and undermined the political cohesion and political role for the once promising party. The Egyptian Patriotic Movement, a political party initiated by former presidential candidate Gen. Ahmed Shafiq, is another example. When Shafiq hinted at his intention to contest the 2018 presidential elections, the regime used its Trojan horses to undermine the party.

The ever-expanding civil society was put under intense pressure after the army takeover in 2011, and the pressure considerably intensified after Mursi's removal. The regime first started by zeroing in on the associations related to the Muslim Brotherhood or other Islamist groups or individuals. The minister of justice established the Committee to Manage Brotherhood Resources. The assets of over 700 of the group's leaders have also been seized. Between December 2013 and November 2017, this massive endeavor resulted in seizing the properties of 1,538 individuals, 1,166 NGOs, 65 corporations, and 21 money exchange companies.[16]

---

[16] *Shrouk*, November 5, 2017.

The regime then expanded the process to non-Islamist NGOs. In May 2017, President Sisi signed Law No. 70. The law criminalizes much of the work of NGOs, firmly controls their funding, and establishes a new entity to oversee civil society organizations dominated by representatives of Egypt's national security agencies, known for their hostility to rights organizations. This law, coupled with massive intimidation strategy, had devastating effects on all NGOs working in Egypt. Many Egyptian NGOs either were forced to close its offices, work without the legal protections, or flee Egypt altogether.[17] Many international NGOs, as well as governmental organizations, decided to relocate outside Egypt and halt any programs in Egypt. The United Nations Development Program's Regional Bureau for the Arab States, International Institute for Democracy and Electoral Assistance (International IDEA), and Konrad-Adenauer-Stiftung are just a few examples of many. Others have stopped their operations in Egypt, waiting to see how the government will enforce the law.[18]

Alongside controlling the state and society, President Sisi is clear about his view of the media. In a public statement, shortly after his inauguration Sisi stated, "The late leader Gamal Abdel Nasser was lucky because he was talking, and the press was with him [no voice of dissent]."[19] The regime implemented a meticulous plan to domesticate the press. This four-step program included: terminating anti-regime print and TV, intimidating independent journalists, establishing a staunchly pro-regime media empire, and limiting citizens' access to information. In fact, Sisi and his MIRA started their efforts to control the media well before his ascendency to power. The process of media control accelerated since the army takeover in 2013. On the same day of Mursi's removal, the military closed seventeen TV stations in addition to closing the offices of the Al-Jazeera network.

The regime's concept of opposition media is quite elaborate. In addition to Islamists, it includes revolutionaries, leftists, and even liberals. The regime had shown quite a low level of tolerance to all types of criticism. It panned many individuals from TV, radio, and printed press. The era when criticism of the leader was permissible that existed since Mubarak's removal and flourished under Mursi is now long gone. The satirical anti-Mursi television host Bassem Yousef is a potent example. After playing a critical role in the anti-Mursi

---

[17] For instance, Cairo Institute for Human Rights Studies (CIHRS) moved to Tunis, Tunisia.

[18] The Ford Foundation, the leading American NGO that worked in the Middle East and North Africa since the early 1950s and maintained an office in Cairo since 1959 have stopped issuing new grants to all organizations inside and outside Egypt.

[19] *Almasry Alyoum*, August 5, 2014.

mobilization, his TV show, *Al-Bernameg*, was frequently jammed and threatened with lawsuits. After Sisi became president in 2014, Youssef was put under intense pressure to terminate the widely popular show. The TV host was first threatened with lawsuits for allegedly insulting Sisi[20] and then was hit with a multimillion-dollar fine.[21] The signals were abundantly clear and the "Egyptian Jon Stewart" fled his homeland for exile in the United States.

Another example of the intimidation strategy is journalist Hossam Bahgat. Bahget, a leading investigative reporter, was detained by the MIRA. The regime was not particularly happy with his reporting on many sensitive issues including a story titled "A Coup Busted?", which detailed the military trial of several army officers convicted by a military court of trying to conspire against the president.[22] Bahget angered the regime as well by debunking the myth of Mursi's release of scores of jihadists accused of engaging in terrorist attacks. Bahgat faced the customary charges of "deliberately broadcasting false news that harms national interests." He was fortunate because his arrest produced an international outcry, including an intervention by the UN Secretary-General, Ban Ki-moon. Bahget was released after only two days in military detention.

This was quite fortunate in comparison to other journalists who have been languishing in pretrial detention, forcibly disappeared, or killed by the security forces. Prominent journalist and researcher Ismail al-Iskandarani has spent years behind bars without being convicted of any offense. Iskandarani, one of the very few journalists that used to cover human rights' violations in the Sinai, is one of many dissident voices that have been silenced amid an intensifying crackdown on independent media.[23] These were not isolated incidents; Reporters without Boarders recounted,

> Egypt is now one of the world's biggest prisons for journalists. Some spend years in detention without being charged or tried. Others face long jail terms

---

[20] *Shrouk*, February 22, 2014.

[21] *Shrouk*, December 22, 2014.

[22] Bahgat is the founder of the Egyptian Initiative for Personal Rights, one of Egypt's most acclaimed human rights organizations. Since 2014 he has worked as a journalist with *Mada Masr*, an independent media outlet known for covering news stories that other parts of the Egyptian press shy away from.

[23] Al-Iskandarani, an independent researcher and a former fellow at the Woodrow Wilson Center and National Endowment for Democracy, ran afoul of the regime and exposed the human rights violations in Sinai. He was detained in November 2015 upon arrival to Egypt to visit his ailing mother. The charges were the most common in post-June 2013 Egypt. Due to membership in an unlawful organization and spreading false news, he has spent years behind bars without being convicted of any offence. *Shrouk*, October 31, 2017.

or even life imprisonment in iniquitous mass trials. Under Gen. Sisi's leadership, the authorities have waged a witch-hunt since 2013 against journalists suspected of supporting the Muslim Brotherhood and have orchestrated a "Sisification" of the media.[24]

Furthermore, an increasingly draconian legislative arsenal poses a clear threat to media freedom. Chief amongst this is the Terrorism Law that includes many stiff penalties for journalists.[25] Under the law, adopted in August 2015, journalists are obliged on national security grounds to report only the official version of "terrorist" attacks and suffer severe penalties if they violate this law. Another law that solidified control is the Unified Media Law.[26] The regime firmly controls the new board created by this legislation with extensive powers to oversee the print and TV media. The president controls the seventeen-member Supreme Council for Media Regulation. He appoints three members, and the tightly controlled House of Representatives selects another three members. Three other members were appointed by virtue of their positions, which they received by presidential decree.

After stamping out undesirable voices, the government moved to fill the void. The presidency decided on a two-way strategy: acquisitions of private TV networks by businessmen linked to the government and the intelligence services[27] and the creation of a new media conglomerate owned and controlled by the regime or its allies. The most notable example is DMC, an extensive TV network with a range of news, sports, and entertainment channels. Dubbed "the mouthpiece of the intelligence services," this one billion EGP enterprise was given preferential treatment in covering news and major sports events. In privately owned stations, "remote control media" became well-known phenomena. Most, if not all, TV hosts and news anchors receive their marching orders from security and intelligence officers or at best practice self-censorship to remain in the regime's good graces.

---

[24] https://rsf.org/en/egypt.

[25] Law 95 of 2015.

[26] Law 92 of 2016.

[27] The administration does not shy from declaring its control over these media outlet. In one notable example, Brigadier General Mohamed Samir, the former spokesman of the Egyptian Armed Forces, was appointed vice-president of *Al-Assema* TV Network. Besides, the former military senior officer was named CEO of the newly established *Al-Safir* news website.

Additionally, the regime has worked vigorously to restrict access to information. A large number of websites that do not conform to the official point of view have been blocked. The state-owned Middle East News Agency quoted "a senior security source" saying that the blocked websites "publish content that supports terrorism and extremism and intentionally propagate lies."[28] The list keeps expanding, but it most certainly includes hundreds of websites.

JUDGES AND THE GENERAL

In implementing this firm consolidation of power strategy, the regime benefited from the collaboration of judiciary. The courts' cooperation with the regime is quite evident in many rulings, statements, and Public Prosecution Department (PPD) orders. The judiciary provided valuable RSFs in service of the regime. This included the SCC, the administrative courts, the criminal courts, and particularly the terrorism circuits, the PPD, and the State Security.

COURTS

Courts enabled the regime to delegitimize the remaining pillars of the Mursi regime. The Freedom and Justice Party (FJP) was dissolved on August 9, 2014, by a ruling from the High Administrative Court (HAC). The court also ordered the confiscation all the FJP's assets and headquarters. The court reasoned that the FJP threatens national unity, social peace, and the democratic system. The court justifications seems more political than legal arguing that the party is faulted for naming the June 30th "Revolution" a coup.[29] The Political Parties Committee petitioned the HAC to disband the Development and Building Party, the political wing of the *Gamaa Islamia*. The HAC's Commissioners Body issued its advisory opinion recommending the approval of such request on the grounds that the party leaders have tried to "destroy the state and igniting a civil war amongst citizens . . . the party is not trustworthy to participate in political life."[30] This party was a strong backer of Mursi's administration and openly declared its opposition to the military takeover.

The courts provided another critical RSF to the regime by ordering the closure of four TV channels, including *Al-Jazeera Mubasher* Egypt and other

---

[28] https://ara.reuters.com/article/ME_TOPNEWS_MORE/idARAKBN18K30X.
[29] *Shrouk*, August 10, 2014.
[30] *Shrouk*, October 22, 2017.

TV channels connected to the Muslim Brotherhood. Besides, a court issued an order to revoke the license of other religious TV channels critical of the new regime.

The courts also refrained from overturning many of the regime's questionable decisions. For instance, Genina challenged his dismissal before the administrative courts. The court refrained from ruling on the dubious sacking on the premise that Genina's four-year term ended. The court, however, wanted to preserve its power in reviewing such decisions in the future. The court reasoned that the president issues such decisions in his administrative, not sovereign, capacity and therefore is subject to judicial review.[31]

The Terrorism Circuits played a highly significant role in vanishing thousands of regime opponents. Either through exceptionally harsh verdicts or lengthy pretrial detention. These circuits, established in 2013, became the backbone of the regime's legal arsenal under Sisi. News coverage reveals that the Terrorism Circuits tried more than 10,000 defendants and issued death sentences in the hundreds. The same handful of judges presided over most high-profile cases. Four circuits gained a reputation for their harsh punishments. In many instances, verdicts were based solely on the State Security's reports and confessions obtained during detention. Many defendants' lawyers argued confessions were made under duress. Presiding judges on these circuits became household names. Mohamed Nagi Shehata,[32] Shaban El-Shami,[33] Hassan Farid,[34] and Mohamed Shrien Fahmi were particularly known for handing down harsh sentences against the opposition.

---

[31] *Shrouk*, February 21, 2017.

[32] Mohamed Nagi Shehata, the flamboyant, self-styled rule of law crusader, chaired the Fifth Criminal Circuit of Giza. Judge Shehata openly proclaimed his support for Sisi. In a lengthy newspaper interview, Judge Shehata did not shy from criticizing the opposition, many TV hosts, and even his colleagues at the Court of Cassation. *El-Watan*, December 12, 2015. No wonder that after these public statements, the Cairo Court of Appeal accepted a challenge to remove Judge Shehata from many cases arguing that he lacks impartiality to rule.

[33] As president of the 15th Criminal Circuit at Cairo Court of Appeal Shaban El-Shami issued many rulings that met the regime's hardline aspirations. Amongst Shami's notable achievements is the death sentence against former president Mursi. He also rejected the public prosecution appeal against releasing former president Mubarak on corruption charges. Judge Shami also affirmed the Public Prosecutor's (PP) orders to seize the financial assets of scores of Brotherhood leaders. Shami was rewarded with an under-secretary of justice position

[34] Hassan Farid, who chairs the 28th Criminal Circuit at Cairo Court of Appeal, ordered the death penalty for thirty people convicted of involvement in the 2015 assassination of the PP. Farid condemned ten Muslim Brotherhood leaders to death on accusations of blocking the Cairo–Alexandria road for seven hours. He kept one teenager for more than 700 days of pretrial detention for wearing a T-shirt that had the slogan "Stop Torture, Nation without Torture." Judge Farid sentenced three journalists to three years in prison in connection with their work for Al-Jazeera English for allegedly reporting "false news."

Mohamed Shrien Fahmi, who chairs the 11th Criminal Circuit at Cairo Court of Appeal is a noteworthy example. Perceived as one of the most talented and able judges of his generation,[35] Fahmi is known for his strict law and order judicial philosophy. Fahmi epitomizes the tight nexus between generals and judges. Fahmi's grandfather was the commander of the cavalry under the monarchy. His father was an army general under the republic. His wife is the daughter of the former State Security Investigations Service (SSIS) Chief Moustafa Abd Elkader. Judge Fahmi was the go-to judge on many high-profile cases in which his jurisprudence was exceptionally clear. He freed many of Mubarak's regime loyalists on corruption and violence charges. On the other hand, he delivered a staggering number of death and life sentences against former president Mursi, many leading Islamists, and different rank and file opposition. Judge Fahmi also investigated the scores of judges accused of being sympathetic to the previous regime. He transferred fifty-nine of them, recommending their dismissal to the disciplinary board. Many were later sacked.

Through the cooperation of the presidents of the Courts of Appeal, the regime was able to centralize all litigation of prominent political dissidents at the hands of the carefully selected judges. The president of Cairo Court of Appeal would habitually choose one of these terrorism circuits to hear a case when the Court of Cassation quashes the conviction of another terrorism circuits. For instance, when the high court reversed Shami's convictions of Mursi and others and ordered a retrial, the new presiding judge was no other than Fahmi.

The overt political positions expressed by these judges and other like-minded on the bench have embarrassed the judicial corps. The High Judicial Council (HJC) have taken actions to limit the coverage of trials. The HJC issued an order to ban media coverage of all trials via audiovisual devices. This decision has stirred much controversy in human rights, media, and judicial circles. It contradicts the provisions of Article 268 of the Code of Criminal Procedure that hearings shall be public except in exceptional cases determined by the court itself. Several judicial councils also issued decisions prohibiting judges from giving statements about legal cases to the press and preventing them from posting about them on social media. Indeed, Public Prosecutor (PP) Nabil Sadek banned all prosecutors from expressing political opinions on social media or making statements to the press.

---

[35] Personal interview with a senior judge at Cairo Court of Appeal, May 6, 2016.

The judiciary issued numerous gagging orders in sensitive cases. Judges and prosecutors have issued media gags on several prominent and controversial cases over the past few years. In many occasions, the suppression orders were related to cases of embarrassing nature to the government. These orders meant that the regime point of view as expressed in the official pronouncements of the courts or the PPD was the only information available to the citizenry. It prevented lawyers and anti-regime activists from presenting their cases in the court of public opinion. These gagging orders included amongst many the following examples:

- President Mursi's alleged espionage
- The 2012 presidential election
- The Council of State bribery scandal
- The assassination of former PP Hisham Barakat
- The detention of former chief of staff of the armed forces Gen. Sami Annan

Pretrial detention is another critical RSF. By using the courts to detain many of the regime's opponents from all walks of life, the government can maintain a claim to legality. The PPD and the courts have arrested thousands opposition activists on questionable legal grounds. Most of the victims are members or supporters of the now-outlawed Muslim Brotherhood, but activists of many political colorations, not only Islamists, have been swept up in the wide-ranging crackdown. Since the army takeover, pretrial detention has become one of the sad facts of life in Egypt. The poignant stories of abuse of pretrial detention are countless. One, however, stands out because it has become an international symbol of Egypt's harsh crackdown on civil society.

Aya Hijazi, a thirty-one-year-old Egyptian-American returned to Egypt after the 2011 uprising in the national euphoria that accompanied Mubarak's removal. She and her husband founded the *Belady Foundation,* an NGO that seeks to shelter and rehabilitate marginalized street children. Amidst the crackdown on civil society organizations, police raided the foundation's premises. Hijazi, her husband, and others working at the foundation were detained. After months of pretrial detention, she was brought before a judge to answer for multiple counts of criminal charges. The judge habitually renewed her detention for three years, until President Trump personally interceded on her behalf during President Sisi's visit to the White House. Two weeks after the Egyptian president returned, the court ordered her release. Hijazi was flown to Washington on an American government airplane to meet with the President Trump in the Oval Office; a meeting that left no doubts who was behind her release.

The courts and PPD performed another critical RSF in service of the regime. The regime took full advantage of the highly hierarchical nature of the PPD (see Figure 9.1). Under PP Sadek, the centralization of the PPD has reached new heights. Rather than having several deputy public prosecutors as was the case under his predecessors, Sadek only appointed a single deputy public prosecutor.[36] To further consolidate power, the deputy public prosecutor also chairs the all-powerful Public Prosecution Inspection Department (PPID). The PPID scrutinize the work of all prosecutors and have been used in the past to badger uncooperative prosecutors. The deputy public prosecutor manages a group of eight First Public Attorneys (one for each Court of Appeal), who supervises the work of Public Attorneys. The later oversee the work of a fleet of prosecutors, deputy prosecutors, and assistant prosecutors. The PP has an ultimate say in all decisions regarding prosecution (or refraining from prosecution) and all prosecutorial decision regarding politically sensitive cases are managed either by the PP's trusted lieutenants in the first district attorneys' offices or are handled directly by the politically reliable State Sesucrity Public Prosecution Department. Inspection of detention centers, mandated by law, was turned into a mere formality. The prosecution manual and unofficial guides prohibit prosecutors from conducting any inspection without prior approval of their superiors. In most occasions, the Public Attorney Offices would inform the governorate police chiefs in advance about the pending inspection. State Security's detention facilities and other unofficial detention centers, where most human rights' violations occur, are never inspected.

The PPD became perceived as a tool of regime oppression. The Mubarak era's claim to legality and due process has faded. The PPD's role in the crackdown against the opposition is transparent even to the casual observer. Dusting the regime reputation before international and domestic public opinion has been another critical service offered by the judiciary. Amid allegations of pervasive torture and maltreatment in prisons and police stations that serviced during President Sisi's visit to France, the PP declared that members of the PPD conducted surprising inspections to twenty-five jails to ensure that the rights of detainees are respected.[37]

The HJC's and other superior judicial bodies' cooperation was key. The Judicial Disciplinary Board fired forty-one judges on accusations of supporting

---

[36] Under Sadek, the PP has direct supervisory authority over five "specialized" prosecution offices; each is managed by one First Public Attorney. The PP office also includes a group of prosecutors that staff his technical office.

[37] *Shrouk*, October 31, 2017.

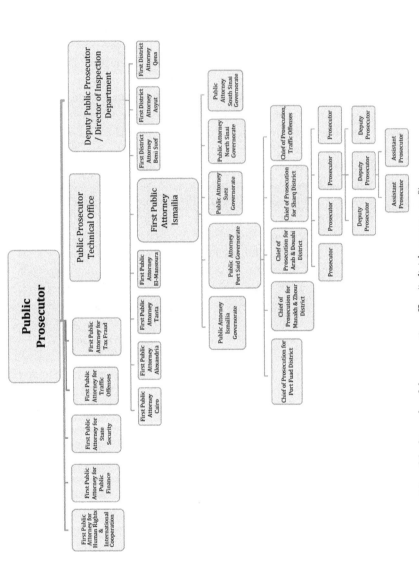

FIGURE 9.1 Map of the hierarchy of the prosecution office (judicial year 2017–2018)

former president Mursi.[38] The steps to intimidate judges went much further than sacking judges accused of Islamist political views. Many liberal judges were removed from office in an episode that brings back memories of the 1960s. The Judicial Disciplinary Board discharged Zakaria Abdul-Aziz, the fervent former president of the Judges Club, on accusations of his alleged calls to attack the SSIS headquarters during the January 25th protests. It seems that the security apparatus did not forget Zakria's role in mobilizing judges during the 2005–2006 judicial uprising. By using the upper echelon of the judiciary to cleanse unhospitable judges, the regime avoided getting entangled in a second "judicial massacre." The HJC, on the other hand, refused to address any complaints against pro-regime judges. The double standards were evident in the HJC refusal to investigate the charges against El-Zend who was accused of interfering in political affairs. The Council of State in 2017 followed in the HJC's footsteps. The Council censured many judges for expressing their views on judicial and public-interest matters.[39]

Nevertheless, this wide-ranging judicial cooperation did not satisfy the regime's appetite for full control.[40] Again, borrowing from Nasser's libretto, the government expanded the domain and reach of exceptional courts. This included the military tribunals and the State Security Courts. The administration also utilized the subservient legislature to implement changes in the Penal Code and the Code of Criminal Procedures to facilitate convictions and undermine the rights of defendants and due process.

The regime in its quest for sustainable control brought back the dreadful State Security Courts. The prime minister issued a decree transferring entire categories of cases to these courts under the state of emergency. The cases transferred included crimes under Law 107 of 2013 on Demonstrations, Law 94 of 2015 on Fighting Terrorism, Law 394 of 1954 on Weapons and Ammunition, Law 113 of 2008 on Freedom of Religion in addition to crimes related to terrorism, threatening state security, and whole sets of other cases.[41] These courts, which lack many of the guarantees of fair trial and its verdicts, cannot be appealed. The president has the sole authority to affirm, shorten, or cancel

---

[38] Presidential Decree No. 192 of 2016 discharged thirty-one judges and Presidential Decree No. 193 of 2016 dismissed thirteen judges.

[39] Personal interview with a member of the Council of State Judges' Club, February 20, 2018.

[40] Sisi made a few overtures to judges. Sisi visited the High Judicial Court (HJC) Headquarter and delivered a speech during the celebration of the judicial day April 23, 2016. In his first speech before the House of Representatives, Sisi alluded in passing to the judiciary stating, "The exalted judicial bench that elevate the voice of truthfulness and enshrine justice in the corners of the country." Sisi speech before the House of Representatives on February 13, 2016.

[41] *Shrouk*, October 8, 2017.

the verdicts. These courts will remain in charge of these cases even after the end of the state of emergency. The PP transferred the case of a Muslim Brotherhood member and twenty-three others to the State Emergency State Court.[42] This was the first to after these dreadful courts were abolished in 2012.

Sisi, very much like Nasser, has expanded the use of military courts where preferred verdicts can be easily secured.[43] While the use of military courts has not vanish since Nasser's death, Sadat and Mubarak only used military tribunals in a limited number of cases. This has changed dramatically under Sisi. Human Rights Watch maintained, "Military courts have tried at least 7,420 Egyptian civilians since October 2014."[44] Benefiting from the generous provisions in the 2014 Constitution, Sisi issued many decrees to expand military courts' jurisdiction. For instance, Decree-Law 136 of 2014 for the Securing and Protection of Public and Vital Facilities.

The law, decreed by Sisi in the absence of a parliament, places all "public and vital facilities" under military protection for two years and directs state prosecutors to refer any crimes at those places to their military counterparts, paving the way for further military trials of civilians. This decree states that the armed forces "shall offer assistance to the police and fully coordinate with them in securing and protecting public and vital facilities," including electricity stations, gas pipelines, oil wells, railroads, road networks, bridges, and any similar state-owned property. The House of Representatives extended the law for five more years, until August 2021. The PPD readily transferred scores of cases to the military courts even though these actions happened before the proclamation of the presidential order.

A military court sentenced deputy Muslim Brotherhood's chief, Khairat Al-Shater, and others to between five and fifteen years of hard labor on accusations of monitoring state institutions and planning to spread anarchy after the army takeover. The principle evidence during the trial came in the form of testimonies from state security officers.[45] Another case involved an attempt assignation of President Sisi and Saudi Crown Prince Mohammed Bin Nayef.[46] Another military court sentenced TV anchor Hussam Abu Abokhary to ten

---

[42] *Shrouk*, November 2, 2017.

[43] The use of the Military Courts intensified after Mubarak's removal. The SCAF made full use of "their courts." Between the January 25, 2011, Revolution and June 30, 2012, when Mursi was inaugurated president, 11,800 Egyptian civilians were tried before military courts. According to Human Rights Watch, the military judiciary conviction rate was 93 percent.

[44] www.hrw.org/news/2016/04/13/egypt-7400-civilians-tried-military-courts

[45] *Shrouk*, March 29, 2017.

[46] *Shrouk*, July 9, 2017.

years of hard labor on accusations of enticing Islamists to attack the State Security Headquarter in Nasser City during the aftermath of the 2011 uprising.[47]

The eagerness of the judiciary and the PPD to transfer cases to the military courts threatened to overwhelm the military justice system. Military tribunals were worried that a flood of less-politically sensitive cases would undermine its ability to adjudicate cases of interest. This has created some preposterous outcomes. In at least one occasion, the Military Court Fourth Circuit refused to adjudicate a case transferred to it from the *Beni Soyif* Criminal Court. Both courts claimed they have no jurisdiction to adjudicate the case. In the end, the State Cases Authority (SCA) had to file a case before the SCC to settle the matter. The SCC had to intervene to set out parameters for the applicability of the expanded jurisdiction of the military courts.[48] The SCC ruled that the regular courts system is responsible for trying cases related to demonstrations.

The regime's control over the different judicial institutions, however, was far from complete. Several criminal circuits outside the handpicked terrorism circuits started to issue rulings to free political detainees. Several brave judges defied the regime. Challenges to the regime's repressive agenda was more ubiquitous in the Court of Cassation. Many of the high court's circuits quashed convictions from lower courts, particularly the terrorism circuits. For instance, the Court of Cassation annulled a life sentence handed to political activist Ahmed Douma in a case related to the cabinet's clashes in 2011. The Court of Cassation quashed the life sentence of fifteen members of the Muslim Brotherhood on accusations of committing violence and demonstrations in the Delta city of *Damanhour*, and membership in an outlawed organization.[49] In addition, the Court of Cassation ruled that the HJC's discretionary power to reappoint judges who assumed executive offices is not unlimited and subject to review by the courts.[50] This ruling was significant because the HJC was very selective in reappointing judges who assumed executive positions: permitting politically reliable judges to return to the bench while refusing to readmit others with ties to the Mursi administration.

One circuit was quite steadfast in its commitment to due process and the rule of law. The circuit chaired by Judge Anas Omara was particularly consistent in overturning convictions from the lower courts in the politically charged cases. Omara was, according to seniority, going to chair the Court of Cassation and the HJC in July 2017. Omara is a staunch defender of judicial

---

[47] *Shrouk*, October 31, 2017.
[48] *Shrouk*, November 6, 2017.
[49] *Shrouk*, November 6, 2017
[50] *Shrouk*, May 1, 2016.

independence. He did not do himself any favor when he ruled to cancel all death penalties based solely on evidence provided by security investigations, overturning many cases involving members of the Muslim Brotherhood. His court established an important legal doctrine that runs contrary to the practices in the terrorism circuits. Omara argued, "The trial court cannot base its verdict on national security department's information. Investigations alone cannot by itself considered evidence or proof of the actions committed by the suspects." Applying this doctrine would undermine a great number of politically related rulings. The regime was also worried that Omara's chairmanship of the HJC might open the door for reinstating judges who opposed the army takeover and were sacked from their judicial posts with diminutive claim to due process.[51]

The "fort of rights and liberties," as the Council of State has been known, was another obstacle in the eyes of the regime. Due to its superior institutional independence and rule of law ideological predispositions, opposition to the regime's repressive agenda was even more widespread in the administrative judiciary. The Court of Administrative Judiciary's (CAJ) circuit, chaired by Yahia Al-Dakroury, delivered rulings that ran counter to the wishes of the regime. Al-Dakroury canceled a decision made by the committee tasked with investigating the funds of the Muslim Brotherhood's members to freeze the assets of several individuals. The confiscation of financial resources was a cornerstone of the regime's strategy to cripple the Brotherhood and Islamic political groups in general. The ruling forced the government to change the law. The new legislation created a judicial rather than administrative committee to oversee this process and allowed accused legal recourse before the courts.

Moreover, Al-Dakroury's court ordered that a travel ban imposed on several journalists, preachers, and activists be lifted. The court order stated:

---

[51] On one hand, Judge Mohamed Abu Al-Ella's recent decisions towed the regime's line. The circuit that he chaired refused the appeals of several individuals condemned to death despite mounting evidence that confessions were extracted under extreme torture. Amnesty International, *Egypt: Seven men facing imminent execution after being tortured in custody*, www.amnesty.org/en/latest/news/2017/06/egypt-seven-men-facing-imminent-execution-after-being-tortured-in-custody/. The same circuit also rejected the motion of the Muslim Brotherhood supreme guide Mohamed Badie, his deputy Khairat al-Shater and others on the Public Prosecution decision to include them on the terrorist list. On the other hand, Abu Al-Ella accepted the appeal on Mubarak's era prime minister Ahmed Nazif against his five-year sentence on corruption charges. Abu Al-Ella's service on the bench was not at all worrisome in the eyes of the regime. He was seconded to work on the Court of Ethics (1995–1999). He then worked in Kuwait for six years (2000–2006) – the maximum period allowed under the law. After 2011, he was selected to chair the committee tasked with reviewing appeals about judicial appointment before 2008. These posts are usually granted to only loyal judges.

"Preventing the claimant from travel encroaches on his constitutional rights granted by the Constitution, including his freedom to travel." In November 2015, Al-Dakroury again issued a ruling obliging the cabinet to disclose financial settlements reached with investors who illegally acquired state-owned lands and public-sector companies. Al-Dakroury urged the government to issue the Freedom of Information Act, under the constitution.

Judge Al-Dakroury also issued an order to cancel the gag order issued by the PP in relation to the 2012 presidential elections.[52] The court argued that the constitution underscores citizens' rights to information, and the criminal investigation is one of the most important sources of information about such an important matter as the presidential elections.[53] Additionally, Al-Dakroury's circuit issued a ruling quashing a decision by the State Security Prosecution Department (SSPD) preventing lawyers from entering the SSPD's headquarter. The court reasoned that such a decision undermines the dignity of lawyers and prevents them from performing their duties in the service of their clients.[54] Because the SSPD handles all politically sensitive cases, this ruling pertains particularly to political detainees, chief amongst them the Islamists.

The first circuit of HAC, responsible for reviewing appeals concerning rights and liberties was noticeably steadfast in its rule of law and rights and liberties stand. This circuit, which customarily is chaired by the president of the Council and includes most senior judges, refused an appeal against the ruling of CAJ quashing a decision by the SSPD preventing lawyers from entering the SSPD's headquarter.

The HAC's First Circuit dealt the security apparatus another legal defeat by issuing a ruling that the Ministry of Interior must reveal the location of a disappeared female doctor that had vanished since April 2014. The court reaffirmed the lower court decision arguing that forced disappearance is a violation of human rights principles and the constitution guarantees against disappearance.

The HAC rebutted the appeal of the PP against a ruling of the administrative court canceling the minister of interior's decision to prevent detainees from making phone calls to their lawyers and relatives. The court ruled that detainees in custody are entitled to no-cost phone calls on constitutional, legal, and humanitarian grounds. The court also reasoned that this right is an international right and that national codes should be amended to

---

[52] *Ahram*, January 20, 2016.
[53] Personal interview with the Council of State's first vice-president Yahia Al-Dakroury, December 2, 2017.
[54] *Shrouk*, September 9, 2017.

correspond to international human rights treaties.[55] This is critical because the security forces regularly use pressure and intimidation to coerce confessions from detainees.

The HAC refused an appeal against the administrative court decision to prohibit police from having permanent posts in public universities.[56] This decision came despite intense media campaign to restore security forces' overt control over university campuses where activists and Islamists had a strong presence. While the previous ruling was clearer cut in its ban, the new ruling, taking into consideration the public mood, permitted the police to intervene to prevent crimes and protect properties and citizens.

The Council also issued many rulings in the domain of socioeconomic rights. One was related to the right to strike. The HAC acquitted seventeen post office workers facing charges of peaceful striking. The court used Article 15 of the constitution to bestow the right, noting that legislators have failed to include it in the civil service law.[57] The ruling maintained, "The legislator was presumed to intervene in regulating the act of striking within the civil service law. In this case, the legislators did not fulfill their obligation, and the court found that the employees did not surpass what within their rights." The court's decision is doubly significant because it makes constitutional rights operative in the absence of laws regulating them. It is also a reversal from a previous stand by the Council that criminalized strikes based on narrow interpretations of Islamic law.

All these rulings, while representing inconveniences to the regime, pale in comparison to the June 21, 2016, ruling. The last straw that broke the camel's back, however, was Al-Dakroury's decision on the maritime border treaty with Saudi Arabia. Al-Dakroury issued a ruling asserting that in signing the *Tiran* and *Sanafir* agreement the regime had violated the constitution. The agreement, signed in April 2016, redraws Egypt's maritime borders and cedes the strategic Red Sea islands to Saudi Arabia. This was an explosive domestic and regional problem for the regime. Domestically, Sisi's nationalist discourse and the perception of the army as the protector of Egypt's sovereignty was brought to severe questions with the surrender of the vital strategic islands that Egypt exercised control over for many decades, islands that Egyptian soldiers lost

---

[55] *Al-Waten*, July 6, 2017.
[56] *Youm7*, December 15, 2014.
[57] The government employees were fired from their jobs at a post office in *Ashmon, Monufiya* by a court verdict issued on January 26, 2015. The verdict claimed they had failed to fulfill the demands of their public-sector jobs, referring specifically to a five-day strike in February 2014.

their lives defending. Relinquishing sovereignty flaw in the face of Sisi's cultivated image as the new Nasser.

In addition to domestic dilemmas created by the ruling and subsequent affirmation by the HAC, the ruling put the regime in a difficult position with its principle regional backer, the Kingdom of Saudi Arabia. Sisi made a personal pledge to the then-deputy crown Prince Mohammad bin Salman to cede sovereignty over the islands to KSA. The rulings infuriated the dashing and powerful Saudi prince. MBS, as bin Salman is commonly known, accused Sisi of duping him. Saudi Aramco stopped supplying Egypt with shipments of petroleum products, and a tug of media war erupted between the two regimes. President Sisi pleaded with the Kuwaiti royal family to intervene. The efforts of the minister of foreign affairs succeeded in easing the tension, and Sisi renewed his commitment to the deal.[58]

The regime had to use questionable legal tactics to ratify the treaty. The government exploited the highly politicized Urgent Matters Circuit to secure a ruling condemning the administrative court and HAC's rulings as infringements on the legislature and executive's foreign policy privileges. This verdict, which most legal experts argued have no legal merit or grounds, was used as a pretext to "manufacture" a jurisprudence dispute. This dispute between the two institutions was then used by the regime to request the intervention of the reliable SCC.

On June 4, 2017, the SCA filled a case on behalf of the Council of Ministers, the House of Representatives, and the defense, foreign, and interior ministries.[59] The SCC's chief justice did the regime bidding by ordering the suspension of all rulings related to the case. The suspension order came as a surprise to experts who follow the slow speed of the high court. The court issued its injunction before the passing of the fourteen days allotted to lawyers to submit their legal briefs. The regime seized on this injunction, rushing the agreement to the House's floor where it was hastily ratified. Then, it was promptly signed by Sisi, creating a *fait accompli*, despite the continuous litigation before the SCC. The regime, however, was not particularly thrilled by the unforeseen delay, legal failures, and public scrutiny. Courts' rulings flew in the face of the regime's consolidation aspirations.

---

[58] Personal interview with a senior official at the Kuwaiti Ministry of Foreign Affairs who participated in the shuttle diplomacy between the two leaders, Kuwait City, November 8, 2017.
[59] SCC Case No. 12 of Judicial Year 39.

THE REGIME TAKES THE GLOVES OFF

The regime's response to these inhospitable judicial decisions was predictable. Media attacks against the courts, and notably the Council of State, exposing corruption charges in the judiciary and using financial pressure against judges.[60] When intimidation and domestication tactics failed to achieve the desired objectives, the regime decided to use the "nuclear option." Borrowing an act from Nasser's playbook, Sisi instructed his deferential legislative majority to present a new draft law that would overturn more than half a century of the seniority-based system to select judicial chiefs.

It seems quite certain that the *Tiran* and *Sanafir* rulings figured profoundly in Sisi's calculation to take such action. A high-ranking former government official who has close professional and family ties to the Council of State has relayed the following story, which explains Sisi's decision to go forward with the law despite the strong opposition. Magdy Al-Agatti, minister of house of representatives affairs and a former senior vice-president of the Council,[61] assured Sisi that the Council would not invalidate the *Tiran* and *Sanafir* agreement. When Al-Dakroury did the opposite, Al-Agatti again reassured the regime that the HAC would "do the right thing." When the HAC reaffirmed the ruling, Al-Agatti was severely criticized for his serious misjudgment. To save his grace, Al-Agatti convinced the president that judges on the HAC were fearful of defying the next president of the Council, i.e., Al-Dakroury. Sisi asked for a way to give the presidency control over the direction of judicial politics.[62] Al-Dakroury was arguably the prime target.[63] Sisi wanted to prevent the appointment of the unwavering Al-Dakroury to the Council's presidency.[64]

---

[60] Despite the constitutional and legislative guarantees of judicial autonomy, a sizable portion of judges' salaries remain firmly under the control of the executive-controlled Ministry of Justice. When judges are perceived favorably, their fringe benefits would increase. When the regime is unsatisfied with the judicial corps in general or a specific institution, these portions of the salaries would be delayed or withhold.

[61] Al-Agatti served as a legal adviser to National Intelligence since 1993. He is known for his close ties to the deep state institutions. He was appointed to the ten-member committee that drafted changes to the 2012 Constitution after the military takeover in 2013.

[62] Personal interview with a former government minister, November 20, 2017.

[63] The regime's effort to domesticate Al-Dakroury included a carrot and a stick. The carrot was to second Judge Al-Dakroury's son to a highly sought-after position in the Supreme Constitutional Court. The stick was carried out by spreading rumors about appointing the son as a judge in the Council despite his poor grades and revealing the substantial income Al-Dakroury received from serving on several government boards included the Central Bank of Egypt.

[64] Al-Dakroury is no revolutionary nor Islamist. He could be described as a typical professional statist-reformer. In November 2012, Al-Dakroury and his family took to Tahrir Square to protest

The legislation endows the president with tremendous powers in appointing the presidents of the Court of Cassation (and HJC), the Council of State, the Administrative Prosecution Authority (APA), and the SCA. The provisions in the new bill are the same. The president of the Republic shall appoint the various chiefs from among three nominees chosen by the respective judicial body's supreme council. The nominations are to be drawn from the judicial body's seven most senior deputy president's and must be sent to the president of the Republic sixty days before the end of the former chairman's term. If no nominations are sent on time, if fewer than three names are sent, or if the nominations otherwise do not conform to the requirements, the president has the discretion to choose any of the seven most senior members in each institution. These changes, hence, undermine the fundamental principle of seniority enshrined in long-established norms, though not in the prevailing legislation.[65]

The draft law was proposed for the first time in June 2016 (the same month of the *Tiran* and *Sanafir* ruling), most likely as a trial balloon to assess the responses of the courts and judges and/or as a warning sign to the judiciary to get its act together and unconditionally support the regime's agenda. The draft law was later proposed again with a few modifications early in 2017. The bill

---

a constitutional declaration issued by former president Mohamed Mursi giving him exceptional powers, such as the right to issue irrevocable laws. At the time, Al-Dakroury said the declaration was "a flagrant interference with Egypt's judicial authority and the work of the judiciary, which transgresses the principle of separation of authorities and puts the president above the law." Al-Dakroury's rulings reflect a deep commitment to the rule of law, separation of powers, and judicialization. Al-Dakroury, following in the footsteps of his idol Al-Sanhuri, seems to very much believe in an active judicial role. Personal interview with first vice-president of the Council of State Yahia Al-Dakroury, December 2, 2017.

[65] The current legal codes, which mostly were inherited from the Nasser and Sadat era, did not codify the prevailing practices. These rules gave the chief executive wide latitude in the appointment process. Article 44 of the Judicial Authority Law (Law No. 46 of 1972), states "Filling judicial posts either through appointment or promotion shall be through a decree from the President of the Republic. The President of the Court of Cassation shall be appointed from amongst the vice presidents after taking the opinion of the High Judicial Council." Article 83 of Council of State Law (Law No. 47 of 1972) proposes, "The President of the Council of State shall be appointed by the President of the Republic from amongst the vice presidents of the Council after taking the opinion of a special general assembly composed of the President of the Council of State, his vice presidents, deputy presidents, and councilors who served at the rank of council for two years." Article 35 of the Administrative Prosecution Authority Law (Law No. 117 of 1958) maintains, "The appointment of the president of the Administrative Prosecution Authority shall be through a decree from the President of the Republic." Article 16 of the State Cases Authority Law (Law No. 75 of 1963) stipulates, "Filling the authority's posts either through appointment or promotion shall be through a decree from the President of the Republic. The President of the Authority shall be appointed from amongst the vice presidents after taking the opinion of the Authority's Supreme Council."

was fast-tracked through the House of Representatives' Legislative Committee and then to the floor without gathering the opinion of the different judicial institutions as mandated by Article 185 of the 2014 Constitution.

In addition to undermining a well-recognized norm, an apparent conflict of interests arises from the appointment of the president of the HJC by the President. The HJC president presides over the special court to try the President were he to commit crimes stipulated in Article 159 of the constitution.[66] Another conflict of interests arises, albeit indirectly, from the appointment of the president of the Council of State by the President. Since the former presides over the HAC's First Circuit that has the sole authority to rule on legal disputes pertaining to presidential elections as well as appeals related to the nullification of the Presidential orders.

The proposed law was met with an uproar from all sectors of the judicial community. Some, however, were more vocal than others. The HJC response was notably muted, the HJC issued a brief communique to the Speaker of the House stating, "I would like to kindly inform you that the HJC in its session on March 12, 2017 rejected the draft law." The Judges Club was more active in its opposition. The Club initially called for a General Assembly to discuss its resignation "in protest against the breach of judicial independence." However, the Club postponed the general assembly indefinitely a few days later when it became clear that the HJC would not support such efforts.[67] The president of the Judges Club Mohamed Abdel-Mohsen sent an open letter to judges bitterly describing the stances of the HJC and the Ministry of Justice.[68]

This timid response is striking if compared with the powerful positions the HJC and the Judges Club took under Mursi. Abdel-Mohsen did point a finger

---

[66] Article 159 stipulates the following: "A charge of violating the provisions of the Constitution, high treason or any other felony against the President of the Republic is to be based on a motion signed by at least a majority of the members of the House of Representatives ... The President of the Republic is tried before a special court headed by the president of the Supreme Judicial Council, and with the membership of the most senior deputy of the president of the Supreme Constitutional Court, the most senior deputy of the president of the State Council, and the two most senior presidents of the Court of Appeals."

[67] The president of the HJC rejected the Judges Club request to use the Court of Cassation headquarter to host the extraordinary general assembly. When the request to convene an extraordinary general assembly was presented to the president of Cairo Court of Appeal, he transferred it on the same day to HJC president Moustafa Shafiq. Judge Shafiq, however, refused to allow the Judges Club to convene a general assembly in the Court of Cassation headquarter in downtown Cairo. Judge Shafiq refused, "Taking into consideration the current circumstances and because of the *refusal of security entities*, we decline to convene the emergency general assembly in the corridors of High Justice House."

[68] *Shrouk*, June 21, 2013.

at senior judges for their timorous response.[69] He compared the positions of the Ministry of Justice and the HJC during the crisis of removal of PP Mahmoud under Mursi and their reaction to the current crisis. The HJC sent the amendments to the judicial authority law in 2013 to the different courts and public prosecution offices all over Egypt asking for their opinion.

The Council of State was the first judicial institution to convene a general assembly to challenge the proposed law. The Council's highest authority sent an official letter to the House was the most elaborate and was signed by all members of the Special Council Administrative Affairs (SCAA). The message was roughly three pages long while letters from the HJC and its counterpart in the APA was just a single sentence long. The Council of State was the most steadfast in its opposition. The Council's legislative division, mandated by the 2014 Constitution to review all legislations, rejected the proposed law on procedural and substantive grounds.[70]

The regime took a plethora of coordinated actions to soften judicial reaction. Conveniently, the ACA, where Sisi's son serves as an officer, unearthed a bribery that implicates the Council's secretary general. This episode was highly publicized and extensively covered in the state-owned media and private newspapers and TV channels. While the allegations only included a handful of Council's staff and only one senior judge, the press dubbed the episode "State Council's bribery."

Another arm-twisting move was to instruct state-controlled media to bring to debate the phenomena of "judicial hereditary," where sons and relatives of judges receive appointment to judicial posts. This is of significance to judges who are keen to provide lucrative employment for their sons and daughters in the exceptionally tight domestic labor market.

It was also notable that pro-reform judges Assem Abd El-Gbar and Hisham Rauf were referred to the disciplinary board a few days after the debate on the proposed law surfaced. The two senior judges (one at the Court of Cassation and the other at Cairo Court of Appeal), were accused back in 2015 of participating in drafting an anti-torture draft law.[71] The investigation continued until March 2016. Abd El-Gbar stated that he believes these actions were taken "likely to exclude us from the judiciary or intimidate judges to prevent them from taking a stand against the intrigues against judges these

[69] Abdel-Mohsen, however, bowed to pressure and refused to coordinate activities with fellow chiefs of judicial clubs. Personal interview with the president of the State Council's Judges Club Samir El-Bahy, December 3, 2017.

[70] *Shrouk*, April 15, 2017.

[71] *Shrouk*, March 30, 2017.

days.[72] Abd El-Gbar and Rauf's day in court was no other than April 24th, a few days of the anticipated parliamentary vote on the judicial law. The formal accusations were all too familiar "intervening in legislative work through the drafting of draft laws and partaking in political action."[73]

The regime spared no pains to ensure that senior judges would not escalate the confrontation. A leading member of the House of Representatives Legislative Committee issued a fiery public statement shortly after the Council of State declared its strong opposition to the proposed law. The statement included veiled and not-so-veiled threats to decrease retirement age for judges on the pretext of equality with other civil servants and ending seconding judges to different government institutions and public companies.[74]

After the House voted on the law, the State Council Club and the Judges' Club, called on Sisi not to ratify the law, to no avail. After Sisi signed the bill into law, the HJC and other judicial councils applied the controversial law and sent the names of its three most senior judges to the president sixty days before the end of the term. The only pocket of resistance was again the Council of State. The Council's general assembly defied the law and nominated Judge Al-Dakroury, the most senior vice-president, alone. This was an implicit rebuke to Law 13 of 2017.[75]

Sisi issued several decisions to appoint the presidents of the different judicial institutions.[76] All four appointees were not the most senior within the respective organizations. As expected, the President of the Republic decided to withhold the appointment of Al-Dakroury and Omara. Ahmed Abu Al-Azm, ranked fourth in the seniority list, received the presidential appointment for

---

[72] http://albedaiah.com/news/2017/04/01/132918.

[73] Abd El-Gabar was blunt in his commentary on the decision stating that "There are two reasons to this case. The first is to cleanse members of the 'judicial independence trend' from the judiciary. Second, is to prevent me from joining the High Judicial Council, especially that I have three more years within the judiciary and will be the first vice-president of the Court of Cassation in the 2019 Judicial Year." *Shrouk*, April 25, 2017.

[74] *Shrouk*, April 3, 2017.

[75] *Shrouk*, May 13, 2017.

[76] The regime was still worried about administrative judges' response to the presidential decree bypassing Al-Dakroury. It prevailed on its allies on the Special Council Administrative Affairs (SCAA) to issue an executive order banning all judges from engaging in any social media outlets. With formal media tightly controlled by the regime, this decision had the intended effect of suppressing all dissenting voices. The SCAA coupled this unprecedented decision with calling some judges before the Council's Inspection Department. These measures had the sole goal of stifling any and all efforts to mount genuine collective opposition. Personal interview with a member of the Council of State's Club Board of Directors, Cairo on July 24, 2017.

president of the Council of State and Judge Abu El-Ala (ranked second in seniority) was appointed president of the HJC and the Court of Cassation.

Many judges interviewed for this book have pointed out to that the changes intended to keep specific judges out of assuming the leadership of the HJC and Council of State. Unlike Omara, who quashed the harsh rulings against anti-regime activists, Abu El-Ala reaffirmed almost all decisions, paving the way for the executions of several individuals. These rulings have made some analysts wonder if there was causation between Judge Abu El-Ala's decisions and Sisi's choice of him. One analysis put it bluntly but in a question format (likely fearing prosecution), "Did the execution rulings paved the way to the presidency of the Court of Cassation in Egypt?"[77]

On the other hand, Abu Al-Azm has been trying to play favorites with the regime.[78] Upon his chairmanship over the Council's legislative division, Abu Al-Azm was rather expediently quickly to review the scores of draft laws. On average the process lasted only fifteen days regardless of the length and complexity of the draft. This quickness was critical in the passing of the changes to the judicial authority's laws. The House sent the proposal to the Council on March 29th. The legislative division could have delayed its response until April 29th. This would have prevented applying the law to the Court of Cassation and other judicial institutions where the presidents were to retire on June 30th. On the contrary, Abu Al-Azm sent the Council's opinion on April 15th, granting the legislative machinery precious added time to pass the proposed law conveniently on the regime timetable.[79] Abu Al-Azm also was publically on record supporting the President of the Republic and the Speaker of the House.

These changes to the law apparently had many clear objectives: punish those high-level judges who dared to deviate from the regime's line, ensure presidential consolidation of power over the courts, and smooth any rough edges prior to the 2018 presidential election and Sisi's second term.[80] In

---

[77] www.sasapost.com/executions-andcourt-of-cassation-in-egypt/ هل مهدت أحكام إعدام المعارضين الطريق لرئاسة محكمة النقض في مصر؟

[78] In the Council's emergency general assembly held to protest the law, the president of the Council's Judges Club, Samir Al-Bahy, asked the seven senior judges to pledge to refuse the presidential nomination if it does not abide by seniority. All the judges except Abu Al-Azm agreed to this. Personal interview with Samir Al-Bahy, December 3, 2017.

[79] The bill was signed into law on April 28, 2017. On April 30th, the HJC sent the nominations of the most senior three deputy presidents to Sisi.

[80] This change was another step in the reconfiguration of the power structure within the regime by limiting the political role of judges. This bill was a continuation of further actions that were taken before including the ouster of minister of justice, Ahmed El-Zend, who presented himself as a strongman in the July 3rd regime. The Ministry of Interior was also a subject of the

addition to demonstrating the reach of the executive in the most sensitive judicial appointments, the new law had the added benefit of using the extensive powers of the judicial chiefs to prevent any pockets of resistance from emerging at the bench. The president of the HJC/Court of Cassation or the Council of State are not merely first among equals. They exercise unmatched control over administrative affairs, appointments, and financial matters. After the assassination of the PP, many members of the HJC nominated certain judges to assume the post. In the end, the big prize went to Nabil Sadek, a close confident of the president of the Court of Cassation who served as head of his technical office.[81]

The regime domination over the judicial institutions is not only a goal in itself but also necessary to ensure control over the electoral contestation processes for the presidency, legislature, and local governments. The 10-members National Elections Authority (NEA), authorized to oversee all national and local elections Article 209 stipulates, the ten members "selected equally from among the vice-presidents of the Court of Cassation, the presidents of the Courts of Appeal, the vice-president of the State Council, the State Cases and Administrative Prosecution, who are to be selected by the Supreme Judicial Council and special councils of the aforementioned judicial bodies."[82]

The regime thoroughly packed the ten-member NEA. The NEA chairman is a known protégé of the minister of justice and a close friend of Sisi's brother (also a senior Court of Cassation judge). The NEA spokesman is no other than Mahmoud Al-Sherif, another known regime supporter and the brother of Ahmed Helmy Al-Sherif, the deputy chair of the House Legislative Committee and the same person who proposed the amendments to the judicial appointment law. Al-Sherif's cousin is the deputy speaker of the House. Another member is Abu Baker Marwan, the brother of former judge turned minister of legal and parliamentary affairs, Omar Marwan. Five other members either served in the Ministry of Justice or are known to be staunch

---

same institutional "claw trimming" with the removal of its Minister Ibrahim. Ibrahim, appointed by Mursi in January 2013, was an important player in the army takeover and the bloody crackdown that unfolded afterward.

[81] Sadek graduated from the Police Academy in 1976. He resigned from his job a few years later as a police officer to pursue a career as a judge. He served in several positions within the judiciary, including chief prosecutor for financial and business affairs during the Mubarak-era. Sadek worked for six years in Qatar as an Appeals Court judge. In Doha, Sadek befriended Sisi's older brother, another Court of Cassation judge.

[82] Article 209 of the 2014 Constitution mandates a presidential decree to appoint members of the NEA. The 2012 Constitution did not require such presidential action. This was another manifestation of expanding presidential powers in the new constitution.

supporters of the regime. In one unusual case, one of the ABA nominees was withdrawn and replaced by another member after adverse security reports about her husband. No wonder that a few nominees declined to accept the nomination for the NEA. One reported, "I decided to turn down the offer to join the NEA because of the overtly political nature of its work which does not align with my judicial work."[83] The value of this regime control over the NEA was evident in how the Authority managed the 2018 presidential elections. The election timetable was perfectly tailored to fit Sisi. The NEA looked eager to remove Sisi's rival, former chief-of-staff of the armed forces Sami Annan from the electoral rolls one day after he was detained by the security forces. The NEA also facilitated the candidacy of the regime's handpicked candidate.

Because the administrative judiciary was the prime target of the law, the newly appointed president of the Council worked laboriously to mold the Council's most critical circuits on the executive size. One crucial change was the reorganization of the HAC's First Circuit responsible for many of the anti-regime rulings.[84] The circuit's packing was entirely transparent. Abu Al-Azm removed all members and replaced them with trusted lieutenants who worked with him previously. Many of them would not typically qualify according to seniority to occupy such critical posts.[85] In addition, the education circuit (rights of political opposition students) and contracts (which invalidated many questionable government's contracts) were also subject to major overhaul.[86]

Abu Al-Azm rammed changes through the Council's General Assembly, where no one was permitted to voice any dissenting voice. Nevertheless, one of the Council's vice-presidents who was passed for a seat on the HAC filed an appeal arguing that the decision should be overturned because it defies the established judicial norms of seniority. The petition also alluded to the fact that members of the Council's general assembly were coerced to support such a decision.[87] Most of these who were appointed to staff the critical first circuit did not meet the qualifications previously set by the SCAA in 2016. They all are junior members of the Council. The Al-Wafd newspaper

---

[83] Personal interview with a former nominee to the NEC, December 27, 2017.

[84] The First Circuit has jurisdiction over many critical matters including appeals pertaining to public rights and liberties, appeals pertaining to political parties, appeals pertaining to presidential, legislative and local elections, appeals pertaining to NGO's, appeals pertaining to trade unions, appeals pertaining to investing, stattlite podcasting, appeals pertaining to citizenship, residency, deportation and prevention from entry to the Egypt.

[85] *Shrouk*, September 23, 2017.

[86] Multiple interviews with judges at the Council of State, September 25, 2017.

[87] *Shrouk*, October 2, 2017.

headline on the story was revealing: "the purge of the HAC's First Circuit in the Council of State Assembly.[88] Of the twelve members that compose the circuit, perhaps only one would qualify based on seniority for such critical assignments. To ensure that future generations of administrative judges will not harbor any unfavorable ideological commitments, the new president increased the weight of security reports in the admission process. The national security apparatus reports is now used as a de facto veto against any applicant to the Council.[89]

The jurisprudential change in the courts and the Council is starting to crystalize. When Al-Dakroury contested the presidential decree before the Council's circuit on Judicial Personal Requests, the Circuit was in no hurry to issue a ruling. After postponing the decision for several times, it transferred it to the SCC. While this is less than ideal for the Abu Al-Azm, the SCC has been known since 2001 for their deference to the executive branch and the court is widely expected either to declare that law constitutional or to keep it on the back burner for years if not decades.[90] The same outcome is expected regarding Judge Omara's appeal. The government is utilizing all delay tactics until July 2018, when Omara reached the mandatory retirement age of seventy and the issue became moot.

Furthermore, the Administrative Court refused to hear a petition against the maritime boarder treaty between Egypt and Cyprus, which many suspects have squandered Egypt's mineral rights.[91] The HAC first circuit rejected an appeal from activist Ahmed Duma against holding his trial in a glass cage. The court argued that it has no jurisdiction to adjudicate this matter.[92] This decision was welcome news for the regime. Since July 2013, all courts' proceedings for leading opposition figures, including President Mursi and the top Brotherhood leadership, prominent liberals, and leftists, were held in glass cages, where the defendants' voices cannot be heard. Lawyers have argued that these conditions violate the defendants' rights to free trial as they cannot hear what takes place outside the cage during the courts' hearings. The Council's First Circuit refused the appeal against the government-preferred candidate, Moussa Moustafa Moussa, on procedural grounds. Allowing Sisi to run against his own handpicked candidate.[93]

---

[88] *Al-Wafd*, September 23, 2017
[89] Personal interview with a member of the Council of State Judges Club, October 23, 2017.
[90] *Shrouk*, November 23, 2017.
[91] *Al-Masry Al-Youm*, August 30, 2017.
[92] *Shrouk*, February 19, 2018.
[93] *Shrouk*, February 21, 2018.

The HJC under Abu El-Ala revived the old claim that the HJC only speak for judges and is the only entity to be consulted on judicial matters. When the House of Representatives introduced an amendment allocating half of all pail money to the Fund for Judges' Health and Social Welfare, many judges were worried that this amendment is going to be perceived as a bribe to judges, who can increase the bail amounts to fill the empty coffers of the Fund. The Judges Club sent a letter to the Speaker of the House protesting the amendment. The HJC president issued a very strongly worded communique. He stated,

> Pertaining to the letter sent by judge Mohamed Abdel Mohsen, the President of Egypt's Judges Club to Dr. Ali Abdel Aal, the Speaker of the House of Representatives, to protest a proposed law to prop the Fund for Judges' Health and Social Welfare, we assert that the High Judicial Council, regardless of its position which it will reveal when it will be brought before it according to the Constitution, it warns that it [HJC] is the only entity that manages judges' affairs and speaks for them according to Article 77–2 of the Judicial Authority Law. No other entity, whatever it might be, should address these matters.[94]

The new judicial chiefs are eager to prove their value to the regime. This carries considerable benefits during their tenure and beyond.[95] Abu Al-Azm's son, a junior judge at the Council of State was seconded to the Suez Canal Company. The minister of justice added seven senior judges to the list of legal arbitrators. The list included the president of the Council of State, the president of the APA, the president of Cairo Court of Appeal, the president of Alexandria Court of Appeal, the president of Tanta Court of Appeal, the president of Mansoura Court of Appeal.[96] The prime minister issued a ministerial decree permitting a SCC's justice to work as a legal adviser to the Kuwaiti parliament.[97]

CONCLUSION

The military–judicial alliance proved vital to shoring up the Sisi regime. The synergy between generals and judges is significant for the two sides. The judiciary, however, lost a substantial part of the widespread support it used to enjoy in the society. Restoring judicial standing would be taxing.

---

[94] *Al-Masry Al-Youm*, February 18, 2018.
[95] On the eve of the presidential election, the HJC president donated 100,000 EGP to Sisi's Fund "Viva Egypt." The HJC also asked judges to donate as well. *Shrouk*, March 25, 2018.
[96] *Shrouk*, November 15, 2017.
[97] Prime Minster Decree No 2212 of 2017.

The judiciary could find itself in an arduous position if the Islamists and their allies come back to the pinnacle of political power.

Social scientists would rarely endeavor into making predictions about mega political events such as institutions' survival or demise. The multiplicity of factors that goes into such analysis and the influence of international, regional, as well as domestic forces make such predictions incredibly risky academic exercise. Nevertheless, if the model presented in this book proves accurate, the inevitable forecast would be the eventual clash between the presidency and the courts, something alongside what happened under Nasser in 1968. As the SCC has demonstrated its loyalty and usefulness to the regime, quite likely it will not be affected. Baring a dramatic change in its jurisprudence, the regime is not expected to undermine the SCC's role, jurisdiction, or institutional independence. The criminal courts also went along with the regime's agenda. Criminal courts, and particularly the Terrorism Circuits, delivered critical RSFs for the regime. This leaves out the Court of Cassation and the Council of State.

The regime has achieved partial control over the Court of Cassation through changing the rules of appointing its president. The handpicked president of the court and the HJC proved his loyalty to the regime on more than one occasion. This, however, might not be enough. The court's high level of institutional autonomy, the reservoir of due process and the rule of law precedents might prove difficult to bend. The regime seems to be aware of these factors. This explains the changes to the Penal Code and Code of Criminal Procedures to facilitate convictions and make it harder for the Court of Cassation to overturn verdicts by the Courts of Appeal.

The Council of State is a bigger problem for the regime. While the handpicked president of the Council has filled critical circuits and influential positions with his protégées, he is unable to force an ideological transformation in the Council. The regime's response to this is hard to predict. The presidency proved less than restrained on more than one occasion. The government can utilize its hegemonic legislative majority to push through constitutional amendments and recast the constitution into a highly authoritarian document.[98] It could also include either limiting the Council's jurisdiction or, at an extreme, abolishing the administrative judiciary altogether and merge its functions with the courts.

This would ensure the regime's triumph in the short term but could prove ruinous in the future. After all, naked force cannot be sustained in the long

---

[98] These amendments could include a reversal of the two-term limits and expand presidential powers.

run without legal cover. Nasser's brute force was disguised by his charisma, socioeconomic achievements and foreign policy success abroad. Sisi is not Nasser, and 2018 is not 1956. Sisi's record in these three fronts is lacking. The general is completely void of charisma. His oratorical gifts are nonexistent and pale in comparison not only to Nasser but even Sadat. In addition, Egyptians have suffered worsening economic situation since July 3rd than any other time in recent memory. The devaluation of the currency, hyperinflation, mounting domestic and international debts, and wasteful spending on mega projects, negates any hope that Sisi would evolve into an enlightened despot along the lines of Pinochet in Chile or Park in South Korea.

Sisi's foreign policy record is also not an exemplary success. The regime failed to protect Egypt's historical water rights. This will surely cause irreparable damage. The surrendering of the vital Red Sea islands undermined Egypt's national security. The regime's counterterrorism policies have created a fertile ground for radicalization. Attacks in the restive Sinai have increased in frequency and intensity since Sisi assumed office. The regime's pursuit of unbounded dominance is turning Egypt into a giant pressure cooker with no judicial safety valve.

That being said, one thing remains certain: judicial politics will remain at the heart of Egypt's contestation processes for years to come. Courts' rulings and actions over the past few years have firmly positioned the judiciary in the cultural and ideological fault lines of a deeply divided society. Judges' future political role is part of a larger debate, of course, about Egypt's past, Egypt's present, and Egypt's future. Judicialization will continue to be significant, profound, and immensely political. This is not going to be the last book on this subject.

References

PERSONAL INTERVIEWS*

Deputy Chief Justice of the Supreme Constitutional Court, March 13, 2018.
Senior judge at Cairo Court of Appeal, multiple interviews in 2016–2018.
Member of the Council of State's Club Board, multiple interviews in 2015–2018.
Judge at Southern Cairo Court of First Instance, multiple interviews in 2014–2017.
Vice president of the Council of State, multiple interviews in 2015–2017.
Nabil Abdel Fattah, assistant director of the Al-Ahram Center for Political and Strategic
    Studies, March 16, 2006.
Judges at the Council of State, multiple interviews in 2014–2016.
Mahmoud Abou- El-Leil, Minister of Justice, May 9, 2006.
Mohamed Maher Abo El-Enin, vice president of the Council of State, November 23,
    2005.
Mahmoud A, board member of the Alexandria Judges Club, multiple interviews in
    2006.
Zakaria Abd Al-Aziz, president of the Judges Club, February 27, 2006.
Mahmoud Abd Altif, vice president of the Council of State, December 17, 2005.
Assim Abd-al-Gabar, vice president of the Court of Cassation, multiple interviews in
    2006.
Abdel-Moneim Abu al-Futuh, member of the Guidance Bureau, Muslim
    Brotherhood, April 3, 2006.
Samir Al-Bahy, president of the Council of State's Judges Club, December 3, 2017.
Mohammed Al-Dakroury, chief legal advisor to President Hosni Mubarak, retired
    senior judge of the Council of State, and secretary of Ethics and Legal Affairs at
    the NDP, March 1, 2006.
Ashraf Al-Baroudi, judge of the Alexandria Court of Appeal, multiple interviews in
    2006.

---

* Names are in alphabetical order with titles at the time of interviews. I also interviewed about
fifty different judges, public prosecutors, administrative prosecutors, and lawyers who spoke on
the condition of anonymity. Due to the heightened risks after July 3, 2013, most interviews
since this date are not identified. Last names of serving judges are also redacted.

Tariq Al-Bishri, former first vice president of the Council of State, May 6, 2006.

Shrief F., judge, multiple interviews in 2005–2017.

Hussam Al-Ghariani, vice president of the Court of Cassation, multiple interviews in 2006.

Anwar Al-Hawari, editor in chief of *Al-Wafd* newspaper, multiple interviews in 2004–2006.

Amro Al-Husani, vice president of the Administrative Prosecution Body, multiple interviews in 2006.

Yahia El-Dakroury, Council of State's first vice-president, December 2, 2017.

Yahia Galal, vice president of the Court of Cassation, multiple interviews 2006.

Sameh Al-Kashef, deputy director of the Judicial Inspection Department, May 9, 2006.

Mahmoud Al-Khodiry, president of the Alexandria Judges Club, multiple interviews in 2006.

Yahia Al-Rifai, former president of the Judges Club, April 5, 2006.

Mostafa Kamel Al-Sayed, human rights activist and professor of political science of Cairo University and the American University in Cairo, multiple interviews, 2004–2015.

Tarek A, judge, multiple interviews in 2006.

Jamal Dahroug, first vice president of the Council of State, December 17, 2005.

Mohamed A, Administrative Prosecution Authority, multiple interviews in 2007–2017.

Yussef A, chief prosecutor at the Court of Cassation, multiple interviews in 2012–2016.

Mohamed Nagui Darbala, vice president of the Judges Club, April 2, 2006.

Amr A, chief prosecutor at the Court of Cassation, multiple interviews in 2010–2013.

Essam El-Erian, spokesman of the Muslim Brotherhood and former MP, April 2, 2006.

Kamal El-Menoufi, Dean of the Faculty of Economics and Political Science, multiple interviews in 2004–2007.

Tawfiq El-Menoufi, vice president of the Administration Prosecution Authority, May 2, 2006.

Essam Tawfiq Farag, president of the Civil Prosecution of the Court of Cassation and board member of the Alexandria Judges Club, multiple interviews in 2006.

Ashraf N, judge, multiple interviews in 2005–2017.

Osama Al-Ghazali Harb, President of the Democratic Front Party, multiple interviews in 2005–2006.

Bahey El-Din Hassan, Director of Cairo Institute for Human Rights Studies, April 3, 2006.

Ali Al-Din Hilal, Minister of Youth and National Democratic Party's General Secretariat Member, multiple interviews in 2005–2017.

Mohamed Kamal, leading member of the National Democratic Party and member of the *Shoura* Council, multiple interviews in 2005–2016.

Abdallah Khalil, lawyer and expert in international human rights law, April 3, 2006.

Mohammed Safi El-Din Kharboush, president of the National Council for Youth, multiple interviews, 2006–2017.

Ahmed Mekki, vice president of the Court of Cassation, multiple interviews in 2006.

Mahmoud Mekki, vice president of the Court of Cassation, multiple interviews in 2006.

Intsar Nasim, Director of the Judicial Inspection Department, Ministry of Justice, May 9, 2006.

Adel Qorah, former President of the Court of Cassation and HJC, member of the *Shoura* Council and the ruling National Democratic Party, February 25, 2006.

Ahmed Saber, spokesman of the Judges Club, multiple interviews in 2006.

Mohammed Al-Sayed Said, deputy-director of *Al-Ahram* Center for Political and Strategic Studies, February 27, 2006.

Abdel Monaim Said, director of *Al-Ahram* Center for Political and Strategic Studies, 27, February 2006.

Ahmed Thabet, Nassri Party member and professor of political science at Cairo University, multiple interviews 2004–2006.

Ahmed Z, judge of the *Damnour* Court of First Instance, multiple interviews 2006.

BOOKS, ARTICLES, AND CHAPTERS

Abd al-Barr, Faruq. *Dawr majlis al-Dawlah al-Misri fi himayat al-huquq wa-al-hurriyat al-`amah* (al-juz' 3). al-Qahirah, Matabi` Sijill al-`Arab, 1998.

*Dawr majlis al-Dawlah al-Misri fi himayat al-huquq wa-al-hurriyat al-`amah* (al-juz' 2). al-Qahirah: Matabi` Sijill al-`Arab, 1991.

*Dawr majlis al-Dawlah al-Misri fi himayat al-huquq wa-al-hurriyat al-`ammah* (al-juz' 1). al-Qahirah: Matabi` Sijill al-`Arab, 1988.

Mawqif `Abd al-Razzaq al-Sanhuri min qadaya al-hurriyah wa-al-dimuqratiyah. al-Qahirah: n. p., 2005.

Abd al-Fattāh, Nabīl, ed. *al-Quḍāh wa-al-iṣlāḥ al-siyāsī.* al-Qahirah: Markaz al-Qahirah li-Dirāsāt Ḥuqūq al-Insān, 2006.

Abd al-Hafiz, Ahmad. *Niqabat al-Muhamin: surat Misr fi al-qarn al-`ishrin.* al-Qahirah Markaz al-Dirasat al-Siyasiyah wa-al-Istiratijiyah, 2003.

Abd al-Hamīd, Husni Darwish. *al-Qadā' hisn al-hurriyat.* al-Qahirah: Dar al-Ma'ārif, 1986.

Abd Allah, Abd al-Ghani Basyuni. *Mabda al-musawah amama al-qada wa-kafalat haqq al-taqadi.* al-Iskandariyah: Munshaat al-Ma`arif, 1983.

Abd al-Mun`im, Ahmad Faris. *al-Dawr al-siyasi li-Niqabat al-Muhamin, (1912–1981).* al-Qahirah: n.p., 1984.

Abd al-Rāziq, Husayn. *Misr fī 18 wa-19 Yanāyir: dirāsah siyāsīyah wathā'iqiyah.* al-Qahirah: Shuhdī, 1985.

Abd al-Salsm, Muhammad. *Sanawat 'asibah: dhikriyat Na'ib 'amm.* al-Qahirah: Dar al-Shuruq, 1975.

Abdel-Fadil, Mahmoud. *Iqtisād al-Misrī bayna al-takhtīt al-markazī wa-al- infitāh al-iqtisādī.* Tarābulus: Ma'had al-Inmā' al-'Arabī, 1980.

Asfur, Muhammad. *Istiqlal al-sultah al-qada'iyah.* al-Qahirah: Matba`at Atlas, 1969.

Asfur, Sa'd, and Muḥsin Khalīl. *al-qada al-Idari.* al-Iskandariyah: Munsha'at al-Ma'arif, 1975.

Ashmawi, Muhammad Sa`id. *`Alá minassat al-qada.* al-Qahirah: Dar al-Hilal, 2000.

Azzuz, Abd al-Rahman. *al-Qada al-sha`bi.* al-Qahirah: Dar Nahdat Misr lil-Tab` wa-al-Nashr, 1977.

Abdel Nasser, Gamal. *Egypt's Liberation: The Philosophy of the Revolution.* Washington, DC: Public Affairs Press, 1955.

Abdel-Fadil, Mahmoud. *The Political Economy of Nasserism: A Study in Employment and Income Distribution Policies in Urban Egypt, 1952–72*. Cambridge: Cambridge University Press, 1980.

Abraham, Henry J. *The Judicial Process*. New York: Oxford University Press, 1998.

Abu al-Majd, Sabri. *Sanawat ma qabla al-thawrah: Yanayir 1930–23 Yuliyu 1952* (al-juz' 1). al-Qahirah: al-Hayah al-Misriyah al-'Ammah lil-Kitab: 1987.

Abu Basha, Hasan. *Mudhakkirat Hasan Abu Basha fi al-amn wa-al-siyasah: Yanayir 1977, Uktubir 1981, Ramadan 1987*. al-Qahirah: Dar al-Hilal, 1990.

Abū Qamar, Maḥmūd Riḍā. *al-Qaḍā' wa-al-wāqi' al-siyāsī: dirāsah taṭbīqīyah 'alá al-qaḍā' ayn al-idārī wa-al-dustūrī fī Miṣr*. al-Qahirah: Jāmi'at 'Ayn Shams, Kullīyat al-Ḥuqūq, 1995.

Abū Ṭālib, Ḥāmid Muhammad. *Nizām al-qaḍā' al-Misrī fī mīzān al-sharī'ah*. al-Qahirah: Dār al-Fikr al-'Arabī, 1993.

Acemoglu, Daron, and James A. Robinson, *Economic Origins of Dictatorship and Democracy*, New York: Cambridge University Press, 2010.

Aḥmad, Rif'at Sayyid. *Thawrat al-Jinarāl: qiṣṣat Jamāl 'Abd al-Nāṣir kāmilah, min al-milād ilá al-mawt, 1918–1970: mawsū'ah fikrīyah wa-siyāsīyah*. al-Qahirah: Dār al-Hudá. 1993.

Al-'Adili, Usamah Ahmad. *al-Nizam al-siyāsī al-Misrī wa-al-tajribah al-lībirālīyah*. al-Jīzah: Maktabat Nahdat al-Sharq, 1996.

Al-Baghdadi, Abd al-Latif. *Mudhakkirāt 'Abd al-Latif al-Baghdadi*. al-Qahirah: al-Maktab al-Misrī al-Hadīth, 1977.

Albertus, Michael, and Victor Menaldo. "Dictators as Founding Fathers? The Role of Constitutions under Autocracy." *Economics & Politics*, 24, no. 3 (2012): 279–306.

Al-Bishri, Tariq, *al-Dimuqratiyah wa-nizam 23 Yuliyu 1952–1970*. al-Qahirah: Dar al-Hilal, 1991.

Al-Bishri, Tariq. al-Qaḍā' al-Miṣrī bayna al-istiqlāl wa-al-iḥtiwā' in ed. Alā' Abū Zayd and Hibah Ra'ūf 'Izzat, *al-Muwāṭanah al-Miṣrīyah wa-mustaqbal al-dīmuqrāṭīyah: ru'á jadīdah li-'ālam mutaghayyir*, al-Qahirah: Maktabat al-Shurūq al-Dawlīyah: 2005.

Al-Dimuqratiyah wa-al-Nasiriyah. al-Qahirah: Dar al-Thaqafah al-Jadidah, 1975.

Al-harakah al-siyāsīyah fī Misr, 1945–1952. al-Qahirah: al-Hay'ah al-Misrīyah al-'Ammah lil-Kitāb, 1972.

Al-Qada al-Misri bayna al-istiqlal wa-al-ihtiwa. al-Qahirah: Maktabat al-Shuruq Al-Dawliyah, 2006.

Dirasat fi al-dimuqratiyah al-Misriyah. al-Qahirah: Dar al-Shuruq, 1987.

Al-Ghiryānī, Tal'at. *Fu'ād Sirāj al-Dīn: ustūrah … ākhir bāshawāt Misr*. al-Qahirah: Dar Sfinks, 1995.

Al-Hakim, Tawfiq. *The Return of Consciousness*. New York: New York University Press, 1985.

Al-Jarihi, Magdi. *Majlis al-Dawlah (Qadai al-mashrū'īyah): al-musāwāh wa-al-ḥurrīyah*. al-Qahirah: Dar el-Tahrir, 2006.

Al-Jarihi, Magdi. al-Maktab al-Fanni, al-Niyabah al-Idariyah. *al-Niyabah al-Idariyah 1954–2004*. al-Qahirah: al-Niyabah al-Idariyah, 2004.

Al-Naqd, Mahkamt. *al-Kitāb al-dhahabī lil-mahākim al-ahlīyah 1883–1933* (al-juz' 1). al-Qahirah: al-Matba'ah al-Ami'ri'yah, 1937.

Al-Kitāb al-dhahabī lil-mahākim al-ahlīyah 1883–1933 (al-juz' 2). al-Qahirah: al-Matba'ah al-Ami'ri'yah, 1938.

Al-Nuwab, Majlis. *Majmu`at madabit*, (Session 3, al-juz' 1). al-Qahirah: al-Matba`ah al-Amiriyah, 1926.

Al-Qasem, Anis. "The Injurious Acts under the Jordanian Civil Code." *Arab Law Quarterly*, 4, no. 3 (August 1989): 183–198.

Al-Quda, Nadi. *Mu'tamar al-'Adālah al-Awwal, 1986: al-Wathā'iq al-asāsīyah: wathā'iq al-jalsatayn, al-iftitāḥīyah wa-al-khitāmīyah*. al-Qahirah: Nadi al-Quda, 1986.

Al-Rāfi'ī, Abd al-Rahmān. *'Asr Ismā'īl*. al-Qahirah: Matba'at al-Nahdah, 1932.

Al-Rifai, Yahia, *Sh'wan regal al-quda'*. al-Qahirah: Nadi al-Quda, 1991.

Al-Rifai, Yahia. *mulḥaq Istiqlāl al-qaḍā' wa-miḥnat al-intikhābāt*. al-Qahirah: al-Maktab al-Miṣrī al-Ḥadīth, 2004.

Al-Rifai, Yahia. *qudah 'di'd al-astbdad*. al-Qahirah: al-Maktab al-Miṣrī al-Ḥadīth, no date.

Al-Rifai, Yahia. *Tashrī'āt al-sulṭah al-qaḍā'īyah mu'allaqan 'alá nuṣūṣihā. Malāḥiq al-ṭab'ah al-thānīyah*. al-Qahirah: Nadi al-Quda, 1991.

Introduction to Hamadah Husni, *'Abd al-Naṣir wa-al-qaḍaā*. al-Qahirah: n. p., 2005.

Al-Sādāt, Anwar. *al-Bahth 'an al-dhāt: qissat hayātī*. al-Qahirah: al-Maktab al-Misrī al-hadīth, 1978.

Wasiyyatī. al-Qahirah: al-Maktab al-Misrī al-hadīth, 1982.

Al-Sanhuri, Nadiyah, and Tawfīq al-Shawi, eds. *'Abd al-Razzāq al-Sanhuri min khilāl awrāqihi al-shakhiīyah*. al-Qahirah: al-Zahrā' lil-I'lām al-'Arabī, 1988.

Al-Sharif, Muhammad. *'Alā hamish al-dustur*. al-Qahirah: n.p., 1938.

Al-shuyukh, Majlis. *al-Dastur: wa-al-qawanin al-muttasilah bih*. al-Qahirah: al-Matba`ah al-Amiriyah, 1938.

Amin, Galal A. *al-Iqtiṣād wa-al-siyāsah wa-al-mujtama' fī 'aṣr al-infitāḥ*. al-Qahirah: Maktabat Madbūlī, 1984.

Amos, Maurice S. "Legal Administration in Egypt." *Journal of Comparative Legislation and International Law*, 3rd Ser., 12, no. 4 (1930): 168–187.

Aruri, Naseer H. "Disaster Area: Human Rights in the Arab World." *MERIP Middle East Report*, 149 (November–December 1987): 6–9, 11–16.

Asfur, Sa'd. *al-qada al-Idari*. al-Iskandariyah: Munsha'at al-Ma'arif, 1975.

Ayyubī, Ilyas. *Ta'rikh Misr fī 'ahd al-Khidiw Isma'il Pasha: min sanat 1863 ila 1879*, part 2. al-Qahirah: Matba'at Dar al-Kutub al-Misrīyah, 1923.

Badawi, Abd al-Hamid. *Majallat Majlis al-Dawla*, al-Sanah 1, (Yanayir 1950).

Badowi, Abd al-Hamid. *athr al-amtizat fi al-qudaa wa al-tashrea' fi misr*, in *al-Kitāb al-dhahabī lil-mahākim al-ahlīyah*, Mahkamt al-Naqd, al-juz' 1. al-Qahirah: al-Matba'ah al-Ami'ri'yah, 1937.

Baha al-Din, Ahmad. *Shar`iyat al-sultah fi al-`alam al-`Arabi*. al-Qahirah: Dar al-Shuruq, 1984.

Bahā' al-Din, Ahmad. *Mu'āwarātī ma'a al-Sadat*. al-Qahirah: Dar al-Hilal, 1987.

Baker, Raymond William. *Sadat and After: Struggles for Egypt's Political Soul*. Cambridge: Harvard University Press, 1990.

Bates, Robert. "Social Dilemmas and Rational Individuals: An Assessment of New Institutionalism" in ed. John Harriss, Janet Hunter, and Colin M Lewis, *The New Institutional Economics and Third World Development*. New York: Routledge, 1997.

Baum, Lawrence. *The Puzzle of Judicial Behavior*. Ann Arbor: University of Michigan Press, 1997.

Beattie, Kirk J. *Egypt during the Nasser Years: Ideology, Politics, and Civil Society*. Boulder, CO: Westview Press, 1994.

Bell, John. *Judiciaries within Europe: A Comparative Review*. Cambridge: Cambridge University Press, 2006.

Berg, Bruce L. *Qualitative Research Methods for the Social Sciences*. Boston, MA: Pearson, 1998.

Bill, James A., and Carl Leiden. *Politics in the Middle East*. Boston, MA: Little Brown, 1979.

Blaydes, Lisa. *Elections and Distributive Politics in Mubarak's Egypt*. New York: Cambridge University Press, 2010.

Boix, Carles. *Democracy and Redistribution*. Cambridge: Cambridge University Press, 2003.

Carles Boix, and Milan W. Svolik. "The Foundations of Limited Authoritarian Government: Institutions, Commitment, and Power-Sharing in Dictatorships." *Journal of Politics*, 75, no. 2 (2013): 300–316.

Bogdan, Robert. "Participant Observation." *Peabody Journal of Education*, 50, no. 4 (July 1973): 302–308.

Boulanger, Christian. "The Charisma of, Rationality in, and Legitimacy through Law: A Neo-Weberian Analysis of Post-Communist Constitutionalism." Unpublished Manuscript, 2001.

Boyle, Kevin, and Adel Omar Sherif, eds. *Human Rights and Democracy: The Role of the Supreme Constitutional Court of Egypt*. London: Kluwer Law International, 1996.

Brinton, Jasper Yeates. "The Closing of the Mixed Courts of Egypt." *The American Journal of International Law*, 44, no. 2 (April 1950): 303–312.

The Council of State in Egypt. Cairo: American Embassy, 1951.

The Mixed Courts of Egypt. New Haven, CT: Yale University Press, 1968.

Brownlee, Jason. *Authoritarianism in an Age of Democratization*. Cambridge, UK: Cambridge University Press, 2007.

Brown, Nathan J. "Arab Administrative Courts and Judicial Control of the Bureaucracy," paper presented to the annual conference of the Structure of Government Section, International Political Science Association, Ben-Gurion University, Israel, February 1997.

"Law and Imperialism: Egypt in Comparative Perspective Retrospective." *Law & Society Review*, 29, no. 1 (1995): 103–126.

"Reining in the Executive: What Can the Judiciary Do?" paper presented to The Role of Judges in Political Reform in Egypt and the Arab World Conference, Cairo, April 1–3, 2006.

"The Precarious Life and Slow Death of the Mixed Courts of Egypt." *International Journal of Middle East Studies*, 25, no. 1 (February 1993): 33–52.

The Rule of Law in the Arab World: Courts in Egypt and the Gulf. Cambridge: Cambridge University Press, 1997.

Brumberg, Daniel. "The Trap of Liberalized Autocracy." *Journal of Democracy*, 13, no. 4 (2002): 56–68.

Bunce, Valerie. *Subversive Institutions: The Design and the Destruction of Socialism and the State*. New York: Cambridge University Press, 1999.

Burgess, Susan. "Beyond Instrumental Politics: The New Institutionalism, Legal Rhetoric, and Judicial Supremacy." *Polity*, 25 (1993): 445–459.

Cannon, Byron. *Politics of Law and the Courts in Nineteenth-Century Egypt*. Salt Lake City: University of Utah Press, 1988.

Casper, Jonathan. "The Supreme Court and National Policy-making." *American Political Science Review*, 70, no. 1 (March 1976): 50–63.

Clayton, Cornell W., and Howard Gillman, eds., *Supreme Court Decision-Making: New Institutionalist Approaches*. Chicago, IL: University of Chicago Press, 1999.

Collier, David. "The Comparative Method," in ed. Ada Finifter, *Political Science: The State of the Discipline II*. Chicago, IL: American Political Science Association, 1993.

Dahl, Robert. "Decision-Making in a Democracy: The Supreme Court as a National Policy-Maker." *The Journal of Public Law*, 6 (Fall 1957): 279–295.

Modern Political Analysis. Englewood Cliffs: Prentice-Hall, 1961.

Ḍayf Allāh, Sayyid Ismāʿīl. *Nazāhat al-intikhābāt wa-istiqlāl al-qaḍāʾ*. al-Qahirah: Markaz al-Qahirah li-Dirāsāt Ḥuqūq al-Insān, 2000.

Dawisha, Adeed, and I. William Zartman, eds. *Beyond Coercion*: The Durability of the Arab State. London: Croom Helm, 1988.

Dekmejian, R. Hrair. *Egypt under Nasir: A Study in Political Dynamics*. Albany: State University of New York Press, 1971.

De Mesquita, Bruce Bueno and Alastair Smith. "Political Survival and Endogenous Institutional Change." *Comparative Political Studies*, 42, no. 2 (2009), 167–197.

Dimitrov, Martin K., ed. *Why Communism Did Not Collapse: Understanding Authoritarian Regime Resilience in Asia and Europe*. New York: Cambridge University Press, 2013.

Domingo, Pilar. "Judicialization of Politics or Politicization of the Judiciary? Recent Trends in Latin America." *Democratization*, 11, no. 1 (February 2004): 104–126.

"Judicialization of Politics: The Changing Political Role of the Judiciary in Mexico," in ed. Rachel Sieder, Line Schjolden, and Alan Angell, *The Judicialization of Politics in Latin America*. New York: Palgrave MacMillan, 2005.

Eisenstein, James, Peter F. Nardulli, and Roy B. Flemming. *The Contours of Justice: Communities and their Courts*. Boston, MA: Little Brown, 1988.

El-Ghobashy, Mona. "Egypt's Paradoxical Elections." *Middle East Report Online* 238 (Spring 2006). Available from: www.merip.org/mer/mer238/elghobashy.html.

Elkins, Zachary, Tom Ginsburg, and James Melton. The Content of Authoritarian Constitutions, in eds. Tom Ginsburg and Alberto Simpser, *Constitutions in Authoritarian Regimes* New York: Cambridge University Press, 2014.

El-Mahdi, Rabab. Egypt: A Decade of Rupture, in eds. Lina Khatib and Ellen Lust, *Taking to the Streets: The Transformation of Arab Activism*. Baltimore: Johns Hopkins University Press, 2014.

The Democracy Movement: Cycles of Protest, in eds. Rabab El-Mahdi and Philip Marfleet, *Egypt: The Moment of Change*. London: Zed Books, 2009.

El-Menoufi, Kamal. "The Orientations of Egyptian Peasants towards Political Authority between Continuity and Change." *Middle Eastern Studies*, 18, no. 1 (January 1980): 82–93.

El-Mikawy, Noha.*The Building of Consensus in Egypt's Transition Process*. Cairo: American University in Cairo: 1999.

El-Nahal, Galal H. *The Judicial Administration of Ottoman Egypt in the Seventeenth Century*. Minneapolis, MN: Bibliotheca Islamica, 1979.

El-Nawawy, Mohammed, and Adel Iskandar. *Al Jazeera: How the Free Arab News Network Scooped the World and Changed the Middle East*. Cambridge: Westview Press, 2002.

El-Sadek, Ali. "Istqlal al-sultah al-qudae 'an al-sultah al-tashreaa'." *al-Majallah al-Jinā'īyah al-qawmīyah* 38, no. 1, 2, and 3 (March, July, and November 1995)

Epp, Charles R. *The Rights Revolution: Lawyers, Activists, and Supreme Courts in Comparative Perspective*. Chicago: University of Chicago Press, 1998.

Epstein, Lee, and Jack Knight. *The Choices Justices Make*. Washington DC: CQ Press, 1998.

Ezrow, Natasha M., and Erica Frantz. "State Institutions and The Survival of Dictatorships." *Journal of International Affairs*, 65, no. 1 (Winter2011): 1–14.

Farahat, Mohamed Nour. "The Rule of Law: Can the Constitution be Unconstitutional?" *Al-Ahram Weekly*, 2–8 February 2006.

Fawzī, Hishām Muḥammad. *Raqābat dustūrīyat al-qawānīn: dirāsah muqārinah bayna Amrīkā wa-Miṣr*. al-Qahirah: Markaz al-Qahirah li-Dirāsāt Ḥuqūq al-Insān, 1999.

Finkel, Jodi S. "Judicial Reform as an 'Insurance Policy' in Mexico in the 1990s: A Supreme Court Willing and Able to Enter the Political Fray," paper presented at the annual meeting of the International Political Science Association Research Committee on Comparative Judicial Studies, University of Parma, Parma, Italy, 2003.

Judicial Reform as Political Insurance Argentina, Peru, and Mexico in the 1990, Notre Dame, IN: University of Notre Dame Press, 2008.

Finklestone, Joseph. *Anwar Sadat: Visionary who Dared*. Essex: Frank Cass, 1995.

Fiss, Owen M. The Right Degree of Independence, in ed. Irwin Stotzky, *The Role of the Judiciary in the Transition to Democracy in Latin America*. Boulder: Westview, 1993.

Fluharty, David Henning. "Charisma as Attachment to the Divine: Some Hasidic Principles for Comparison of Social Movements of Gandhi, Nasser, Ben-Gurion, and King," Ph.D. diss., University of New Hampshire, 1990.

Frantz, Erica, and Natasha Ezrow. *The Politics of Dictatorships: Institutions and Outcomes in Authoritarian Regimes*. Boulder, CO: Lynne Rienner, 2011.

Frantz, Erica, and Andrea Kendall-Taylor. "A Dictator's Toolkit: Understanding How Co-optation Affects Repression in Autocracies." *Journal of Peace Research* (2014): 51, 332–346.

Friedland, Martin L. *A Place Apart: Judicial Independence and Accountability in Canada*. Ottawa: Canadian Judicial Council, 1995.

Friedrich, Carl J., and Zbigniew K. Brzezinski. *Totalitarian Dictatorship and Autocracy*. New York: Praeger, 1961.

Gallagher, Mary, and Jonathan K. Hanson. "Coalitions, Carrots and Sticks: Economic Inequality and Authoritarian States." *PS: Political Science & Politics*, 42, no. 4 (2009): 667–672.

Authoritarian Survival, Resilience, and the Selectorate Theory, in ed. Martin K. Dimitrov, *Why Communism Did Not Collapse: Understanding Authoritarian Regime Resilience in Asia and Europe*. New York: Cambridge University Press, 2013.

Gandhi, Jennifer, and Adam Przeworski. "Cooperation, Cooptation and Rebellion under Dictatorships." *Economics and Politics*, 18, no. 1 (March 2006), 1–26.

"Authoritarian Institutions and the Survival of Autocrats." *Comparative Political Studies*, 40, no. 11 (November 2007): 1279–1301.

Gandhi, Jennifer. *Political Institutions under Dictatorship*. Cambridge, UK: Cambridge University Press, 2008.

Gates, John "Theory, Methods, and the New Institutionalism in Judicial Research." in *The American Courts: A Critical Assessment*, ed. John Gates and Charles A. Johnson. Washington DC: CQ Press, 1991.

Geddes, Barbra "What Do We Know about Democratization After Twenty Years?" *Annual Review of Political Science*, 2 (1999): 115–144.

Gibson, James L. "Challenges to the Impartiality of State Supreme Courts: Legitimacy Theory and "New-Style" Judicial Campaigns." *American Political Science Review*, 102, no. 1 (February 2008): 59–75.

"From Simplicity to Complexity: The Development of Theory in the Study of Judicial Behavior." *Political Behavior*, 5, no. 1 (1983): 7–49.

Gillman, Howard, and Cornell Clayton, eds. *The Supreme Court in American Politics: New Institutionalist Interpretations*. Lawrence: University Press of Kansas, 1999.

Goldberg, Ellis. *Tinker, Tailor, Textile Worker*. Berkeley: University of California Press. 1986.

Guarnieri, Carlo, and Patrizia Pederzoli. *The Power of Judges: A Comparative Study of Courts and Democracy*. Oxford: Oxford University Press, 2002.

Ḥāfiz, 'Ulwī. *al-Fasād*. al-Jīzah: al-Sharikah al-'Arabīyah al-Duwalīyah lil-Nashr wa-al-I'lām, 1991.

Hamzawy, Amr. "Opposition in Egypt Performance in the Presidential Election and Prospects for the Parliamentary Elections." *Policy Outlook*, Carnegie Endowment for International Peace, Democracy, and Rule of Law Project, (October 2005): 6.

Hasan, Ammar Ali. *Wizarat al-'Adl*. al-Qahirah Markaz al-Dirasat al-Siyasiyah wa-al-Istiratijiyah, 2003.

Ḥasan, Iṣām al-Dīn Muḥammad. *Shuhūd 'ayān 'alá al-intikhābāt al-barlamānīyah al-Miṣrīyah li-'ām 2005*. al-Qahirah: al-Majmū'ah al-Muttaḥidah, 2006.

Hassan, Essam Edin, ed. *Features of the Mass Media Landscape in Morocco, Egypt and Jordan: General Conclusions*. Cairo: CIHRS, 2007.

Hassūnah, Isam. *23 Yūliyū– wa-'Abd al-Nasir: shahādatī*. al-Qahirah: Markaz al-Ahram lil-Tarjamah wa-al-Nashr, 1990.

Heikal, Muhammad Hasanayn. *Ahādīth fī al-'āsifah*. al-Qahirah: Dar al-Shurūq, 1987. *Uktubir 73: al-silah wa-al-siyasah*. al-Qahirah: Markaz al-Ahram lil-Tarjamah wa-al-Nashr, 1993.

Heydemann, Steven, and Reinoud Leenders, eds. *Middle East Authoritarianisms: Governance, Contestation, and Regime Resilience in Syria and Iran*. Stanford, CA: Stanford University Press, 2013.

Hilāl, Alī al-Dīn. *Taṭawwur al-niẓām al-siyāsī fī Miṣr, 1803–199*. al-Qahirah: Markaz al-Buḥūth wa-al-Dirāsāt al-Siyāsīya, 1997.

Hilāl, Riḍā Muḥammad. "mawqif Lajnat shu'ūn al-aḥzāb min Ṭalabāt ta'sīs al-aḥzāb al-ṣaghīrah," in ed. Amr Hashim, *al-Ahzab al-saghirah wa-al-nizam al-hizbi fi Misr,*. al-Qahirah: Markaz al-Dirasat al-Siyasiyah wa-al-Istiratijiyah, 2003.

Hilal, Ali al-Din, Moustafa Kamel Sayed, and Ikram Badr al-Din. *Tajribat al-dimuqratiyah fi Misr, 1970–1981.* al-Qahirah: al-Markaz al-'Arabi lil-Bahth wa-al-Nashr, 1982.

Hilbink, Lisa. *Judges beyond Politics in Democracy and Dictatorship: Lessons from Chile.* Cambridge: Cambridge University Press, 2007.

Hill, Enid. "Al-Sanhuri and Islamic Law." *Cairo Papers in Social Science.* Cairo: American University in Cairo, 1987.

——— "Courts and the Administration of Justice in the Modern Era," in ed. Nelly Hanna, *The State and Its Servants: Administration in Egypt from Ottoman Times to the Present.* Cairo: The American University in Cairo Press, 1995.

——— "The Golden Anniversary of Egypt's National Courts." in ed. Jill Edwards, *Historians in Cairo: Essays in Honor of George Scanlon.* Cairo: American University in Cairo Press, 2002.

——— *Mahkama! Studies in the Egyptian Legal System, Courts and Crimes, Law and Society.* London: Ithaca Press London, 1979.

Hinnebusch, Jr, Raymond A. *Egyptian Politics under Sadat: The Post-populist Development of an Authoritarian-Modernizing State.* Cambridge: Cambridge University Press, 1985.

Hirschal, Ran. *Towards Juristocracy, The Origins and Consequences of the New Constitutionalism.* Cambridge, MA: Harvard University Press, 2004.

Hirschl, Ran. "The New Constitutionalism and the Judicialization of Pure Politics Worldwide. " *Fordham Law Review,* 75, no. 2 (2006): 721–754.

Hoyle, Mark S. W. "The Mixed Courts of Egypt: An Anniversary Assessment." *Arab Law Quarterly,* 1, no. 1 (November 1985): 60–68.

Hoyle, Mark. *Mixed Courts of Egypt.* London: Graham & Trotman, 1991.

Husni, Hamadah. *'Abd al-Nāṣir wa-al-qaḍā': dirāsah wathā'iqīyah.* al-Qahirah: n. p., 2005.

Imam, Abd Allah. *Inqilab al-Sadat: ahdath Mayu 1971.* al-Qahirah: Dar al-Khayyal, 2000.

Imām, Abd Allāh. *Madhbahat al-qada'.* al-Qahirah: Maktabat Madhbūlī, 1976.

Imām, Abd Allāh. *Salāh Nasr yatadhakkar: al-mukhābarāt wa-al-thawrah.* al-Qahirah: Mu'assasat Rūz al-Yūsuf, 1984.

Imam, Hamadah. *al-Jins al-siyasi: al-'alaqah al-khafiyah bayna al-sultah wa-al-sihafah wa-al-fannanat.* al-Jīzah: Madbuli al-Saghir, 2002.

Imarah, Muhammad. *al-Duktur 'Abd al-Razzaq al-Sanhuri: Islamiyah al-dawlah, wa-al-madaniyah, wa-al-qanun.* al-Qahirah: Dar al-Rashad, 1999.

Imām, Sāmiyah Said. *Man yamliku Miṣr?: dirāsah taḥlīlīyah lil-uṣūl al-ijtimā'īyah li-nukhbat al-infitāḥ al-iqtiṣādī fī al-mujtama' al-Miṣrī, 1974–1980.* al-Qahirah: Dar al-Mustaqbal al-'Arabi, 1986.

Israeli, Raphael. *"I, Egypt": Aspects of President Anwar al-Sadat's Political Thought, Jerusalem Papers on Peace Problems.* Jerusalem: Magnes Press, Hebrew University, 1981.

——— "The Pervasiveness of Islam in Contemporary Arab Political Discourse: The Cases of Sadat and Arafat," in ed. Ofer Feldman and Christ'l De Landtsheer, *Politically*

Speaking: A Worldwide Examination of Language Used in the Political Sphere. Westport, CT: Praeger, 1998.

Jackson, Donald W. "Judicial Independence in Cross-National Perspective," in ed. American Bar Association, *Judicial Independence: Essays, Bibliography, and Discussion Guide.* Chicago, IL: American Bar Association, 1999.

Jamal, Yaḥyá. *al-Qānūn al-dustūrī :maʿa muqaddimah fī dirāsat al-mabādi' al-dustūriyah al-ʿāmmah.* al-Qahirah: Dārr al-Naḥḍah al-'Arabīyah, 1995.

Jamiʿ, Mahmud. *`Araftu al-Sadat: nasf qarn min khafaya al-Sadat wa-al-Ikhwan.* al-Qahirah: al-Maktub al-Misri al-Hadith, 1998.

Jindi, Abd al-Halim. *Nujum al-muhamah fi Misr wa-Urubba: al-Halbawi, al-Sanhuri, Mustafá Marʿi, Marshal Hawl, Hanri Rawbayr.* al-Qahirah: Dar al-Maʿarif, 1991.

Jirishah, Ali. *Fi al-zinzanah.* al-Qahirah: Dar al-Shuruq, 1975.

Kassem, Maye. *In the Guise of Democracy: Governance in Contemporary Egypt.* Reading, UK: Ithaca Press, 1999.

Khan, Paul W. "Independence and Responsibility in Judicial Rule," in ed. Irwin Stotzky, *The Role of the Judiciary in the Transition to Democracy in Latin America.* Boulder, CO: Westview, 1993.

Khānkī, Azīz. *al-Mahākim al-mukhtalitah wa-al-mahākim al-ahlīyah: mādīhā, hādirhā, mustaqbalahā.* al-Qahirah: al-Matbaʿah al-'Asrīyah, 1939.

Kienle, Eberhard. *Grand Delusion: Democracy and Economic Reform in Egypt.* London: I. B. Tauris & Company, 2001.

Kulliyat al-Huquq. *al-Mutamar al-`Ilmi al-Awwal li-Kulliyat al-Huquq: dawr al-Mahkamah al-Dusturiyah al-`Ulya fi al-nizam al-qanuni al-Misri.* al-Qahirah: Jamiʿat Hulwan, 1998.

Lacouture, Jean. *The Demigods: Charismatic Leadership in the Third World.* New York: Knopf, 1970.

Landry, Pierre. The Institutional Diffusions of Courts in China: Evidence from Survey Data, in eds. Tom Ginsburg and Tamir Moustafa, *Rule by Law: The Politics of Courts in Authoritarian Regimes.* Cambridge: Cambridge University Press, 2008.

Langohr, Vickie. "Cracks in Egypt's Electoral Engineering: The 2000 Vote." *Middle East Report Online,* November 7, 2000.

Larkins, Christopher M. "Judicial Independence and Democratization: A Theoretical and Conceptual Analysis." *The* American Journal of Comparative Law, 44, no. 4 (Autumn 1996): 605–626.

Law, David S., and Mila Versteeg. Constitutional Variations among Strains of Authoritarianism, in eds. Tom Ginsburg and Alberto Simpser, *Constitutions in Authoritarian Regimes.* New York: Cambridge University Press, 2014.

Leenders, Reinoud. Prosecuting Political Dissent: Courts and the Resilience of Authoritarianism in Syria," in eds. Steven Heydemann and Reinoud Leenders, *Middle East Authoritarianisms: Governance, Contestation, and Regime Resilience in Syria and Iran.* Stanford: Stanford University Press, 2014.

Liebesny, Herbert J. *The Law of the Near & Middle East: Readings, Cases, & Materials.* Albany: State University of New York Press, 1975.

Lust-Okar, Ellen. *Structuring Conflict in the Arab World: Incumbents, Opponents, and Institutions.* Cambridge: Cambridge University Press, 2005.

Magaloni, Beatriz. *Voting for Autocracy: Hegemonic Party Survival and Its Demise in Mexico.* Cambridge, UK: Cambridge University Press, 2006.

"Credible Power-Sharing and the Longevity of Authoritarian Rule." *Comparative Political Studies*, 41 (2008): 715–741.

Magaloni, Beatriz, Enforcing the Autocratic Political Order and the Role of the Courts, in eds. Tamir Moustafa and Tom Ginsburg, *Rule by Law: The Politics of Courts in Authoritarian Regimes*. Cambridge: Cambridge University Press, 2008.

Mahoney, James, and Dietrich Rueschemeyer. "Comparative Historical Analysis: Achievements and Agendas," in ed. James Mahoney and Dietrich Rueschemeyer, *Comparative Historical Analysis in the Social Sciences*. Cambridge: Cambridge University Press, 2003.

Mahoney, James. "Strategies of Causal Inference in Small-N Analysis." *Sociological Methods and Research*, 28, no. 4 (May 2000): 387–424.

Majlis al-Sha'b, al-Lajnah al-Tashrīīyah. *al-Qawanin al-asasiyah al-mukammilah lil-dustur: ma'a mudhakkirathā al-idahīyah wa-taqarir Lajnat al-Shu'ūn al-Tashri'iyah wa-munaqashat al-majlis*, (al-juz' 2). al-Qahirah: al-Hay'ah al- 'Ammah li-Shu'ūn al-Maṭābi' al-Amīrīyah, 1974.

Mallat, Chibli. "*Constitutional Law in the Middle East: The Emergence of Judicial Power*." University of London, SOAS Law Department Working Papers, Working Paper no. 3 (February 1993).

Mansfield, Peter. *Nasser's Egypt*. Baltimore: Penguin, 1965.

Mansur, Ahmad Subhi, ed. *Dawr al-qada fi da`m thaqafat al-mujtama` al-madani: halaqat niqashiyah*. al-Qahirah: Markaz Ibn Khaldun lil-Dirasat al-Inmaiyah, 1997.

Marvell, Thomas B. *Appellate Courts and Lawyers: Information Gathering in the Adversary System*. Westport, CT: Greenwood Press, 1978.

Marx, Karl, and Friedrich Engels. *The Communist Manifesto*. New York: Monthly Review Press, 1964.

Mayhew, David R. *Divided we Govern: Party Control, Lawmaking, and Investigations, 1946–1990*. New Haven, CT: Yale University Press, 1991.

McDermott, Anthony. *Egypt from Nasser to Mubarak: a Flawed Revolution*. London: Croom Helm, 1988.

Mekki, Ahmed. al-ṣidām bin al-niẓām al-Nāṣiri wa al-quḍāt, in ed. Nabīl `Abd al-Fattāh. *al-Quḍāh wa-al-iṣlāḥ al-siyāsī*. al-Qahirah: Markaz al-Qahirah li-Dirāsāt Ḥuqūq al-Insān, 2006.

Mill, John Stuart. *Collected Works of John Stuart Mill*, vol. 21. ed. J. M. Robson. Toronto: University of Toronto Press, 1963.

Moustafa, Tamir. "Law versus the State: The Expansion of Constitutional Power in Egypt, 1980–2001." Ph.D. diss. University of Washington, 2002.

    The Struggle for Constitutional Power: Law, Politics, and Economic Development in Egypt. New York: Cambridge University Press, 2007.

Muhammad, Anwar. *Shuhud 'asr al-Sadat*. al-Qahirah: Dar Ayh Imm lil-Nashr wa-al-Tawzi', 1990.

Murad, Abd al-Fattah. *al-Mukhalafat al-tadibiyah lil-qudah wa-a`da' al-niyabah: dirasah tahliliyah wa-ta'siliyah muqaranah*. al-Iskandariyah: `A. al-F. Murad, 1993.

Murphy Walter F., and Joseph Tanenhaus. "Public Opinion and the United States Supreme Court: Mapping of Some Prerequisites for Court Legitimation of Regime Change." *Law & Society Review*, 2, no. 3 (May 1968): 357–384.

Murray-Brown, Jeremy, Raymond H. Anderson, and Henry Fonda. *Nasser People's Pharaoh*. Northbrook: Nielsen-Ferns International and New York Times Productions, 1979.

Muti'i, Lam'I. *Haulai al-rijal min Misr*. al-Qahirah: al-Hayah al-Misriyah al-'Ammah lil-Kitab, 1987.

Naguib, Mohammed. *Kalimati lil-ta'rikh*. al-Qahirah: Dār al-Kitāb al-Namūzaji, 1975.

Najib, Muḥammad Fatḥi. *al-Tanẓim al-qadai al-Misri*. al-Qahirah: Dar al-Ṭiba'ah al-Ḥadithah, 1998.

Nasar, Mumtaz. *Ma'rakat al-'adalah fi Misr*. al-Qahirah: Dar al-Shurūk, 1974.

Neuman, William Lawrence. *Social Research Methods: Qualitative and Quantitative Approaches*. Boston, MA: Allyn and Bacon, 2000.

North, Douglas, and Barry Weingast. "Constitution and Commitment: The Evolution of Institutions Governing Public Choice in Seventeenth-Century England." *The Journal of Economic History*, 49, no. 4 (December 1989): 803–832.

North, Douglass C. *Structure and Change in Economic History*. New York: W. W. Norton, 1981.

Nutting, Anthony. *Nasser*. New York: E. P. Dutton, 1972.

O'Donnell, Guillermo. *Modernization and Bureaucratic-Authoritarianism: Studies in South American Politics*. Berkeley, CA: Institute of International Studies, 1973.

Olson, Mancur. "Dictatorship, Democracy, and Development." *American Political Science Review*, 87, no. 3 (September 1993), 567–576.

Osiel, Mark J., "Dialouge with Dictators: Judicial Resistance in Argentina and Brazil." *Law and Social Inquiry*, 20, no. 2 (Spring 1995).

Pasha, Nubar. *Nūbār fī Misr, 'arḍ wa-taqdīm Nabīl Zakī Nabīl Zakī*. al-Qahirah: Mu'assasat Akhbār al-Yawm, 1991.

Pereira, Anthony W. *Political (In)Justice: Authoritarianism and the Rule of Law in Brazil, Chile, and Argentina*, Pittsburgh, PA: University of Pittsburgh Press, 2005.

Peerenboom, Randall P. *Asian Discourse of Rule of Law*. London: Routledge, 2004.

Pepinsky, Thomas. "The Institutional Turn in Comparative Authoritarianism." *British Journal of Political Science*, 44, no. 3 (July 2014): 631–653.

Perlmutter, Amos. *Egypt, the Praetorian State*. New Brunswick: Transaction Books, 1974.

Pierson, Paul, and Theda Skocpol. "Historical Institutionalism in Contemporary Political Science," in ed. Ira Katznelson and Helen V. Milner, *Political Science: The State of the Discipline*. New York, NY: Norton, 2002.

Powell, Ivor. *Disillusion by the Nile: What Nasser Has Done to Egypt*. London: Solstice Production, 1967.

Przeworski, Adam. The Games of Transition, in eds. S. Mainwaring, G. A. O'Donnell, and J. S. Valenzuela, *Issues in Democratic Consolidation: The New South American Democracies in Comparative Perspective*. Notre Dame, IN: University of Notre Dame Press, 1992.

Qatri, Mahmoud. *Tazwīr Dawlah: shihādāt. al-istibdād wa-tazwīr al-intikhābāt*. al-Jīzah: Markaz al-Mustaqbal al-Miṣrī, 2005.

Quinlivan, James T. "Coup-proofing: Its Practice and Consequences in the Middle East." *International Security*, 24, no. 2 (Fall 1999): 131–165.

Ra'fat, Wahid. *Dirāsāt fī ba'd al-qawānīn al-munazzimah lil-hurrīyāt*. al-Iskandarīyah: Munsha'at al-Ma'ārif, 1981.

Fusul min Thawrat 23 Yulyu. al-Qahirah: Dar al-Shuruq, 1978.

Radwan, Fathi. *72 shahran ma'a 'Abd al-Nasir.* al-Qahirah: Dar al-Hurriyah, 1986.

Ragin, Charles C. *The Comparative Method: Moving Beyond Qualitative and Quantitative Strategies.* Berkeley: University of California Press, 1987.

Rawls, John. *A Theory of Justice.* Cambridge: Harvard University Press, 1999.

Reid, Donald M. *Lawyers and Politics in the Arab World, 1880–1960.* Minneapolis, MN: Bibliotheca Islamica, 1981.

Roberson, B. A. "The Emergence of the Modern Judiciary in the Middle East: Negotiating the Mixed Courts of Egypt," in ed. Chibli Mallat, *Islam and Public Law.* London: Graham & Trotman, 1993.

Root, Hilton L., and Karen May. Judicial Systems and Economic Development, in eds. Tom Ginsburg and Tamir Moustafa, *Rule by Law: The Politics of Courts in Authoritarian Regimes.* Cambridge: Cambridge University Press, 2008.

Rosberg, James. "Roads to the Rule of Law: The Emergence of an Independent Judiciary in Contemporary Egypt." Ph.D. diss. MIT, 1995.

Rowland, C. K., and Robert A. Carp. *Politics and Judgment in Federal District Courts.* Lawrence: University Press of Kansas, 1996.

Russell, Peter H., and David M. O'Brien, eds. *Judicial Independence in the Age of Democracy: Critical Perspectives from around the World.* Charlottesville: University Press of Virginia, 2001.

Rutherford, Bruce K. *Egypt after Mubarak: Liberalism, Islam, and Democracy in the Arab World.* Princeton: Princeton University Press, 2008.

"The Struggle for Constitutionalism in Egypt," Ph. D. diss., Yale University, 1999, 286–287.

Safran, Nadav. *Egypt in Search of Political Community.* Cambridge: Harvard University Press, 1961.

Said, Atef Shahat. "dor Nadi al-qudah fi ta'ziz istqlal alquda wa al'ashalh alsiasi," in ed. Nabil Abdel Fattah, *dwar al-qudah fi al-aslah al-siasi.* al-Qahirah: Markaz al-Qahirah li-Dirāsāt Ḥuqūq al-Insān, 2006.

"The Judges Club of Egypt: A Space for Defending Democracy and Independence of the Judiciary." MA Thesis, American University in Cairo, 2004.

Salah, Abdullah. "al-dawr al-siyāsī lal-qaḍa' al-Miṣrī," in *al-Taṭawwur al-siyāsī fī Miṣr, 1982–1992,* ed. Muḥammad Ṣafī al-Dīn Kharbūsh. al-Qahirah, Jāmi'at al-Qahirah, Kullīyat al-Iqtiṣād wa-al-'Ulūm al-Siyāsīyah, Markaz al-Buḥūth wa-al-Dirāsāt al-Siyāsīyah, 1994.

Ṣāliḥ, Ibrāhīm Alī. *al-Wajīz fī sharḥ qānūn al-Mudda'ī al-'Āmm al-Ishtirākī.* al-Qahirah: 'Ālam al-Kutub 1986.

Salim, Latifah Muhammad. *Tarikh al-qadai al-Misri al-hadith, al-juz'* 1, 1875–1914. al-Qahirah: al-Hayah al-Misriyah al-'Ammah lil-Kitab: 2000.

Tarikh al-qadai al-Misri al-hadith, al-juz' 2, 1914–1952. al-Qahirah: al-Hayah al-Misriyah al-'Ammah lil-Kitab: 2000.

Salīm, Muḥammad al-Sayyid. *al-Taḥlīl al-siyāsī al-Nāṣirī: dirāsah fī al-'aqā'id wa-al-siyāsah al-khārijīyah.* Bayrūt: Markaz Dirāsāt al-Waḥdah al-'Arabīyah, 1983.

Scheb II, John M., Thomas D. Ungs, and Allison L. Hayes, "Judicial Role Orientations, Attitudes and Decision Making: A Research Note." *The Western Political Quarterly,* 42, no. 3 (September 1989): 427–435.

Segal, Jeffrey, and Harold J. Spaeth. *The Supreme Court and the Attitudinal Model.* New York: Cambridge University Press, 1993.

Shalakany, Amr. "'I Heard It All Before': Egyptian Tales of Law and Development." *Third World Quarterly*, 27, no. 5 (July 2006): 833–853.

Shambayati, Hootan, "A Tale of Two Mayors: Courts Politics in Iran and Turkey." *International Journal. Middle East Studies*, 36, no. 2 (2004): 253–275.

Shapiro, Martin. Courts in Authoritarian Regimes, in eds. Ginsburg and Moustafa, *Rule by Law: The Politics of Courts in Authoritarian Regimes*. Cambridge: Cambridge University Press, 2008.

Shapiro, Martin, and Alec Stone Sweet. *On Law, Politics, and Judicialization*. Oxford: Oxford University Press, 2002.

Courts: A Comparative and Political Analysis. Chicago, IL: University of Chicago Press, 1981.

Sharqāwī, Su'ād, and Abd Allāh Nāṣif. *Nuẓum al-intikhabāt fī al-'ālam wa-fī Miṣr*. al-Qahirah: Dar al-Nahḍah al-'Arabīyah, 1994.

Sharqāwī, Su'ād. *Nisbīyat al-ḥurrīyāt al-'ammah wa-in'ikāsātuhā 'alá al-tanẓīm al-qānūnī*. al-Qahirah: Dār al-Nahḍah al-'Arabīyah, 1979.

Sherif, Adel Omar. "Attacks on the Judiciary: Judicial Independence – Reality or Fallacy?" in ed. Eugene Cotran, *Yearbook of Islamic and Middle Eastern Law*, Volume 6, 1999–2000. London; Kluwer Law International, 2001.

Shetreet, Shimon, and Jules Deschênes Dordrecht, eds. *Judicial Independence: The Contemporary Debate*. Boston, MA: Martinus Nijhoff Publishers, 1985.

Shetreet, Shimon, and Christopher Forsyth, eds. *The Culture of Judicial Independence: Conceptual Foundations and Practical Challenges*. Boston, MA: Martinus Nijhoff Publishers, 2012.

Shuhayb, Abd al-Qādir. Muḥākamat al-infitāḥ al-iqtiṣādī fī Miṣr. Beirut: Dār Ibn Khaldūn 1979.

Sieder, Rachel, Line Schjolden, and Alan Angell, eds. The Judicialization of Politics in Latin America. New York: Palgrave Macmillan, 2005.

Silverstein, Gordon. Singapore: The Exception That Proves Rules Matter, in eds. Tom Ginsburg and Tamir Moustafa, *Rule by Law: The Politics of Courts in Authoritarian Regimes*. Cambridge: Cambridge University Press, 2008.

Ṣiyām, Sirrī. "al-Qaḍā' al-Tabī'ī al-Musāwāh amāma al-qaḍā" in ed. Badr Minyāwī, *al-Musāwāh amāma al-qaḍā*. al-Qahirah: al-Markaz al-Qawmī lil-Buhūth al-Ijtimā'īyah wa-al-Jinā'īyah, 1991.

Smith, Benjamin. "Life of the Party: The Origins of Regime Breakdown and Persistence under Single-Party Rule." *World Politics*, 57 (2005): 421–451.

Smith, Charles Anthony. "Credible Commitments and the Avoidance of War: The Role of the Judiciary in emerging Federations and Re-emerging Nations." Ph.D. diss. University of California – San Diego, 2004.

Springborg, Robert. *Mubarak's Egypt: Fragmentation of the Political Order*. Boulder: Westview Press. 1989.

St. John, Robert. *The Boss: The Story of Gamal Abdel Nasser*. New York: McGraw-Hill, 1960.

Stone Sweet, Alec. *Governing with Judges: Constitutional Politics in Europe*. Oxford: Oxford University Press, 2000.

Stovall, Howard L. "Arab Commercial Laws–Into the Future." *The International Lawyer*, 34 (Fall 2000): 839–847.

Tanneberg, Dag, Christoph Stefes, and Wolfgang Merkel. "Hard Times and Regime Failure: Autocratic Responses to Economic Downturns." *Contemporary Politics*, 19, no. 1 (2013): 115–129.

Tashakkori, Abbas, and Charles Teddlie. *Mixed Methodology: Combining Qualitative and Quantitative Approaches*. Thousand Oaks, CA: Sage Publications, 1998.

Tate, C. Neal, and Torbjorn Vallinder, eds. *The Global Expansion of Judicial Power*. New York: New York University Press, 1995.

Tiefer, Charles. "Egypt's Parliamentary Election Ends on an Undemocratic Note." Available from: www.forbes.com/sites/charlestiefer/2015/12/21/egypts-parliamentary-election-ends-on-an-undemocratic-note/#f29872755a56

Vogel, Frank E. *Islamic Law and Legal System: Studies of Saudi Arabia*. Leiden: Brill, 2000.

Volpi, Frédéric, and Francesco Cavatorta, eds. *Democratization in the Muslim World: Changing Patterns of Authority and Power*. New York: Routledge, 2007.

Ubayd, Muḥammad Kāmil. *Istiqlāl al-qaḍā': dirāsah muqāranah*. al-Qahirah: Nādī al-Quḍāh, 1991.

Wahbī, Azzah. *al-Sulṭah al-tashrīʿīyah fī al-niẓām al-siyāsī al-Miṣrī baʿda Yūliyū 1952*. al-Qahirah: Markaz al-Dirāsāt al-Siyāsīyah wa-al-Istirātījīyah, 1993.

Weber, Max. "Politics as a Vocation." In ed. H. H. Gerth and C. Wright Mills, *From Max Weber: Essays in Sociology*. New York: Oxford University Press, 1977.

The Theory of Social and Economic Organization. trans. by A. M. Henderson and Talcott Parsons. New York: Oxford University Press, 1947.

Wickham, Carrie Rosefsky. *Mobilizing Islam: Religion, Activism and Political Change in Egypt*. New York: Columbia University Press, 2002.

Wright, Joseph. "Do Authoritarian Institutions Constrain? How Legislatures Affect Economic Growth and Investment." *American Journal of Political Science*, 52 (2008): 322–343.

Wright, Joseph, and Abel Escribà-Folch. "Authoritarian Institutions and Regime Survival: Transitions to Democracy and Subsequent Autocracy," *British Journal of Political Science*, 42, no. 2 (April 2012): 283–309.

Wynn, Wilton. *Nasser of Egypt; the Search for Dignity*. Cambridge: Arlington Books, 1959.

Yūnus, Sharīf. *Istiqlāl al-qaḍā*. al-Qahirah: Markaz al-Qahirah li-Dirāsāt Ḥuqūq al-Insān, 2007.

Yūsuf, Hāmid Ahmad. *ʿAbd al-Nāsir wa-aqzām al-sultah*. al-Iskandarīyah: Dar al-Huda lil-Matbuʿat, 1989.

Zahran, Gamal. "al-dawr al-siyāsī lal-qaḍaʾ al-Miṣrī fī sunʾ al-qarār," in ed. Alī al-Dīn Hilāl, *Al-Niẓām al-siyāsī al-Miṣrī: al-taghayyur wa-al-istimrār*. al-Qahirah: Maktabat al-Nahḍah al-Miṣrīyah, 1988.

Zayani, Mohamed. "Introduction–Al Jazeera and Vicissitudes of the New Arab Mediascape," in ed. Mohamed Zayani, *The Al Jazeera Phenomenon: Critical Perspectives on New Arab Media*. Boulder, CO: Paradigm Publishers, 2005.

Zayyāt, Muḥammad Abd al-Salām. *al-Sādāt, al-qināʾ wa-al-ḥaqīqah*. Kitāb al-Ahālī, raqm 18. al-Qahirah: Jarīdat al-Ahālī, 1989.

Miṣr ilá ayn: qirāʾāt wa-khawāṭir fī al-dustūr al-dāʾim 1971. al-Qahirah: Dār al-Mustaqbal al-ʿArabī, 1986.

Zelditch, Morris. "Some Methodological Problems of Field Studies." *American Journal of Sociology*, 67, no. 5 (March 1962): 566–576.

Index

CPSIA information can be obtained
at www.ICGtesting.com
Printed in the USA
BVHW091827110522
636808BV00007B/56